Research on China's Strategy and Policy in Northeast Asia

RESEARCH ON CHINA'S STRATEGY AND POLICY IN NORTHEAST ASIA

Liu Qingcai

Translated by Duan Feng and Zhang Jie

NEW JERSEY · LONDON · SINGAPORE · BEIJING · SHANGHAI · HONG KONG · TAIPEI · CHENNAI

Published by

World Scientific Publishing Co. Pte. Ltd.
5 Toh Tuck Link, Singapore 596224
USA office: 27 Warren Street, Suite 401-402, Hackensack, NJ 07601
UK office: 57 Shelton Street, Covent Garden, London WC2H 9HE

Library of Congress Control Number: 2024042807

British Library Cataloguing-in-Publication Data
A catalogue record for this book is available from the British Library.

中国东北亚战略与政策研究
Originally published in Chinese by Economic Science Press
Copyright © Economic Science Press 2016

RESEARCH ON CHINA'S STRATEGY AND POLICY IN NORTHEAST ASIA

Copyright © 2025 by World Scientific Publishing Co. Pte. Ltd.

All rights reserved. This book, or parts thereof, may not be reproduced in any form or by any means, electronic or mechanical, including photocopying, recording or any information storage and retrieval system now known or to be invented, without written permission from the publisher.

For photocopying of material in this volume, please pay a copying fee through the Copyright Clearance Center, Inc., 222 Rosewood Drive, Danvers, MA 01923, USA. In this case permission to photocopy is not required from the publisher.

ISBN 978-981-98-0538-9 (hardcover)
ISBN 978-981-98-0539-6 (ebook for institutions)
ISBN 978-981-98-0540-2 (ebook for individuals)

For any available supplementary material, please visit
https://www.worldscientific.com/worldscibooks/10.1142/14103#t=suppl

Desk Editors: Nambirajan Karuppiah/Kura Sunaina

Typeset by Stallion Press
Email: enquiries@stallionpress.com

Preface

Northeast Asia holds a prominent position in China's diplomatic strategy in terms of geopolitics. This is a place where the world's major powers and strategic interests converge. Since the end of the Cold War, the situation in Northeast Asia has undergone significant changes and is in a period of significant historical transformation. The bipolar pattern in Northeast Asia has ended, and a new pattern of competition and cooperation among China, the United States, Japan, and Russia is taking shape. In 2010, China surpassed Japan to become the world's second-largest economy, which is changing the pattern of international power in Northeast Asia. China has actively pursued major-country diplomacy with Chinese characteristics, promoted the construction of a community with a shared future in China's neighborhood, and implemented a more active foreign policy in Northeast Asia. As a country from outside the region, the United States plays a vital role in Northeast Asia. The Obama administration's "Asia-Pacific rebalancing" strategy was mainly aimed at Northeast Asia, anchoring the US strategy of moving eastward. The United States has continuously consolidated and strengthened its bilateral military alliances with Japan and the Republic of Korea (ROK). It has also strengthened its forward military deployment in the two countries. Japan's Abe government actively implemented a "normal nation" policy,* amended the Pacifist Constitution, lifted the ban on collective self-defense, and passed a series

---

*Japan's military power has been seriously restricted since World War II as the punishment for its invasion to the Asian countries. It has been deprived of the rights of a normal country. Japan is now trying to regain the rights as normal country with the approval of the United States.

of security laws to make Japan a new political and military power. Russia is a country spanning Eurasia and has important national interests in Northeast Asia. Russia actively participates in Northeast Asia affairs and regards the region as an important channel for its integration into the Asia-Pacific region, actively developing cooperation between its East Siberia and the Far East regions and Northeast Asia.

There are long-standing historical problems in Northeast Asia, including the nuclear crisis in the Democratic People's Republic of Korea (DPRK) and the Korean Peninsula issue, and territorial sovereignty and maritime rights disputes, reflecting the new changes in the international system and the geostrategic game among major powers in the region. The historical problems still influence relations among countries in Northeast Asia. Japan's post-war introspection, the Korean Peninsula issue, and the island disputes are all remnants of World War II. After the end of the Cold War, these past problems were still unresolved and grew into complex practical problems in Northeast Asia. The DPRK and the ROK in the Korean Peninsula have been facing a long-term confrontation. The Korean War has been in a suspended state for 70 years and no peace treaty has been signed yet. The United States has stepped up its military deployment in the ROK and has frequently held large-scale joint military exercises, all of which have increased the external pressure on the DPRK's national security. The DPRK is determined to conduct nuclear and missile tests to improve its national defense capability. The DPRK's nuclear deterrence policy and war brinkmanship have escalated tensions on the Korean Peninsula. There are also disputes over the delimitation of islands and seas in Northeast Asia, including the four islands dispute (called the Northern Territories in Japan and the Southern Kurils in Russia) between Russia and Japan, the Diaoyu Dao dispute and the delimitation of the East China Sea between China and Japan, and the dispute over a set of islands (called Dokdo in Korean and Takeshima in Japanese) between the ROK and Japan. These disputes directly affect the development of relations between countries in the region.

As an important country in Northeast Asia, China has critical national interests concerning politics, economy, security, and culture in Northeast Asia. The complicated situation in Northeast Asia poses severe challenges to China's national sovereignty, security, and development interests. To create a peaceful, stable, and prosperous international environment in Northeast Asia, China needs to implement a more active strategy and policy in accordance with its major-country diplomacy. In response to the transformation of the international system and the changes in the situation in Northeast Asia, this book discusses the political, economic, security, and cultural relations in Northeast Asia, with important insights into hot-button issues, peppered with policy research, theoretical analysis, and a comprehensive, in-depth, and systematic study of China's strategy and policy in the Northeast Asian region.

In terms of research objectives, this book discusses China's strategic vision for Northeast Asia. Adhering to the new concept of major-country diplomacy with Chinese characteristics and building relations with neighboring countries based on the principles of amity, sincerity, mutual benefit, and inclusiveness, China proposes a foundation of mutual trust with economic cooperation and institution-building to create a new international order in Northeast Asia. Therefore, it is necessary to reject a zero-sum game and realize collaboration based on a balance of interests. Beyond the Cold War mentality and military confrontation policies, we should establish new concepts of cooperative and common security and jointly safeguard peace and stability in Northeast Asia. Based on the principles of international law, we should establish a code of conduct and an international mechanism for Northeast Asian countries to achieve long-term stability, development, and prosperity. China's high status in Northeast Asia determines that it will adopt an active Northeast Asia policy. As a responsible country, China plays the role of initiator, shaper, and builder in the region with the aim of creating a good geopolitical foundation and developmental environment for its own peaceful development.

Our prominent theme in this book is the transformation of Northeast Asia's international system and China's strategic choices. This book analyzes the structural transformation of the international system in Northeast Asia, studies China's identity and role, opportunities and challenges, national interests and strategic objectives, and discusses the construction of a new international order in Northeast Asia. In this book, two hot spots are discussed: the DPRK nuclear crisis and the disputes of the Northeast Asian countries over the territorial sovereignty and maritime rights. These are the sensitive issues that directly affect peace and stability in this region. We should solve these problems through diplomatic channels in a peaceful way. There are also three basic issues in this region. The first issue is the security threats in Northeast Asia and the construction of security mechanisms. This book analyzes both security and non-traditional security threats and puts forward some ideas and measures to maintain peace and stability including the construction of security mechanisms.

The second issue is the energy security challenge, which requires the establishment of an energy cooperation system. The third issue is trade, investment, and regional economic cooperation in Northeast Asia. Under the framework of the Belt and Road Initiative, trade and investment are facilitated, connectivity and free trade are developed, and regional economic cooperation is strengthened.

From the perspective of major-country diplomacy with Chinese characteristics, this book conducts an in-depth and systematic study of China's strategy and policy in Northeast Asia. We try to combine theoretical research with applied, strategic, and policy research to comprehensively analyze China's place in Northeast Asia. This book uses various research methods, combining systematic analysis, qualitative analysis, normative research, and empirical research. Based on various analyzed criteria, China's strategy and policy in Northeast Asia are deemed to be stable, sustainable and predictable, ensuring the realization of its goals in the region.

As the international system in Northeast Asia is in a period of transformation, the foreign policies and relations of various countries are undergoing significant adjustments and changes, which have increased points of dispute in Northeast Asia. We strive to seek long-term, balanced, and pragmatic solutions for these issues. In this regard, the first issue is that the transformation of the international system in Northeast Asia depends on the changes in the balance of power among the major powers in the region. The Asia-Pacific strategies of the US and China–US strategic relations are important influencing factors. This gives Northeast Asia a variety of choices and possibilities in terms of the direction and order of transformation of the international system. The second issue is the security dilemma in Northeast Asia. Due to the lack of mutual trust, the construction of a regional security mechanism is not possible at present, even though such a mechanism will be conducive to the maintenance of peace and stability in Northeast Asia. However, the US–Japan and US–ROK bilateral military alliances pose a significant impediment. The third issue is the DPRK nuclear crisis, which is a volatile situation. The DPRK nuclear crisis and the Korean Peninsula issue are the major regional issues affecting the peace and stability of Northeast Asia as well as China's national security. With the Six-Party Talks on the DPRK nuclear issue being stalled, the process of solving the nuclear issue through multilateral diplomacy has been blocked. China is trying to find solutions to the problem by establishing a peace mechanism in Northeast Asia. The fourth issue is the ongoing development of economic integration in Northeast Asia. Trade and investment by countries in Northeast Asia are increasing, leading to closer interdependent relationships. However, the level of regional economic integration and institutional development is poor, which directly affects financial security, energy security, economic and trade cooperation, and international competitiveness in Northeast Asia. Based on the comparative advantages of the economies of various countries, we have put forward policies and plans to promote economic and trade integration and cooperation in Northeast Asia, starting with energy and financial cooperation, the development of trade and investment facilitation, and the construction of free trade areas.

The study of China's strategy and policy in Northeast Asia is closely linked with the situation in the world and international trends. In 2008, the global financial and economic crisis hit the US economy hard, and the European Union was caught in a sovereign debt crisis. This has fully exposed the severe drawbacks of the western free-market economic system. The overall rise of the emerging economies in the world has led to an equalization of the international balance of power. The establishment of the G20 led to a fundamental change in the global governance structure. As the world's second-largest economy, China plays an increasingly important role in promoting world economic cooperation and development. In 2013 and 2014, the central government held special peripheral meetings and foreign affairs meetings and put forward a new concept of building relations with neighboring countries based on amity, sincerity, mutual benefit, inclusiveness, and the concept of building a shared future. At the same time, President Xi Jinping put forward the development strategy of the Belt and Road Initiative. The promotion of China's status as a major power in Northeast Asia has been a significant development in recent times as it has led to the evolution of China's major-country diplomacy with Chinese characteristics.

To complete this project, we consulted with well-known scholars from domestic research institutions and formed a strong research team with the personnel from the School of Public Administration and the Northeast Asian Studies College, Jilin University. The team consists of professors and scholars who have long been engaged in political, economic, security, and cultural research in Northeast Asia. During the implementation of the project, we carried out extensive academic exchanges and conducted scientific research and policy consultation. To this end, the research group held five national and international academic conferences, published more than 70 papers in authoritative local journals, and submitted a number of policy research and consultation reports to the Ministry of Foreign Affairs.

This book — *Research on China's Strategy and Policy in Northeast Asia* — is the final result of the above-mentioned major research project supported by the Ministry of Education of the People's Republic of China. The final research result was officially submitted on August 20, 2015 and passed expert appraisal in February 2016. We have extensively drawn on the suggestions of experts and published this book after much revision and improvement. This academic work condenses the collective wisdom of many experts. It is currently the first scholarly monograph in China that comprehensively and systematically studies China's foreign policy in Northeast Asia. Through much research and analysis, we strive to provide conceptual thoughts, diplomatic wisdom, and policy suggestions for China's foreign policies and practices in Northeast Asia and further promote academic research on this extensive subject. However, due to the limitations of theory and policy, there will inevitably be omissions and improprieties for which criticism is welcome.

About the Translators

Duan Feng obtained his Ph.D. from Sichuan University and is now Professor of English and Translation Studies at the same university. He has published three monographs on translation studies entitled *New Development in Translation History of China*, *Cultural Translation in the Literature of Chinese Ethnic Minorities*, and *Study on Literary Translation Subjectivity from the Cultural Perspective*. He has translated various books, including *The Internationalization of China's Economy*. His articles have appeared in both Chinese and international journals and he is a member of several Chinese academic associations involving translation studies and TEFL.

Zhang Jie is a professor at Chengdu University of Technology and holds the job title of Executive Translator. She has translated more than 20 English books, including *Green Transformation in China: Understanding China's Ecological Progress*, *China: Whole-Process People's Democracy*, and *China, Land of Ceremony and Propriety*. She is now working on a translation project sponsored by the National Social Science Fund of China.

About the Author

Liu Qingcai, Ph.D., is Professor, Doctoral Supervisor, and former Chairman of the Academic Committee of the School of Public Administration at Jilin University. He has also served as a part-time professor at the Northeast Asian Research Center, Jilin University, and the School of Political Science and Public Administration, China University of Political Science and Law. He has dedicated his career to the study of Northeast Asia issues, publishing more than 50 academic papers on related topics. His edited works include *The Geopolitics of Northeast Asia in the Early 21st Century: Regional Politics and Relations among Nations* and *Study of Russia's Northeast Asia Policy: Geopolitics and State Relations*. He also co-authored *Russia in the 1990s: Politics, Economy, and Diplomacy* and *Geopolitics in Northeast Asia and China's Geostrategy*.

Contents

Preface v

About the Translators xi

About the Author xiii

Chapter 1 Transformation of International System in Northeast Asia and China's Strategic Choice   1
- 1.1 Transformation of the International System, Problems in Northeast Asia, and Challenges Facing China   2
- 1.2 China's National Interests in Northeast Asia   12
- 1.3 China's Role in Northeast Asia   33
- 1.4 China's Strategic Conception of Northeast Asia   50

Chapter 2 Security Challenges in Northeast Asia and China's Security Strategy   85
- 2.1 Security Situation and Challenges in Northeast Asia   86
- 2.2 China's Security Interests and Security Strategy in Northeast Asia   96
- 2.3 The Mode and Vision of Promoting the Construction of a Security Mechanism in Northeast Asia   117

Chapter 3 Disputes Over Territorial Sovereignty and Maritime Rights and Interests in Northeast Asia and China's Strategy and Countermeasures — 137
  3.1 Disputes Over Territorial Sovereignty and Maritime Rights and Interests in Northeast Asia and Their Impact — 138
  3.2 China's Territorial Sovereignty and Maritime Rights and Interests in Northeast Asia and its Strategic Choice — 153
  3.3 China's Strategy and Countermeasures to Resolve the Diaoyu Dao Issue Between China and Japan — 169
  3.4 China's Strategy and Countermeasures for Resolving the China–Japan Disputes Over Maritime Rights and Interests in the East China Sea — 177

Chapter 4 Energy Security in Northeast Asia and China's Energy Cooperation Policy — 187
  4.1 Energy Security Situation and Energy Strategy of the Northeast Asian Countries — 188
  4.2 Energy Cooperation and Competition between Countries in Northeast Asia — 209
  4.3 China's Strategies and Policies for Energy Cooperation in Northeast Asia — 221

Chapter 5 Economic and Trade Relations in Northeast Asia and China's Regional Cooperation Policy — 237
  5.1 Economic and Trade Cooperation in Northeast Asia Under the Conditions of Economic Globalization — 237
  5.2 Investment Facilitation and FTA Cooperation of International Trade Centers in Northeast Asia — 270
  5.3 China's Strategic Conception of Promoting Trade and Investment Facilitation and Regional Cooperation in Northeast Asia — 295
  5.4 The Construction of the China–Japan–ROK FTA and China's Strategic Countermeasures — 313

Bibliography — 333

Index — 357

Chapter 1

Transformation of International System in Northeast Asia and China's Strategic Choice

Since the end of the Cold War in 1991, with the disintegration of the Soviet Union, particularly in the 21st century, the situation in Northeast Asia has undergone significant changes. While the strategic situation in Northeast Asia remains stable and controllable as a whole, the international system in the region is experiencing a historic transformation, showing a trend of multi-polarization. In this process, a variety of security dilemmas and challenges have affected the security of Northeast Asia. Currently, the most critical unstable factors are the Korean Peninsula issue, various territorial sovereignty issues, and maritime rights disputes. Despite security problems popping up from time to time, the economy in Northeast Asia is developing steadily. Countries in this region have become important economic and trade partners, forming a close and interdependent relationship. After the global financial and economic crisis in 2008, Northeast Asia has gradually grown into a powerful engine and driving force for world economic development.

Northeast Asia is a region where many major powers in the world are concentrated and where the interests of those countries converge. At the same time, Northeast Asia is also an important arena for cooperation, competition, and strategic games among major powers. China is an important country in Northeast Asia and has strategic interests in this region. It is of vital geopolitical basis for China to establish major-country diplomacy with Chinese characteristics and realize peaceful development. China also aims to build relations with neighboring countries in Northeast Asia based on amity, sincerity, mutual benefit, and inclusiveness and actively promote the construction of a new type of international order in Northeast Asia.

1.1 Transformation of the International System, Problems in Northeast Asia, and Challenges Facing China

After the end of the Cold War, the bipolar pattern of the world ended and instead a trend of multi-polarization emerged. In Northeast Asia, with the rapid development of China, the international balance of power underwent significant changes, which required considerable adjustment from the international community. The trend of multi-polarization in Northeast Asia has been conducive to the establishment of a new type of international order with mutual-benefit cooperation. However, it has also led to systematic conflicts, bringing about structural contradictions and disputes between big and emerging powers, causing security dilemmas among big powers, and making the situation in Northeast Asia highly unstable. At present, the security dilemma, hot-button issues, and various countries' adjustments of their international strategies in Northeast Asia are essentially causing a seismic-level transformations of the international system in Northeast Asia. The transformation of the international system in Northeast Asia and the complicated regional situation are new problems and challenges facing China's diplomacy. It requires us to evaluate the situation calmly and objectively, weigh the pros and cons, explore the law, and make analyses and judgments from the perspective of major-country diplomacy with Chinese characteristics.

1.1.1 Transformation and structural conflict of international system in Northeast Asia

Since the end of the Cold War, especially since the beginning of the 21st century, the international system in Northeast Asia has undergone a significant period of historic transformation. New changes have taken place, making the situation in this region very complicated and uncertain. The basis and starting point for China to determine its diplomatic strategy and policy in Northeast Asia are to conform to the trend of times in the transformation of international system, to adapt to the new changes in the situation, and to cope with the newly arising problems and challenges in the area.

1.1.1.1 *The international order in Northeast Asia is in an important period of historic transformation*

Since the end of the Cold War, the international system in Northeast Asia has undergone significant historical changes. The original balance of international power was broken. The international pattern is now moving toward multi-polarization and the national strategies of various countries have considerably adjusted their foreign policies accordingly.

First of all, in the international system of Northeast Asia, the balance of power among regional powers has changed significantly. The so-called "power" not only refers to economic strength and military strength but also includes soft power such as regional influence and cultural charisma. Specifically, among the major powers in Northeast Asia, China, the United States, Japan, and Russia have undergone major changes, which is mainly manifested in the fact that the gap in national strength between China and the United States is narrowing and China has overtaken Japan and Russia to become the new power in Northeast Asia. China's economy has developed rapidly and surpassed Japan as the world's second-largest economy and the largest economy in Northeast Asia in 2010. China's military strength is also continuously increasing. With the increasing army expenditure, the level of military modernization and national defense capability is improving continually. In particular, China's ability to cruise and to ensure offshore defense has been improving. China's military strength to safeguard national sovereignty and territorial integrity as well as maintain regional peace and stability has been strengthened. China's influence in Northeast Asia is also continually increasing. It played a central role in easing tensions in the Korean Peninsula and in coordinating the Six-Party Talks in Beijing to resolve the nuclear crisis relating to Democratic People's Republic of Korea (DPRK). In contrast, Japan has lost its position as the largest economic power in Northeast Asia, and its economy has been in a state of depression and stagnation for a long time. In diplomacy, Japan has long followed the United States and has no independent diplomatic strategy and policy, which is not conducive to its influence in Northeast Asia. Russia has implemented an active policy in Northeast Asia since the collapse of the Soviet Union. However, due to the long-term economic stagnation and backwardness in Russia's Far East, the level of economic and trade cooperation between Russia and Northeast Asia is relatively low, which dramatically limits Russia's position and influence in Northeast Asia. The United States is a foreign country to Northeast Asia, but it is an essential presence in the international system in Northeast Asia. Through its bilateral military alliance with Japan and the Republic of Korea (ROK) and its long-term military presence in those countries, the United States has exerted a significant influence on the international pattern and regional security in Northeast Asia. With China's rapid economic development, the economic gap between China and the United States is narrowing. At present, the ability of the United States to control and dominate the Northeast Asian region is seriously weakened. The United States has always worried that China will replace its position as the leading country in the Northeast Asian region in the future.

Secondly, Northeast Asia is moving toward multi-polarization. In Northeast Asia, the bipolar pattern dominated by the United States and the Soviet Union during the Cold War ended, and Russia completely abandoned its confrontation policy toward the United States. The rapid growth of China has fundamentally transformed the landscape of US unipolar hegemony. To this end, the United States has continuously strengthened its bilateral military alliance with Japan and the ROK in Northeast Asia. As two powers in the world and two permanent members of the UN Security Council, China and Russia are independent poles in the world and Northeast Asia. China and Russia have established a comprehensive strategic partnership of cooperation and actively carried out coordination and cooperation in regional affairs, which effectively balances and restricts the US intention to seek regional hegemony and limits the role of the US–Japan and US–ROK bilateral alliances in regional affairs. Therefore, a relatively balanced state of strategic power in Northeast Asia has been formed, and a multi-polar equilibrium pattern in Northeast Asia has emerged.

Finally, the transformation of the international system in Northeast Asia is at a critical crossroads. It involves the choice of a global system model: one is to adapt to the development trend of multi-polarization in Northeast Asia and establish a multi-polar and balanced international system pattern. This multi-polar and balanced international system will be the basis for establishing equality, mutual trust, good neighborliness, friendship, and mutual-benefit cooperation. In this regional international system, the cooperation and common governance of the major powers are not a zero-sum game, let alone a winner-take-all strategy but involve win-win cooperation to build a peaceful, stable, and prosperous regional order. The other is the hegemonic system dominated by the US unipolarity, that is, the so-called "Pax Americana." Under this system, the United States acts as the regional leader, and the bilateral military alliance established by the United States with Japan and the ROK will serve as the basis for regional security. The United States is committed to incorporating regional powers such as China and Russia into the US-led system to avoid any possible challenges to the US leadership. Under this system, countries are not equal, and the United States will be the leader. In terms of development path and ideology, dependent countries will lack autonomy, and the development mode of the United States will be widely encouraged in Northeast Asia. In terms of security, the United States does not maintain collective security in a real sense, but gives priority to ensuring security with its allies, and takes the establishment of bilateral military alliances and absolute military dominance as the basis for US regional hegemony. This system does not conform to the interests of China, Russia, and other countries, nor does it conform to the trend of democratic development of the international system.

The choice of the two modes of the international system in Northeast Asia is directly related to how one intends to construct the global system and order in this region. One is the regional international system and order characterized by multi-polar balance, mutual respect, equal consultation, and win-win cooperation among regional powers. The other is the "Pax Americana," which establishes the US unipolar system and order. Under the trend of multi-polarization in Northeast Asia, promoting the establishment of a multi-polar and balanced democratic order has become an essential choice for China's strategy in Northeast Asia.

1.1.1.2 *Structural conflicts brought about by the transformation of the international system in Northeast Asia*

The transformation of the international system in Northeast Asia is mainly manifested in the regional power dynamics and major changes in the international pattern. The transformation involves adjustments and changes in the status as well as the roles of the countries in Northeast Asia. Therefore, the countries in Northeast Asia actively carry out strategic and policy adjustments to urge the international system to change to a direction more in line with their interests. Due to the differences in principles and structural conflicts among the major powers in Northeast Asia on issues such as system role, power distribution, and regional order, Northeast Asia entered a period of turbulence in the process of system transformation.

Firstly, major powers in Northeast Asia have made significant strategic adjustments. With the shift in the balance of international forces in Northeast Asia and the new changes in the pattern of the global system, the major powers in Northeast Asia have made further strategic and policy adjustments to adapt to the changes in the international system in the region. They have actively defended their national status and interests. China has emerged as a major power in Northeast Asia. It has conducted active diplomacy among major powers in Northeast Asia. It plays the role and fulfills the responsibility of a builder and shaper of the system in maintaining peace and stability in Northeast Asia and promoting cooperation and development. Japan is trying to get rid of its position and limitation as a defeated country after World War II and become a regional political and military power through the normal nation or country policy/ strategy. Japan's Abe government revised its Pacifist Constitution and forced the adoption of a new security legislation, which involved a series of measures all aimed at serving Japan's new strategic goal of being perceived as a big country. With the world's political and economic focus shifting to the Asia-Pacific region, Russia has begun to implement a more active Asia-Pacific and Northeast Asia policy on the basis of its geopolitical reality across Eurasia, seeking to integrate into Northeast Asia and actively participate in the regional affairs. The United States has adopted the policy of "pivot to Asia" and worked for a new "Asia-Pacific rebalancing" strategy. In Northeast Asia, the United States has continuously consolidated and strengthened its bilateral military alliances, i.e., the US–Japan alliance and the US–ROK alliance, to safeguard its hegemonic position and leadership.

Secondly, the "Thucydides' Trap" between China and the United States has been brought about by the transformation of the Northeast Asian system. At present, the interests of China and the United States are deeply intertwined, and the basis for common interests and cooperation is constantly expanding. However, China is actively promoting the construction of a new type of international order in Northeast Asia, which will undoubtedly pose a challenge to the hegemonic position of the United States in the region, thus triggering a structural conflict or confrontation between China and the United States. Therefore, breaking the so-called "Thucydides' Trap" theory and the logic of the tragedy of great power politics, and establishing a new type of China–US great power relationship in Northeast Asia is an epoch-making topic.

Finally, the transformation of the Northeast Asian system gives rise to the regional security dilemma due to a lack of security cooperation in Northeast Asia. Frequent conflicts have arisen due to the security dilemma among major powers. Therefore, during the period of system transformation in Northeast Asia, the strategies and policies of all countries in the region have undergone significant adjustments and changes.

The US military strategy has shifted its focus to the Asia-Pacific region and has continuously consolidated and strengthened its bilateral military alliance with Japan and the ROK. After President Obama came to power, the US government announced the implementation of the "pivot to Asia" policy and worked out the "Asia-Pacific rebalancing" strategy. The United States continues to increase its forward military deployment, hold frequent joint military exercises, and raise the level of arms and military cooperation. There is a trend of political deviation toward the right in Japan. The Abe administration had actively promoted the revision of Japan's pacifist constitution, lifted the ban on collective self-defense, and changed Japan's post-war defense policy. In September 2015, the Abe administration forcibly passed a new security bill to expand the defense scope of Japan's Self-Defense Forces and broke through various restrictions on Japan's overseas military operations. The military alliance and military policy between the United States and Japan have obvious purpose and target. It increases the external threat to the national security of China and Russia, which will undoubtedly arouse the vigilance and precaution of China, Russia, and other countries and is not beneficial to regional peace and stability. Both *National Security Strategy of the United States* and *the US Quadrennial Defense Review* have reported doubts and precautions about the process, transparency, and intention of China's military modernization. *Defense of Japan* and *the National Defense Program guidelines* released by the Japanese government mention "the Military Threat of China." In Northeast Asia, there have been wars between Russia and Japan as well as between the United States and Japan. Japan has a history of being defeated; China, the DPRK, and the ROK have a history of being invaded by foreign enemies. The history of this complicated relationship makes Northeast Asian countries very sensitive to the issues of national independence, sovereignty, and security. The return of the United States to Asia, Russia's "turning to East," the development of China, Japan's change in strategy, and the competition between the DPRK and the ROK for dominance in the process of unification of the Korea Peninsula have all contributed to the uncertainty, instability and fragility of the security situation in Northeast Asia. This security dilemma thus results in a severe lack of trust among major powers, intensifies the regional arms race, and has complicated the regional security situation grievously.

1.1.2 Security issues and challenges in Northeast Asia

The security situation in Northeast Asia is generally stable and in control, but might not remain so. Influenced by many factors such as historical issues, the Cold War mentality, the security dilemma, the Korean Peninsula issue, and territorial disputes, there are many security risks and challenges in Northeast Asia. If any strategic misjudgment or improper handling occurs, conflicts would intensify and lead to regional wars.

Firstly, the legacy of the Cold War is still lingering in Northeast Asia. The Cold War has been over for more than 30 years, but the Cold War mentality still exists in Northeast Asia. The bloc politics, alliance policies, military superiority policies, containment strategies, ideologies and value diplomacy practiced during the Cold War are still prevalent, exerting an overwhelming impact on the relations of countries in the region. The North–South tension in the Korean Peninsula during the Cold War has not changed, and a state of high tension prevails. Neither the United States nor Japan has diplomatic relations with the DPRK. The United States and Japan continue their hostile containment policies toward the DPRK. The United States continues to maintain and strengthen the bilateral military alliance with Japan and the ROK as to maintain its military advantage in Northeast Asia. These Cold War policies do not accord with the changes in Northeast Asia and they are still an essential factor affecting the peace and security in this region.

Secondly, the Korean Peninsula issue is a severe threat to peace and stability in Northeast Asia. The DPRK and the ROK remain in a state of high tension and confrontation. The denuclearization of the Korean

Peninsula is still a major security issue. The DPRK nuclear issue has undergone fundamental changes. The DPRK has changed from carrying out nuclear energy development programs to mastering nuclear weapons technology and has a small number of miniature nuclear warheads. It is still developing and testing missile technology. The DPRK has broken through the nuclear threshold to become a nuclear state with nuclear weapons and nuclear strike capability. As the situation in the Korean Peninsula is volatile, the DPRK's possession of nuclear weapons will pose a serious threat to peace in the Korean Peninsula and security in Northeast Asia. At present, the Six-Party Talks on the DPRK nuclear issue as initiated by Beijing have been stalled and have not been formally restarted since 2008. As a result, the denuclearization process of the Korean Peninsula has been stranded. Comprehensive measures must be taken to ease the DPRK–ROK relations in the Korean Peninsula and make the United States and Japan abandon their policy of refusing to recognize the DPRK. Promoting the establishment of a cooperation mechanism in the Korean Peninsula and the Northeast Asian region will help resolve the DPRK nuclear issue, eliminate the danger of nuclear proliferation, and realize peace and stability in the Korean Peninsula and Northeast Asian region.

Thirdly, disputes over territorial sovereignty and maritime rights and interests in Northeast Asia have become major obstacles to the development of national relations. At present, China and Japan have disputes over Diaoyu Dao and the East China Sea demarcation. Russia and Japan have disputes over the northern territories. The ROK and Japan have disputes over the sovereignty of a set of islands, called Dokdo in Korean and Takeshima in Japanese. Most of these territorial disputes are long-standing problems that have become serious obstacles to the development of relations among the involved countries. Due to the territorial dispute in the north, more than 70 years after the end of World War II, Russia and Japan have still not signed a post-war peace treaty. The illegal "purchasing" of Diaoyu Dao by the Japanese government in 2012 triggered a fierce debate between China and Japan over the Diaoyu Dao issue. To this end, Japan has strengthened its military deployment in the East China Sea and China has continuously increased its naval strength to adequately safeguard its territorial sovereignty and maritime rights and interests. The Chinese government's maritime police vessel regularly cruises the waters of Diaoyu Dao, causing friction between Chinese and Japanese ships. The dispute over a set of islands (called Dokdo in Korean and Takeshima in Japanese) between the ROK and Japan has also resulted in estrangement and tension between the ROK and Japan. These territorial disputes are regarded as the core interests of the respective countries and have become potential hidden dangers that can lead to regional conflicts.

Fourthly, the internal and external policies of the Abe administration aroused strong opposition and serious unease from neighboring countries, which resulted in a series of issues such as Japan's reflection on the history of the war, visits to the Yasukuni Shrine, and the "comfort women" issue. The aggression of the Japanese militarists in the past had caused disasters in Asian countries; in particular, the aggression against China, caused more than 35 million Chinese casualties. The Japanese invaders also forced women from the DPRK, the ROK, and China to serve as "comfort women" and tortured them. However, the Japanese government tried its best to cover up and evade these heinous crimes of aggression and has openly denied the history of aggression and the crime of forcibly recruiting "comfort women." Senior officials of the Japanese government and members of parliament have publicly and collectively paid homage to the Yasukuni Shrine to honor several Class-A war criminals. This act has hurt the feelings of the Asian people, especially those in Northeast Asia. What is even more alarming is that Japan's rightist politics and the rise of militarism may also become a new source of war and pose a new threat to Northeast Asia.

The rightist politics in Japan are of great concern. The Abe administration pushed to amend the pacifist constitution, lift the ban on collective self-defense, and amend the security-related laws, all of which could lead to military power. Japan's lifting the right to war set forth in its peace constitution has gradually enabled it to abandon its security policy of exclusive self-defense and become a potential threat to regional security.

1.1.3 Economic cooperation and integration in Northeast Asia

During the Cold War, there were two kinds of economic systems and structures in Northeast Asia, in which the level of economic and trade development in the countries was relatively low. With China's reform and opening up, especially after the collapse of the Soviet Union, China, Russia, Mongolia, and other countries have achieved economic transformation and started to shift to the market economy, which has created basic conditions for the development of economic and trade cooperation among countries in Northeast Asia.

The Asia-Pacific region is the most dynamic in the world in terms of economic development. Northeast Asia is an essential engine of economic growth in the Asia-Pacific region, which could lead to economic and trade cooperation. In Northeast Asia, there are economically and technically developed countries such as Japan and the ROK, countries with rich natural resources such as Russia, and countries with abundant human capital and vast markets such as China. China, Japan, the ROK, and Russia all have rich foreign exchange reserves and huge investment potentials.

Countries in Northeast Asia such as China, Japan, the ROK, Russia, and Mongolia have become important trade partners to each other. China is the largest trade partner of the other countries in Northeast Asia. The areas of cooperation are expanding and the interdependence is deepening.

After the global financial and economic crisis in 2008, countries in Northeast Asia actively carried out trade settlements in local currencies, implemented currency swaps, and strengthened cooperation in the financial field to avoid financial risks. On June 1, 2015, China and the ROK formally signed a Free Trade Agreement (hereinafter called "China–ROK FTA"), which covers many fields such as trade in goods, trade in services, investment, and rules. In terms of tariff concessions, after a 20-year transition period, the FTA agreed to implement zero tariffs on more than 90% of tax items and about 90% of imported goods in the two countries. It is of great significance for improving the level of trade cooperation between China and the ROK, promoting the development of trade between the two countries, and supporting the negotiation of free trade agreements among China, Japan, and the ROK.

At present, the level of economic integration in Northeast Asia still needs to be improved. Compared with Europe and Southeast Asia, Northeast Asia lags in the construction of free trade areas and commercial communities. China and the ROK have already signed the FTA. However, after years of negotiations, a China–Japan–ROK FTA has still not occurred. There is still a long way to go to establish a Northeast Asia free trade area and a Northeast Asia regional economic union or economic community. The Tumen River regional cooperation actively promoted by the Chinese government might not proceed due to the complicated regional situation. The lack of an economic cooperation mechanism in

Northeast Asia substantially limits the economic autonomy of Northeast Asia, making it difficult to resist the possible impacts of global financial and economic risks.

The development of economic cooperation in Northeast Asia has deepened the intersection and integration of the interests of all countries in the region, promoted economic growth and prosperity in Northeast Asia, and contributed to the maintenance of regional peace and stability. However, close economic and trade relations have also brought about fierce economic competition and triggered financial friction and conflicts. The construction of free trade areas is based on the principles of equality, mutual benefit, and win-win cooperation. However, there is still a dispute over economic dominance in Northeast Asia. The United States actively promotes the high-standard Trans-Pacific Partnership Agreement (TPP) in the Asia-Pacific region, with the obvious intention of sidelining and containing China. The United States and Japan refused to join the Asian Infrastructure Investment Bank (AIIB) initiated by China, with the intention of stopping China from dominating regional economic cooperation. The dispute over regional economic dominance and various worries or distrust have severely hindered the development of economic integration in Northeast Asia.

1.2 China's National Interests in Northeast Asia

Northeast Asia holds a prominent position in China's peripheral diplomacy and is an essential geopolitical basis for China's peaceful development. China is located in the east of Eurasia and on the west bank of the Pacific Ocean. It is a big Asian country with a long borderline and a massive neighborhood. Northeast Asia, where China is located, has a concentration of major powers and is the region where power and national interests are closely intertwined. Northeast Asia has the most dynamic economy and is the region where China's closest foreign trade partners are situated. The security situation in Northeast Asia is also very complex. The external threats and challenges to China's national security mainly come from this region.

China is an important country in Northeast Asia. Its national interests can be expressed in terms of political interests, economic interests, security interests, and cultural interests. Therefore, effectively safeguarding and realizing its national interests are important goals of China's Northeast Asia strategy and policy.

1.2.1 China's political interests in Northeast Asia

China's political interests in Northeast Asia mainly refer to the interests of national sovereignty. Sovereignty is a country's supreme authority to handle internal and external affairs independently. National sovereignty can be divided into internal sovereignty and external sovereignty. Internal sovereignty refers to the country's independent right to choose its social and political system and development path. Cultural traditions and values are respected. The country has the supreme power to make internal decisions without any external interference. External sovereignty is manifested in the independent judgment of foreign policies, the maintenance of the sovereign equality of the country, and the guarantee of fundamental rights such as national sovereignty and territorial integrity.

Northeast Asia is a region of pluralism and diversity. Countries in this region have very different histories and development paths as well as social and political systems. Their religions, cultures, and ideologies have diverse characteristics. The countries are also very different in size and strength. Northeast Asia embraces economically developed countries, emerging economies, and economically backward countries. There are both western democratic countries and countries with socialist systems. In terms of religious beliefs, there are Christianity, Catholicism, Eastern Orthodox, and Buddhism, as well as Confucian culture. In Northeast Asia, there are the world and regional powers such as China, Japan, and Russia, as well as small countries such as the DPRK and Mongolia. Geographically, the United States is outside the region of Northeast Asia; however, it is also an important country that cannot be excluded in Northeast Asian geopolitics. Effectively safeguarding China's political interests has become an important goal of China's Northeast Asia strategy and policy.

1.2.1.1 *Establishing China's status and influence as a major power in Northeast Asia*

In the international system of Northeast Asia, the status of a big country implies certain power distribution and stratification of prestige. As far as power distribution is concerned, it involves the construction of an international pattern in Northeast Asia. It could be a pattern where the United States acts as the only monopoly or a pattern where large powers representing multiple poles coexist. As far as power distribution is concerned, it involves construction of an international pattern in Northeast Asia. It could be the pattern of powers dominated by the US monopoly or the pattern of coexistence of multipolar powers. Prestige rating shows influence of a powerful country and represents its soft power. It also demonstrates its ability to inspire, get together, attract and lead as a powerful country in the region. The status of a country in the regional international system involves a pattern of power distribution, which determines a country's identity and role in regional affairs, such as a dominator or subordinator, leader or follower. Prestige rating indicates a country's influence. The higher the prestige rating, the greater the influence. The establishment of a country's international status and influence is an important political act for a country. It forms the basis for the implementation of a country's foreign policy and the maintenance and realization of national interests.

At present, China is attempting to establish its status as a major power and enhance its influence. Since the 18th National Congress of the Communist Party of China (CPC), the Chinese government has determined the strategic orientation of establishing major-country diplomacy with Chinese characteristics and has put forward a new concept of building relations with neighboring countries based on the principles of amity, sincerity, mutual benefit, and inclusiveness. The major-country diplomacy with Chinese characteristics is manifested at all levels of global, regional, and inter-state relations. The establishment of China's status as a major power in Northeast Asia is an important geopolitical strategy. China's diplomatic principles of amity, sincerity, mutual benefit, and inclusiveness and its foreign policy of creating an amicable, secure, and prosperous neighborhood constitute its neighboring foreign policies as a major power. It shows the ability and willingness of the Chinese government to provide public goods to the surrounding areas, and its responsibility as a major power in maintaining regional peace and stability and promoting regional economic development and prosperity.

Judging from the comparison of international power in Northeast Asia, China fully possesses the strength of a regional power and is constantly strengthening its regional influence. In Northeast Asian affairs, China should not be absent. It is not only an equal participant but also a builder and initiator. China should participate in regional affairs on an equal footing, oppose US regional hegemony and power politics in Northeast Asia, enhance the establishment of rules and regimes, and promote the establishment of new international relations and international order in Northeast Asia.

1.2.1.2 *Upholding socialism with Chinese characteristics*

Globalization and informatization are the trends of the times in the development of contemporary international relations. They involve merging all countries in the world into a unified global system, making it impossible for any country to be alone. This system also continuously promotes the establishment of generalized principles of international law and codes of conduct, so that no country can surpass the rules of the international institutions. However, the trend of globalization has not obliterated the essence and characteristics of the diversity of the world. The differences in historical traditions, social, and political systems, economic development, cultural and educational levels, religious beliefs, and value patterns of various countries make it impossible for all countries in the world to adopt the same development path and mode. The choice of development path and mode for each country is deeply rooted in its national history and political reality. Northeast Asia is characterized by political and cultural diversity. There are capitalist countries and socialist countries coexisting. As for the social value, some countries adhere to the western value system and some embrace the socialist value system.

During the Cold War, the two major blocs led by the United States and the Soviet Union were on opposing sides of social systems and ideological lines. After the collapse of the Soviet Union, the confrontation between the two systems of the East and the West disappeared. However, the United States did not let go of restrictions and containment policies on socialist countries. The expansion strategy implemented by the United States is the so-called value diplomacy aimed at socialist countries. In essence, the United States is imposing its development model on all countries in the world, especially socialist countries. It also regards China and other socialist countries as new threats, leading to the "China threat" theory.

Socialism with Chinese characteristics is the historical choice of the Chinese people. It is the path and mode of development with Chinese characteristics as explored by the Chinese people under the leadership of the Communist Party of China (CPC). It is the political foundation and institutional guarantee for the realization of China's political democracy, social stability, economic development, legal perfection, and civilized progress. Fighting against the denigration, westernization, and subversion of China's political system by external forces, defending China's socialist system, and enhancing its superiority and attractiveness are all of national political interest to China.

1.2.1.3 Defending China's national unity and territorial integrity

National reunification and territorial integrity are the fundamental symbols of national sovereignty, which means that a sovereign country has effective jurisdiction and rule over its territorial scope. National reunification means that a sovereign country has a unified national political entity and a unified central power. The opposite of national reunification is national secession, which means that a unified sovereign state has two or more political entities and authorities at the same time.

Therefore, it is imperative for China to uphold the one-China principle, firmly oppose foreign interference and separatist activities, actively promote the peaceful development of relations across the Taiwan Straits on the basis of the 1992 Consensus, and resolutely safeguard China's national reunification and territorial integrity.

There are territorial disputes between China and its neighboring countries. It is a national political interest issue concerning the territorial integrity of China. In Northeast Asia, China and Russia have entirely solved their border problem. However, there are still disputes over the ownership of islands and the maritime demarcation between China and Japan and China and the ROK. China and Japan have dramatic differences over the Diaoyu Dao issue and the demarcation of the East China Sea. In 2012, Japan tried to take possession of the disputed islands through illegal "nationalization" of Diaoyu Dao, breaking the consensus of "shelving differences and seeking joint development." Diaoyu Dao and its affiliated islands are an integral part of China's territory. China has indisputable territorial sovereignty over Diaoyu Dao. There are also serious disputes between China and Japan over the delimitation of the exclusive economic zone and the continental shelf in the East China Sea. There are also disputes between China and the ROK on the demarcation of the Yellow Sea and the Suyan Rock. All these disputes concern China's core national interests in safeguarding territorial sovereignty and maritime rights and interests.

1.2.2 China's economic interests in Northeast Asia

With the deepening of economic globalization and regional economic integration, countries around the world are paying more and more attention to regional development. Northeast Asia is the region with the fastest global economic growth, the most dynamic development, the most growth potential, and the most development prospects in the 21st century. China is an important country in Northeast Asia and has important economic interests in the region. China is making effort to deepen economic cooperation, prevent various economic risks, and improve the economic competitiveness in Northeast Asia so as to create a good regional environment for its economic development and build a foundation for economic progress.

1.2.2.1 *Northeast Asia is important to China's economic development*

Northeast Asia is the fastest-growing region in the world economy. After the global financial and economic crisis in 2008, the US economy has been declining and Europe's economy has been stagnating. However, the economy in Northeast Asia has maintained rapid growth and has become a powerful engine for global economic development; the economies in Northeast Asia, i.e., China, the ROK, Russia, and Mongolia, all resumed their growth rapidly and maintained a strong momentum of development. In 2013, the gross domestic product (GDP) of the six countries in Northeast Asia was close to US$17.5 trillion, accounting for nearly a quarter of the world's total. Four of the top 15 countries in terms of the world's GDP were located in Northeast Asia.[1] The economies of Northeast Asian countries are highly complementary. There are developed countries, emerging economies, and developing countries in this region. Japan and the ROK have abundant capital and advanced technology and management experience, but both are facing the reality of scarce resources. Russia is rich in mineral resources, but its Far East is sparsely populated and its social economy and infrastructure are relatively backward. China is rich in natural and human resources, with rapid economic growth and vast trade and investment markets. Mongolia is rich in mineral resources and has determined a strategy of rejuvenating the country through mineral resources. The DPRK has also established an economic policy of carrying out foreign trade and international economic

---

[1] Opening a New Era of Peace and Cooperation in Northeast Asia (2014). Keynote Speech by Assistant Foreign Minister Qian Hongshan at the Opening Ceremony of the 2014 Northeast Asia Peace and Cooperation Initiative Forum, website of the Ministry of Foreign Affairs of the People's Republic of China, http://www.fmprc.gov.cn/mfa_ehn/ziliao_611306/zyjh_611308/t1204796.shtml, October 28, 2014.

cooperation. Thus, Northeast Asia has opened up an extensive development space for China to carry out regional economic and trade cooperation.

China and all other countries in Northeast Asia have been important economic and trade partners, forming a close interdependent relationship. In 2014, China was Japan's largest trading partner, with a trading volume of US$307.48 billion. China was Japan's largest importer and second-largest exporter.[2] In 2014, China became the ROK's largest trading partner with a trade volume of US$235.4 billion. China was the ROK's largest exporter and importer.[3] The bilateral trade volume between China and the ROK exceeded the total trade volume between the ROK and the United States, the ROK and Japan, and the ROK and Europe as a whole in the same period. The trade volume between China and Russia in 2014 was US$88.4 billion. China is Russia's largest importer and second-largest exporter.[4] In 2014, China and Russia signed a gas purchase contract worth US$400 billion. Russia will export 38 billion cubic meters of natural gas to China annually through the Eastern Route Gas Pipeline for 30 years.

Regional economic cooperation is essential for foreign economic cooperation. Therefore, the development of regional economic cooperation is the primary choice for foreign trade and economic cooperation. Northeast Asian countries are the remarkable economic and business partners of China. They have formed close economic and trade cooperation relations and created an excellent regional environment for China's economic development and foreign economic cooperation.

---

[2] Overview of Japan's Trade in Goods and Bilateral Trade Between China and Japan in 2014, website of the Ministry of Commerce of the People's Republic of China, http://countryreport.mofcom.gov.cn/record/view110209.asp?news_id=43691, April 27, 2015.

[3] Overview of the ROK's Trade in Goods and Bilateral Trade Between China and the ROK in 2014, website of the Ministry of Commerce of the People's Republic of China, http://countryreport.mofcom.gov.cn/record/view110209.asp?news_id=42573, January 21, 2015.

[4] Overview of Russia's Trade in Goods and Bilateral Trade Between China and Russia in 2014, website of the Ministry of Commerce of the People's Republic of China, http://countryreport.mofcom.gov.cn/record/view110209.asp?news_id=43256, April 10, 2015.

1.2.2.2 Deepening the economic cooperation and realizing the economic integration in Northeast Asia

The economic and trade cooperation among the countries in Northeast Asia has developed fast and is continuously improving due to the effect of economic globalization and regional integration. To promote trade and investment cooperation, China and the other countries in Northeast Asia have established bilateral dialogues and coordination mechanisms at different levels. To cope with the global financial crisis in 2008 and guard against financial risks, China signed currency swaps and trade settlement agreements with Japan, the ROK, and Russia. Countries in Northeast Asia have taken a series of measures such as implementing active opening policies, reducing tariffs and trade barriers, and expanding market access to develop trade relations. They have promoted trade facilitation, implemented connectivity, and expanded regional trade and investment. Northeast Asia has also begun the negotiation process for a free trade area. The China–ROK FTA was formally signed in 2015. China, Japan, and the ROK are still in the process of negotiations for an FTA.

Northeast Asia is yet to accommodate a multilateral economic and trade cooperation mechanism and is still limited to bilateral economic and trade cooperation. To deepen regional economic and trade cooperation and integration, it is also necessary to establish a multilateral regional economic cooperation mechanism among the countries in this region.

1.2.2.3 Maintaining economic interests and jointly preventing various economic risks

The economic risks involved in Northeast Asia mainly include guarding against financial risks and maintaining energy security and market stability. China should take adequate measures to deal with economic risks to protect the steady and healthy development of China's economy.

Firstly, Northeast Asia should maintain financial stability and jointly guard against financial risks. China's financial security faces multidimensional challenges from the financial environment in Northeast Asia. Northeast Asia is a newly emerging region in the world economy, with two major economies, China and Japan, as well as the economically developed ROK. The financial markets of Northeast Asian countries are closely interwoven, and the imbalance of a country's local market could quickly become a regional crisis. The Southeast Asian financial crisis in 1997 and the global financial crisis in 2008 were destructive to the economies of Northeast Asian countries, indicating that the countries in the region lack financial systems and have imperfect financial systems and weak financial regulation. The imperfection of financial cooperation mechanisms and the lack of financial risk prevention mechanisms make the region powerless to resist the impact of regional and global financial crises. There are also many problems in the domestic financial system of China. Since China's accession to the World Trade Organization (WTO), challenges in the financial field have emerged one after another. The financial crimes targeting China are very prominent and China's financial security problems need to be tackled immediately. Moreover, the domestic financial policies of some neighboring countries will also affect China's financial security. In particular, Japan has repeatedly adopted a policy of letting the yen depreciate during its domestic economic recession, letting the crisis spill over into its neighborhood, posing a threat to the stability of financial markets in Northeast Asia, including China.

Secondly, China must safeguard its energy interests. With the rapid development of China's economy, the consumption of mineral resources has soared. Strategic energy sources such as oil and natural gas still rely heavily on imports. This situation highlights the urgency of ensuring economic resource security. China's ongoing exploration of oil and natural gas in the East China Sea has, to a certain extent, expanded its access to strategic resources. Guaranteeing the effective and steady supply of energy resources will be the top priority in the future. Also, the demand for energy resources in Northeast Asian countries is increasing, and China is facing fierce challenges from regional competition for energy resources. In the asymmetric interdependence of energy relations, China is vulnerable to any risk to its energy supply. Any restriction or impact on the supply of oil and gas resources or the safety of the transportation routes will hit the domestic economy. At the same time, the increase in the overall energy demand in Northeast Asia has led to a rise in conflicts in the energy field, such as the conflicts and differences between China and Japan over the oil transmission lines in Russia's Far East. Even many regional conflicts, such as the Diaoyu Dao issue between China and Japan, affect energy competition.

Finally, China must maintain market stability in Northeast Asia. Market security mainly includes domestic market investment and foreign market competition. In Northeast Asia, the United States, Japan, and the

ROK are important investors in the market in China. These countries are all at the forefront of investment in China. For China's economic development, maintaining a favorable environment for foreign investment and ensuring the stable capital source are important foundation, and the safety of the domestic market also acts as an important guarantee. In addition, China's economic structure is similar to that of many neighboring countries. The market competition covers numerous aspects, such as technology, capital, talents, and market share. The market competition is also increasingly fierce. Ensuring an edge in the market competition and expanding China's market share in Northeast Asia are related to China's economic interests in Northeast Asia and the country's economic development. Although the scale of China's foreign trade has expanded, its international competitiveness has not increased correspondingly. Northeast Asian countries are generally highly dependent on foreign trade, and the competition in the regional market is fierce, which brings enormous competitive pressure to Chinese industries. In particular, the devaluation effect caused by the financial crisis will also bring challenges to the price competitiveness of Chinese commodities as the world's economies gradually recover from the crisis. At the same time, foreign-funded enterprises from Northeast Asia, especially Japan and the ROK, will enter and grab the Chinese market, thereby affecting China's national industries and causing potential problems for the domestic industries in China.

1.2.3 China's security interests in Northeast vAsia

National security interest is an essential prerequisite for a country's survival and development, and it is a fundamental guarantee of national sovereignty and rights. China is an important country in Northeast Asia and has essential national security interests in this region. China's security interests in Northeast Asia are closely related to the security situation and challenges in this region and are mainly manifested in safeguarding national sovereignty and territorial integrity, effectively defending national security, actively responding to various non-traditional security threats and challenges, and creating a peaceful, stable, and harmonious regional environment for political stability, economic and social development, cultural prosperity and neighborly diplomacy.

1.2.3.1 Strengthening national defense security and safeguarding territorial and maritime security

National defense security is the most basic security aspect of a country. It refers to effectively defending against the invasion by foreign enemies and safeguarding the national territory and border security. In Northeast Asia, China is facing a complicated security situation and ensuring national security is an essential military strategic task.

First of all, the US "Asia-Pacific rebalancing" strategy poses an external military threat to China's national security. After the collapse of the Soviet Union and the end of the Cold War, the US military strategic focus began to shift to the Asia-Pacific region. After Barack Obama came to power in 2009, he decided on a "pivot to Asia" policy and implemented a new "Asia-Pacific rebalancing" strategy. Despite the overall shrinking of US military expenditures, the US continues to strengthen its military presence and deployment in the Asia-Pacific. Six of the 11 US aircraft carriers are deployed in the Asia-Pacific region, and the most advanced US combat aircraft, submarine, and warship as well as advanced military equipment are based in Guam, Japan, and the ROK to achieve forward military deployment. On July 20, 2015, the US Navy issued its "Navigation Plan" (NAVPLAN), which stated that the US Navy would comprehensively strengthen its military deployment in the Asia-Pacific region, for which the most advanced weapons and equipment of the US Navy would be deployed, such as F-35 Lightning II, F/A-18E/F Super Hornet, and P-8A Poseidon Patrol.[5]

The shift of the US military's focus to the Asia-Pacific region is intended to contain China. The US believes that China's military modernization is a challenge to the US military dominance in the Asia-Pacific region, and it thus regards China as a country capable of posing a threat to the US with "anti-access and area-denial" weaponry. According to the *Quadrennial Defense Review* published by the US Department of Defense in 2010, the United States was to develop a new joint air–sea battle concept to defeat adversaries across a range of military operations, including

---

[5] Xie Zhao, U.S. F-35C Carrier Aircraft to Deploy in Asia Pacific to Ensure Long-range Strike on China's Coast, website of China News Network, http://www.chinanews.com/mil/2015/07-23/7422383.shtml, July 23, 2015.

adversaries "equipped with sophisticated anti-access and area denial capabilities."[6]

The effective way to safeguard China's national security interests is not conflict and confrontation, but to build up military trust, properly handle differences, prevent misjudgment, establish a crisis management and control mechanism, and promote the establishment of a new model of major-country relationship between China and the United States.

Secondly, Japan's new defense policy poses a threat to China's national security. The Abe administration seeks to get rid of the institutional constraints after World War II and implements a policy of regarding Japan as a normal nation and pursuing military power. The Abe administration pushes for amending the pacifist constitution, giving up the exclusive defense policy, lifting the ban on collective self-defense, and removing legal obstacles relating to the use of force and sending troops overseas. Japan tries to get rid of its identification of being a defeated country in World War Two and strengthen its military force as a normal country. On July 1, 2014, the Abe administration passed the Decision of Japan's National Security Council, which was a cabinet resolution to amend the constitutional interpretation and lift the ban on collective self-defense, meaning that Japan decided to abandon its postwar exclusive defense policy. The resolution relaxed the conditions and scope of Japan's use of force. Japan can use force not only when it is attacked but also when countries with close ties to Japan are attacked by force and Japan's survival is threatened. In the past, Japan's use of force to defend itself was strictly limited to its neighborhood. But now it has expanded its scope to the world. On August 5, 2014, the Japanese government released the Defense of Japan 2014 resolution, which for the first time added amendments to the constitutional interpretation and lifted the ban on collective self-defense. On May 14, 2015, the Abe administration passed a series of security regulations related to the exercise of the right to collective self-defense and submitted them to the lower house of Japan's parliament for deliberation. The lower house of Japan forcibly passed a new security legislation on July 16, 2015. The new security legislation comprises a series of bills, including one new law and ten legal amendments. This new security legislation establishes

---

[6] Liu Haiyang, Changes in U.S. Military Power after the Cold War, Ping Huang and Ni Feng, eds., *Research Report on U.S. Issues* (2013), Beijing: Social Sciences Academic Press (China), 2013, p. 131.

Japan's legal right to exercise collective self-defense and expand the overseas military operations of the Self-Defense Forces. The Abe administration, therefore, has completely abandoned the pacifist constitution and the exclusively defense-oriented strategy through government resolutions and the security legislation and has gradually sought to make Japan a military power.

Japan's defense policy has the strategic intention of guarding against China. Japan does not pose a direct military threat to China's national security. However, within the framework of the US–Japan alliance, disputes and conflicts between China and Japan are in danger of triggering conflicts between China and the US. Therefore, we should promote the establishment of a China–Japan security dialogue and control mechanism to prevent the escalation of tensions and confrontations between China and Japan and avoid military conflicts.

Finally, China should safeguard its security strategic space. With the development of the world's new military revolution, weaponry has gradually become more accurate, intelligent, invisible, and unmanned. The national security strategy and national defense policy of China have also undergone significant adjustments to adapt to the new changes in weaponry and war patterns. China keeps on carrying out the strategic military policy of active defense. By broadening its strategic vision and renewing its strategic thinking, China has built up and is managing a comprehensive defense system consisting of preparation for and termination of war, deterrent and actual combat, shaping situation and controlling risk, containing war and winning war. Based on the strategic environment in Northeast Asia, to adequately protect China's eastern territory and maritime security, China has continuously adjusted and optimized its military and strategic layout. The Chinese Navy has begun to shift from the previous offshore defense strategy to a combination of offshore defense and open sea defense to improve its strategic deterrent and counterattack capabilities. China's air force has changed from a homeland defense type to a combination of attack and defense.[7]

With the expansion of China's foreign trade and investment, it has become highly dependent on international energy and resources. As its overseas interests continue to expand, it is becoming more and more critical to safeguard China's maritime rights and interests and the safety of its

---

[7] *White Paper on China's Military Strategy*, Chinese Central Government's Official Website, http://www.gov.cn/zhengce/2015-05/26/content_2868988.htm, May 26, 2015.

strategic naval routes. The goal of China's maritime security is not only to protect the offshore waters but also to break through the offshore defense, move towards the Pacific Ocean and the Indian Ocean, and expand the strategic depth of protecting China's maritime borders. To this end, China has established the East China Sea Air Defense Identification Zone as an extension of the defense area, effectively safeguarding China's maritime security.

1.2.3.2 *Protecting Chinese citizens and ensuring social security*

It is a country's vital responsibility to protect the life and property of its citizens overseas and safeguard the legitimate rights and interests of its enterprises and companies. This responsibility forms an integral part of the national security interests. Trade, investment, and personnel exchanges between China and the countries in Northeast Asia are frequent and close. It has become an important part of China's national security interests to protect the personal property and safety of Chinese citizens, safeguard the legitimate rights and interests of Chinese enterprises, ensure non-discrimination and fair competition opportunities, prevent the infiltration and subversion of hostile foreign forces, and maintain social and political stability.

China's contacts with the countries in Northeast Asia are increasingly close. More and more Chinese citizens are working, studying, and travelling in Northeast Asian countries. The number of Chinese citizens visiting Japan, the ROK, the DPRK, Russia, and Mongolia has increased significantly. In 2014, 6.1 million Chinese citizens visited the ROK,[8] 2.41 million visited Japan, and 1.2 million visited Russia. The number of young Chinese students studying in Japan, Russia, and the ROK is also increasing year on year. Due to the need for investment, project contracting, and labor employment contracts, some Chinese citizens are engaged in engineering technology and labor services in Northeast Asian countries, such as engineering projects and agricultural labor contracts in Russia and mineral resources exploration and development projects in Mongolia.

---

[8] A Survey of China's Attitude to Travel in the ROK: Travel to the ROK is Expected to Recover, People's Daily Online, http://travel.people.com.cn/n/2015/0708/c41570-27271186.html, July 8, 2015.

Chinese citizens in these countries may encounter criminal cases such as theft, robbery, and murder, as well as maltreatment and illegal detention. Therefore, the Chinese government and the governments in Northeast Asia should strengthen coordination and cooperation, safeguard the legitimate rights and interests of Chinese citizens, protect their property, and ensure their safety.

With the rapid development of China's economy, China has become a major manufacturing country, a major trading country, and a significant investment country in the world, and its trade and investment cooperation with countries in Northeast Asia has been continuously expanding. China has become the largest trading partner of all the countries in Northeast Asia, one of the largest import and export target countries for goods trade, and one of the largest investment destinations for Japan and the ROK. China has also begun to invest in countries in Northeast Asia and has expanded the China–Russia and China–Mongolia cooperation in the field of investment. There is fierce market competition in Northeast Asia. It is important to safeguard the legitimate rights and interests of Chinese enterprises in competition as well as in economic and trade aspects following WTO agreements and investment protection agreements. China is making efforts to ensure that Chinese enterprises receive fair and equal treatment in other countries and participate in fair competition without discrimination. It is also acting to make sure that the legitimate interests and various rights of Chinese firms are adequately protected. At present, all countries in Northeast Asia have joined the WTO and China has signed trade agreements and investment protection agreements with countries in Northeast Asia. This improves the standardization and institutionalization of economic and trade cooperation and helps to protect the interests of China's foreign trade companies.

China has relatively complicated ethnic and cultural relations with the neighboring Northeast Asian countries. For example, the eastern regions of Jilin and Liaoning provinces are populated by the Korean ethnic group, which is culturally similar to the populations of the DPRK and the ROK. In this regard, we should ensure normal exchanges between China, the DPRK and the ROK, and promote and expand economic cooperation and cultural exchanges. At the same time, we should also crackdown on illegal immigration, transnational crimes, drug trafficking, commercial smuggling, and other illegal and criminal activities to protect the security and social order in the border areas between China and the DPRK. Besides, the Mongolian ethnic groups in China and Mongolia are also related by race, history, and culture. With the continuous expansion of China–Mongolia economic, trade, and personnel exchanges, efforts should be made to remove the contradictions and conflicts as well as the various so-called "China threat." Conditions should be created for China and Mongolia to develop good neighborly and friendly relations and deepen all-round cooperation in political, economic, and cultural fields.

1.2.3.3 *Safeguarding peace and security in Northeast Asia*

The area surrounding a country is its great living environment and development space. Maintaining good neighborly relations and friendly cooperation with neighboring countries and establishing a peaceful and stable regional environment are essential guarantees for safeguarding and realizing national security interests. Northeast Asia, as a whole, has maintained a state of peace and stability. However, the peace and stability are very fragile, and there are still various security threats and challenges. The security situation in Northeast Asia is mainly affected by the situation in the Korean Peninsula, the DPRK nuclear issue, and the island disputes among various countries. It is one of China's most important national security strategies to ease tensions in the Korean peninsula, peacefully resolve the DPRK nuclear issue and territorial disputes among countries, actively safeguard peace and stability in Northeast Asia, and create a good regional and international environment for China's peaceful development.

Firstly, we should safeguard peace and stability in the Korean peninsula. The Korean Peninsula and China are linked by mountains and rivers. The situation in the Korean Peninsula is directly related to China's national security. The Korean War that took place in the 1950s directly threatened the security of China's northeast border. Since the armistice, the two sides are still in a state of military confrontation, and their armament levels are continuously escalating. More than 30 years after the end of the Cold War, the United States has not established diplomatic relations with the DPRK. It continues to implement a policy of isolation and sanctions against the DPRK. The US military alliance with the ROK and its military deterrence policy have directly increased tensions in the Korean Peninsula. The Korean Peninsula is the meeting point of the geostrategic interests of the countries in Northeast Asia. The situation in the Korean Peninsula and its changes directly affect the relations among the countries in Northeast Asia and the peace and stability in Northeast Asia.

Tensions in the Korean Peninsula are an essential threat to peace and security in Northeast Asia and also pose a serious challenge to China's national security. Relieving tensions on the Korean Peninsula, promoting the establishment of a peace system in the Korean Peninsula, and supporting the independent, peaceful reunification process between the two sides of the Korean Peninsula are rational choices to solve the Korean Peninsula Issue and safeguard peace and stability in the region. China actively maintains order and security in the Korean Peninsula, promotes dialogue and cooperation between the DPRK and the ROK, and promotes the relaxation of tensions in the Korean Peninsula. It has a positive effect on maintaining peace and stability in Northeast Asia.

Secondly, we should promote the peaceful resolution of the DPRK nuclear issue. The DPRK nuclear issue is a severe threat to the security of Northeast Asia. China has always insisted on the denuclearization of the Korean Peninsula, and at the same time stands for resolving the nuclear crisis in DPRK through peaceful negotiations and opposes the use or threat of force. China actively advocates and promotes the Six-Party Talks to resolve the DPRK nuclear crisis and has achieved phased results. At present, the Six-Party Talks in Beijing on the DPRK nuclear issue have stalled, but this in no way means that a peaceful solution to the DPRK nuclear issue has reached a dead end. The fundamental relaxation of tensions in the Korean Peninsula, the promotion of the establishment of a peace system in the Korean Peninsula, the establishment of a security cooperation mechanism in Northeast Asia, and the normalization of relations between the United States and Japan and the DPRK will help to finally resolve the DPRK nuclear issue, thus preventing the issue from escalating into regional conflicts.

Finally, we should handle territorial disputes in Northeast Asia properly. There are island disputes among various countries in Northeast Asia, such as the territorial dispute over four islands (called the Northern Territories in Japan and the Southern Kurils in Russia) between Russia and Japan, disputes over the Diaoyu Dao and the delimitation of the East China Sea between China and Japan, the territorial dispute over a set of islands (called Dokdo in Korean and Takeshima in Japanese) between the ROK and Japan, the dispute over the boundary between the DPRK and the ROK, and disputes over the delimitation of the Yellow Sea and Suyan Rock between China and the ROK. The island disputes between neighboring countries in Northeast Asia are long-standing issues left arising from the different interpretations and applications of the international law of the sea. As these islands are related to national territorial sovereignty, national defense security, and marine interests, they have become very sensitive issues in the relations between countries. These island disputes seriously affect the relations between countries in Northeast Asia and threaten peace and stability in the region.

The territorial dispute over four islands (called the Northern Territories in Japan and the Southern Kurils in Russia) between Russia and Japan is a remnant of World War II. As a result of the territorial dispute, Russia and Japan have not signed a peace treaty for more than 70 years. The territorial dispute between Russia and Japan has severely affected the strategic mutual trust and national relations between the two countries. The Diaoyu Dao issue between China and Japan is also a historical issue. The illegal "purchase" of islands by the Japanese government in 2012 exacerbated the Diaoyu Dao issue between the two countries. It caused a severe setback of China–Japan strategic and mutually beneficial relations. The dispute over a set of islands (called Dokdo in Korean and Takeshima in Japanese) between the ROK and Japan has also severely affected the development of the ROK–Japan relations.

Island disputes among countries in Northeast Asia are the fuse that may lead to military conflicts among nations. Proper handling of island disputes among countries is an important topic facing all countries. The Chinese government adheres to the principle of peaceful settlement of territorial disputes, emphasizes that history, law, and reality should be fully respected, and opposes the use or threat of force. The purpose of the Chinese government's claim is to prevent territorial disputes from threatening and undermining regional peace and stability.

1.2.4 China's cultural interests in Northeast Asia

China is an ancient civilization with a 5,000-year history. The Chinese nation has created a rich culture. Chinese culture embodies the spirit of the Chinese nation, national wisdom, and national creation. Chinese culture embodies the spirit, wisdom and creation of the Chinese nation. It is the spiritual driving force for the Chinese people to unite as one and strive for the better future. The Chinese culture has a far-reaching influence on all countries in Northeast Asia, which has led to the formation of close cultural relations. China's cultural interests in Northeast Asia consist of expanding cultural exchanges between China and other countries in the region, promoting China's distinctive culture, enhancing China's soft power in Northeast Asia, and finally furthering the development and prosperity of Chinese culture.

1.2.4.1 Spreading Chinese culture and building a bridge to the Northeast Asian countries

Countries in Northeast Asia have ethnic groups that are closely related, economies that are linked, and cultures that are also interlinked. The Chinese culture has had a profound influence on Japan, the ROK, the DPRK, and Mongolia. The Chinese culture has impacted living customs, social ethics, ideology and morality, humanistic spirit, political thought, literature and art, science education, national governance, and international exchanges in China. Today, political, economic, and cultural exchanges between China and the countries in Northeast Asia continue to expand. It is becoming more and more essential to carry forward and disseminate the distinctive Chinese culture.

Disseminating Chinese culture is an essential part of China's foreign policy. Cultural exchanges of countries involve people-to-people interactions, which leads to a meeting of hearts and minds. Culture is the bridge and link between people. In Northeast Asia, Chinese culture has a unique advantage. The cultures of all countries in Northeast Asia contain the spirit of Chinese culture. Actively promoting and carrying forward Chinese culture in Northeast Asia can lead to strengthening mutual understanding, expanding broad consensus, promoting friendship among people of all countries in Northeast Asia, and developing friendly relations among countries.

Chinese culture advocates harmonious values. In its foreign policy, China advocates "coexistence of all in harmony" and "harmony in the world." In its culture, it emphasizes that "a broad mind achieves greatness" and inclusiveness. In its national relations, it advocates "harmony" and "win-win cooperation." Today, China's good neighborly diplomacy based on amity, sincerity, mutual benefit, and inclusiveness embodies the traditional thoughts of Chinese culture. Expanding cultural exchanges can enable countries in Northeast Asia to enhance trust, friendship, and cooperation.

1.2.4.2 Maintaining historical justice and protecting Chinese heritage

China has a history of thousands of years of close contact with Northeast Asian countries. The Northeast Asian region has gone through historical changes such as the change of dynasties, territories changing hands, and the migration of people. There have been many disputes about the history of countries, relations between countries, and cultural interactions between countries in Northeast Asia. However, some debates on historical and cultural issues will inevitably bear political overtones and will be tampered with for political needs. Maintaining fairness in the relations between the countries in Northeast Asia and dealing with these issues rationally are important to safeguard China's cultural interests and deepen the cultural exchanges among the countries in Northeast Asia.

There is a dispute about Koguryo's history between Chinese and ROK scholars. Chinese scholars insist that the Koguryo Kingdom was one of the local regimes established by ethnic minority groups in northeast China. Some ROK scholars believe that the Koguryo Kingdom was the birthplace of the Koryo Kingdom and is thus a part of Korean history. This debate involves the issue of the historical sites of Koguryo City and tombs in Ji'an City, Jilin Province. China completed the application for World Heritage status on July 1, 2004, and at the 28th session of the World Heritage Committee of the United Nations Educational, Scientific and Cultural Organization (UNESCO), its application for inclusion in the World Heritage List was approved. Due to the cultural similarities between China and the ROK, there is also a big dispute over the application to the world's intangible cultural heritage list. For example, the ROK has succeeded in applying its Gangneung Danoje Festival as the world's intangible cultural heritage while as everyone knows that Dragon Boat Festival (*Duanwu*) is a traditional Chinese festival. These examples remind us to strengthen the research, protection, and application of China's excellent traditional culture to further promote the historical inheritance of Chinese civilization.

The war of aggression started by Japan caused much harm to Asian peoples, in particular the war of aggression against China, which caused 35 million casualties and property losses of US$600 billion in China. However, Japan's right-wing forces and Abe administration did everything possible to avoid responsibility and distort the history of aggression. The history textbooks compiled by Japan's right-wing forces openly distort the history of Japan's aggression, describing Japan's invasion in Asia as the "liberation of Asia," downplaying the appalling Nanjing Massacre as the "Nanjing incident" caused by Chinese resistance, describing Japan's invasion as "entering," and openly denying the forced recruitment of "comfort women."[9] This has not only caused great psychological harm to the people of all countries that have been invaded by Japan but has also warned us to uphold historical justice, restore the true history, and let people remember history and cherish peace.

1.2.4.3 Enhancing the soft power of Chinese culture

According to hard power criteria such as the economy and military, China has become a big country in Northeast Asia. However, China's soft power still needs to be improved. Cultural soft power can be expressed as an excellent national image — the attraction, charisma, and influence of China's political system and culture and art.

Firstly, we should promote cultural diversity and inclusiveness. Cultural diversity is the primary feature of human society and the fundamental driving force of cultural development. Human civilization and culture have developed and prospered by seeking common ground while maintaining differences and learning from each other. Cultural diversity requires mutual respect for each country and people's social systems, values, and independent choices of development path. China's socialist system is a historic choice made by the Chinese people. Recent history has proved that it is a social model and development path that conforms to China's national characteristics. China opposes the value diplomacy and democratic diplomacy promoted by the United States and Japan, which impose their values and development patterns on other countries. In essence, the United States and Japan are treating their value diplomacy as the culture diplomacy and using it as a tool in their foreign policy and an essential means to contain China.

Secondly, we should expand cultural exchanges between China and countries in Northeast Asia. In recent years, cultural exchanges between China and the countries in Northeast Asia have been continuously expanded, and intergovernmental cultural coordination and cooperation mechanisms have been established. China and the countries in Northeast Asia often hold cultural exchange activities such as film festivals and art

---

[9] Cao Pengcheng, The Problem of Japanese History Textbooks. *Xinhua New Agency*, http://news.xinhuanet.com/ziliao/2005-04/06/content_2791899_4.htm, April 6, 2005.

festivals. China has also established several Confucius Institutes in the ROK, Japan, Russia, Mongolia, and other countries to teach Chinese to students and help spread Chinese culture. China's cultural diplomacy and cultural exchange activities have helped the spread of Chinese culture in Northeast Asia, deepened people's understanding of China's cultural spirit, literature, and art, and enhanced the trust and friendship between China and people in Northeast Asia.

Finally, we should maintain the positive image of China. A country's image can fundamentally enhance its international reputation, international attraction, and global appeal. With the continuous expansion of cultural exchanges between China and countries in Northeast Asia, China's national image is increasingly improving. However, in the national image survey conducted by foreign media and public opinion agencies, respondents from Japan and the ROK had a low and unfavorable opinion of China and there were still various so-called "China threat" theories.

There may be many reasons why China's national image is not highly valued in Japan and the ROK, such as Resentment caused by China's rapid economic development, the wave of nationalism in countries in recent years, and misleading propaganda by the media. Therefore, strengthening cultural exchanges between China and Japan and the ROK, enhancing mutual trust and friendship, and establishing a good national image are important goals for China's soft power development.

1.3 China's Role in Northeast Asia

The role of a nation is the identity of a nation in the international order. Due to the different national roles, the national interests, goals, and functions are different. Studying China's role in the international system of Northeast Asia is a prerequisite for the study of China's strategy and policies in Northeast Asia. A clear role orientation indicates a clear direction and leads to a clear goal. China has experienced a major change and has changed status from a challenger to a participant and builder in the international system of Northeast Asia. China, as a responsible big country in Northeast Asia, is playing an active and constructive role in maintaining peace and stability, promoting cooperation and development, and promoting the construction of the international system and order in Northeast Asia.

1.3.1 Change of China's role in the international system in Northeast Asia

China is an important country in Northeast Asia. In the international system in Northeast Asia, China's role orientation and role allocation determine its position and function. It directly affects China's national interests and strategic choices. China's role is both positioned by its self-identity and allocated by the international system of the region. It is not only based on China's own comprehensive strength but also formed in the process of interaction among countries in Northeast Asia.

China's role in Northeast Asia is changing. First, China, as an emerging power, has become a big country in Northeast Asia. Second, China has become a participant, builder, and initiator in the international system in Northeast Asia.

1.3.1.1 *Setting up a major-power status in Northeast Asia*

Countries are important actors in international relations. According to the principle of sovereign equality, each country is an equal member of the international community, and all countries, regardless of size and strength, are equal in status. However, due to the different strengths of each country, their roles and influence in international affairs are different. In contemporary international relations, major powers in the world play a leading role in foreign affairs. World powers set the rules and maintain the order accordingly. These international rules reflect and represent the will and interests of the world's major powers. At the same time, they also need to be in line with the interests of most countries and be recognized and supported by most countries in the world. China insists on the central position and leading role of the United Nations in contemporary international affairs. At the same time, we cannot deny the important role of world powers in solving major international problems. The active participation of world powers in the coordination and resolution of international affairs not only means that they are safeguarding their countries and realizing their national interests but also means that they are shouldering international responsibility.

The position of a world or regional power is mainly based on its national strength or comprehensive national strength. According to the national strength assessment system, the comprehensive national strength of a country is manifested not only by hard power, such as natural resources, population, industrial base, economic aggregate, military strength, and scientific and technological level, but also by soft power. The national strength is relative and it is obtained through comparison with the strength of other nations. So strength assessment in a scientific and objective way is the important basis for self-identity awareness.

China is a large country in Northeast Asia with great resources and a large population. More than 40 years after the reform and opening up, China has rapidly risen as an emerging world power. China's GDP ranks behind that of the United States. It overtook Japan in 2010 and is now the largest economy in Northeast Asia. According to the statistics of the International Monetary Fund, the GDP of the United States in 2015 was US$17.95 trillion, China's was US$10.98 trillion, Japan's was US$4.12 trillion, Russia's was US$1.32 trillion, and the ROK's was US$1.38 trillion.[10] China's GDP is equivalent to the sum of GDP of some countries in Northeast Asia such as Japan, Russia, and the ROK. China's innovation capability is continuously increasing and its equipment manufacturing industry is becoming more and more important in the world. China's military modernization process is accelerating and its defense capability is rapidly increasing. China's international image continues to improve, especially its influence in Northeast Asia. China's comprehensive strength and influence in Northeast Asia exceed those of other Northeast Asian countries, which have created a strong foundation for China to establish its status as a major country in Northeast Asia.

President Xi Jinping called for major-country diplomacy with Chinese characteristics at the Central Conference on Work Relating to Foreign Affairs in November 2014. It is important for China's role in the contemporary international system and it also has great significance in establishing China's diplomatic status as a major power in Northeast Asia. The establishment of China's diplomatic status as a major power in Northeast Asia is fully in line with the trend of multi-polarization of the international system in Northeast Asia and also reflects China's international status and influence in Northeast Asia. It means that China, as a regional power, will participate more actively in Northeast Asian affairs, play a more constructive role in maintaining peace and stability, and play a more important leading role in promoting the transformation of the international system and the construction of the international order.

---

[10] International Monetary Fund, World Economic Outlook Database April 2016, April 12, 2016, http://www.imf.org/extemal/pubs/ft/weo/2016/01/weodata/index.aspx.

1.3.1.2 Assigning China's role in the Northeast Asian international system

The role of countries in the international system usually means two things: First, it refers to the role in the global pattern, such as the two superpowers of the United States and the Soviet Union as the two poles in the bipolar pattern; second, it refers to the role and function of a country in the international system, such as challengers, participants, builders, initiators, and other roles. China's role in the global network of Northeast Asia refers to China's position and role in Northeast Asia in different historical periods. This kind of role is a conscious policy choice. It is constructed in the process of interaction between countries in the region and is also manifested in its actual influence on the regional international system and order.

The international system in Northeast Asia has gone through two major historical stages: the Cold War and the post-Cold War period. During the Cold War, the world established a bipolar pattern between the United States and the Soviet Union, forming two major political and military blocs headed by the United States and the Soviet Union. In Northeast Asia, this period was characterized by fierce confrontation and a power struggle between the two major political and military blocs of the United States and the Soviet Union. The struggle for hegemony between the two superpowers could have triggered a war in Northeast Asia. The United States, Japan, and other countries imposed isolation and blockade policies on China. In the late 1970s, China implemented the policy of reform and opening up and began to gradually integrate into the international system, actively improving its relations with the countries in Northeast Asia. China then established diplomatic relations with Japan, the United States, and the ROK; China–Soviet and China–Mongolian relations were normalized.

During the Cold War, China was also a challenger to the international system in Northeast Asia. China publicly opposed the United States and Soviet Union. The Cold War ended, the danger of US–Soviet hegemony and wars in Northeast Asia was eliminated. Major changes have since taken place in the international pattern in Northeast Asia. China has rapidly developed into an emerging major country in Northeast Asia and the world. China's role in Northeast Asia's international system has also changed from challenger to defender and builder, and China has begun to take the initiative to assume the responsibility of a major country in Northeast Asia. China has always insisted that the United Nations possess the leading role in solving international and regional affairs. China is trying hard to firmly maintain the international order established in Northeast Asia after World War II, actively coordinate and solve the Korean Peninsula issue, promote the resolution of the DPRK nuclear crisis, and coordinate and solve other disputes and conflicts in Northeast Asia. China is playing an important role in keeping the peace and stability and helping economic development and prosperity in Northeast Asia.

1.3.2 China as the defender of the international system and order in Northeast Asia

China is a major country in Northeast Asia. It has adhered to the path of peaceful development, actively participated in coordinating and solving the Korean Peninsula issue, and actively maintained order in Northeast Asia after World War II. It has made important contributions to the peace, stability, development, and prosperity in this region.

1.3.2.1 *Acting as a positive force for peace and development in Northeast Asia*

In the 21st century, China has rapidly risen. At this time, various forms of the "China threat" theory have emerged in Northeast Asia. The so-called "military threat," "population threat," and "economic threat" of China are constantly disseminated. Some of these public opinions and ideological trends are based on a kind of inertial thinking. Some people believe that China will inevitably expand to the surrounding areas and the world as the old empire did, thus regarding China's rapid rise as a new threat to the countries in the region. At the same time, it could be a malicious propaganda due to some countries' strategic need to contain China. They regard China's rapid and powerful development as a new threat and challenge. All kinds of "China threat" theories are very harmful and will have a negative impact on the trust and cooperation between China and the countries in Northeast Asia.

In order to eliminate all kinds of worries, misunderstandings, and hostile propaganda and show the world China's adherence to the foreign policy of peace, the Chinese government published the white paper entitled *China's Peaceful Development* in 2005 and 2011 respectively, in order to show the world that China will unswervingly adhere to the path of peaceful development. China's peaceful rise is not a threat to the world and regional peace, but a positive force for the world and regional peace and development.

China's adherence to the path of peaceful development stems from Chinese cultural tradition. China is a peace-loving nation, and its cultural tradition emphasizes "coexistence of all in harmony" and "harmony in the world." China firmly grasps the theme of the times of peace and development, adheres to the principle of acting in accordance with the situation instead of acting against the situation, and seizes the opportunity of peace to develop itself. The experience of China's rapid rise shows us that there can be no development without peace. China can only take the road of peaceful development if it wants to achieve the goal of a prosperous, strong, democratic, civilized, and harmonious modern socialist country.

History and reality have determined that China must adhere to the path of peaceful development and actively safeguard the peaceful development environment in Northeast Asia. China does not seek regional hegemony. China did not seek hegemony in the past, does not seek hegemony now, and will never seek hegemony in the future. The successful experience of China's peaceful development is to break the so-called law that "powerful countries must seek hegemony." In *China's peaceful development*, the Chinese government made it clear that "China is committed to pursuing defense policy which is defensive in nature" and that "the fundamental purpose of modernizing the Chinese armed force is to safeguard China's sovereignty, security, territorial integrity, and interests of national development." It also stated that "China will not engage in the arms race with any other country, and it does not pose a military threat to any other country."[11] Therefore, China, as an emerging power in Northeast Asia, is not a threat to regional peace, but a positive force and an important guarantee for maintaining and realizing peace and stability in Northeast Asia.

1.3.2.2 Actively maintaining peace and stability in Northeast Asia

Maintaining peace and stability in Northeast Asia is an important condition for China's peaceful development and is a major part of China's

---

[11] *China's Peaceful Development*, Chinese Central Government's Official Website, http://www.gov.cn/zhengce/2011-09/06/content_2615782.htm, September 6, 2011.

foreign policy. It is not only in line with China's national sovereignty, security, and development interests but also in line with the common interests of all countries in Northeast Asia. The security situation in Northeast Asia is grave and complicated. It is China's duty-bound responsibility to actively coordinate and resolve the contradictions and conflicts in Northeast Asia and maintain peace and stability in Northeast Asia.

The Korean Peninsula issue and the DPRK nuclear crisis are hot-button issues in Northeast Asia and the greatest threats to peace and security. The Korean Peninsula issue concerns the DPRK and the ROK. It involves easing tensions in the Korean Peninsula and realizing the independent and peaceful reunification of the two sides. The Korean War ended 70 years ago. The DPRK and the ROK have been divided, and the situation in the Korean Peninsula is very tense. The DPRK insists on "Military-First Politics" (Songun Politics) and actively develops missiles and nuclear weapons technology. The ROK has continuously strengthened its military alliance with the United States. The United States continues to maintain a large-scale military presence in the ROK and strengthen forward military deployment. The ROK and the United States frequently hold large-scale military exercises. The Cheonan incident and the shelling of Yeonpyeong Island in 2010 almost triggered a war between the DPRK and the ROK. The Korean Peninsula issue is a legacy of the Cold War and a product of the two superpowers' fight for influence in Northeast Asia. Today, although the Soviet Union has disintegrated, the Korean Peninsula issue is still a complicated geostrategic issue, and the US Northeast Asia strategy is an important external force that affects the situation in the Korean Peninsula.

China and the Korean Peninsula are linked by mountains and rivers, and China maintains good relations with the DPRK and the ROK. On the Korean Peninsula issue, China does not condone confrontation and conflict between the DPRK and the ROK, but actively eases tensions in the Korean Peninsula, strives to diminish disputes between the DPRK and the ROK, and supports the independent and peaceful reunification of the DPRK and the ROK through negotiations based on sovereign equality and no interference from external forces.

The DPRK nuclear crisis is a major threat to the peace and security of the Korean Peninsula and Northeast Asia. On the one hand, the DPRK's development of nuclear weapons and missile technology will aggravate tensions in the Korean peninsula and may lead to conflicts and wars, thus undermining the peaceful situation in Northeast Asia; on the other hand, it endangers safeguarding the denuclearization system in Northeast Asia. Under the Treaty on the Non-Proliferation of Nuclear Weapons, the DPRK, the ROK, and Japan have all pledged to become non-nuclear states. The DPRK's determination to violate the Treaty to develop and possess nuclear weapons will undoubtedly pose a threat to other non-nuclear countries. The consequences may lead to further nuclear proliferation, prompting the ROK and Japan to seek nuclear weapons. It may also lead the United States and the ROK to adopt preemptive tactics and carry out military strikes against the DPRK. Either way will worsen the situation in the Korean Peninsula and in Northeast Asia. China has insisted on the denuclearization of the Korean peninsula. It has firmly opposed the use of force or the threat of force and advocated a peaceful settlement of the DPRK nuclear issue through negotiations. It has actively promoted the Six-Party Talks in Beijing on the DPRK nuclear issue, proposing the establishment of a peace system in the Korean Peninsula and a peace and security mechanism in Northeast Asia to create conditions for the final resolution of the DPRK nuclear issue and the denuclearization of the Korean Peninsula. The Six-Party Talks in Beijing on the DPRK nuclear issue have avoided military conflicts and have also created a way to solve regional problems through multilateral negotiations. What China has done shows that China is an active defender of peace and security in Northeast Asia and that it is playing a positive role in maintaining peace and stability in Northeast Asia.

1.3.2.3 *Actively maintaining the order in Northeast Asia after World War II*

After the end of the Cold War, the bipolar pattern ended, and the international system in Northeast Asia entered an important period of transition. Japan's politics have since then shifted to the right. The Abe administration attempted to deny Japan's history of wars of aggression and the post-war arrangements in Northeast Asia. Defending the victory of the war against Japanese invasion and maintaining the post-war world order in Northeast Asia has become an important task for countries in the region in order to keep peace and stability. This involves a series of issues such as the legal effect of important agreements signed by allies opposing German fascism and Japanese militarism during the war, the post-war arrangements for territory returned by Japan and ceded from Japan, the determination of the nature of Japan's war of aggression, and Japan's accountability for the war and compensation. These issues directly affect the peace and stability in this region. In recent years, the territorial dispute over four islands (called the Northern Territories in Japan and the Southern Kurils in Russia) between Russia and Japan, the Diaoyu Dao issue between China and Japan, the dispute over a set of islands (called Dokdo in Korean and Takeshima in Japanese) between the ROK and Japan, and Japan's reflection on war have all caused conflict in Northeast Asia. The Abe administration denied the history of aggression in Northeast Asia.

The territorial dispute over four islands (called the Northern Territories in Japan and the Southern Kurils in Russia) between Japan and Russia and the Diaoyu Dao issue between China and Japan involve the validity of the Yalta Agreement and the Potsdam Proclamation in international law. According to the Potsdam Proclamation, which urged Japan to surrender, Japan had to return to China all the territories taken from China. Based on the Yalta Agreement and the Potsdam Proclamation, it is clear that the United States violated a series of agreements. It had no right to transfer a territory native to China to Japan for administrative jurisdiction without China's permission. The territorial dispute over four islands (called the Northern Territories in Japan and the Southern Kurils in Russia) between Russia and Japan also directly concerns the effectiveness of the Yalta Agreement in international law. These important agreements form the international legal basis for the post-war order in Northeast Asia. Therefore, it is an important task to uphold the legal validity of these international legal documents and safeguard the post-war order established on the foundation of these international legal documents.

The Abe administration evaded the disastrous consequences of Japan's war of aggression on Asian countries. Japan openly denied atrocities including the Nanjing Massacre and the forced recruitment of "comfort women." Its political leaders openly visited the Yasukuni Shrine, which honors Class-A war criminals. The year 2015 marked the 70th anniversary of the victory in the Anti-Japanese War. At this important historical moment, the Japanese government's right-leaning deviation cannot but arouse high vigilance. China insists that Japan recognize the nature of the war of aggression and urges Japan to apologize for the war. China cannot forget the history. The past is a guide to the future. History is a mirror, and how we judge history determines the direction of the future. By constantly reflecting on the history of Japan's invasion of China, we can avoid a tragic repetition of history and achieve lasting peace between China and Japan.

1.3.3 China as the builder of the international system and order in Northeast Asia

After the end of the Cold War, the international system in Northeast Asia was in a period of historical transformation. China actively advocated abandoning the Cold War mentality and promoting the construction of a just and reasonable international system and order in Northeast Asia.

1.3.3.1 *Actively promoting the construction of new international order in Northeast Asia*

The Cold War is over. Cold War thinking and the related military alliances, power politics, and military confrontation policies still exist in Northeast Asia. The Korean Peninsula issue, the arms race among major powers, the regional security dilemma, and the legacy of World War II have become severe obstacles to the development of international relations. These problems seriously threaten peace and stability in Northeast Asia. Adapting to the trend of the times of peace and development, promoting the construction of a new type of international order in Northeast Asia has become a significant issue facing all countries.

China actively advocates building a new type of international order of equality, mutual trust, inclusiveness, mutual learning, and mutually beneficial cooperation in international relations and making joint efforts to uphold international fairness and justice: "In promoting equality and mutual trust, we should observe the purposes and principles of the Charter of the United Nations, and support equality among all countries, big or small, strong or weak, rich or poor. We should advance democracy in international relations." "In promoting inclusiveness and mutual learning, we should respect diversity of civilizations and development paths, respect and safeguard the rights of all peoples to independently choose their social system and development path, learn from others to make up for our shortcomings, and advance human civilization." "In promoting mutually beneficial cooperation, we should raise awareness about human beings sharing a community of common destiny. A country should accommodate the legitimate concerns of others when pursuing its own interests; and it should promote common development of all countries when advancing its own development."[12]

---

[12] Hu Jintao, Firmly March on the Path of Socialism with Chinese Characteristics and Strive to Complete the Building of a Moderately Prosperous Society in All Respects,

China has actively promoted countries in Northeast Asia to jointly build a new type of international order. In the China–Russia Joint Statement on Deepening the Comprehensive Strategic Partnership and Promoting Win-Win Cooperation, issued on May 9, 2015, China and Russia jointly proposed to promote the establishment of a new type of international order. China and Russia called on all countries to respect each other's sovereignty and territorial integrity, respect each other's core interests and major concerns, respect the social system and development path chosen independently by the people of all countries, and oppose acts of subversion of legitimate political power. They called on all countries to abide by the Charter of the United Nations, the Five Principles of Peaceful Coexistence and other basic norms of international law and international relations, and earnestly implement international treaties. They also advocated the concept of peaceful development and win-win cooperation, promoting multi-polarization of the world and promoting democratization and rule of law in international relations as the basic direction of foreign policy. China and Russia insisted that countries resolve differences and disputes through political and diplomatic channels. They opposed zero-sum games and a winner-takes-all Cold War mentality. They also opposed the use of force or threat of force and opposed the imposition of unilateral sanctions and threats of sanctions. They insisted that countries respect cultural differences and diversity of civilizations and promote constructive cooperation among different civilizations.[13]

On July 4, 2014, President Xi Jinping visited the ROK and delivered a speech entitled "Creating a Future for China-ROK Cooperation and Promoting Prosperity in Asia" at Seoul National University. President Xi Jinping stressed that "in international relations, all countries should abide by international law and the basic norms governing international relations, and uphold the principles of fairness, justice, and equality among nations" to bring "mutual benefits" and lead to "win-win solutions."[14] China and

---

Report to the Eighteenth National Congress of the Communist Party of China, Beijing: People's Publishing House, 2012, p. 47.

[13] China-Russia Joint Statement on Deepening the Comprehensive Strategic Partnership and Promoting Win-Win Cooperation, website of the Ministry of Foreign Affairs of the People's Republic of China, http://www.fmprc.gov.cn/mfa_chn/zyxw_602251/t1262144.shtm, May 9, 2015.

[14] Xi Jinping, "Creating a Future for China-ROK Cooperation and Promoting Prosperity in Asia--Speech at Seoul National University in the ROK," website the Ministry of

the ROK stated in the China–ROK Joint Statement that the two countries will build a mature strategic partnership based on mutual trust, strengthen cooperation to promote peace and stability in the Korean Peninsula and in Northeast Asia, work together to promote economic integration in East Asia and the recovery of the world economy, and play a leading role in the growth of the regional and world economies. China and the ROK should work together to strengthen the emotional ties between the two countries and peoples and build a relationship of mutual trust to further strengthen the cooperation between the two sides on various regional and international issues so as to contribute to the peace and stability of Northeast Asia and the development and common prosperity of the world.[15]

1.3.3.2 *Actively advocating a new security concept*

After the end of the Cold War, Northeast Asia was still facing a severe security situation. Traditional security threats were intertwined with non-traditional security threats. Beyond the Cold War mentality, establishing a new security concept and jointly dealing with various security threats and challenges through cooperation have become the only way for countries to maintain peace and security in Northeast Asia and promote development and prosperity in Northeast Asia.

On July 31, 2002, the Chinese government issued China's Position Paper on the New Security Concept, which comprehensively discussed China's policy and practice on the new security concept and elaborated on the new security concept of mutual trust, mutual benefit, equality, and cooperation. On October 24, 2013, at a seminar on neighborhood diplomacy, President Xi Jinping further elaborated that "We must make efforts to promote regional security cooperation, which is needed by both China and our neighboring countries. A new outlook on security is required that features mutual trust and reciprocity, based on equality and cooperation. We must develop a comprehensive security strategy with neighboring countries, actively participate in regional and sub-regional security initiatives, push forward cooperation and enhance mutual

---

Foreign Affairs of the People's Republic of China, http://www.fmprc.gov.cn/mfa_dhn/ziliao_611306/zyjh_611308/tl171668.shtml, July 4, 2014.

[15] Joint Statement between the People's Republic of China and Republic of Korea, *Xinhua News Agency*, http://news.xinhuanet.com/world/2014-07/03/c_1111449615.htm, July 3, 2014.

trust."¹⁶ On May 21, 2014, at the fourth summit of the Conference on Interaction and Confidence Building Measures in Asia held in Shanghai, President Xi Jinping delivered a speech actively advocating the establishment of a common, comprehensive, cooperative, and sustainable Asian security concept.

In a joint statement on Comprehensive Deepening of Strategic Cooperation Partnership, issued on September 27, 2010, China and Russia jointly advocated the establishment of internationally recognized basic principles of security cooperation, consisting of respect for each other's sovereignty, independence and territorial integrity, and non-interference in each other's internal affairs. These principles also include adhering to the principle of equality and indivisible security, sticking to the national defense policy of defensive nature, renouncing the use of force or the threat with force, fighting against taking or supporting any action that may subvert the governments of other countries or undermine the stability of other countries, resolving differences peacefully through political and diplomatic means, strengthening cooperation in dealing with non-traditional security threats, and carrying out bilateral and multilateral military cooperation that does not target third countries. China and Russia also actively advocate the establishment of an open, transparent, and equal security and cooperation framework in the Asia-Pacific region.¹⁷

In Northeast Asia, China not only advocates a new security concept but also actively promotes the establishment of a peace and security mechanism. On the Korean Peninsula issue, China adheres to the principles of sovereign equality and non-interference in internal affairs and opposes the use or threat of force. It advocates a peaceful settlement of the DPRK nuclear issue through diplomatic negotiations. China has actively promoted the Six-Party Talks on the DPRK nuclear issue, making it an important mechanism and platform for multilateral security dialogue and cooperation in Northeast Asia. China and Russia jointly advocated the establishment of the Shanghai Cooperation Organization (SCO), which

---

¹⁶Xi Jinping, Diplomacy with Neighboring Countries Characterized by Friendship, Sincerity, Reciprocity and Inclusiveness, October 24, 2013, *The Governance of China*, Beijing: Foreign Languages Press, 2018, p. 328.

¹⁷Joint Statement of the People's Republic of China and the Russian Federation on Comprehensive Deepening of Strategic Cooperation Partnership, website of the Ministry of Foreign Affairs of the People's Republic of China, http://www.fmprc.gov.cn/chn/pds/ziliao/1179/t756814.htm, September 27, 2010.

fully embodies the new security concept advocated by China. The SCO is based on the principles of "mutual trust, mutual benefit, equality, joint consultation, respect for cultural diversity and aspiration for collective development" and "making joint efforts to maintain and ensure peace, security and stability in the region"[18] and takes the path of common security, comprehensive security, cooperative security, and sustainable security. The practice has proved that the SCO has played an active role in strengthening mutual trust among its member states, promoting cooperation in political, economic, security, and cultural fields, jointly cracking down on the three forces of terrorism, separatism, and extremism, and maintaining regional peace and security.

1.3.3.3 *Actively promoting mutually beneficial and win-win regional economic cooperation*

China and the countries in Northeast Asia have become important economic and trade partners, forming a community of mutual economic dependence and interests. It is the shared vision of all the countries in Northeast Asia to go with the development trend of economic globalization and regional integration, eliminate various political factors and external interference, deepen economic and trade cooperation, and realize joint development and mutual benefit.

Firstly, the economic and trade cooperation between China and the countries in Northeast Asia should continue to develop. China is the ROK's largest trading partner. The trade volume between China and the ROK is equal to the total trade volume between the ROK and the United States, Japan, and Russia. In 2015, the trade volume between China and the ROK reached US$275.8 billion. China and the ROK have established an economic and trade communication and coordination mechanism at the ministerial level and a mechanism for direct trading of renminbi and the South Korean Won.

China is Russia's largest trading partner, and the two countries set a development target of reaching a bilateral trade volume of US$200 billion by 2020. China and Russia have established a regular meeting mechanism

---

[18] Declaration on the Establishment of the Shanghai Cooperation Organization, website of Shanghai Cooperation Organization, http://www.sectsco.org/CN11/show.asp?id=100, June 15, 2001.

between their prime ministers. This mechanism includes a committee for regular meetings between the prime ministers, which is further divided into sub-committees on trade and economy, science, finance, nuclear energy, communication and information technology, energy, transportation, aerospace, environmental protection, civil aviation, and customs. In recent years, China–Russia cooperation in the field of energy has been expanding. In 2009, China and Russia signed an oil trade agreement after which Russia started exporting 15 million tons of oil to China every year through the oil pipeline from Skovorodino to Daqing, with a contract period of 20 years. In 2011, Russia officially started supplying oil to China through this oil pipeline. In May 2014, China and Russia signed the Purchase and Sale Agreement for the Russian Gas Supply via the Eastern Route, with a total value of US$400 billion. Russia will supply 38 billion cubic meters of natural gas to China every year through the Eastern Route gas pipeline for 30 years. In 2009, the governments of China and Russia also approved the Program of Cooperation between the Northeast of the People's Republic of China and the Far East and Eastern Siberia of the Russian Federation (2009–2018) to promote cross-regional cooperation between the Eastern Russia and Northeast China.

The economic and trade cooperation between China and Mongolia has been continuously strengthened. The two sides have actively promoted mutually beneficial cooperation in mineral resources, infrastructure construction, and finance, aiming to bring the bilateral trade volume to US$10 billion by 2020.

China and Japan are important trading partners. Due to political factors, the trade volume between China and Japan has declined in recent years. However, Japan is still China's largest trading and investment partner in Northeast Asia.

Secondly, China has made great efforts to promote economic cooperation with Japan and the ROK, and the cooperation in Tumen River sub-region. China is actively promoting trilateral cooperation among China, Japan, and the ROK. China, Japan, and the ROK are important trading partners. Economic and trade cooperation among China, Japan, and the ROK is an important engine of regional cooperation in Northeast Asia. In 1999, the "10 + 3" framework between Association of Southeast Asian Nations (ASEAN) and China, Japan, and the ROK initiated a meeting mechanism for leaders of China, Japan, and the ROK. Starting from 2008, the leaders of China, Japan, and the ROK were to meet in rotation in China, Japan, and the ROK. The leaders of China, Japan, and the ROK issued the Joint Statement for Tripartite Partnership in 2008, the Joint Statement on the Tenth Anniversary of Trilateral Cooperation in 2009, and the Trilateral Cooperation Vision 2020 in 2010. China, Japan, and the ROK declared they would further strengthen economic and trade ties, deepen interest integration, strengthen financial cooperation, and create an attractive trade and investment environment. In May 2012, the Agreement on Promoting, Facilitating and Protecting Investment among the Government of the People's Republic of China, the Japanese Government, and the Government of the Republic of Korea (hereinafter to be referred as the China–Japan–ROK Investment Agreement) was signed. In May 2014, the China–Japan–ROK Investment Agreement formally entered into force. It was to establish a more stable and transparent investment environment for investment cooperation among the three countries. However, in recent years, the cooling of China–Japan political relations has severely affected trilateral cooperation among China, Japan, and the ROK.

China actively promotes cooperation and development in the Tumen River region. The Greater Tumen Initiative (GTI) (originally known as the Tumen River Area Development Program) was initiated by the United Nations Development Program in 1991. It takes the Tumen River basin as its core area, which includes Northeast China, coastal cities of the DPRK and the ROK, Mongolia, and the Far East of Russia, and promotes the development of regional cooperation. At present, the Tumen River regional cooperation mainly includes China, the ROK, Mongolia, and Russia, and ministerial-level consultative commission meeting has been established. On September 17, 2014, the 15th Meeting of the GTI Consultative Commission was held in Yanji City, Jilin Province, China. The meeting issued the Yanbian Declaration. Under the cooperation mechanism of the GTI, Northeast Asian countries have carried out practical cooperation in transportation, tourism, trade facilitation, and energy. China actively supports the GTI, which will aid economic and trade cooperation between Northeast China and the Northeast Asian countries, open up a transportation channel from Jilin Province to coastal countries, and accelerate the economic development and prosperity of the countries in the region through subregional cooperation. However, due to the tension in the Korean Peninsula and the negative attitude of Japan, the Tumen River regional cooperation has been going slowly with less effect.

Finally, China has promoted the establishment of a China–ROK free trade area and a China–Japan–ROK free trade area, with the GDP of the three countries reaching US$16.5 trillion, accounting for about 90% of East Asia's GDP. However, the trade volume of China, Japan, and the ROK only accounts for less than 20% of the total foreign trade volume of the three countries, which means there is great potential for cooperation and development. The establishment of the China–Japan–ROK free trade area has met the requirements of economic globalization and trade liberalization. It has realized the free flow of trade, investment, and personnel. It is of great significance for the economic development of China, Japan, and the ROK and of Northeast Asia and the entire Asian region.

On June 1, 2015, the governments of China and the ROK formally signed the Free Trade Agreement between the Government of the People's Republic of China and the Government of the Republic of Korea (hereinafter to be referred as the China–ROK FTA), which is the first step toward the establishment of a free trade area between China and the countries in Northeast Asia. As early as in 2004, China and the ROK started a feasibility study on a free trade agreement. In 2012, the two countries officially started negotiations on a free trade agreement. After 14 rounds of negotiations, the two countries finally reached a free trade agreement. The China–ROK FTA covers a wide range of areas such as trade in goods, trade in services, and investment. The liberalization ratio of trade in goods between the two sides exceeds 90% of taxable items and 85% of trade volume, making it a free trade agreement with a high level of openness. The China–ROK FTA will create a broad development space for the development of China–ROK economic and trade relations, and will also play a role in promoting and demonstrating the establishment of a free trade area among China, Japan, and the ROK.

China, Japan, and the ROK are still negotiating a free trade agreement. Since 2002, China, Japan, and the ROK have begun a feasibility study on the establishment of a free trade area. In November 2012, China, Japan, and the ROK officially started free trade agreement negotiations. The Conference of Chief Negotiators for the 7th Round of China–Japan–ROK Free Trade Area Negotiations was held in Seoul from May 12 to 13, 2015. China, Japan, and the ROK are the driving forces of Asian economic integration. The establishment of a free trade area among China, Japan, and the ROK will not only further deepen the economic and trade cooperation among the three countries but also play a leading role in promoting the development of a comprehensive economic partnership between China, Japan, the ROK, and ASEAN.

1.4 China's Strategic Conception of Northeast Asia

China's strategy and policy in Northeast Asia are to serve its Two Centenary Goals.[19] We should hold high the banner of peace, development, cooperation, and mutual benefit, take into account both international and domestic situations, make full use of both international and domestic resources, adapt to the trend of the times of peace and development, and cope with the new challenges brought about by the transformation of the international system and changes in the situation in Northeast Asia. From the perspective of safeguarding and realizing China's national interests in Northeast Asia, China's strategy and policy in Northeast Asia are determined based on its status as a major country in the region and its role as a defender and builder of regional order. China's strategic goal in the Northeast Asia region is to maintain peace and stability, promote economic development and prosperity, promote the construction of a democratic, just, and harmonious international order, and create a good neighboring international environment for its peaceful development and the great rejuvenation of the Chinese nation.

1.4.1 Guidelines for China's strategy in Northeast Asia

China's strategy in Northeast Asia is determined under the guidance of China's national strategy and diplomatic strategy layout. Northeast Asia occupies a prominent position in China's neighborhood diplomacy and forms an important geopolitical basis for China's peaceful development. We should hold high the banner of peace, development, cooperation, and mutual benefit. Establishing a community with a shared future will be the important guiding thought of China's strategy in Northeast Asia.

1.4.1.1 *Clarifying the important position of Northeast Asia*

Neighborhood diplomacy occupies an essential position in China's overall diplomacy. Neighborhood diplomacy is an important geopolitical basis for China to carry out the diplomacy of big countries and developing

---

[19]To finish building a moderately prosperous society in all respects by the time the Communist Party of China celebrates its centenary in 2021; and to turn China into a modern socialist country that is prosperous, strong, democratic, culturally advanced, and harmonious by the time the People's Republic of China celebrates its centenary in 2049.

countries. On October 24, 2013, China held a symposium on relations with neighboring countries during which President Xi Jinping delivered an important speech, analyzed the situation around China, and determined the strategic objectives and basic principles of China's neighboring diplomatic work. President Xi Jinping pointed out, "the CPC Central Committee defined, planned, and carried out a series of major diplomatic initiatives, paying particular attention to neighboring countries." "Regions around our borders are strategically significant to our country in terms of geography, the environment, and relationships."[20]

Northeast Asia occupies an important position in China's neighboring region. Northeast Asia is a densely populated region of world powers, including major world economies, major military powers, major resource-rich countries, and populous countries. In 2013, the GDP of the six countries in Northeast Asia was nearly US$17.5 trillion, accounting for nearly a quarter of the global economy. Four of the top 15 countries in world GDP are located in Northeast Asia.[21] During the global financial and economic crisis in 2008, the economy in Northeast Asia continued to grow at a high speed and became a major engine of global economic recovery. Northeast Asia is one of the regions with the most vitality and potential for economic development in the world. It is also important to support China's rapid economic development.

Northeast Asia is also one of the regions with the most complicated surrounding environments. The international system in Northeast Asia is in an important period of historic transition. In connection with this, the structural contradictions, the strategic game of big powers, historical issues, the Cold War mentality, territorial disputes, and other contradictions and conflicts in Northeast Asia are intertwined, severely complicating the security situation in Northeast Asia. The United States returned to Asia and implemented the "Asia-Pacific rebalancing" strategy. Japan tried its best to get rid of the post-war system and intended to become a military power again by adopting the policy of regarding itself as a normal country.

---

[20] Xi Jinping, *The Governance of China (I)*, Beijing: Foreign Languages Press, 2018, p. 325.
[21] Qian Hongshan, Opening a New Era of Peace and Cooperation in Northeast Asia: Keynote Speech by Assistant Foreign Minister Qian Hongshan at the Opening Ceremony of the 2014 Northeast Asia Peace and Cooperation Forum, website of the Ministry of Foreign Affairs of the People's Republic of China, http://www.fmprc.gov.cn/mfa_chn/zi]iao_611306/zyjh_611308/t1204796.shtml, October 28, 2014.

Hot-button issues such as the Korean Peninsula issue, territorial disputes, and historical issues in Northeast Asia continue to ferment. The mutual influence and overall effect of structural contradictions and practical problems can easily lead to military conflicts in Northeast Asia. The series of disagreements and disputes in Northeast Asia are directly related to China's sovereignty, security, and development interests, so China is an important stakeholder. Therefore, among Northeast Asia, Southeast Asia, South Asia, West Asia, Central Asia, and other neighboring regions, Northeast Asia is of special significance to China.

Northeast Asia provides China with geographical advantages and development opportunities for economic development and international cooperation, but it also brings about various regional security threats and challenges. Thus, it is crucial for us to study the current situation carefully, look to the whole world, and take an overall view to finally create a prospective strategy and policy for Northeast Asia.

1.4.1.2 *Serving China's peaceful development strategy*

China has set the Two Centenary Goals. President Xi Jinping pointed out that "the strategic purpose of our neighborhood diplomacy is driven by and must serve the two centenary goals and our national rejuvenation."[22] To this end, China needs to create an international strategic space for peaceful development, to implement a win-win opening strategy, and to create a stable surrounding international environment.

Peace and development are still the themes of the 21st century. Another world war is unlikely in the foreseeable future. This provides China with a strategic opportunity to realize peaceful development. Maintaining and making good use of the important strategic opportunity for China's peaceful development is the key to ensuring the realization of the Two Centenary Goals. China's peaceful development strategy involves "striving for a peaceful international environment to develop itself, and promoting world peace through its own development."[23] Without peace and stability in the surrounding areas, there would be no

---

[22] Xi Jinping, *The Governance of China (I)*, Beijing: Foreign Languages Press, 2018, p. 326.
[23] White Paper on *China's Peaceful Development Road*, Chinese Central Government's Official Website, http://www.gov_cn/zhengce/2015-12/22/content_2615756.htm, December 22, 2005.

peaceful international environment for China. To maintain peace and stability in Northeast Asia and enhance cooperation and development in the region, one needs to actively safeguard and make use of the strategic opportunities for peaceful development and create a good surrounding international environment for China's peaceful development. Therefore, China's Northeast Asia strategy involves peaceful development and a stable surrounding environment.

1.4.1.3 *Holding high the banner of peace, development, cooperation, and mutual benefit*

China has always held high the banner of peace, development, cooperation, and mutual benefit, which is the basic policy of China's foreign policy. Peace, development, cooperation, and mutual benefit embody China's wisdom. Peace is the guarantee of development. Development is the foundation of peace. Cooperation is an important way to achieve peace and development. Winning together is China's ultimate goal. China's strategy and policy in Northeast Asia should implement the diplomatic policy of peace, development, cooperation, and mutual benefit.

China firmly pursues an independent foreign policy of peace and good neighborliness and friendship with its neighbors and partners. China advocates the peaceful settlement of international disputes and opposes resorting to or threatening force. It adheres to the new concept of building relations with neighboring countries based on amity, sincerity, mutual benefit, and inclusiveness in Northeast Asia. It seeks no hegemony or expansion, and actively safeguards peace and stability in Northeast Asia.

Development is the foundation of peace and an essential condition for lasting peace. China pursues a win-win strategy of opening up and adheres to the principle of equality, mutual benefit, and joint development. The Northeast Asian countries are highly complementary in economy with close economic ties and deep interdependence. Promoting economic development and prosperity in Northeast Asia can create broad development and cooperation space for China's economic development and prosperity. China's development depends on the common development of all countries. China's development will provide a broad trade and investment market for all countries in Northeast Asia. Through deepening cooperation, we can achieve joint development, jointly contribute to peace, and benefit people.

Cooperation is the only way to achieve peace and development. Strengthening and deepening global and regional international cooperation are necessary in dealing with various traditional and non-traditional security threats and challenges or dealing with the impact of the global economic crisis and fierce international competition. The Northeast Asian countries have established various political, economic, military, and cultural cooperation relations. Now, the task before us is to continuously enhance mutual trust and deepen and expand cooperation fields and space. We need to deepen trust through cooperation, deepen cooperation through trust, and jointly safeguard peace and development in the region.

Achieving win-win results through cooperation is the basic concept of China's foreign policy. In the era of globalization, the interests of all countries intersect and merge with each other. China advocates abandoning the zero-sum game rule to achieve win-win, multi-win, and all-win results through cooperation instead of a winner-takes-all principle. In Northeast Asia, we will carry out cooperation based on the principle of mutual benefit so that all countries in the region will benefit from China's development and China will gain opportunities for cooperation and development from the development of all countries in the region.

1.4.2 Basic objectives of China's strategy in Northeast Asia

China's strategy in Northeast Asia is secondary to China's grand strategy of peaceful development in the world. It is the basic goal China wants to achieve in Northeast Asia based on the changes in the situation in the region and from the perspective of safeguarding and realizing China's national interests in Northeast Asia. At present, China's strategic problems in Northeast Asia are mainly manifested in three aspects. The first is to maintain peace and stability in Northeast Asia and safeguard China's national sovereignty, security, and development interests. The second is to promote economic development and prosperity in Northeast Asia and create a broad development space for China's stable and rapid economic development. The third is to promote the construction of a democratic, just, and harmonious international system and order in Northeast Asia and to establish an institutional guarantee for lasting peace and common prosperity in Northeast Asia.

1.4.2.1 *Maintaining peace and stability in Northeast Asia*

Northeast Asia, as a whole, has maintained a state of peace and stability. The rapid economic development in Northeast Asia and the deepening economic cooperation among various countries all benefit from peace and stability in the region. Peace and stability in Northeast Asia are also an important guarantee to effectively safeguard China's sovereignty, security, and development interests. However, Northeast Asia is also facing severe security situations and challenges, and there are unfavorable factors affecting peace and stability in the region. For this reason, China should regard the maintenance of peace and stability in Northeast Asia as an important goal and task.

First of all, China should safeguard the friendly relations between countries in Northeast Asia. The establishment of good neighborliness and friendly international relations is an important foundation for peace and stability in Northeast Asia. China has normalized its state relations with all countries in Northeast Asia and has established various forms of partnership with Russia, Japan, the ROK, Mongolia, and the DPRK. China has also signed the Treaty of Good Neighborliness and Friendly Cooperation with Russia and Mongolia. These not only show the rising level of China's relations with Northeast Asian countries but also indicate a solid political and legal foundation for the stable development of international relations.

There are also various contradictions and disputes in international relations in Northeast Asia, which have become obstacles affecting the development of the region. The Korean War ended 70 years ago. However, the United States and Japan have still not established diplomatic relations with the DPRK. It has been more than 70 years since the victory of World War II. However, Russia and Japan have not signed the post-war peace treaty due to the territorial dispute over four islands (called the Northern Territories in Japan and the Southern Kurils in Russia). These unfavorable factors have affected the development of relations among countries in Northeast Asia. In recent years, the Diaoyu Dao issue between China and Japan caused a serious decline in the relations between the two countries and greatly increased the risk of friction and conflict. This not only affects the mutual trust between China and Japan but also seriously affects the economic and trade cooperation between the two countries.

As an important country in Northeast Asia, China has long implemented an independent foreign policy of peace, good neighborliness, and friendship with its neighbors. As a responsible major country in Northeast Asia, China actively maintains good international relations, actively coordinates and resolves differences and disputes among nations, promotes the construction of new international relations, and ensures the stable and healthy development of international relations in Northeast Asia.

Secondly, China should safeguard peace and stability in Northeast Asia. Since the end of the Cold War, Northeast Asia has maintained a peaceful and stable situation, with no significant military conflicts or wars. The situation in the Korean Peninsula is however in a precarious state. The Cheonan incident and the shelling of Yeonpyeong Island that occurred in 2010 were quickly brought under control and did not escalate. Maintaining peace and stability in Northeast Asia is in line with the security and development interests of all countries in the region. China has played an active role in maintaining peace and stability in Northeast Asia. China actively advocates the principles of peaceful coexistence and non-interference in internal affairs, and promotes the peaceful settlement of state disputes through diplomatic negotiations, without the use or threat of force. China and other countries in Northeast Asia have established various forms of strategic dialogue mechanisms, security prevention, and liaison mechanisms. It not only helps to promote exchanges and trust between countries but also effectively prevents emergencies.

The United States is a key factor affecting peace and stability in Northeast Asia. The United States has continuously consolidated and intensified its bilateral military alliance with Japan and the ROK. The Obama administration determined the "Asia-Pacific rebalancing" strategy, shifting the focus of US military strategy to the Asia-Pacific region and strengthening its forward military deployment in Northeast Asia. The Obama administration's Asian policy had a strategic intention to contain and prevent China. It also makes the structural contradiction between an established power and an emerging power, the US and China, respectively, increasingly prominent. The United States is deeply involved in disputes over the rights of islands and seas between China and Japan, the Philippines, and other countries, thus increasing the risk of military conflicts between China and the United States, which is not conducive to peace and stability in Northeast Asia.

Peace and stability in Northeast Asia are directly related to China's security interests. The key to resolving the structural contradictions and conflicts in Northeast Asia is to enhance the strategic trust among the countries in Northeast Asia and build a new model of major-country relationship between China and the United States, which features harmony, peace, mutual respect, and win-win cooperation. Actively promoting the security dialogue among the major powers in Northeast Asia and establishing a security cooperation mechanism will be the best way to maintain peace and stability in the region.

Finally, the situation in Northeast Asia will remain stable and controllable. There are many hot-button issues in Northeast Asia: the territorial disputes over four islands (called the Northern Territories in Japan and the Southern Kurils in Russia) between Russia and Japan, the China–Japan dispute over the Diaoyu Dao and the demarcation of the East China Sea, the dispute over a set of islands (called Dokdo in Korean and Takeshima in Japanese) between the ROK and Japan, the dispute over the border between the DPRK and the ROK, and the dispute over the delimitation of the Yellow Sea and Suyan Rock between China and the ROK. In recent years, these disputes over the delimitation of islands and seas have severely affected relations between countries in Northeast Asia. If not handled properly, they may aggravate the tensions between countries and cause conflicts. The Korean Peninsula issue and the Taiwan question are the most sensitive issues affecting peace and stability in Northeast Asia. The DPRK and the ROK are still in a state of military confrontation and tension. The US military alliance policy with the ROK and the US sanctions and containment policy against the DPRK have further exacerbated the tension in the Korean Peninsula. The Taiwan question also faces considerable uncertainty. China's determination to safeguard national sovereignty and reunification will not change. Change in the Taiwan situation and intensification of the Taiwan separatist activities will most likely aggravate the situation in the Taiwan Strait and eventually lead to tensions and conflicts in China–US relations.

China actively participates in the settlement of disputes in Northeast Asia, supports the inter-Korean dialogue, and eases the situation in the Korean peninsula. China opposes the use of force or the threat of force, has promoted the establishment of the Beijing Six-Party Talks on the DPRK's nuclear issue, and intends to peacefully solve the DPRK nuclear issue through multilateral diplomatic negotiations. China also actively advocates the settlement of territorial disputes among countries in Northeast Asia through negotiations and opposes the use of force or war. On the Taiwan question, China has strengthened economic and trade ties and personnel exchanges by developing trust between the two sides of the Taiwan Strait to safeguard peace in the Taiwan Strait and finally achieve national reunification by peaceful means. Strengthening the strategic coordination and cooperation between China and the United States is an essential factor in maintaining peaceful development on the two sides of the Taiwan Strait and realizing peaceful reunification of the two sides.

1.4.2.2 Promoting economic development and prosperity in Northeast Asia

The world economy is still undergoing profound adjustments after the global financial and economic crisis in 2008. The growth rate of the world economy is lower than expected and economic recovery is progressing slowly. Economic trends and policy orientations in major economies such as the United States, the European Union (EU), and Japan continue to diverge. The uncertainty of the international economic environment will have a significant impact on the economic development of Northeast Asia. Facing the new international economic situation and challenges, countries in Northeast Asia should continue to maintain close economic and trade cooperation, deepen economic integration, maintain stable and rapid economic growth, enhance global economic competitiveness in Northeast Asia, and promote economic development and prosperity in the region. Economic development and prosperity in Northeast Asia can create a large development space for China's rapid economic growth, which will further promote growth in the region.

First, countries should maintain close economic and trade relations in Northeast Asia. Countries in Northeast Asia are all important economic and business partners, and their mutual trade and investment are expanding. We must continue to maintain the momentum of development and realize joint expansion. In 2015, China's foreign trade maintained steady growth and continued to maintain its position as the world's largest trading nation in goods. However, the era of high-speed growth is over. It has now entered a new normal of steady growth in foreign trade. China is the largest trading partner for the countries in Northeast Asia. It is very important to continue maintaining close trade relations among the countries in Northeast Asia. Japan, the ROK, and Russia are China's three most significant trading partners in the region. In recent years, influenced by the world economic situation, the trade volume between

China and the three countries has declined to various degrees. According to the statistics from the General Administration of Customs of the People's Republic of China, the bilateral trade volume between China and Japan in 2015 was US$278.66 billion, down 10.2% year on year: China exported US$135.67 billion to Japan, down 9.2% and imports from Japan totaled US$142.99 billion, down 12.2%. The bilateral trade volume between China and the ROK in 2015 was US$275.81 billion, down 5.5% year on year: China's export to the ROK was US$101.29 billion, up 1.0% and imports from the ROK totaled US$174.52 billion, down 8.2%. The bilateral trade volume between China and Russia in 2015 was US$68.06 billion, down 28.6% year on year: China's export to Russia was US$34.78 billion, down 35.2% and imports from Russia were US$33.28 billion, down 20.0%.[24]

The trade volume between China and countries in Northeast Asia has declined due to various international and domestic factors. Japan's economic fluctuation and the deterioration of China–Japan political relations are the main reasons for the decline in the China–Japan trade volume. The sharp drop in China–Russia trade volume in 2015 was due to the serious impact of the Ukraine crisis and the drop in global oil prices. As a result of the Ukraine crisis, western countries led by the United States imposed economic sanctions on Russia, which severely hit the Russian economy. Besides, the international oil price dropped sharply, causing Russian oil export earnings to drop dramatically. According to data released by the International Monetary Fund, Russia's GDP in 2015 was US$1.32 trillion, down 3.7% year on year. For the first time in nearly ten years, Russia's GDP was surpassed by that of the ROK.[25] The grim economic situation in Russia will also influence China–Russia economic and trade relations.

Maintaining the steady growth of trade volume between China and countries in Northeast Asia is an essential condition for China's rapid economic development. China and Japan are important trading partners. Strengthening mutual trust between China and Japan and striving to improve China–Japan relations will contribute to the stable and healthy

---

[24] Table of Total Value of Imports and Exports by Country (Region) (U.S. Dollars) in February 2015, The General Administration of Customs of the People's Republic of China, http://www.customers.gov.cn/publish/portal0/tab49667/info785160.htm, January 21, 2016.

[25] International Monetary Fund, *World Economic Outlook Database, April 2016*, http://www.imf.org/external/pubs/ft/weo/2016/01/weodata/index.aspx, April 12, 2016.

development of economic and trade ties between the two countries. Western sanctions and the fall in international oil prices will severely impact Russia's economy. However, the characteristics of economic complementarity between China and Russia have not changed. By promoting investment and cooperation in major projects between China and Russia, economic and trade relations will grow steadily between the two countries. Countries in Northeast Asia should also actively create conditions to improve the trade and investment environment, open markets to each other, further strengthen connectivity, simplify customs procedures, and expand cooperation in the investment field to maintain stable development of economic and trade relations.

Secondly, China should promote stable and rapid economic development in Northeast Asia. Northeast Asia's economy is full of vitality and has great potential for development. It is also highly complementary. After the global financial and economic crisis in 2008, the economy of Northeast Asia resumed growth first and became a massive engine for global economic growth. Dealing with the complicated environment of the world economy and promoting the stable and healthy development of the economy in Northeast Asia will be essential conditions to ensure the stable and rapid growth of China's economy.

The world economy is in the process of recovery and growth after the global financial crisis. The US economy has begun to show vitality and economic growth. Economic growth in the Euro area is sluggish, and the economies of the core countries are almost stagnant. Economic growth in emerging economies and developing countries has slowed down. Affected by the overall weakness of the international economy and sluggish growth, the economic growth in Northeast Asia is also gradually slowing down. After more than 20 years of rapid economic growth, China has entered a new normal of economic development, shifting from high-speed growth to medium-speed growth. China's economy grew by 7.3% in 2014 and 6.9% in 2015. The slowdown of China's economic growth is influenced by international factors as well as China's laws. At present, China's GDP has reached US$10 trillion, which is 13% of the world's GDP[26]; China's economy is too large to maintain a high growth rate all the time. It must have a process of decreasing growth rate. In addition, China's economy also has problems such as insufficient domestic demand

---

[26] Xinhua Net, Illustration of the Annual NPC and CPPCC Sessions in 2015, Beijing: People's Publishing House, 2015, p. 67.

and overcapacity. China's economy is undergoing structural adjustment and moving "from an extensive model that emphasized scale and speed to a more intensive one emphasizing quality and efficiency, and from being driven by investment in production factors to being driven by innovation."[27] The Abe administration in Japan adopted an economic stimulus policy to get rid of the economic deflation that plagued Japan and boost Japan's economic recovery. However, the effect was not noticeable enough. Japan's economic growth rate was 1.4% in 2013, falling to –0.0% in 2014 and only 0.5% in 2015.[28] The main reasons for the decline in Japan's economic growth were the decline in domestic consumption demand, weak international exports, the decline in industrial production, and massive public debts. The Abe administration of Japan further pushed forward structural reforms to reverse the economic downturn. The overall economic situation in the ROK was stable and positive. The economic growth rate in the ROK was 2.9% in 2013, 3.3% in 2014, and 2.6% in 2015.[29] Further recovery of the international market led to a sharp rebound in the ROK's manufacturing exports. The restoration of the ROK's real estate market drove domestic consumption. The overreliance of the ROK's economy on the international market and weak domestic demand made the ROK's economy somewhat fragile and volatile. For example, the ROK's industrial growth above scale declined in 2015 due to negative growth in its export scale. As a result of western sanctions and the sharp drop in international oil prices in 2014, Russia's economy also suffered a severe setback. The annual economic growth rate was about 0.6%, down 0.8% from 2013. The exchange rate of the Russian ruble dropped sharply. On January 1, 2015, the official exchange rate announced by the Central Bank of the Russian Federation was 56.2 rubles to 1 US dollar and 68.3 rubles to 1 Euro.[30] Compared with the exchange rate at the beginning of 2014, the ruble nearly doubled its value against

---

[27] Towards a Community of Common Destiny and A New Future for Asia, keynote speech by Chinese President Xi Jinping at the Boao Forum for Asia Annual Conference 2015, http://finance.sina.com.cn/china/20150328/1052183357.html, March 28, 2015.

[28] International Monetary Fund, *Regional Economic Outlook: Asia and Pacific*, http://www.imf.org/external/pubs/ft/reo/2016/apd/eng/pdf/areo0516.pdf, April 2016.

[29] *Ibid.*

[30] The official exchange rate announced by the Central Bank of the Russian Federation was 56.2376 rubles to 1 US dollar and 68.3681 rubles to 1 Euro. http://www,interax,ru/business/416461, [EB/OL], December 31, 2014

the US dollar and the Euro. Russia's inflation reached 11.4% in 2014.[31] In 2014, Russia's exports were US$500 billion and imports US$310 billion, with imports and exports falling by 2.2% and 2.3%, respectively.[32]

The economies of all countries in Northeast Asia are facing various risks and challenges at home and abroad. Eliminating trade protectionism, opening domestic markets to each other, expanding cooperation in trade and investment, and coordinating monetary and tariff policies will lead to stable and healthy economic development in Northeast Asia. Chinese President Xi Jinping pointed out the following in his keynote speech at the 2015 annual meeting of the Boao Forum for Asia: "This new normal of the Chinese economy will continue to bring more opportunities of trade, growth, investment and cooperation for other countries in Asia and beyond. In the coming five years, China will import more than US$10 trillion of goods, Chinese investment abroad will exceed US$500 billion, and more than 500 million outbound visits will be made by Chinese tourists. China will stick to its basic state policy of opening up, improve its investment climate, and protect the lawful rights and interests of investors. I believe that together, the people of Asian countries could drive this train of Asia's development to take Asia to an even brighter future."[33]

Finally, we should promote the development of economic integration in Northeast Asia. The development of economic globalization has not only closely linked the economies of various countries and formed a close interdependent relationship but also caused the economic development of multiple countries to be deeply influenced by international economic competition and circumstances. Strengthening regional economic cooperation and realizing regional economic integration are essential ways to ensure regional economic development and prosperity and enhance the country's international competitiveness. Under the complicated situation and challenges of the global economy, it is crucial for us to enhance economic integration in Northeast Asia.

---

[31] Russia's annual inflation is 11.4%. http://www.interfax.ru/business/416458, [EB/OL], December 31, 2014.
[32] Commercial and Financial Ministry predicts in 2015 Russia's GDP will fall by 0.8%. http://itar-tass.com/ekonomika/1616644, [EB/OL], December 2, 2014.
[33] Towards a Community of Common Destiny and A New Future for Asia, keynote speech by Chinese President Xi Jinping at the Boao Forum for Asia Annual Conference 2015, http://finance.sina.com.cn/china/20150328/1052183357.html, March 28, 2015.

Northeast Asia has an endogenous power to develop economic integration. Countries in Northeast Asia are facing the arduous task of ensuring stable economic growth. Strengthening economic integration in Northeast Asia can create a functional development space for economic development of all countries. Northeast Asia has a vast market, abundant resources, advanced technology and manufacturing, sufficient capital, and high-quality human resources. If these aspects are integrated through regional economic integration, stable economic growth of the Northeast Asian countries can be guaranteed, overall competitive advantage can be promoted, and economic development and prosperity can be promoted.

Northeast Asia has a good foundation for economic integration. All countries in Northeast Asia have become important trading partners and their cooperation in trade and investment has been continuously expanding. Based on bilateral cooperation, the Northeast Asian countries are also actively developing multilateral economic cooperation, such as China–Japan–ROK economic cooperation, China–Mongolia–Russia economic cooperation, and Russia–DPRK–ROK economic cooperation. China and the ROK have officially signed a bilateral free trade agreement. China, Japan, and the ROK are still negotiating a free trade agreement. Countries in Northeast Asia actively carry out multilateral cooperation under the framework of the Asia-Pacific Economic Cooperation and ASEAN Plus Three (APT). However, the level of economic integration in Northeast Asia is still relatively low and cannot meet the objective requirements of the development of regional integration. Liu Jianchao stated the following at the Binhai Conference in 2014: "In front of the far-reaching impact of the international financial crisis, the Northeast Asian countries should help each other, strengthen policy coordination, make good use of their comparative advantages, continuously explore strategic points of mutually beneficial cooperation, further improve trade and investment liberalization and facilitation in Northeast Asia, and push regional economic integration to a new level."[34] Northeast Asian countries should strengthen mutual trust, continuously improve the economic systems and foreign trade policies, and promote the establishment and development of economic cooperation mechanisms.

---

[34] Liu Jianchao, Speech at the 2014 Binhai Conference on Peace and Development in Northeast Asia, website of the Ministry of Foreign Affairs of the People's Republic of China, http://www.fmprc.gov.cn/mfa_chn/wjbxw_602253/t1201237.shtml, October 16, 2014.

1.4.2.3 Establishing a new order in Northeast Asia

Northeast Asia's regional system is in a period of historical transition. As a big country in Northeast Asia, China actively promotes the establishment of a new order in the region, not only to better safeguard and realize China's national interests but also to ensure that it fulfills its responsibility as a major country. China should adapt to the trends of the times and put forward a "China Solution" for the construction of a new order in Northeast Asia according to the latest changes in the international system in the region. The establishment of a new international order in Northeast Asia is mainly manifested in the norms of international relations and the establishment of international mechanisms. The goal of promoting the establishment of a new international order in Northeast Asia is to promote a more democratic, harmonious, just, and inclusive region so as to realize the lasting peace and shared prosperity.

Firstly, based on the UN Charter and the principles of international law, we should establish a code of conduct for relations between countries in Northeast Asia. After World War II, to maintain and realize the permanent peace in the world, the allies established the United Nations, signed the UN Charter, and confirmed a post-war world order. The UN Charter and its principles of international law have become the basic norms for coordinating international relations. Based on the UN Charter, China, India, Myanmar, and other countries jointly advocated and put forward the Five Principles of Peaceful Coexistence. To build a new international order in Northeast Asia, we must continue to adhere to and abide by the UN Charter, international law, and other international norms. Countries in Northeast Asia should adhere to the principle of mutual respect for sovereignty and territorial integrity, respect each other's social system, ideology, and choice of development path, and not impose their social model and values on others. We should ban support for separatist activities and oppose undermining the national unity and territorial integrity of other countries. Countries should not infringe upon each other or interfere in each other's internal affairs. All countries should adhere to the peaceful settlement of disputes between countries, not use force or threaten to use force, and not interfere in other countries' internal affairs by means of infiltration, threats, and inducements to subvert other countries' legitimate governments. All countries should develop equal and mutually beneficial national relations and realize peaceful coexistence. We should respect each other's national interests and major concerns, actively carry out mutually beneficial cooperation, develop friendly relations between countries, and realize coexistence and joint development.

The norms of international relations in Northeast Asia can be expressed in bilateral or multilateral treaties and joint statements. A code of conduct for relations between Northeast Asian countries can be established based on the UN Charter, and the principles of international law should become the basic norm to be followed by all countries in the region in the establishment of a new order.

Secondly, we should promote the establishment of a new type of international order in Northeast Asia. In international relations in Northeast Asia, there is still a Cold War mentality. The policies of strengthening military alliances, seeking military superiority, pursuing power politics, and seeking regional hegemony are still popular. The establishment of a new international order in Northeast Asia requires the establishment of win-win cooperation, based on the spirit of the UN Charter and the principles of international law.

In Northeast Asia, countries have established close political, economic, military, and cultural relations. Their interests intersect and merge, and their mutual dependence is deepening. They have formed a community with shared future and are bound together for good or ill. The new changes in international relations require us to keep pace with the times, abandon the traditional "law of the jungle," discard the "zero-sum game" and "winner-takes-all" mentality, and establish a new type of Northeast Asia with win-win cooperation as the core.

Politically, we should respect each other's sovereignty and equality, abandon the traditional alliance and confrontation policies, ensure that no country seeks hegemony, and oppose power politics. Beyond the differences in social system and ideology, we should develop trust, good neighborliness, and friendly international relations based on the principles of international law.

Economically, we should develop a sense of community of shared interests and develop economic cooperation in all fields of trade and investment to achieve complementary advantages and joint development. We will develop economic relations based on equality, mutual benefit, and win-win cooperation.

In terms of security, we should abandon the Cold War mentality and establish a new security concept. Peaceful settlement of disputes between countries is possible if it does not involve the use or threat of force and rejects the establishment of one's own security based on threatening the safety of other countries. According to the new concepts of common security, cooperative security, comprehensive security, and sustainable security, a national security relationship in Northeast Asia will be established.

Culturally, we should practice tolerance and mutual learning and adhere to the spirit of openness and tolerance. We must respect the cultural diversity of Northeast Asia, not impose our ideology on others, and not engage in value diplomacy. To achieve mutual communication, we should learn from each other's strong points.

Thirdly, we should establish a cooperation mechanism in Northeast Asia. Promoting the establishment of a cooperation mechanism in Northeast Asia is an essential component of the establishment of an international order in the region. The regional cooperation mechanism in Northeast Asia is a platform for dialogue and cooperation for all countries. Northeast Asia has established multilateral dialogue and cooperation mechanisms, such as the Shanghai Cooperation Organization, the China–Japan–ROK Summit, and the Beijing Six-Party Talks on the DPRK nuclear issue. Besides, China, Japan, and the ROK have also established a dialogue and cooperation mechanism under the ASEAN-led APT framework. However, the Northeast Asian region has not yet created a cooperation mechanism covering all the countries. Due to the lack of systems in Northeast Asia, stability, peace, and development are extremely fragile. Any military or security emergencies may lead to an escalation of conflicts and loss of control.

The cooperation mechanism in Northeast Asia can include dialogue on the topics of politics, economy, security, and culture. It can be divided into functional cooperation mechanisms, institutional cooperation mechanisms, and regional mechanism. In addition to the countries in the region, the cooperation mechanism can also involve countries from outside the region.

In designing the framework of the cooperation mechanism in Northeast Asia, first of all, we should promote the establishment of a regular high-level meeting mechanism for all countries in the region. The initial stage can involve foreign ministers with a gradually upgrading to meetings of national leaders. The high-level formal meeting mechanism in Northeast Asia offers allows countries to interact on topics of regional politics, economy, security, culture, and diplomacy. It also provides a platform for countries to negotiate and solve regional issues. Second, we should promote the establishment of a regional economic cooperation mechanism, for example, a trade and investment cooperation mechanism attended by the ministers of economy and commerce to coordinate and promote cooperation in economy and trade, investment, currency, finance, customs duties, and logistics. Third, security dialogues should be established, wherein meetings are attended by senior officials from the defense, border defense, and public security departments. Exchange and cooperation should be carried out in strengthening military trust, establishing military early warning systems, preventing unexpected incidents, assisting in rescues at sea, and cracking down on the forces of terrorism, separatism, extremism, and international crimes.

Northeast Asia's cooperation mechanisms can be established step by step. According to the wishes of various countries, a functional dialogue and cooperation mechanism should be established first and then an institutional cooperation mechanism should be gradually set up, adhering to the principles of voluntary participation, multilateral cooperation, openness and transparency, equality and mutual benefit, and win-win cooperation.

1.4.3 Ways to implement China's strategy in Northeast Asia

The goal of China's Northeast Asia strategy is to maintain peace and stability, promote economic development and prosperity, and encourage the construction of a new international order in Northeast Asia that is democratic, just, harmonious, and inclusive. China's strategy in Northeast Asia is not only to realize its goal of peaceful development and modernization but also to conform to the fundamental interests of all countries and people in Northeast Asia by means of active cooperation.

1.4.3.1 *Building a framework for cooperation among major powers in Northeast Asia*

The implementation of China's northeast Asia strategy should follow the path of win-win cooperation. There is a need to realize China's strategic vision for Northeast Asia through strategic cooperation among the major powers in the region. This mainly involves the United States, Russia, Japan, and the ROK. The United States is a foreign country to Northeast Asia. However, it is an essential force in the international pattern of Northeast Asia and its position, interests, and influence in Northeast Asia cannot be neglected. In the strategic framework of China's cooperation among the Northeast Asian powers, China–US relations are the pillar, China–Russia relations are the prop, and the relations among China, Japan, and the ROK are the foundation.

First of all, we will promote the construction of a new model of major-country relationship between China and the United States. The United States is a superpower and an important influential force in Northeast Asia. The United States has important political, economic, and security interests in Northeast Asia. Countries in Northeast Asia are important trading partners of the United States. The United States maintains bilateral military alliances with Japan and the ROK and has military bases and troops in these two countries. Promoting the construction of a new model of major-country relationship between China and the United States is a priority for China's Northeast Asia strategy. As China is an emerging power and the United States is a defending power, it is imperative to avoid falling into the "Thucydides' Trap." China's push to build a new model of major-country relationship involves harmony, peace, mutual respect, and win-win cooperation between China and the United States.

China's strategic goal in Northeast Asia is not to seek regional hegemony, but to be a responsible regional power. In Northeast Asia, China is trying hard to avoid a new China–US confrontation. China and the United States should respect each other's national interests and major concerns and actively cooperate with each other. China and the United States are actively collaborating in maintaining peace and stability in the Korean Peninsula and in resolving the DPRK nuclear issue through the Beijing Six-Party Talks. However, there are severe differences between China and the United States over the Diaoyu Dao issue between China and Japan, arms sales to China's Taiwan region by the US, and the South China Sea issue. Despite the differences, China and the United States have extensive common interests and a solid foundation for cooperation in Northeast Asia. The strategic points of convergence between the two countries are far greater than their differences. The mechanism of regular meetings between the heads of state of China and the United States, the device of strategic and economic dialogue between the two countries, and the close channels of dialogue and communication between the two countries are all conducive to deepening understanding, enhancing trust, reducing misunderstandings, resolving conflicts, and promoting cooperation. The foundation for building a new type of China–US relations among major powers lies in seeking common ground while reserving differences and in seeking peace while being different. On November 12, 2014, when meeting with the then US President Obama, Chinese President Xi Jinping pointed out that the broad Pacific Ocean is large enough to accommodate both China and the US. The two sides should commit themselves to active interaction in the Asia-Pacific region, encourage inclusive diplomacy, and jointly play a constructive role in regional peace, stability, and prosperity.[35] China and the United States are not gearing up for a new major power confrontation in Northeast Asia, but are working together to build a peaceful, stable, and prosperous Northeast Asia.

Secondly, we should strengthen the comprehensive strategic partnership of cooperation between China and Russia. Russia is a world power and an important country in Northeast Asia. Spanning Eurasia, Russia has implemented an active Asian policy. China and Russia transcend differences in social systems and ideologies and actively cooperate. The two countries actively carry out coordination and cooperation in international affairs and have similar or identical positions on many major international and regional issues. Chinese President Xi Jinping pointed out the following: "The relationship between China and Russia is one of the most important bilateral relationships in the world. It is also the best relationship between major countries. A strong and high-performance relationship like this not only serves the interests of our two countries but also provides an important safeguard for maintaining the international strategic balance as well as peace and stability in the world."[36]

The Shanghai Cooperation Organization jointly initiated by China and Russia has played an active role in cracking down on the three forces of terrorism, separatism, and extremism, maintaining regional peace and security, and promoting regional economic cooperation and development. China and Russia have actively coordinated their stances on the DPRK nuclear issue and have played an important role in maintaining peace and stability in the Korean Peninsula. They have also actively promoted the establishment of an open and transparent cooperation framework in the

---

[35] Liu Hua, Xi Jinping Emphasized to Push Forward the Construction of New-type Major Country Relations between China and the United States from 6 Key Perspectives, Xinhuanet, http://news.xinhuanet.com/politics/2014-11/12/c_1113220972.htm, November 12, 2014.

[36] Xi Jinping, *The Governance of China (I)*, Beijing: Foreign Languages Press, 2018, pp. 301–302.

Asia-Pacific region. Russia is a positive force in maintaining a strategic balance in Northeast Asia. Strengthening the strategic cooperative partnership between China and Russia in Northeast Asia will be of considerable significance to the implementation of China's Northeast Asia strategy.

Finally, we should promote trust and cooperation among China, Japan, and the ROK. These are the three major countries in Northeast Asia. Their cooperation is an important foundation for building an international system and order in Northeast Asia. Building a new model of the China–Japan–ROK relationship is an important step to implement China's Northeast Asia strategy. At present, the framework for a cooperation mechanism among China, Japan, and the ROK has been formed, which involves summits, 18 ministerial meetings in the fields of diplomacy, economy and trade, science and technology, and culture, and more than 50 working-level meetings. In September 2011, the China–Japan–ROK Trilateral Cooperation Secretariat was established in Seoul. A broad consensus has been reached on maintaining peace and security in Northeast Asia and promoting regional economic development and prosperity. The goal is to build an all-round cooperative partnership. At present, China, Japan, and the ROK still need to deepen their cooperation in the following aspects: First, strategic mutual trust needs to be built and the worries of China and the ROK about Japan's future choices need to be allayed, in relation to Japan's reflection on its history of aggression and preventing Japan's political right deviation and militarism. China, Japan, and the ROK should ensure mutual support for peaceful development and seek no hegemony or expansion in Northeast Asia. Second, we should promote the construction of the China–Japan–ROK cooperation mechanism, strengthen the construction of cooperative rules and regulations, and enhance mutual trust among countries. Third, China, Japan, and the ROK should speed up the construction of a free trade area, deepen economic integration and cooperation, and promote regional economic development and prosperity. Fourth, we should promote and expand cultural exchanges among China, Japan, and the ROK to establish a broad social foundation for trilateral cooperation.

1.4.3.2 *Strengthening security cooperation in Northeast Asia*

The security situation in Northeast Asia is delicate and complicated, and peace is very fragile. The structural conflicts brought about by the transformation of the international system in Northeast Asia, the security dilemma and fierce arms race of major powers, the Korean Peninsula issue and territorial disputes among countries, and various other security issues can all be considered major issues facing the countries in Northeast Asia. To deal with these security threats and challenges, we must go beyond the traditional security concept and the traditional security pattern, establish a new security concept, strengthen international security cooperation in Northeast Asia, and promote the establishment of a security cooperation mechanism.

Firstly, we should bring forth a new security concept in Northeast Asia. Having the same opinion is an essential ideological basis for multilateral cooperation. Security cooperation in Northeast Asia needs to reach a certain level in order to be recognized. At present, the traditional concept of security still occupies a dominant position in international relations. It involves building a strong military force to ensure national security and seeking military superiority as a country's military and strategic goal. Some countries still adhere to the traditional military alliance policy and continue to consolidate and strengthen bilateral and multilateral military alliances. These conventional security theories and policies used to be significant. However, in the new era of diversified security subjects and threats, it is no longer possible to fully meet the new security challenges by continuing the traditional military power policies. Therefore, we need to change the conventional security concept, abandon the Cold War thinking, and establish a new security concept. China is an active advocate of the new security concept. As early as 2002, the Chinese government published a position paper on the new security concept, actively advocating "mutual trust, mutual benefit, equality, and cooperation." At the Conference on Interaction and Confidence Building Measures in Asia (CICA) held in Shanghai, China, in May 2014, Chinese President Xi Jinping proposed a "common, comprehensive, cooperative and sustainable" Asian security concept. These security concepts advocated by the Chinese government conform to the trend of the times and reflect the security interests of most countries. It is an important ideological basis to strengthen security cooperation in Northeast Asia and promote the establishment of a security cooperation mechanism.

According to the new security concept of "mutual trust, mutual benefit, equality, and cooperation" advocated by the Chinese government, all countries should establish strategic mutual trust without mutual suspicion or hostility. We should adhere to the principle of mutual benefit and respect security interests and major concerns of other countries. While realizing their security interests, all countries should treat each other as equals, respect each other, and refrain from interfering in each other's internal affairs. We should actively carry out security cooperation, settle disputes by peaceful means, and conduct extensive consultations and cooperation on security issues of common concern.

The concept of "common, comprehensive, cooperative, and sustainable" advocated by the Chinese government has created a roadmap toward Asian security that is mutually beneficial. Common security emphasizes that security should be universal. According to Xi Jinping, "We cannot just have the security of one or some countries while leaving the rest insecure, still less should one seek the so-called absolute security of itself at the expense of the security of others."[37] Regional security means that all countries have equal rights and responsibilities and should respect each other's legitimate security concerns. Comprehensive security considers traditional security and non-traditional security issues in an overall way to implement comprehensive policies and coordinate governance. Cooperative security emphasizes the realization of national and regional security through dialogue and cooperation. It is different from security by alliance. It requires the active participation and cooperation of countries in the region and takes the road of win-win cooperation. Sustainable security means emphasizing the maintenance of lasting peace and security in the region. We should pay attention to both development and security so that they can promote each other and achieve long-term peace and stability in the region.

Secondly, we should establish an international code of conduct in Northeast Asia as it can form the basis of international law for security cooperation in the region. To strengthen security cooperation in Northeast Asia, China and Russia have actively advocated the establishment of a code of conduct for security in Northeast Asia. In a Joint Statement by the People's Republic of China and the Russian Federation on the Comprehensive Deepening of Strategic Cooperation Partnership issued on September 27, 2010, an initiative on internationally recognized basic

---

[37] Xi Jinping, New Asian Security Concept for New Progress in Security Cooperation: speaks during the fourth summit of the Conference on Interaction and Confidence Building Measures in Asia, website of the Ministry of Foreign Affairs of the People's Republic of China, http://www.fmprc.gov.cn/mfa_chn/ziliao_611306/zt_611380/dnzt_611382/yxhy_667356/zxxx/t1158070.shtml, May 21, 2014.

principles was put forward to be followed in developing bilateral and multilateral security cooperation. These basic principles include respect for each other's sovereignty, independence, and territorial integrity, non-interference in each other's internal affairs, adherence to the principle of equality, indivisible security, a national defense policy of a defensive nature, non-use of force or threat with force, refraining from taking or supporting any actions aimed at overthrowing the governments of other countries or undermining the stability of other countries, resolving differences through peaceful means through diplomacy in accordance with the principles of mutual understanding and compromise, and carrying out bilateral and multilateral military cooperation that does not target third countries.[38]

These internationally recognized codes of conduct proposed by China and Russia are based on the UN Charter and the principles of international law. These basic principles should be formally established as the norms of international law in Northeast Asia and can be established by signing a Northeast Asia Security Charter. The Charter can be an open international convention that all countries in the Northeast Asia region and other countries outside the region can sign and participate in. The participants must pledge to abide by the provisions of the charter, enjoy relevant rights, and fulfill corresponding obligations.

Finally, a security cooperation mechanism in Northeast Asia should be established. Countries in Northeast Asia have conducted extensive dialogue and cooperation to enhance strategic mutual trust. In their meetings and joint communiqués, leaders of all countries expressed their willingness to develop partnerships and support peaceful development. For example, former US President Obama made it clear that the United States does not seek to contain China and the rise of a strong and prosperous China can strengthen the international community.[39] The China–Japan Joint Statement on All-round Promotion of Strategic Relationship of Mutual Benefit shows that China and Japan are not threats to each other

---

[38] Joint Statement of the People's Republic of China and the Russian Federation on Comprehensive Deepening of Strategic Cooperation Partnership, website of the Ministry of Foreign Affairs of the People's Republic China, http://www.fmprc.gov.cn/chn/pds/ziliao/1179/t756814.htm, September 27, 2010.

[39] The White House Office of the Press Secretary. Remarks by President Barack Obama at Suntory Hall, https://www.whitehouse.gov/the-press-office/remarks-president-barack-obama-suntory-hall, November 14, 2009.

and can support each other's peaceful development.[40] Countries have also established strategic and security dialogue mechanisms, such as the China–US Strategic and Economic Dialogues, the China–Russia Strategic and Security Consultation, the China–Japan Defense and Security Consultation, the China–ROK High-level Strategic Dialogues, the Russia–Japan Strategic Dialogues, and the Russia–ROK Strategic Dialogues. It is worth emphasizing that all countries in Northeast Asia have expressed their positive desire to enhance mutual trust and maintain peace and stability. However, the construction of a security dialogue and cooperation mechanism is pending. To truly solve the problem of strategic mutual trust, we also need to establish rules. It is necessary to build a security dialogue and cooperation mechanism in Northeast Asia. Therefore, it is necessary to create a trust mechanism, an early warning and control mechanism, and a security cooperation organization in Northeast Asia.

Dialogue and cooperation on trust and disarmament in the military field should be carried out, including an exchange of visits by leaders of military departments, mutual notification of military information, and invitations to observe military exercises. Through negotiations, an agreement on trust-building in the military field in Northeast Asia can be signed. The agreement will clearly stipulate that countries in the region will not use or threaten to use force against each other; limit the scale, geographical scope, and number of military exercises; and inform each other of important military deployments, military exercises, and missile launches. It will also ask that countries involved should increase openness and transparency in the military field, restrict military deployment and military activities, and increase military trust and predictability of military operations. Arms control and disarmament negotiations will be held on issues such as preventing the proliferation of weapons of mass destruction and deploying regional anti-missile systems.

Preventive diplomacy and management mechanisms should be established. Countries in Northeast Asia should hold regular meetings of ministers and senior officials on foreign affairs, national defense, public security, border defense, and other aspects. Regular meetings are mainly for information exchange, prevention of regional military conflicts,

---

[40] China-Japan Joint Statement on All-round Promotion of Strategic Relationship of Mutual Benefit, website of the Ministry of Foreign Affairs of the People's Republic of China, http://www.gov.cn/jrzg/2008-05/07/content_964157.htm, May 7, 2008.

coordination, settlement of regional disputes, and non-traditional security cooperation. At present, the regional security problems to be solved are mainly emergencies that may arise from tensions in the Korean Peninsula, escalation of military confrontations, nuclear leakage and catastrophic consequences that may result from the DPRK's nuclear test and missile launches, the serious threats that may be posed to regional security, and the impact of the US deployment of a regional anti-missile defense system on the regional strategic balance.

A specific organization should be gradually established whose aim is to develop strategic mutual trust and friendly relations among its member countries. Each member state guarantees non-aggression and non-interference in each other's internal affairs. They should respect the core interests and legitimate concerns of all countries, resolve disputes among countries peacefully through negotiations, and refrain from the use or threat of force against each other. They should strengthen military trust and disarmament and carry out military exchanges and cooperation. They should strengthen cooperation in non-traditional security areas, jointly crack down on the three forces of terrorism, separatism, and extremism, and deal with the challenges of transnational crimes and various global issues. Coordination and cooperation will be carried out in areas of energy security, food security, environmental security, public health security, economic security, and financial security. The organization will establish decision-making and leadership, formulate statutes and rules, and establish enforcement and supervision agencies. As for the agreements and resolutions signed by the organization, the member states participating in the signing must abide by and implement them, and supervise the implementation.

1.4.3.3 *Deepening economic cooperation in Northeast Asia*

Countries in Northeast Asia have established close economic cooperation and become important trading partners with each other. On this basis, it is also necessary to further promote regional economic integration and cooperation in Northeast Asia and enhance the level of trade and investment cooperation. The important development directions for strengthening the economic cooperation in Northeast Asia are to promote the construction of the Silk Road Economic Belt in Northeast Asia, enhance the cooperation in the development of the Tumen River region, and deepen economic cooperation among China, Japan, and the ROK.

Firstly, we should work to build the Silk Road in Northeast Asia. In 2013, Chinese President Xi Jinping put forward the Belt and Road Initiative (BRI). On March 5, 2015, Premier Li Keqiang put forward the task of working with the "relevant countries in developing the Silk Road Economic Belt and the 21st Century Maritime Silk Road." In March 2015, the Chinese government issued its Vision and Actions on Jointly Building Silk Road Economic Belt and 21st-Century Maritime Silk Road, which is a strategic plan and development blueprint that takes the historic Silk Road as a bridge and link. It adheres to the spirit of the Silk Road, involving "peaceful cooperation, openness and tolerance, mutual learning and mutual benefit and win-win cooperation," and connects the three continents of Asia, Europe, and Africa through the Silk Road Economic Belt and the Maritime Silk Road. By establishing infrastructure, it strengthens connectivity and facilitates trade to realize common development and prosperity.

Northeast Asia is an essential area in China's BRI development plan. The construction of the Silk Road Economic Belt in Northeast Asia will promote the development of regional economic integration. China's BRI has received support from countries in Northeast Asia. On May 8, 2015, China and Russia signed the Joint Statement on Cooperation on the Construction of a Joint Eurasian Economic Union and Silk Road Projects. Russia expressed its support for the construction of the Silk Road Economic Belt. The two countries will strive to connect the construction of the Silk Road Economic Belt with the construction of the Eurasian Economic Union to ensure sustained and stable regional economic growth, strengthen regional economic integration, and safeguard regional peace and development.[41] At the second meeting of heads of state of China, Russia, and Mongolia on July 10, 2015, Chinese President Xi Jinping put forward the construction of the Silk Road Economic Belt initiative, proposing to "link the Silk Road Economic Belt with Russia's construction of the Railway across Eurasia and Mongolia's Prairie Road initiative, and push forward the construction of China-Russia-Mongolia

---

[41] China-Russia Joint Statement on Cooperation on the Construction of Joint Eurasian Economic Union and the Silk Road Projects, website of the Ministry of Foreign Affairs of the People's Republic of China, http://www.fmprc.gov.cn/mfa_chn/zyxw_602251/t1262143.shtml, May 9, 2015.

Economic corridor."[42] The Chinese proposal received positive responses from the presidents of Russia and Mongolia. The establishment of the Asian Infrastructure Investment Bank (AIIB) is an important step in the development of the Belt and Road Initiative. In 2013, China initiated the establishment of the AIIB, mainly to support infrastructure construction and develop connectivity. In December 2015, the AIIB was formally established with 57 founding members signing the Articles of Agreement of the Asian Infrastructure Investment Bank, including Russia, the ROK, and Mongolia. The BRI proposed by China conforms to the development requirements and cooperation aspirations of all countries in the region. It will play a significant role in promoting regional economic cooperation in Northeast Asia.

Secondly, we should work to promote the construction of a major channel for the Tumen River regional cooperation. In 1991, the United Nations Development Program initiated the establishment of the Tumen River development project. Since the implementation of the Tumen River Area Development Program (TRADP), certain achievements have been made in promoting regional economic cooperation along the Tumen River including the construction of a regional cooperation mechanism. The Chinese government has taken a series of important measures to promote regional cooperation in the Tumen River region. On August 30, 2009, China's State Council approved an Outline of the Tumen River Region Cooperation Development Framework: The Changchun–Jilin–Tumen Development and Opening-up Pilot Zone. In April 2012, China's State Council approved the establishment of the China Tumen River Region (Hunchun) International Cooperation Demonstration Pilot Zone. The outline stipulates that the construction of the Changchun-Jilin-Tumen Development and Opening-up Pilot Zone shall be taken as the main body to promote the construction of internal and external transportation channels, to establish the cross-border economic cooperation zone, and to improve the level of Tumen River regional cooperation and development.[43] In 2013, the Chinese government put forward the development

---

[42] Xi Jinping (2015). Attends the second meeting of the heads of state of China, Russia and Mongolia, People's Daily Online, http://citiccard.politics.people.com.cn/n/2015/0710/c1024-27281577.html, July 10, 2015.

[43] Outline of the Tumen River Region Cooperation Development Framework: Changchun-Jilin-Tumen Development and Opening-up Pilot Zone, Sina, http://jl.sina.com.cn/yanbian/jjyb/2014-07-14/68.html, July 14, 2014.

strategy of BRI. It involves four provinces in the northeast part of China. It will significantly promote the construction of the Tumen River regional sea and air international transportation corridor and improve regional economic cooperation.

Under the framework of the BRI, the construction of a sealand transportation corridor linking China, Russia, the DPRK, and the ROK and the construction of a Eurasian continental bridge linking China, Russia, and Mongolia will be furthered promoted. Heilongjiang Province has put forward the idea of China-Russia joint construction of the Eastern Land and Sea Silk Road Economic Belt. Jilin Province has linked the China-Russia joint construction of Zarubino Port with the construction of a pilot area for the development and opening up of Changchun-Jilin-Tumen area, thus enabling Jilin Province to change its lack of access to the sea and gain a strategic channel for international transportation.

China and Russia are actively cooperating in infrastructure construction involving railways, bridges, and seaports to establish strategic transport links between China and Russia and between Asia and Europe. China State Railway Group Co., Ltd. and Russian Railways have reached a strategic cooperation agreement to develop infrastructure and transportation. The railway companies of the two countries plan to build infrastructure to increase railway capacity and international traffic volume between the two countries. On October 13, 2014, during the 19th regular meeting between Chinese and Russian prime ministers, China and Russia signed a Memorandum of Understanding in the Sphere of High-speed Railway involving the National Development and Reform Commission, the Ministry of Transport of the Russian Federation, China State Railway Group Co., Ltd., and Russian Railways. The purpose of the document is to plan for a Euro-Asian high-speed railway transportation corridor from Moscow to Beijing, including giving priority to the implementation of a Moscow–Kazan high-speed railway project. China and Russia are building a cross-border railway bridge in Tongjiang to improve their transit capacity. It is a railway bridge located in Tongjiang city in China and Nizhneleninskoye in Russia. In February 2014, the Tongjiang cross-border railway bridge entered the construction phase. At present, China and Russia mainly have three railway transportation routes, namely, the Manzhouli–Zabaykalsk, Suifenhe–Grodekovo, and Hunchun–Makhalino routes. The Tongjiang cross-border railway bridge is another important cross-border transportation route. It will promote trade and personnel exchanges between Northeast China and Russia's Far East and form another major international intermodal link between China's northeast railway network and Russia's Siberian railway. China and Russia are actively promoting the construction of maritime transportation routes and will jointly build the Zarubino Port. Russia supports China's plan to build a Maritime Silk Road and actively promotes cooperation in building a northern maritime corridor. The construction of the Zarubino Port is a major cooperation project. On May 20, 2014, the Jilin Provincial Government and Russia's Summa Group signed a framework agreement on cooperation in the construction of the Zarubino Port, with plans to build it in Troitsy Bay, a coastal border region of Russia. It is an important international freight port mainly for container transportation, including container terminals, special grain terminals, and multifunctional maritime terminals, with a designed annual cargo throughput capacity of 60 million tons. The Zarubino Port is 18 kilometers from China's border. It will promote economic and trade cooperation between Northeast China and the Russian Far East, open sea routes to Jilin Province, and establish a northern Maritime Silk Road linking the Asia-Pacific region and Europe.[44]

Finally, we should deepen the trilateral economic cooperation among China, Japan, and the ROK, the three major economic powers in Northeast Asia. Their total economic volume accounts for 90% of the trade volume of East Asia, 70% of the trade volume of Asia, and over 20% of the trade volume of the world.[45] China, Japan, and the ROK are important trading partners. In 2015, the total trade volume of the three countries reached US$625.7 billion.[46] Over the years, China has become the largest trading partner of Japan and the ROK. Japan and the ROK are China's second- and third-largest trading partners. China, Japan, and the ROK are the supporting forces for East Asian economies and the core forces for promoting the economic integration process in East Asia and the

---

[44] Liu Qingcai and Liu Tao, The Development Strategy of Russian Far East Region and China-Russia Regional Cooperation under the Background of Western Sanction, *Northeast Asia Forum*, 2015, 3.

[45] Assistant Foreign Minister Liu Jianchao Attends the Nineth Northeast Asia Trilateral Forum, website of the Ministry of Foreign Affairs of the People's Republic of China, http://www.fmprc.gov.cn/mfa_chn/wjbxw_602253/t1148853.shtml, April 21, 2014.

[46] Vice Minister of Ministry of Foreign Affairs Zhang Yesui: The total trade volume of the three countries reached as high as US$625.7 billion in 2015. China Radio International, http://news.cri.cn/20160429/119491f1-6042-b606-83a3-e79113c720c9.html. August, 29, 2016.

Asia-Pacific region. The Regional Comprehensive Economic Partnership (RCEP) and Free Trade Area of the Asia-Pacific (FTAAP) promoted by ASEAN depend to a large extent on economic cooperation among China, Japan, and the ROK. Therefore, further deepening of cooperation among China, Japan, and the ROK is the requirement to maintain the stable economic growth of the three countries, promote the economic development and prosperity of Northeast Asia, and establish a foundation for the economic integration of East Asia. At present, efforts to deepen economic cooperation among China, Japan, and the ROK are focused on promoting the construction of a free trade area.

China, Japan, and the ROK should actively promote the construction of a China–Japan–ROK FTA. As early as 2002, the leaders of China, Japan, and the ROK proposed the idea of building a free trade area for which the official negotiation was launched in 2012. By May 2015, a meeting of chief representatives during the 7th round of negotiations was held. The talks covered trade in goods, trade in services, investment, the scope of the agreement, and other related issues. The establishment of the China–Japan–ROK FTA is mutually beneficial. It will further open the market, provide trade liberalization and facilitation, give full play to the complementary advantages of the economies of the three countries, and promote the development of economic and trade relations among the three countries. The establishment of the free trade area will also boost the economic and foreign trade growth of the three countries.

China, Japan, and the ROK have different levels of economic development and industrial structures and have their own comparative advantages. The principles of mutual benefit should be fully considered. For some highly sensitive products, doors can be gradually opened. In May 2012, China, Japan, and the ROK formally signed an Agreement for the Promotion, Facilitation, and Protection of Investment, providing an important foundation for the construction of a free trade area. China and the ROK signed the Free Trade Agreement on June 1, 2015, which will help push forward the negotiation of China–ROK FTA and provide useful experience for the construction of China–ROK FTA.

The economic cooperation among China, Japan, and the ROK still has great potential and room for development. It is necessary to deepen the cooperation among the three countries. China, Japan, and the ROK should create connectivity and more convenient conditions for trade, establish unified authentication standards, and establish a seamless logistics system. They can promote economic restructuring, enterprise transformation and upgrading, and carry out mutually beneficial cooperation in the fields of green- and low-carbon enterprises, energy conservation and environmental protection, finance, smart cities, social security, medical care, and high and new technologies.[47]

1.4.3.4 Enhancing China's soft power in Northeast Asia

China is a big country in Northeast Asia. To play its role effectively, China also needs to enhance its soft power. Through the implementation of a good foreign policy, China's image as a big country with benevolence and good neighborliness will be established, and the so-called "China threat" theory in some countries in Northeast Asia will be eliminated. Through the active public diplomacy of China, the affinity of the people of various countries in Northeast Asia towards China has been increased and China's influence as a big county in the region has been enhanced.

First of all, we should advocate win-win cooperation and build a new image of a major country with Chinese characteristics. China is a big emerging economy in Northeast Asia. China's rapid rise has aroused the concern of some countries in the region. At the same time, various so-called "China threat" theories have emerged. To dispel all kinds of doubts, the Chinese government published a White Paper called *China's Peaceful Development* in 2005 and 2011. The Chinese government solemnly declared that China will unswervingly follow the path of peaceful development, developing itself by maintaining a peaceful international environment and developing itself. The path of peaceful development chosen by China is based on China's national conditions and conforms to the trend of the times. It is also deeply rooted in China's culture of "harmony." In China's traditional culture, it advocates "harmony for good," "harmony for all nations," and "harmony for the whole world," conducts "benevolent governance," and opposes hegemony and tyranny. It is different from western traditional thoughts of "seeking hegemony" and engaging in "power politics." China actively advocates win-win cooperation instead of a zero-sum game. The traditional Chinese culture has had a profound

---

[47] Keynote Speech by Chief Member Tang Jiaxuan at the Opening Ceremony of the 5th New Japan-China Friendship Committee for the 21st Century, website of the Ministry of Foreign Affairs of the People's Republic of China, http://www.fmprc.gov.cn/mfa_chn/ziliao_611306/zyjh_611308/t1216306.shtml, December 3, 2014.

influence on the early thoughts and cultures of Japan, the ROK, the DPRK, and Mongolia.

China, as an emerging power in Northeast Asia, is not a new threat to other countries, but a positive force to maintain peace and stability in Northeast Asia. China is a responsible power in Northeast Asia. China will not monopolize regional affairs or seek regional hegemony. China does not favor any one country in Northeast Asia but respects the core interests and major concerns of all countries. China opposes the use of force and advocates the peaceful settlement of various disputes through negotiation and consultation. China has actively promoted the establishment of a more just and reasonable international system and international order in Northeast Asia so as to safeguard peace and stability in the region.

Secondly, China should adhere to the diplomatic concept of building relations with neighboring countries based on amity, sincerity, mutual benefit, and inclusiveness and implement a good and friendly foreign policy. China and the countries in Northeast Asia have formed a close interdependent relationship and established a common destiny of being bound together for good or ill. The Chinese government has established a foreign policy of "being good to our neighbors, taking our neighbors as partners," and "bringing harmony, stability, and prosperity to the neighborhood."

In October 2013, at a symposium on relations with neighboring countries, President Xi Jinping systematically elaborated on China's neighborhood diplomacy in the new era and put forward new ideas of building relations with neighboring countries based on amity, sincerity, mutual benefit, and inclusiveness. The core idea is to insist on good neighborliness, sincerity, mutual benefit, tolerance, and openness. Efforts should be made to disseminate China's diplomatic thoughts and policies into a common concept and code of conduct to be followed and upheld by all countries in Northeast Asia. Xi Jinping stated the following on China's Northeast Asian neighbors: "And we hope that China will have a stronger affinity with them, and that our appeal and our influence will grow."[48]

Finally, we should actively carry out public diplomacy to enhance the soft power of Chinese culture by expanding people-to-people exchanges

---

[48] Xi Jinping, Diplomacy with Neighborhood Countries Characterized by Friendship, Sincerity, Reciprocity and Inclusiveness, *The Governance of China (I)*, Beijing: Foreign Languages Press, 2018, p. 327.

and improving the public perception of China among the people of other Northeast Asian countries. At present, we have very close contact with countries in Northeast Asia, and China's image and prestige are constantly improving. However, people in some countries still have doubts about China. The index of trust and goodwill toward China is low. There is still a certain market for various "China threat" theories. These problems are not part of the mainstream, but their impact cannot be underestimated, and we need to take them seriously. We should actively carry out public diplomacy, expand cultural exchanges between China and countries in Northeast Asia, and enhance China's cultural soft power to eliminate the influence of various negative factors.

China has established an intergovernmental coordination mechanism for people-to-people exchanges and cooperation with countries in Northeast Asia and has drawn up various action plans for the same. China has established Confucius Institutes in all countries in Northeast Asia to help local people learn about the Chinese language, culture, and thoughts. China and other countries in Northeast Asia have successively held various cultural exchange activities. These public diplomatic practices and people-to-people exchanges help to eliminate all kinds of negative impressions of China, deepen mutual understanding between China and the peoples of the countries in Northeast Asia, enhance trust and friendship, and consolidate the social foundation for long-term stable development of China and the countries in Northeast Asia.

Chapter 2

Security Challenges in Northeast Asia and China's Security Strategy

Northeast Asia is a region where the world's major powers are concentrated, where the strategic interests of the world's major powers intersect and converge, and where the security situation is extremely difficult and complicated. Structural conflicts, security dilemmas, and arms races, the Cold War mentality, long-standing historical problems, the Korean Peninsula issue, the DPRK nuclear crisis, and territorial sovereignty and maritime rights disputes among countries in Northeast Asia have all become serious threats to the security of the region. There are also three forces of terrorism, separatism, and extremism in Northeast Asia, as well as various non-traditional security issues such as economic security, energy security, food security, ecological security, information security, and public health security. These security issues are a mixture of historical and practical issues. Traditional security threats and non-traditional security threats are intertwined, making the security threats facing Northeast Asia complex. Faced with new security threats and challenges, we need to abandon the traditional Cold War mentality, abandon the traditional security model of alliance, bring forth a new security concept, and highlight cooperative and common security. Promoting the establishment of a multilateral security cooperation mechanism is essential for maintaining peace and stability, and achieving long-term stability and prosperity in Northeast Asia.

2.1 Security Situation and Challenges in Northeast Asia

Northeast Asia is one of the regions with the most complicated and sensitive security situations. It is the meeting point of the strategic interests of the world's major powers. Compared with other regions of the world, Northeast Asia is a typical place where heterogeneous political civilizations coexist. Conflicts caused by different civilizations, different ideologies, and different stages of development are prominent in the region. The coexistence of heterogeneous political civilizations and incompatible strategic objectives has made Northeast Asia notable. It has restricted cooperation among countries in the region and hindered the development of mutual trust. However, the low level of political mutual trust also causes the conflict of the countries in Northeast Asia when they are deciding their own security strategy.

2.1.1 Cold War legacy in Northeast Asia and the US containment policy

At the beginning of the 21st century, the Cold War legacy in Northeast Asia continued to ferment, leading to frequent international conflicts. During the Cold War, in order to confront the Soviet Union and contain China, the United States built a security and military alliance with Japan and the ROK, creating a pattern of confrontation between Chinese mainland and Taiwan region and the DPRK and the ROK. After the end of the Cold War, changes took place in Northeast Asia. In order to maintain the position of the world's only superpower, the United States took strategic measures to strengthen the Cold War alliance and turned its focus to China. Even today, both land and sea conflicts continue to exist. At present, there are disputes between China and Japan over the rights and interests of the Diaoyu Dao and the East China Sea, as well as differences in the perception of historical issues. There is dissension between Russia and Japan over the ownership of four islands, called the Northern Territories in Japan and the Southern Kurils in Russia. Japan and the ROK also have disputes over a set of islands, called Dokdo in Korean and Takeshima in Japanese. The South and North of the Korean Peninsula have been divided for a long time. These problems are all the legacies of the Cold War and threatened peace and security in Northeast Asia.

Removing the Cold War legacy has become an unavoidable problem facing the governments of Northeast Asian countries. However, due to the new changes in the political and security situation in the world, in particular in the Northeast Asian region, western countries led by the US and Japan started to consider China as their main rival. So, the problems between China and Japan and China and the United States have become crucial problems in the development of Northeast Asia. Thus, the United States and Japan have shifted their national strategies from the Soviet Union to China. The territorial disputes and conflicts between Japan and the ROK and Japan and Russia can be set aside for the time being. However, the disputes between China and Japan and the Korean Peninsula issue are actively hindering peaceful development in the region. Behind the conflicts between China and its neighboring countries, we can see the shadow of the US through its "Asia-Pacific rebalancing" strategy. The essence of the US' "Asia-Pacific rebalancing" strategy is to restrain China's rise in the region. Its available strategy support comes from the ASEAN countries such as the Philippines, Vietnam, and Myanmar in Southeast Asia and Japan and the ROK in Northeast Asia. The US–Japan alliance and US–ROK alliance are the two arms of the US to exert its influence in Northeast Asia, and as it is pointed out, "a typical alliance must have a certain country or a certain group of countries as its target."[1] During the Cold War, the Soviet Union was the target, but now it is China. The danger of the Cold War legacy in Northeast Asia is that the long-standing historical problems can be manipulated by political opponents to achieve their strategic goals. The problems among the countries in Northeast Asia can be solved by future generations. However, the resurgence of these age-old problems in current times has been triggered by both the domestic and foreign factors. There is strategic competition as well as strategic dependence among countries. A country's long-term strategy should not be blinded by the current problems. We should deal with crises calmly and resolve strategic conflicts through cooperation. Countries in Northeast Asia should realize that the security of the region is the precondition for their survival, development, and safety. Problems, contradictions, and conflicts among countries should be resolved fairly

---

[1] Hans Morgenthau, Politics Among Nations: The Struggle for Power and Peace (7th Edition), Translated by Xu Xin, Hao Wang, Li Baoping. Beijing: Peking University Press, 2006, p. 220.

and reasonably within the area through inter-country consultations. We should guard ourselves against any pretext or excuse used by other forces to interfere in the affairs of the region. As far as the essence of the alliance between the US and Japan and the US and the ROK is concerned, Japan and the ROK are not on the same level as the United States in many aspects such as politics, the economy, and the military. Both Japan and the ROK need to rely on the United States for their security. Given the current geopolitical environment in Northeast Asia, especially the conflict between China and Japan, Russia and Japan, the ROK and Japan, China and the ROK, the DPRK and Japan, and the DPRK and the ROK, the US uses Japan and the ROK to contain China and uses its alliances to subconsciously restrict and control the development orientation of both countries, which has become increasingly obvious in the US' Asia-Pacific rebalancing strategy.

2.1.2 Security dilemmas and confrontations in Northeast Asia

Due to the lack of institutional arrangements, Northeast Asia is full of unstable variables. At present, the countries in Northeast Asia are dealing with serious "security dilemmas." Northeast Asia is a region with the most widespread and prominent security dilemmas as mentioned earlier. The DPRK nuclear issue is a hot-button topic. It affects the entire Northeast Asia region and the world as it involves nuclear security. A settlement of the DPRK nuclear issue cannot be achieved overnight. It requires sincerity and patience from all parties, and the security concerns of all relevant countries should be equally considered. By making use of the settlement of the DPRK nuclear crisis, we can build an institutionalized order of sustainable peace and common security in Northeast Asia. However, there is always a gap between wishes and reality. The DPRK adopted "Military-First Politics," tested nuclear weapons, and made every effort to enlarge its armed forces. This is a consequence of the ROK–US alliance and their intention to control the Korean Peninsula. In the eyes of the DPRK leaders, everything that the ROK and the United States have done is hostile, which will aggravate the situation. Similarly, in the ROK and the United States, doubts and fears about the DPRK's national defense policy have led to the continuous enhancement of military security alert levels and the constant improvement of the quality and level of military equipment. It can be said that among the newly industrialized countries, the ROK has devoted incomparable human, material, financial, and energy resources to its own security, as has the DPRK. These are the inevitable results of the difficult security situation in this region. The security dilemma between the DPRK and the ROK in the Korean Peninsula concerns not only the two parties but all countries in Northeast Asia, thus expanding the bilateral security dilemma to a multilateral one. Northeast Asia has truly become an unstable region.

The dilemma of China–Japan relations and the opposition between the two countries' geostrategies are also some of the crucial causes of the insurmountable security dilemma in Northeast Asia. The geopolitical contradiction between China and Japan is manifested in several aspects, the root of which is historical. The so-called geopolitical conflicts are fundamental conflicts of interests between neighboring countries in a relatively independent political and geographical region. There are strategic differences based on economic, political, and security interests. The geopolitical conflicts between China and Japan have deepened the security dilemma in Northeast Asia.

2.1.3 Non-traditional security threats in Northeast Asia

In Northeast Asia, non-traditional security issues involve resources, environment, network security, organized crime, and other aspects, and have shown an increasingly prominent development trend. If countries in Northeast Asia do not take strong measures to prevent and solve these problems, they will pose a threat to the development, stability, and security in the entire region.

Firstly, from the perspective of resources, the resource storage of the countries in Northeast Asia is very unbalanced. Some rare and strategic resources, such as China's rare earth and Russia's oil and gas resources, have become the targets of competition among countries in the region. As it is said in the book *Our Common Future*, "such conflicts are likely to increase as these resources become scarcer and competition for them increases."[2] The competition between China and Japan over China's rare earth export policy and the competition over Russia's oil pipeline all

---

[2] Our Common Future, The World Commission on Environment and Development, 1987, p. 239.

prove that the scarcer the resources, the more intense the competition, and the greater the possibility of conflict.

Secondly, countries in Northeast Asia are faced with the threat of the deteriorating living environments. As a result of global warming, some natural disasters caused by extreme weather are constantly occurring in Northeast Asian countries. For example, the frequent occurrence of sandstorms is a prominent manifestation of environmental deterioration in Northeast Asia. According to relevant data published by the United Nations, sandstorms occur more than 180 times a year around the world. Since the second half of the 20th century, extremely large sandstorms have frequently occurred in some countries and regions in Northeast Asia. The frequency of occurrence has increased from 8 times per year in the 1960s to more than 20 times per year since the 1990s, and the scope of spread and losses caused is also getting larger. The impact of sandstorms has already broken expanded, covering many countries in Northeast Asia. If the governments of Northeast Asian countries do not take adequate measures to curb its spread, there will be a new crisis in the ecological environment of the region.

Thirdly, cross-border pollution and the transfer of hazardous substances will also lead to conflicts between countries, posing a threat to regional stability and security. For example, nuclear power plant safety and nuclear waste pollution will affect regional security and inter-state relations. During the Cold War, the Soviet Union secretly dumped a large amount of nuclear waste into the Sea of Japan. After the incident came to light in 1993, Japan intervened with Russia and protested against the act. In March 2011, the Fukushima nuclear power plant leakage accident caused by an earthquake and tsunami not only caused heavy losses in Japan but also triggered a security panic in many neighboring countries.

Fourthly, the ecological crisis is worsening. Economic development of countries in the region is leading to the destruction of resources and the environment. If countries do not take common measures to stop the destruction, ecological degradation will threaten the peace and international relations in Northeast Asia. According to *Ci Hai*, the encyclopedia, "the ecological crisis is caused by the humanity's blind and excessive production activities. During the latent period, the damage is often hard to detect, such as forest dwindling, grassland degradation, soil erosion, desert expansion, water depletion, abnormal climate, imbalance of ecological balance, etc."[3]

---

[3] *Ci Hai* condensed version, Shanghai: Shanghai Lexicographical Publishing House, 1999, p. 1498.

In the 21st century, with the rise of environmental diplomacy, a country's ecological image has become an important symbol of the country on the international stage. Some western scholars have put forward the so-called theory of interference for international environmental to go with the transnational nature of ecological threats. They believe that a single country cannot protect against environmental damage within its territory. Some scholars even suggest that the United Nations should increase its environmental protection function. As Crispin Tickell says, "if one country's environmental problems affect the interests of other countries, the Security Council should naturally authorize actions to maintain international peace and security."[4] The deterioration of the ecological environment has caused new potential safety hazards to China and the whole region.

Fifthly, with the development of information technology and the popularization and application of the Internet, network security has become a heated issue in various countries. Due to the openness of the Internet, it has become one of the main battlefields of e-commerce and information warfare in various countries. For example, on April 23, 2013, the Associated Press released a statement on its Twitter account, which was hacked, that the White House was attacked and President Obama was injured. As soon as the fake information was released, the S&P 500 stock index fell 14 points in 5 seconds and its market value evaporated by US$136.5 billion. The Dow Jones Industrial Average fell 143.5 points or 0.98%. Li and Fu have explained that "cyber threats mainly include hacking, spreading viruses, theft and corruption in the financial field, launching denial-of-service attacks to break down the target system. Terrorists use information technology and the internet to make plans, raise funds, spread public opinions and communicate, spread false advertisements to defraud money, steal political, military, and commercial secrets, and carry out information warfare."[5] Network security is now an important agenda for countries all over the world. Dealing with the challenges in this field has become an important topic for governments all over the world, especially for security departments. Countries in Northeast Asia are also facing severe challenges.

Sixthly, with the rapid development of globalization, networking, information technology, and communication technology, organized

---

[4] Crispin Tickell, "The Inevitability of Environmental Security," *Threats without Enemies*, ed. Gwyn Prints, London: Earthscan, 1993, pp. 9–23.

[5] Li Wei and Fu Chunhua Non-traditional Security and International Relations, *Global Strategic Structure*, Beijing: Current Affairs Press, 2000, p. 493.

transnational crime has become malignant tumor in the international community. It not only endangers social order but also poses a threat to national security. At the present stage, transnational crimes are mainly manifested in the increasing collusion among criminal organizations of various countries and the increasing internationalization of criminal activities, such as drug smuggling, transnational kidnapping, money laundering, and smuggling, which have become new hazards that endanger social stability, affecting the relations between countries and triggering international disputes. If not eliminated, these will threaten normal exchanges between countries and even destroy the existing cooperation and trust between countries. In the era of globalization and informationization, the whole world is a big family connected to each other. The world has become smaller and the "interdependence" between countries is stronger. The past domestic problems have become regional or global problems today, and non-traditional security issues are more common. Therefore, many countries have agreed to strengthen coordination, communication, and cooperation in these fields. In terms of non-traditional security, Northeast Asia is facing the same or even similar threats as other regions in the world. Dealing with those challenges and threats has become a problem that the countries in Northeast Asia need to face and solve.

2.1.4 Challenges posed by the US hegemony policy in Northeast Asia

China is the geopolitical center of Northeast Asia, and its "peaceful rise" has become the biggest threat to the United States' hegemonic system. For China, which is committed to building a pluralistic and balanced security order in Northeast Asia, the US' hegemonic attempt and its "Asia-Pacific rebalancing" strategy are undoubtedly major challenges.

The US–Japan alliance poses a threat to China's security. The US–Japan military alliance was originally intended to contain China. After the Cold War, due to China's rapid development, the United States adjusted its military deployment in Northeast Asia to safeguard its global and regional hegemony. The United States has placed the focus of its security strategy on Northeast Asia, especially strengthening and adjusting its military alliance, and has put China on its target list. The United States has made use of the fact that China–Japan strategic alliance has not yet been established and created the alleged "threat" of China to Japan to amend the Japan–US security treaty and the defense cooperation guidelines. Expanding the scope of US–Japan alliance directly challenges China's basic security interests. On April 27, 2015, the United States and Japan held the US–Japan Security Committee (US–Japan 2 + 2) foreign and defense ministerial consultations in New York, revising the Guidelines for US–Japan Defense Cooperation. This new edition lifted the geographical restrictions on the operations of Japan's Self-Defense Forces, allowing Japan to play a more offensive role in the world. President Barack Obama said that the two countries will cooperate in a wider area after finalizing the new agreement, which will help the United States adjust its military deployment in the Asia-Pacific region, which includes responding to maritime security challenges and disaster emergencies. On May 14, a series of security bills related to the exercise of the right to collective self-defense were passed at the interim cabinet meeting held by the Japanese government. According to the new security bill, Japan's long-standing post-war policy of "exclusive defense" will be entirely modified. On June 10, 2015, the plenary session of Japan's Senate passed the Law on the Establishment and Amendment of the Ministry of Defense, formally abolishing the "civilian leadership" system. In fact, it canceled the superior position of civil service officials in the Ministry of Defense over the military officials and abolished an important line to prevent the Self Defense Forces from acting arbitrarily. The US hegemonic policy has also contributed to Japan's security threat to China. Due to the absolute and conflicting nature of the dispute over oil and gas resources in Diaoyu Dao and the East China Sea between China and Japan, the United States will be directly involved in any possible China–Japan military conflict in the name of fulfilling its alliance obligations. This more direct and realistic security challenge greatly increases China's difficulty in defending itself. The US is using Japan as a proxy to bait China in any future conflict. This intensifies the possibility of a direct China–US conflict. Therefore, this is the most serious security threat and challenge to China.

The US Taiwan policy is the biggest obstacle to China's reunification through its "Taiwan Relations Act" and the policy of protecting Taiwan. The China-US relationship that the United States wants to build is one of contact and containment, that is to contain China while cooperating with China. The fundamental purpose is to prevent China from rising to become the enemy of the hegemonic strategy of the United States. In the sense of strategic coordination, the longer the Taiwan issue drags on, the more unfavorable it will be to China's development and security. This is what the United States wants most. On the one hand, the United Sates has limited strategic cooperation with China to absorb and utilize the latter's energy and influence; one the other hand, the United States is using the Taiwan question to contain China and prevent China from becoming powerful. The United States is using the Taiwan question to further its regional hegemony and global hegemony ambitions. This is naturally endangering China's interests and is a key test to China's peaceful rise.

The United States regards its influence in the Korean Peninsula as the key to establishing hegemony in Northeast Asia. The position of the United States in the security structure of Northeast Asia, in particular the Korean Peninsula, is based on the US–ROK military alliance and its military and political presence on the Peninsula. The US military presence in the ROK directly threatens the DPRK's security and indirectly challenges China's security interests. Geographically, China and the DPRK are linked by mountains and rivers and the two countries are closely related with each other in terms of security interests. A direct threat to the DPRK's security is an indirect threat to China's security. The United States is the initiator and beneficiary of the North Korea–South Korea confrontation. The pattern of the confrontation in the Korean Peninsula is in line with the hegemonic interests of the United States. The political situation in Northeast Asia has changed since the end of the Cold War and the confrontational relations between the DPRK and the ROK have begun to ease, but the United States does not want the Peninsula to be unified as that would put the region beyond its control. Comparatively speaking, the divided Korean Peninsula is the basis of the military alliance between the United States and the ROK and is also the reason for the United States to maintain its military presence on the Peninsula. If the Korean Peninsula is reunified, the United States may lose an important strategic fulcrum in Northeast Asia due to the uncertainty of its future policy orientation. Therefore, the United States will try its best to maintain the current pattern in the Korean Peninsula, i.e., one of conflict between the North and South. The US has rejected the DPRK government's long-standing desire for "talks," which fully reflects the US strategy toward the DPRK. The situation of high pressure and long-term tension might lead to war or chaos. However, no matter whether form the turmoil in the Korean Peninsula takes, it will undoubtedly indirectly threaten China's security.

The influence of the United States in Mongolia also poses an indirect challenge to China's security. After the Cold War, the US began to quickly influence Mongolia, and US–Mongolia political and military relations developed rapidly. The relationship between the United States and Mongolia brings forth a challenge to China's peripheral security. Mongolia plays a very important role in China's geosecurity. Due to the need to contain China strategically, the United States has never stopped looking for containment points around China. Naturally, Mongolia's strategic value has not been ignored. Since the 1990s, the United States has been actively developing military exchanges and cooperation with Mongolia, and attempting to weaken China–Mongolia relations and alienate China. At present, Mongolia is striving to maintain a balanced relationship with the major powers in Northeast Asia. Due to its geographical advantages, China–Mongolia and Russia–Mongolia relations enjoy relative priority. However, the balance is often dynamic, and the advantage of relative priority may be lost due to changes in competition. Even though China–Mongolia relations are always positive, if the balance changes favorably towards the US, China's security interests will be weakened objectively. Any inclination of Mongolia to the side of the United States will cause an indirect counterbalance and challenge to China's security interests. This is not a problem that China should take lightly. Therefore, China should maintain its policy toward Mongolia, promote continuous expansion, deepen China–Mongolia relations, consolidate the foundation of peripheral security in a rational way, and resist the indirect threat to China's security from the US.

US hegemony is a strategic challenge to China's security. In recent years, the number of US military forces in the Pacific has been continuously adjusted. The US has shifted its focus to the Northwest Pacific, reaching Northeast Asia, and has made China the target of its deterrence tactics. Relying on its Japan and ROK military alliances, the United States has created a military chain to block China on the outer edge of China's eastern and southeastern maritime borders. This chain extends southward and connects with the islands in Southeast Asia. It encircles China's core area of coastal defense interests, objectively hindering China's access to the open sea and hampering China's strategy of becoming a naval power. In competition with China, the United States has taken the "zero-sum game" rules. The United States infringes on the strategic resources of China to stifle its peaceful rise, creates continuous security pressure on

China's politics, economy, and military, and undermines China's overall progress. China must remain aware of the strategic challenges from the United States, flexibly respond to the changes, adjust its own objectives in a timely manner, control the pace of internal affairs and diplomacy, and seek security and development in a steady way. It is necessary to accurately identify the US tactics against China and counter the strategic challenges to China's security.

2.2 China's Security Interests and Security Strategy in Northeast Asia

China is an emerging economy in Northeast Asia and has essential security interests in the region. China's national security requires that "all national security work shall adhere to the overall national security view, regard people's security as the tenet, regard political security as the fundamental, regard economic security as the basis, regard military, cultural, and social security as the safeguard, and by promoting international security, maintain national security in all fields, build a national security system, and walk a path of national security with Chinese characteristics."[6] From the perspective of geopolitics, Northeast Asia is located to the east and north of China. China shares borders with Russia and Mongolia on land. As the China–Russian border is 4,350 kilometers long and the China–Mongolia border 4,700 kilometers long, peace and friendship between China, Russia, and Mongolia are crucial to the security of China's northern territory. The Korean Peninsula is a barometer of security and stability in Northeast Asia because the issue of the Korean Peninsula plays a vital role in Northeast Asia and concerns the peaceful development of all countries in the region. The Taiwan issue relating to China's reunification is a core issue of China's sovereign security. China and Japan face each other across the sea, with a strip of water in between, with the Diaoyu Dao issue directly affecting the sovereignty and maritime security of the two countries. The confrontations between the two countries in recent years have become an essential part of the security dilemma in Northeast Asia. While China and Russia are deepening their strategic partnership, China is also actively improving and promoting its security

---

[6]The National Security Law of the People's Republic of China, Xinhua Net, http://news.xinhuanet.com/legal/2015-07/01/c1115787801_2.htm, July 1, 2015.

cooperation with the United States. However, the "Asia-Pacific rebalancing" strategy of the United States will intensify the strategic game in Northeast Asia, affecting China's national security interests and security strategy in this region.

2.2.1 China's traditional security interests in Northeast Asia

In July 2009, State Councilor Dai Bingguo summarized China's core national interests in the China–US Economic Dialogue as safeguarding, firstly, national security, secondly, national sovereignty and territorial integrity, and finally sustainable and stable development of the economy and society.[7] The National Security Law of the People's Republic of China, promulgated on July 1, 2015, defines national security as "a status in which the regime, sovereignty, unity, territorial integrity, welfare of the people, sustainable economic and social development, and other major interests of the state are relatively not faced with any danger and not threatened internally or externally and the capability to maintain a sustained security status."[8] China's security interests in Northeast Asia cover four dimensions, namely, political security, military security, economic security, and ecological security. Specifically, China's security interest in the region is expressed in the following four aspects.

2.2.1.1 *China's sovereign security*

Sovereign security involves China's right to handle internal and external affairs independently and forms the cornerstone of China's security interests in Northeast Asia, including the security of China's state system, governmental system, and political system. In the international political system, the distinctive character of China's social and political system is a socialist system with Chinese characteristics. China's political characteristics have shaped its unique development. Northeast Asia has become a "living fossil" of the Cold War in the early 21st century due to the two

---

[7] Chen Yue, China's Current Diplomatic Environment and Its Correspondence, *Contemporary International Relations*, 2010, 11: 4.
[8] The National Security Law of the People's Republic of China, Xinhua Net, http://news.xinhuanet.com/legal/2015-07/ 01/c1115787801_2.htm, July 1, 2015.

social systems, two ideologies, and two economic and social development modes in this region.

The actual threat to China's political security interests in Northeast Asia lies in the fact that the United States and other western countries are playing the leading roles in the contemporary international system. They have attempted to stifle China's rise. They have repeatedly challenged China, damaging China's national interests and interfering in China's national sovereignty.

China is surrounded strategically by countries with heterogeneous social systems in Northeast Asia. Prejudice and hostility against China's political system persist in the United States and Japan. The ideological struggle in Northeast Asia did not end with the Cold War.

2.2.1.2 *China's territorial integrity and national unity*

China's security interests in Northeast Asia refer to China's territorial integrity and national unity free of invasion and threat by the outside forces. Morgenthau once pointed out that the essential issue for a country is its survival.[9] National territorial integrity and national unity are fundamental issues related to the survival and development of a country and are the basis for realizing other interests. In Northeast Asia, the threat to China's integral territorial interests comes from maritime territory disputes with neighboring countries. There exists a dispute between China and Japan over the Diaoyu Dao issue and the delimitation of the continental shelf in the East China Sea. There are also great differences between China and the ROK on sovereignty over the Yellow Sea and the Suyan Rock. In the dispute between China and Japan over the Diaoyu Dao, Japan not only unjustly seized Diaoyu Dao but also attempted to make the illegal possession legal and effective. This damages China's national maritime interests and security interests.

National reunification is the top priority of a nation-state and an important component of China's security interests in Northeast Asia. After World War II, the United States established its dominant position in the Pacific region. Through its maritime deterrence strategy, the United States limited China's sphere of influence to the landmass of Northeast Asia. The United States has implemented a policy that is in conflict with China's

---

[9]Hans Morgenthau, The national interest of the United States. American Political Science Review, 1988, 46, p. 961.

political strategy. The Taiwan issue highlights the geopolitical game between China and the United States in Northeast Asia. The US policy on Taiwan has seriously harmed China's aim of national reunification.

It is important to properly handle the existing territorial and maritime rights disputes with neighboring countries and safeguard national sovereignty and territorial security. In Northeast Asia, the territorial and maritime disputes between China and Japan have seriously threatened China's territorial integrity and the region at large. Now, Japan has readjusted its military policy, increased its military spending, expanded its military strength, and implemented a strategy of becoming a military power. The Diaoyu Dao issue between China and Japan continues to intensify, directly threatening China's territorial integrity and national security. In particular, in 2012, Japan once again broke the consensus between China and Japan to "shelve the dispute" over Diaoyu Dao and announced the implementation of the so-called "nationalization" by violating China's territorial sovereignty. With the normalization of Chinese ships and planes cruising in Diaoyu Dao, the dispute between China and Japan is continuing to intensify. Territorial disputes pose a direct and serious threat to national security, and the friction they bring about can easily lead to direct military conflicts. As an armed conflict is not in the actual interests of China or Japan, the Diaoyu Dao issue is unlikely to lead to a large-scale war between the two sides. At the same time, a low-intensity and small-scale military conflict cannot be ruled out.

As far as the future direction is concerned, the dispute between China and Japan over Diaoyu Dao is difficult to completely resolve in the foreseeable future, but the friction between the two countries will likely be normalized. On the one hand, since the Liberal Democratic Party came to power in Japan at the end of 2012, the right deviation of Japanese politics has become more obvious and the influence of the right-wing forces has continued to rise. If the Japanese government's tough policy toward China is put into practice, the situation will definitely lead to the continued aggravating of the Diaoyu Dao issue, worsening the tension between China and Japan. On the other hand, with the continued rise of China, neighboring countries, including Japan, are more worried that China will "retrieve" the disputed islands, reefs, and sea areas after becoming stronger, thus creating a sense of crisis and urgency due to which their need to actively fight for and expand power has increased.[10] Therefore, Japan is

---

[10] Zhang Xuegang, China's Border Sea Situation and Policy Choice. *Contemporary International Relations*, 2012, 8: 16.

likely to take a tougher stance and take more offensive actions on the Diaoyu Dao issue. The Diaoyu Dao issue between China and Japan will cause a deadlock in China–Japanese relations, challenging China's security interests in Northeast Asia for a long time. In July 2015, Japan's lower house passed a new security bill. Chinese scholars believe that Japan may not only take part in unnecessary wars in the future but could also regard certain neighboring countries as its enemies and undermine regional peace and stability. The new security bill serves the US military strategy of promoting a rebalance of power in the Asia-Pacific region, which, together with Japan's trend towards remilitarization, will act as a trigger for further military tensions in the Asia-Pacific region. Japan's militarist tendencies are highly alarming.[11]

Under the "Asia-Pacific rebalancing" strategy, the United States continues to move its strategic focus eastward, exerting a profound impact on China's peripheral security. On January 5, 2012, the United States released its new military strategy report "Sustaining US Global Leadership: Priorities for 21st Century Defense," proposing to further consolidate its existing alliances in the region and expand cooperation with emerging countries. On June 3, 2012, the US Secretary of Defense Leon Edward Panetta formally proposed the "Asia-Pacific rebalancing" strategy, "the goal of which is to insert the United States into this region in a positive way and make it lead the 'game' in the Asia-Pacific region so that the United States can play an indispensable leading role in Asia." The "rebalancing" strategy has become a new version of the US strategy of "pivot to Asia-Pacific," which aims to realize US hegemony over the region by strengthening the deployment of the US military in the Asia-Pacific. With this strategic concept, the United States has continuously strengthened its strategic deployment in the Asia-Pacific region, including Northeast Asia, and strengthened its alliance with Asian allies such as Japan and the ROK while streamlining its defense budget and making strategic contractions from Europe and the Middle East. The Obama administration has repeatedly stressed that the US–Japan alliance is the cornerstone of Asia-Pacific security, due to which Japan clearly regards China as an important threat. The US strategy allying with Japan and suppressing China has had a profound negative impact on China's national security interests. Chen has

---

[11] Lyu Yaodong, Wang Huibo, Japan's House of Representatives Passes New Security Bill That Allows Attack without Being Attacked, China Net, http://news.china.com/international/1000/20150715/20016035_all.html#page_2, July 15, 2015.

pointed out that"the high-intensity military layout of the United States in the Asia-Pacific region clearly reflects the strengthening of the US military precautions against China, which will inevitably cause greater military pressure on China and increase the risk factor of military conflicts with the United States. It should be noted that the United States is seeking to build an upgraded version of the Asia-Pacific alliance strategy, that is, to strengthen the trilateral cooperation between the United States, Australia and Japan."[12] In October 2014, the then US Vice President Biden claimed that, by 2020, the United States would have 60% of its naval resources and airpower stationed in the Pacific region. The United States is strengthening its deterrent capability against the DPRK's nuclear ambitions, expanding the US–Vietnam cooperative relationship, and seizing the "historic opportunity" to establish a new relationship with Myanmar.[13] US leaders have repeatedly stated that the "Asia-Pacific rebalancing" strategy is not aimed at China, but military deployment in the region and strengthening military alliances with Northeast Asian countries point to China being in their crosshairs. China's peaceful development is facing increasing political and military pressure from the US "Asia-Pacific rebalancing" strategy, which has strengthened US security dominance in East Asia and weakened China's influence.

2.2.1.3 *China's peaceful economic and social development environment*

Economic security is related to the development of a country. Together with political, territorial, and sovereign security, it constitutes the core national security interest. Northeast Asia is an important area for China's foreign trade and economic cooperation and provides a base for China's peaceful development. With China's establishment of a market economy system, its national economic interests are inextricably linked with those of other countries in the world. However, there is a long maritime island chain in China's coastal geographical vicinity, extending from the ROK,

---

[12] Chen Jimin, The US Asia-Pacific Rebalancing Strategy and Its Challenges to China. *Study Times*, http://www.cntheory.com/zydx/2015-02/ccps150210WOGJ.html, February 10, 2015.
[13] Bridget Hunter, Biden Outlines U.S. Foreign Policy for Rapidly Changing World, http://iipdigital.usembassy.gov/st/english/article/2014/10/20141003309340.html#ixzz3dkmmO0DF, October 3, 2014.

Japan, and the Philippines to Indonesia. China has disputes with some countries along this island chain relating to maritime territory, marine resources, and maritime rights and interests. The United States began to build a Pacific Island chain to encircle China and the Soviet Union during the Cold War, which it still uses to target China. Now, China has an increasing need for overseas trade and resources; therefore, the protection of China's maritime security interests is related to China's rise.

The biggest challenge to China's economic and social development interests in the 21st century comes from the US policy of strengthening hegemony in Northeast Asia. Against the background of the global financial crisis, the success of China's model and China's rise as a superpower have led to the United States recognizing China as a threat. Hegemony is the core interest of the US. Once a country challenges the position of the US, it will take various measures to eliminate the threat. As long as China continues to grow, the United States will pursue a policy of engagement and containment toward China no matter how much China expresses its goodwill. In 2006, the US Defense Department's Quadrennial Defense Review stated that China, as a major emerging power, "has the greatest potential to compete militarily with the United States. If the United States does not take countermeasures, China is likely to develop destructive military technologies, thus breaking the US advantage in traditional weapons."[14] In March 2011, the US Defense Intelligence Agency Director Ronald Burgess said that China was the biggest threat to the United States. At present, China is still focusing on the Taiwan issue, but will expand its basic goal from regional growth to international growth. Chinese leaders will continue to increase their own advantages while looking for weaknesses of potential rivals.[15] In recent years, the focus of US military deployment has begun to shift to the Asia-Pacific region, and its military deployment in the area is mainly concentrated in Northeast Asia, which poses a direct threat to China's peaceful development. In the National Security Strategy published in May 2010, the Obama administration affirmed the strategic goal of "world leadership" insisted upon by successive US administrations, stressing that the United States should continue

---

[14] The U.S. Department of Defense. Quadrennial Defense Review. http://www.defenselink.mil/qdr/report/Report20060203.pdf, February 6, 2006.
[15] Eli Lake, China deemed the biggest threat to the US, The Washington Times. http://www.washingtontimes.com/news/2011/mar/10/china-deemed-biggest-threat-to-us/?page=all, March 10, 2011.

to strengthen its military alliance with Pacific countries.[16] In January 2012, Obama published *Sustaining US Global Leadership: Priorities for 21st Century Defense*, which pointed out that "the United States has played a leading role in the transformation of the international system over the past sixty-five years... We will emphasize our existing alliances, which provide a vital foundation for Asia-Pacific security."[17] The strengthening of US relations with Japan, the ROK, ASEAN countries, Australia, and India, along with its arms sales to China's Taiwan region, shows that the US is building a strategic containment chain to prevent the rise of China.

Tensions between China and Japan are also threatening China's opportunity for peaceful development. A peaceful and stable surrounding environment has been the key to China's rise. However, the lack of strategic mutual trust between China and Japan and a potential confrontation have aggravated the deterioration of China's security environment in Northeast Asia. Other areas of conflict involve the South China Sea, the China–India border, and the Korean Peninsula issues, increasing security cost for China. Japan recognizes the unipolar hegemony of the United States, pursues a diplomatic strategy supporting the establishment of unipolar world order by the United States, and places great hopes on the realization of Japan's ambition as a political power under the leadership of the United States. The rise of the Democratic Party of Japan and Yukio Hatoyama's resignation show that, according to Jin, "Japan's demand for security support from the United States exceeds its efforts to seek a 'normal nation,' and any attempt to destabilize the US-Japan alliance will face great resistance."[18] Japan's diplomatic strategy of aligning with the United States and opposing China poses a real threat to China's security environment and interests in Northeast Asia. The structural contradiction and mutual suspicion between China and Japan have led to a deteriorating relationship between the two sides. After the end of the Cold War, while Japan's status as a powerful nation was returning, China had already become a major power in the world. China's GDP in 2010 caught up with

---

[16] The White House, National Security Strategy. http://www.whitehouse.gov/sites/defauh/files/rss_viewer/national_security_strategy.pdf, May 2010.

[17] The White House, Sustaining U.S. Global Leadership: Priorities for 21st Century Defense. http://www.defense.gov/news/Defense_Strategic_Guidance.Pdf. January 2012.

[18] Jin Canrong, The New Situation of China's Diplomacy in 2010. *Contemporary International Relations*, 2010, 11: 7.

and surpassed that of Japan for the first time in more than 100 years ever since 1840. The Japanese government created the "China threat." This will inevitably lead the Japanese government to take policy measures to guard against China. It will take diplomatic actions such as Japan–US military integration, oppose the lifting of the EU ban on arms sales to China, and propose the concept of a "Japan–US–Australia–India value alliance," thus triggering potential confrontation in China–Japan strategic relations. China–Japan relations evolved from a "strategic partnership" during the Cold War to "competition" in the post-Cold War era. Conflicts of national interest often lead to countervailing factors in the relations between the two countries.

2.2.1.4 *China's military security in Northeast Asia*

China's military security in Northeast Asia mainly refers to the protection of China's territory from threats and infringement by other countries' military forces, military alliances, and the surrounding military environment. Military security is necessary for the realization of national security interests and involves a country's basic survival issues. In this era, the environment in Northeast Asia includes the geopolitical pattern of "one superpower plus three powers," the US–Japan–ROK alliance that is attempting to contain China, and further development of new military reforms in the world. China thus has to guard against military threats, safeguard homeland security interests, prevent nuclear proliferation and arms races, and maintain stability in the neighborhood. Needless to say, China's military security in Northeast Asia is facing the following challenges:

(1) The US military presence in Northeast Asia and the bilateral military alliance system led by the US pose a serious challenge to China's security. Protecting China's geo-military security interests in Northeast Asia requires us to enhance our effective deterrent capability of military forces to offset the military superiority of hostile military groups, ensure secure borders, and ensure the existence of geostrategic buffer zones.
(2) The proliferation of mass destruction weapons, especially nuclear weapons, in China's surrounding areas will undermine the stability in Northeast Asia as well as the balance of the regional military power structure, and could lead to China facing a regional nuclear arms race. It is in China's interest to build a peaceful and stable surrounding

security environment by effectively preventing nuclear proliferation in Northeast Asia.

(3) Regional hot-button issues challenge China's security in Northeast Asia. The crisis in the Korean Peninsula has continuously intensified tensions, directly threatening China's national security interests. The Korean Peninsula is very important to China's national security. In modern times, the Korean Peninsula crisis has dragged China to the brink of war several times. At the beginning of the 21st century, the DPRK is of great strategic significance to China's national security when there exist the US-Japan-ROK alliance and the military bases along the Pacific island chain with containing China as the aim. Any conflict in the DPRK will endanger the safety of northeast China. Any crisis in the Korean Peninsula will directly harm China's national security interests.

2.2.2 China's non-traditional security interests in Northeast Asia

China's security interests in Northeast Asia include not only traditional security fields like political security, military security, social security, and geopolitical security but also non-traditional security interests, namely, economic security and ecological security as described in the following.

2.2.2.1 *China's economic security interests in Northeast Asia*

It is important to ensure China's financial security. Finance is the lifeblood of the national economy, and the financial system is the functional system for allocating social capital and resources, as well as an intermediary between various economies within the country.[19] All sectors of the national economy interact with each other through the financial system. Therefore, the stability and safety of the financial system are directly related to the overall safety of the national economy. China's economic security interests in Northeast Asia consist of preventing regional financial risks by resisting and eliminating all kinds of threats and infringements to ensure normal financial functioning in China.

---

[19]Lei Jiasu, *Theory and Method of National Economic Security*, Beijing: Economic Science Press, 2000, pp. 89–90.

China should also safeguard its energy security. The rapid industrialization of China has created the current economic structure with high energy demand. Under this structure, energy security is an increasingly unavoidable problem on which the steady development of the national economy is based. Northeast Asia is important for China's diversified energy supply strategy. As far as this region is concerned, China's energy security involves oil and gas resources On the one hand, there should be a stable and reliable source of energy in Northeast Asia to ensure the regular supply of oil and gas; on the other hand, there should be a smooth and safe energy transportation channel in Northeast Asia to ensure the transportation safety of the resources.

China needs to ensure its industrial security so that its domestic industries can maintain healthy and stable development in an open international economic and trade system, as well as maintain independent industrial status and competitive advantages. China's industrial security is mainly manifested in foreign trade and business activities in this region and the good functioning of domestic industries free from unfair competition by imported products and import surges. This will safeguard the independent position and competitive advantage of Chinese industries in regional competition to ensure the overall coordinated and sustainable development of the national economy.

China should safeguard its ecological security interests in Northeast Asia, thereby guaranteeing that the ecological environment in the region is free from the pollution and destruction. Ecological security is in the interests of national health and quality of life, as well as sustainable social and economic development. Ecological security may be of a low priority in terms of overall security interests. However, the destruction of the ecological environment may cause chain reactions and have indirect effects on national political security, military security, and economic security. Therefore, the importance of ecological security cannot be ignored.

China's ecological security interests in Northeast Asia mainly include two aspects: atmospheric ecological security and marine ecological security. Atmospheric ecology is an overall system that transcends national borders. Air movement enables air pollution in one country to travel long distances to another country, resulting in cross-border air pollution.[20] The air pollution caused by countries in Northeast Asia can destroy the

---

[20] Zhang Haibin, Review and Prospect of Environmental Cooperation in Northeast Asia, *The Journal of International Studies*, 2000, 2: 76.

ecosystem of the whole region and endanger the environment on which other countries depend for their survival and development. Currently, the atmospheric and ecological problems in Northeast Asia are mainly manifested in sandstorms and acid rain. In particular, the cross-border spread of acid rain has a great negative impact on China's ecological environment, national life, and economic and social development. Maintaining atmospheric ecological safety is an important part of China's security interests. As for marine ecological security, pollutants released by human activities into the ocean will destroy the marine ecosystem, damaging the quality of seawater and producing a series of negative consequences. The sea areas in Northeast Asia (the Yellow Sea and the Sea of Japan) are semi-closed, with relatively weak self-regulation capacity, along with serious pollutant emissions by coastal countries. This has led to continuous deterioration of marine ecology. The destruction of regional marine ecology will hinder China's marine activities like fishing, damage China's seawater and environmental quality, and endanger China's national health. Therefore, maintaining the safety of marine ecology is another important aspect of China's ecological security interests in Northeast Asia.

Finally, China should also safeguard information security, referring to the protection of the national information system. Information security involves information system security, database security, personal privacy protection, commercial information security, and state secrets protection. In the process of informationization, countries all over the world are highly dependent on information networks for everything. Information networks are like the nervous system of the body. However, information security issues have emerged. Improving China's independent research and development capability for information technology and strengthening the construction of network security are important components of China's non-traditional security interests in Northeast Asia.

2.2.2.2 *The existing threats to China's economic security interests in Northeast Asia*

China's financial security faces multi-dimensional challenges. As the financial markets of Northeast Asian countries are closely linked, the imbalance of a country's local market can easily spread to other countries. At the same time, the unsound financial cooperation mechanism and the lack of financial risk prevention in Northeast Asia make the region unable to resist the impact of the global financial crisis effectively. Besides, the domestic financial policies of some neighboring countries will also affect China's financial security. Japan, in particular, has repeatedly adopted a policy of letting the Japanese yen depreciate during its domestic economic recession, exporting the crisis to its neighbors and posing a threat to the stability of financial markets in Northeast Asia, including China.

China's energy security faces the challenge of regional energy competition. China is sensitive to the asymmetric interdependence of energy relations and is vulnerable to energy supply risks. Any restriction on oil and gas resources and transportation lines will hit China's domestic economy. At the same time, an increase in the overall energy demand in Northeast Asia has led to an increase in conflicts in the energy field, such as the differences between China and Japan over the oil transmission lines in Russia's Far East. Even many regional conflicts (such as the dispute between China and Japan over Diaoyu Dao) have their origins in energy competition.

China's industrial security faces severe challenges from the competition in the Northeast Asian market. Although the scale of China's foreign trade has expanded, its international competitiveness has not increased correspondingly.[21] Northeast Asian countries are generally highly dependent on foreign trade and the competition in the regional market is fierce, causing relatively great competitive pressure on Chinese industries. In particular, the devaluation effect caused by the financial crisis will also bring challenges to the price competitiveness of Chinese commodities as the economies of various countries recover after the crisis. At the same time, the entry of foreign-funded enterprises from Northeast Asia into the Chinese market, especially those from Japan and the ROK, will definitely impact China's national industries.

China's ecological security interests in Northeast Asia are facing real threats. First, cross-border air pollution is an urgent ecological disaster facing China. In Northeast Asia, power plants and factories burning fossil fuels in various countries discharge a large number of pollutants such as sulfur into the air. Air movement enables air pollutants from one country to spread to neighboring countries, resulting in cross-border air pollution. These pollutants have caused widespread acid rain in Northeast Asia and also pose a threat to China's atmospheric and ecological security. Besides, sandstorm is another representative phenomenon of air pollution in

---

[21] Liu Yiting, Seven "Potential Crises" in China's Economic Security, *China Quality Daily*, March 6, 2006.

Northeast Asia. The yellow sand from the Mongolia Plateau and even Siberia can have a negative impact on the atmospheric environment in northern China. Besides, regional marine pollution is also a severe threat to China's ecological security in Northeast Asia. The sea in Northeast Asia is enclosed on most sides and weak in self-regulation, which makes it vulnerable to pollution and destruction. In recent decades, with the industrial development of countries in the region, the marine ecological environment in Northeast Asia has been increasingly polluted and destroyed. The dumping of pollutants from land, exploitation of offshore oil, especially oil spills, and various forms of ship pollution have worsened the marine environment in Northeast Asia, which is manifested in red tides, oil pollution, plastic pollution, and accumulation of toxic substances. Marine pollution is persistent, widespread, and difficult to control, which endangers the balance of the marine ecosystem and poses severe challenges to China's ecological security.

China's information network faces major challenges. China faces competition from countries in the region in the field of information network security. China's National Computer Network Emergency Response Technical Team/Coordination Center pointed out in 2012 that many infiltrations and attacks against China's network infrastructure had been detected from time to time. Although no serious harm was done, high-level and organized network attacks pose serious challenges to the security of network infrastructure.[22] On June 9, 2013, US intelligence agent Edward Snowden voluntarily disclosed secret documents of the US National Security Agency on the "Prism" surveillance program to *The Guardian* and *The Washington Post*. Since George W. Bush's reign in 2007, the US National Security Agency and the Federal Bureau of Investigation had launched a secret project codenamed Prism, which monitored 10 types of data, including videos, pictures, and mail, through access to the central servers of 9 US companies, including Microsoft, Yahoo, Google, and Apple, to gather intelligence and monitor the public's network activities. The "Prism" affair revealed that the US government had been monitoring and infiltrating China and other countries' network systems for a long time. In the sector of network security, the United States, on the one hand, tried every means to steal Chinese intelligence

---

[22] National Computer Network Emergency Response Technical Team/Coordination Center of China, Overview of China's Internet Network Security Situation 2012, http://www.cert.org.cn/publish/main/upload/File/201303212012CNCERTreport.PDF, June 9, 2013.

and carried out large-scale state hacking, endangering China's network security; on the other hand, the United States also claimed to be a cyber guard and accused China of attacking US cybersecurity. In the past 15 years, the US intelligence agency Tailored Access Operations (TAO) has successfully infiltrated China's computer and telecommunications systems and obtained "the best and most reliable information"[23] about what is happening in China.

The "Prism" affair sounded the alarm for China's national information security. Products of Cisco, Microsoft, Google, Qualcomm, Intel, Apple, Oracle, IBM, and other US companies are widely used in China's national information infrastructure. Almost all the government, customs, postal, financial, railway, civil aviation, medical, military, and police departments use products of American companies. In the financial industry, the data centers of China's four major commercial banks all use Cisco equipment, which accounts for more than 70% of equipment used in the financial industry and over 50% in the customs, public security, armed police, industry and commerce, education and other government agencies. In the railway system, Cisco's share of equipment usage is about 60%. In civil aviation, all equipment used is from Cisco. Cisco products account for more than 60% of equipment used in airports, docks, and ports. In the oil industry, manufacturing, light industry, and tobacco industries, Cisco's share exceeds 60%, and many enterprises and institutions use only Cisco equipment. In the media, Cisco's share of equipment usage has reached more than 80%.[24] The widespread use of American information products in key sectors in China poses potential risks to China's national information security.

2.2.3 Rational thinking on China's security strategy in Northeast Asia

China's national security strategy is an overall plan to safeguard the national security interests of the country. The country's strategic decisions on politics, military affairs, economy, diplomacy, science and technology, and social development should be guided by and coordinated with

---

[23] Ding Liangheng, The US Secret Agency Blasted "Cyber Attack on China" for 15 Years. China Net, http://news.china.com/international/1000/20130613/17887101.html, June 13, 2013.

[24] Bai Zhaoyang, Cisco, IBM, Microsoft, and Other Five Major US Enterprises' Infiltrating China's Network Reflecting Hidden Worries, Xinhua Net. http://news.xinhuanet.com/fortune/2013-06/25/c_124905600.htm?Prolongation=1, June 25, 2013.

its strategy. The goal of China's Northeast Asia security strategy is to maintain peace, stability, development, and prosperity, promote friendly exchanges among peoples, prevent regional emergencies, and prevent hostile forces from undermining peace and security in the region.

2.2.3.1 *China's security environment in Northeast Asia*

China is located in the eastern part of Eurasia and is an important country in Northeast Asia. Peace and development in Northeast Asia are closely related to China's prosperity and stability as China is an integral part of the geopolitical environment of the region. In recent years, peace has prevailed in Northeast Asia. China's security in Northeast Asia faces three challenges: the US "Asia-Pacific rebalancing" strategy, China–Japan diplomatic friction, and the DPRK nuclear issue.

The "rebalancing" strategy of the United States aimed at maintaining its leading position in the Asia-Pacific region is still in progress. Preventing the rise of China in Northeast Asia is the core goal of the "rebalancing" strategy of the United States. The strategy has encouraged the development of right-wing conservative forces in Japanese politics. After the generational change in leadership in Northeast Asian countries, the nuclear crisis in the Korean peninsula remains deadlocked and the Six-Party Talks have stalled.

The Diaoyu Dao issue has caused China and Japan to be in a state of political, diplomatic, and security confrontation. Relations between the ROK and the DPRK have eased, and China–Russia, China–ROK, and China–Mongolia relations are running smoothly; a new model of major-power relationship between China and the US is being explored. The economic development of East Asian countries is still undergoing transformation. Nationalism and maritime awareness continue to rise and disputes over maritime sovereignty remain. The behavior of the United States, the world's only superpower, in preventing the rise of China has constructed a geopolitical environment in Northeast Asia in which some countries are using the United States to oppose China. The main opponents of China's rise are the United States and Japan.

2.2.3.2 *The concept of China's Northeast Asia security strategy*

The National Security Law of the People's Republic of China, promulgated on July 1, 2015, stipulates that "National security shall be maintained by insisting on mutual trust, mutual benefits, equality, and cooperation, actively participating in security exchange and cooperation with foreign governments and international organizations, and fulfilling international security obligations to promote common security and maintain world peace."[25] The concept of China's Northeast Asia security strategy is to adhere to the five principles of mutual respect for sovereignty and territorial integrity, mutual non-aggression, mutual non-interference in internal affairs, equality and mutual benefit, and peaceful coexistence among the countries in Northeast Asia. China will actively promote mutual respect, mutual trust, and equal consultation in the development of politics among the countries in Northeast Asia so as to jointly promote the democratization of international relations in the region. As for economic development, China will develop a cooperative and complementary relationship with Northeast Asian countries and take efforts to help their economies develop in the direction of mutual benefit. As for culture, China respects the differences and diversity of cultural development in different countries and is willing to learn from other cultures and seek common ground while maintaining its uniqueness. As for security, China will enhance mutual trust and cooperation, reduce differences and resolve disputes, and jointly safeguard peace and stability in Northeast Asia. In terms of environmental protection, China will adhere to the principle of common but differentiated responsibilities in environmental governance and protection in Northeast Asia. China will promote mutual assistance and joint efforts among Northeast Asian countries to realize cooperation in environmental management and protection and cooperate with these countries to deal with both regional and global climate changes.

China's security strategy in Northeast Asia should focus on comprehensive security, pursue common security, and promote cooperative security. In the face of the serious security dilemmas in Northeast Asia, countries in this region should "remove the cold war mentality, abandon ideological prejudice, and establish a new concept of mutual aid and win-win cooperation."[26] They should also undertake multilateral cooperation to maintain and realize common security. Only by such acts can countries

---

[25] The National Security Law of the People's Republic of China, Xinhua Net, http://news.xinhuanet.com/legal/2015-07/01/c1115787801_2.htm, July 1, 2015.
[26] Speech by Chinese Foreign Minister Yang Jiechi at the First Lanting Forum. People's Daily Online, http://world.people.com.cn/GB/157578/13372720.html, December 2, 2010.

in Northeast Asia achieve the goals of preventing conflicts, avoiding wars, and maintaining peace and prosperity.

2.2.3.3 The goal and path of China's security strategy in Northeast Asia

The ultimate goal of China's security strategy in Northeast Asia is to safeguard the Chinese people's right to choose their own social system and development path and not to allow other countries and forces to interfere in China's internal affairs. China will resolutely safeguard its core interests such as national unity and territorial integrity in Northeast Asia from damage and infringement and ensure the implementation and enforcement of China's foreign policy in Northeast Asia. China's security strategy will provide security for friendly cooperation with all Northeast Asian countries to uphold the Five Principles of Peaceful Coexistence. It will support the Chinese government in resolving contradictions and differences among the countries in Northeast Asia through dialogue and peaceful negotiation to contribute to peace and security in the region.

Therefore, China should rely on the China–Russia strategic cooperative partnership, actively develop its national relations with the ROK, the DPRK, and Mongolia, and actively build a new type of relationship with the United States and Japan.

China should develop a strategic partnership of cooperation with Russia and promote collaboration between the two countries in safeguarding peace and development in Northeast Asia. In recent years, the strategic mutual trust between China and Russia has been continuously strengthened; economic, trade, and energy cooperation has been continuously expanded; and non-governmental exchanges have never been more active. The two countries support each other on issues concerning their core interests, including national sovereignty, unity, and territorial integrity, and actively advocate world multi-polarization of international relations to promote the establishment of a more just, reasonable, and democratic international political and economic order to promote lasting peace and common prosperity.[27] The significance of the China–Russian strategic cooperative partnership at the regional level lies in the balance it provides

---

[27] Joint Statement of the People's Republic of China and the Russian Federation on Comprehensive Deepening of Strategic Cooperation Partnership, Chinese central

in Northeast Asia in the maintenance of peace, stability, and prosperity. China–Russian relations are also beneficial to the security interests of the two countries and will enhance the international status and influence of the two countries.

China will continue to deepen its strategic partnership with the ROK. In 2013, China and the ROK issued the China–ROK Joint Statement for the Future and the Action Plan to Enrich the China–ROK Strategic Cooperative Partnership. These two statements have defined a new blueprint and direction for the construction and promotion of "China–ROK relations." China and the ROK have a high degree of consensus on the denuclearization of the Korean Peninsula and opposition to the Japanese government's denial of its historical aggression. On June 1, 2015, China and the ROK formally signed a free trade agreement, injecting new impetus into bilateral development. The benign interaction between China and the ROK is helpful in limiting the US–Japan–ROK alliance.

China is actively developing comprehensive strategic cooperation with Mongolia, which is an important neighbor. The boundary line between the two countries is 4,700 kilometers long, and they share broad consensus on many issues related to the security of Northeast Asia. Both countries advocate the denuclearization of the Korean Peninsula. The continuous development of China–Mongolia cooperation will play a positive role in promoting the construction of a multilateral security cooperation mechanism in Northeast Asia.

China is exploring the possibility of improving China–DPRK relations. China's peaceful development strategy needs good relations with the DPRK because it needs stability in the Korean Peninsula. On the premise that the DPRK blocks nuclear testing, China should take measures to improve relations.

The construction of a new type of major-country relationship between China and the United States is an essential basis for realizing China's strategic goal of security in Northeast Asia. China and the United States have a wide range of common interests in Northeast Asia and the world at large. Strengthening China–US strategic dialogue and communication and expanding military exchanges and cooperation will help reduce misunderstandings and enhance trust, which will help to expand

government's official website, http://www.gov.cn/ldhd/2010-09/28/content_1712072.htm, September 28, 2010.

China–US cooperation in the field of security. The key to strengthening the strategic cooperation between China and the United States is to abandon the Cold War mentality, get rid of the "Thucydides' trap," and build a new model of major-country relations featuring no conflict, no confrontation, mutual respect, and win-win cooperation between the two countries.

China strives to develop good strategic reciprocal relations with Japan. In recent years, China–Japan relations have been declining because of Japan's "purchase" of the disputed islands. The relations between the two countries have deteriorated greatly. As both China and Japan are major powers in Northeast Asia, the result of the troublesome relations can only be destructive. The fundamental reason for the worsening of China–Japan relations is Japan's change in its diplomatic policy. During the Abe administration, Japan amended its Pacifist Constitution, lifted the ban on collective self-defense, and forcibly passed a new security bill. Japan must deeply reflect on its history, adhere to peaceful development, and, more importantly, win the trust of all countries in Northeast Asia through practical actions.

2.2.3.4 *China's security strategy choice in Northeast Asia*

The 2013 White Paper on China's National Defense, "The Diversified Employment of China's Armed Forces," pointed out the following: "It is China's unshakable national commitment and strategic choice to take the road of peaceful development. China unswervingly pursues an independent foreign policy of peace and a national defense policy that is defensive in nature."[28]

First of all, China should continue to follow the path of peaceful development in Northeast Asia. Guided by the diplomatic concepts of "good neighborly friendship and partnership," China has been building relations with neighboring countries based on amity, sincerity, mutual benefit, and inclusiveness. China will strictly abide by its good neighbor policy to strengthen the foundation of peace and stability in Northeast Asia. Through good neighborly diplomacy, a geopolitical environment of equality, mutual benefit, and mutual trust will be created, and countries in

---

[28] Defense White Paper: The Diversified Employment of China's Armed Forces, the Ministry of National Defense of the People's Republic of China, http://www.mod.gov.cm/affair/2013-04/16/content_4442839.htm, April 16, 2013.

the Northeast Asian region will jointly realize peace, stability, and prosperity.

Secondly, China's military security policy in Northeast Asia should adhere to defensive ideals, strive to achieve a balance of strategic forces, and seek peace through strength. However, China should continuously strengthen its military strength in the course of peaceful development and strive to modernize its armed forces. To achieve a strategic balance of power in Northeast Asia, China should enhance strategic deterrence with military strength and seek peace in this manner. China is committed to the peaceful settlement of territorial disputes and creating an amicable, secure, and prosperous neighborhood.

Finally, solving the problem of security in Northeast Asia depends on China's use of its diplomatic policy. The structural contradiction between hegemonic and rising powers in Northeast Asia does exist. The United States, Japan, and other countries in Northeast Asia have always paid special attention to the subtle changes in China's foreign policy with doubtful eyes. They accept that China's economic development is an undeniable fact but spare no effort to prevent China's military rise. They are trying to perfect an island chain containment network before the modernization of China's military power, forcing China to accept to become a "caged tiger." In order to solve the security dilemma and realize China's peaceful rise, we need theoretical and practical innovation in diplomacy. China's diplomatic strategy in the 21st century should aim to cooperate with various international forces to promote multi-polarization of international relations. The international political and economic effect of China's rise should be a move away from a unipolar world to a possible multipolar coexistence. China's road to rising determines the contradiction between China-US, the rising power and the hegemonic power. However, China plays its role in the international system not as a substitute for US hegemony, but a builder for a multi-polar world. China–US relations should avoid the "Thucydides' Trap." The trend of multi-polarization in international relations has constructed a buffer zone for conflicts between hegemonic power and rising power. However, the central theme of the peaceful development in the contemporary world, the interdependent interest ties in international relations in globalization, the beneficiary identification of China in the contemporary global system environment and the non-expansion feature of Chinese history and culture bring about China's choice of a peaceful rise and determine low intensity conflicts and close cooperation in many fields in the contemporary China–US relations.

The way forward for China and Japan lies in the joint efforts by the two countries to build a strategic relationship of mutual benefit.

2.3 The Mode and Vision of Promoting the Construction of a Security Mechanism in Northeast Asia

As a region where the strategic interests of China, the United States, Japan, and Russia collide, Northeast Asia has a complicated security situation. The complexity of relations and the dynamic nature of the power structure make it difficult to effectively solve the current complicated regional security problems under the existing security structure. There is a lack of security cooperation and institutional arrangements in Northeast Asia. The decentralized power structure makes it a challenge to coordinate and control the existing conflicts of interest effectively.[29] Promoting regional security cooperation and building a local security mechanism are the unavoidable practical needs of Northeast Asian countries. Based on the consideration of national interests, countries in Northeast Asia have also advocated promoting the construction of regional security mechanisms. There is an objective need and subjective desire to promote the construction of a security mechanism in Northeast Asia. Normative discussion and empirical research on this security mechanism are necessary. This section discusses the security mechanism in Northeast Asia from the aspects of objectives and principles, structure and function, mode selection, and construction paths.

2.3.1 Objectives and principles of the security mechanism in Northeast Asia

The security mechanism in Northeast Asia is different from military alliance. It aims to maintain peace and stability in Northeast Asia, promote dialogue and cooperation, and establish international codes of conduct and norms. It is based on the principles of equality, trust, mutual benefit,

---

[29] Huang Fengzhi and Jin Xin, A Multidimensional Survey of China's Security Interests in Northeast Asia, *Northeast Asia Forum*, 2011, 2: 5.

and cooperation and realizes common security through equal consultation and cooperation.

2.3.1.1 *The goal and principle of the security mechanism of Northeast Asia*

(1) Safeguarding peace and stability in Northeast Asia: Peace and development remain the themes of the present era, but the Cold War mentality still puzzles Northeast Asia. Various issues inherited from the past continue to ferment, hot-button issues explode from time to time, and territorial disputes are difficult to resolve. In particular, the Korean Peninsula has become a "powder keg." The DPRK, the ROK, Japan, Russia, China, and the United States are playing a special game, which is the remnant of the Cold War in the micro world and is still continuing.[30] The goals of the security mechanism in Northeast Asia are to build an effective platform for rational communication and cooperation among countries in this region, to provide a possible path to peacefully resolve conflicts among countries, to control international crises, and to prevent regional wars. If the security mechanism in Northeast Asia can operate smoothly, regional tensions can be effectively relieved, regional hotspot issues such as the DPRK nuclear issue can be peacefully resolved, possible regional military conflicts and nuclear arms races can be effectively eliminated, and thus the stable development of relations among countries can be promoted. The security mechanism in Northeast Asia provides a favorable conditions for the development and prosperity of all countries.

(2) Ensuring common security of all countries in Northeast Asia: The most basic purpose of the international security mechanism is to meet the security needs of member states.[31] The primary goal of the security mechanism in Northeast Asia is to ensure common security of all countries in the region. White paper on China's Peaceful Development says that "regarding common security, all countries share a common stake in the era of economic globalization. The international community

---

[30] Barry Buzan and Ole Waever, *Regions and Powers: The Structure of International Security*. Translated by Pan Zhongqi *et al*. Shanghai: Shanghai People's Publishing House, 2010, p. 144.

[31] Tang Yongsheng and Xu Qiyu, *To Obtain the Balance in the Complexity*, Beijing: World Affairs Press, 2004, p. 15.

should heighten awareness of common security. Countries should safeguard their own security while respecting others' security."[32] At present, with the development of regionalization, the security interest of a country is becoming more and more regional and Northeast Asia is no exception. Countries in Northeast Asia are facing the same regional security situation and common security threats, including military security threats caused by territorial disputes, economic threats caused by energy shortages and trade disputes, and environmental threats caused by ecological damage and climate change. In the field of traditional security, arms control has not been possible in Northeast Asia and there has also been a counter-disarmament trend, in particular in the field of nuclear arms. With regard to the DPRK nuclear issue, if the relevant parties fail to communicate effectively and handle the crisis, there will be a profound negative effect on the security of the Northeast Asian region. The present situation will even increase the possibility of a regional nuclear race and intensify the challenges to the security of the region. The security mechanism in Northeast Asia should alleviate and eliminate the security issues in the region and reduce the possibility of regional war.

(3) Regulating the diplomatic actions of Northeast Asian countries: The biggest function of the international mechanism is to "restrict and regulate the actions of the international communities."[33] In the absence of a security mechanism in Northeast Asia, the unpredictability of diplomatic actions of various countries is high, mutual trust among countries is lacking, and zero-sum games are prevalent. The establishment and effective operation of a security mechanism in Northeast Asia will promote the formation of a series of universally binding principles, rules, and norms, thus restricting the diplomatic actions of countries in the region. The benign operation of the security mechanism in Northeast Asia can enable countries to gradually internalize the code of conduct in the field of security into their own ideas, allow countries to carry out diplomatic actions under the effective

---

[32] White Paper on *China's Peaceful Development*, the State Council Information Office of the People's Republic of China, http://www.scio.gov.cn/zxbd/nd/2011/Document/1006416/1006416_3.htm.

[33] Stephen Krasner, ed., *International Regime*. Cornell University Press, 1983, p. 62, quoted from Ni Shixiong. *Contemporary Western Theory of International Relations*, Shanghai: Fudan University Press, 2004, p. 376.

regulation, and improve the predictability of the security behavior and security interaction of Northeast Asian countries.

2.3.1.2 *Principles of the security mechanism in Northeast Asia*

(1) The principles of inclusiveness and equality: The security mechanism in Northeast Asia should first uphold the basic principles of inclusiveness and equality. On the one hand, we should adhere to the principle of inclusiveness and build a security framework that can cover all countries in Northeast Asia, rather than an outward-oriented confrontational mechanism targeting specific countries in the region. The construction of the security mechanism in Northeast Asia cannot be at the expense of intensifying disputes. On the other hand, we should stick to the principle of equality and sincere mutual support and maintain that all countries, big or small, strong or weak, rich or poor, are equal members of the international community.[34] We should oppose the intention and behavior of seeking hegemony in Northeast Asia through regional security mechanisms. Through the construction of the security mechanism in Northeast Asia, countries should not impose their will on other countries but should realize equal consultation and cooperation.

(2) The principle of win-win cooperation: Hu Jintao says that "cooperation and win-win mean that we should develop the awareness of community with a shared future for mankind. A country should accommodate the legitimate concerns of others when pursuing its own interests; and it should promote common development of all countries when advancing its own development."[35] The security mechanism in Northeast Asia should ensure that all countries in the region can maximize their own security interests through international cooperation so that all parties can benefit together. The anarchy of the international community makes countries regard safeguarding national security interests as a zero-sum game, which is even more prominent in Northeast Asia where there is no security mechanism. The

---

[34] Hu Jintao, Firmly March on the Path of Socialism with Chinese Characteristics and Strive to Complete the Building of a Moderately Prosperous Society in All Respects-Report to the 18th National Congress of the Communist Party of China (November 8, 2012), *People's Daily*, November 18, 2012.

[35] *Ibid.*

Northeast Asian countries have maintained their national security interests through self-help, and the most important means is to enhance their own military strength, which traps them in a regional security dilemma. At present, there are a series of regional security problems in Northeast Asia. Countries in the region are facing many common threats. No country can cope by itself. So, security cooperation among countries is necessary. The security mechanism in Northeast Asia can ensure that countries in the region exchange information and coordinate their interests within the framework of the mechanism, avoid zero-sum games in the security field, promote security cooperation among countries, and realize mutual benefits.

(3) The principle of comprehensive management: The security mechanism in Northeast Asia should comprehensively deal with traditional security threats and non-traditional security challenges in the region and realize the comprehensive management of regional security. In the field of traditional security, the remnants of the Cold War in Northeast Asia are still obvious, the threat of regional conflicts has not disappeared, and the security dilemma is difficult to ease; in the field of non-traditional security, economic security, social security, environmental security, and other issues are complex and new security threats are constantly emerging. Non-traditional security in the region focuses on the financial crisis, energy shortage, deterioration of the ecological environment, terrorism and proliferation of weapons of mass destruction, illegal immigration, epidemic diseases, etc.[36] The transnational nature of non-traditional security threats and the difficulty of solving them have made it impossible for the countries in Northeast Asia to deal with them alone. As they face common non-traditional security threats, countries need to jointly manage various issues of regional security through extensive security cooperation based on comprehensive regional security within the framework of regional security mechanisms.

(4) The principle of consensus: The security mechanism in Northeast Asia should implement cooperation and solve problems under the principle of consensus among all countries in the region. Security in Northeast Asia has an important impact on all countries in the region. Only by taking into account the security interests of all countries in the region can the security mechanism in Northeast Asia operate

---

[36] Xiao Xi, Non-traditional security of Northeast Asia: Its problem domain and cooperation models, *Northeast Asia Forum*, 2010, 2: 5.

effectively. Under the framework of the security mechanism in Northeast Asia, all countries should fully communicate and negotiate, express their demands, and coordinate the security interests of all parties to reach a consensus and carry out multilateral security cooperation. The security mechanism in Northeast Asia should attach importance to contracts and consensus to solve specific security problems and protect the security interests of all countries adequately.

2.3.2 The structure and function of the security mechanism in Northeast Asia

The security mechanism in Northeast Asia is a cooperative system composed of principles, rules, norms, and decision-making systems, which can be divided into functional security mechanisms and institutional security mechanisms. Its function is to create a platform for dialogue and cooperation among members, establish a code of conduct, mediate differences and conflicts, and promote dialogue and collaboration. The security mechanism in Northeast Asia is a platform to provide equivalent information, carry out equal exchanges, enhance mutual trust, and encourage discussion and cooperation. It is an institutional arrangement to coordinate and resolve differences and disputes, and prevent and control crises.

2.3.2.1 *Structure of the security mechanism in Northeast Asia*

The security mechanism in Northeast Asia should have a complete structure to realize all-round, multi-level, and multi-channel regional security cooperation to comprehensively deal with and effectively solve various security problems in Northeast Asia. With new thinking on security featuring mutual trust, mutual benefit, equality, and coordination, we should no longer regard the regional security mechanism as a simple one-dimensional model but include diversified cooperation models. The cooperation model of the new security concept should be flexible and diverse, including multilateral security mechanisms with strong binding force, multilateral security dialogues, bilateral security consultations, and unofficial security dialogues of an academic nature.[37] The security mechanism

---

[37] China's Position Paper on the New Security Concept, Website of the Ministry of Foreign Affairs of the People's Republic of China, http://www.fmprc.gov.cn/mfa_chn/ziliao_611306/tytj_611312/t4549.shtml, July 15, 2015.

in Northeast Asia should be a composite structure covering diversified cooperation modes. Its specific structure can be discussed from two dimensions: horizontal governance fields and vertical subjective layers.

(1) The horizontal structure of the security mechanism in Northeast Asia: The security mechanism in Northeast Asia should include crisis management mechanisms, nuclear non-proliferation mechanisms, and arms control mechanisms. The first issue is the crisis management mechanism. In Northeast Asia, there is a general lack of strategic mutual trust in the bilateral relations between China and the United States, China and Japan, China and the ROK, the DPRK and the ROK, Japan and the ROK, Japan and Russia, and the United States and Russia. The opposition and competition in security interests have led to high uncertainty in regional security. For example, the situation on the Korean Peninsula has been tense for a long time, and the territorial sovereignty disputes among the Northeast Asian countries have been heating up. In this security situation, there is always the possibility of international crises and conflicts. In the framework of the security mechanism in Northeast Asia, complete bilateral and multilateral crisis management mechanisms should be established to form institutionalized consultation channels to deal with and avoid crisis escalation. The second issue is the nuclear non-proliferation mechanism. The existence of the DPRK's nuclear issue has had a serious negative impact on Northeast Asia and even made it difficult to rule out the dangers of nuclear proliferation and a nuclear arms race. The establishment of a nuclear non-proliferation mechanism in Northeast Asia with the participation of China, the United States, Russia, Japan, the ROK, the DPRK, and Mongolia is an important guarantee for the security of Northeast Asian countries.[38] An important point in the construction of the security mechanism in Northeast Asia is to strengthen the nuclear non-proliferation mechanism within the region based on the Treaty on the Non-Proliferation of Nuclear Weapons and the Comprehensive Nuclear Test Ban Treaty. The third issue is the arms control mechanism. Apart from nuclear arms control, arms control of conventional weapons is also very important to Northeast Asia. There are many powerful military forces and advanced

---

[38] Huang Fengzhi, Gao Ke, and Xiao Xi, *Study on Security Strategy in Northeast Asia*, Changchun: Jilin People's Press, 2006, p. 400.

military equipment in Northeast Asia. Arms control in Northeast Asia has shown a reverse disarmament trend, making it difficult to resolve the security dilemma. Especially in recent years, with China's growth and military modernization, the United States has accelerated the shift of military and strategic focus, implemented the strategy of "pivot to Asia-Pacific," and strengthened its forward military deployment in Northeast Asia, which have intensified the instability of the security situation in Northeast Asia and the risks of a regional arms race. An effective arms control mechanism has become a must for security in Northeast Asia.

(2) The vertical structure of the security mechanism in Northeast Asia: The security mechanism in Northeast Asia should include both intergovernmental and non-governmental "track-II" mechanisms. The first mechanism is the intergovernmental mechanism, which is the main component of the security mechanism in Northeast Asia. Although the security mechanism in Northeast Asia can include various international actors, sovereign states will be the major actors of security cooperation. There is no doubt that the security mechanism should be dominated by the intergovernmental security cooperation and dialogue. The Beijing Six-Party Talks on the DPRK nuclear issue was a core mechanism for security consultation and collaboration in Northeast Asia. The second mechanism is a non-governmental "track-II" mechanism. The "track-II" mechanism involves semi-official and non-governmental participants, including current or former government officials, researchers from government think tanks, scholars in related fields, and business elites. Because of their special background or public office status, the participants have personal or organizational relationships with the security policy decision-makers in their respective governments.[39] The "track-II" mechanism can influence the security policies of Northeast Asian governments. The inclusion of channels and platforms for "track-II" diplomacy in the Northeast Asian security mechanism can provide an auxiliary channel for dialogue and consultation on regional security issues and contribute to security coordination and cooperation among Northeast Asian countries.

---

[39] Yu Changshen, "Track-II" diplomacy and security cooperation in the Asia-Pacific region. *Southeast Asian Studies*, 2003, 5: 44.

2.3.2.2 Functions of the security mechanism in Northeast Asia

(1) The function of conflict management: There are a series of contradictions and problems in Northeast Asia that affect the stability of the security order and may lead to international conflicts, including structural contradiction between US hegemony and China's rise, the Korean Peninsula issue, the Taiwan issue, and complicated territorial disputes among Northeast Asian countries, such as the Diaoyu Dao issue, the territorial dispute over a set of islands (called Dokdo in Korean and Takeshima in Japanese), and the territorial dispute over four islands (called the Northern Territories in Japan and the Southern Kurils in Russia). Frequent conflicts and confrontations have become a prominent feature of the current security situation in Northeast Asia. Conflict management is an essential function of the security mechanism. The implication of conflict management covers conflict prevention, conflict avoidance, conflict containment, conflict transformation, conflict reconciliation, and conflict resolution.[40] Conflict management covers the entire cycle of international conflicts, including pre-conflict prevention, conflict management, and post-conflict peace-building. The Northeast Asian regional security mechanism is committed to preventing conflicts between countries that endanger the regional security order. The effective operation of the security mechanism in Northeast Asia will prevent and control conflicts within the region, avoid large-scale armed conflicts among countries in the region, and realize regional peace and stability to the greatest extent.

(2) The function of ensuring security: Safeguarding the security of Northeast Asia cannot depend on hegemonic stability or balance of power. The belief of hegemonic stability cannot be fully realized in Northeast Asia, and the security system in Northeast Asia cannot form a regional alliance that can balance the hegemonic power outside the region. The rapid rise of China, the United States' "pivot to Asia," and its implementation of the "Asia-Pacific rebalancing" strategy have deepened the structural contradictions within the Northeast Asian regional system. In the Northeast Asia region, it is difficult to obtain an effective security guarantee by relying solely on the function of the

---

[40] Niklas Swanström, *Regional Cooperation and Conflict Management: Lessons from the Pacific Rim*. Department of Peace and Conflict Research, Uppsala University, Report No. 64, 2002, p. 20.

system's structure. It is necessary to resort to the international system, that is, the security mechanism in the Northeast Asia region. The security mechanism in Northeast Asia provides security for all Northeast Asian countries. This security function should cover both traditional and non-traditional security issues. The traditional security function of the security mechanism in Northeast Asia is to prevent and eliminate the threats and hidden dangers in the political and military security fields in Northeast Asia through coordination and cooperation among the countries in Northeast Asia. The non-traditional security function is to deal with and solve the problems and challenges in the areas of economic security, social security, and ecological security in Northeast Asia.

(3) The function of trust-building: Countries in Northeast Asia have long been influenced by ideological opposition or historical feuds. They are suspicious and fearful of each other and generally regard each other as potential threats. There is a general lack of strategic mutual trust in the bilateral relations between China and the United States, China and Japan, China and the ROK, the DPRK and the ROK, Japan and the ROK, Japan and Russia, and the United States and Russia, which aggravates the security situation in the region.[41] Eliminating mutual suspicion and building strategic mutual trust are important functions of the security mechanism in Northeast Asia. Through systematic communication and exchange, the regional security mechanism should convey reliable information, increase the transparency of all parties, eliminate misjudgment of each other's strategic intentions, and avoid security dilemmas caused by asymmetric information. The effective operation of the security mechanism in Northeast Asia can gradually resolve unnecessary misunderstandings, suspicion, fear, and hostility among countries in the region, enhance mutual understanding and trust, and lay a foundation for further regional security cooperation. The operation of the security mechanism in Northeast Asia is conducive to the realization of the political goal of "Consultation and dialogue" "to enhance mutual trust, reduce differences and settle disputes. Use or threat of use of military force should be avoided."[42]

---

[41] Huang Fengzhi, Jin Xin, A Multidimensional Survey on China's Security Interests in Northeast Asia, *Northeast Asia Forum*, 2011, 2: 5.

[42] White Paper on *China's Peaceful Development*, the State Council Information Office of the People's Republic of China, http://www.scio.gov.cn/zxbd/nd/2011/Document/1006416/1006416.htm.

As the hot-button issues in Northeast Asia have erupted frequently in recent years, the importance and urgency of trust-building cannot be understated.

2.3.3 The selection of a model for the security mechanism in Northeast Asia

International security mechanisms have many specific models, including the collective security model, such as the United Nations; the military alliance model, such as the North Atlantic Treaty Organization; and the multilateral cooperation model, such as the Shanghai Cooperation Organization. The formation of a model of international security mechanism depends on the power structure, relationships, shared notions, institutional linkages, external environment, and domestic politics of member countries. The selection of a model for the security mechanism in Northeast Asia should be based on the history and reality of the region. We should neither blindly pursue the idealistic model nor rigidly stick to the realpolitik dogma of a zero-sum game.

2.3.3.1 *Comparison and selection of security mechanism models in Northeast Asia*

The collective security model, military alliance model, and multilateral cooperation model are alternative models of the security mechanism in Northeast Asia. In the following, we will examine these models from normative and practical aspects to show that multilateral cooperation is the most reasonable choice for the security mechanism in Northeast Asia.

(1) The collective security mechanism: Collective security is a kind of security system that protects the national security of each country using collective force to deter or stop possible invaders and acts of aggression.[43] The collective security mechanism in Northeast Asia is an idealized model remote from reality. From a normative point of view, it conforms to the principles of equality and inclusiveness, win-win cooperation, and so on. It can resolve the security dilemma in Northeast Asia and safeguard the security of the region. However,

---

[43] Ni Shixiong *et al.*, *Contemporary Western Theory of International Relations*, Shanghai: Fudan University Press, 2004, p. 376.

from a practical point of view, it is not a reasonable choice to construct a collective security mechanism in Northeast Asia. On the one hand, the collective security mechanism has its own inherent defects that cannot be avoided. As Kissinger revealed, the weakness of collective security lies in the fact that the interests of all countries are rarely consistent and security is not impeccable. Therefore, the members of a comprehensive collective security system are more likely to sit idly by than to take joint actions.[44] On the other hand, the complicated security environment in Northeast Asia determines that an effective collective security mechanism cannot be established in the foreseeable future. Conflicts of interest and disputes in Northeast Asia are deeply rooted, and strategic mutual trust and identity are seriously lacking. There are still many kinds of bilateral and trilateral relations in Northeast Asia. They are intertwined and mutually restricted, making it difficult to form consensus in terms of a regional security system. The construction of a collective security mechanism will this not be possible in the near future.

(2) The military alliance mechanism: A military alliance is a formal alliance formed between two or more sovereign countries by using force to deal with external threats.[45] In Northeast Asia, there are now two bilateral military alliances — one between the United States and Japan and the other between the United States and the ROK. The United States even regards these alliances as "the foundation of Asian security"[46] and continuously strengthens them. However, whether from the perspective of what it ought to be or what it is, the military alliance model is not a reasonable choice for the security mechanism in Northeast Asia. From the perspective of what it ought to be, the military alliance mechanism violates the basic principles of equality, tolerance, and win-win cooperation. A military alliance is closed and exclusive. Alliance countries will exclude other countries from participating in regional security affairs and will not accommodate all countries in Northeast Asia. Judging from its goal, what the military

---

[44] Henry Kissinger, *Diplomacy*. Translated by Gu Shuxin, Lin Tiangui. Haikou: Hainan Publishing House, 1998, p. 81.
[45] Glenn H. Snyder, *Alliance Politics*. Ithaca: Cornell University Press, 1987, p. 4.
[46] The White House, *National Security Strategy*, http://www.whitehouse.gov/siles/default/files/rss_viewer/national_security_strategy.pdf, May 2010.

alliance wants to achieve is not common security equally shared by all countries, but absolute security enjoyed unilaterally. In terms of its methods, the military alliance takes the third party as the target country and seek the military advantage over the target country, which destroys the principle of win-win cooperation. From the perspective of what it is, there are four strategic competitive relationships in Northeast Asia between the United States, China, Japan, and Russia. The structural conflicts of strategic interests among the major powers cause the conflict of their security strategies. The military alliance mechanism bases its security interests on exerting negative influence on the third party countries. It seeks the security of alliance countries unilaterally without taking into account the interests of all the Northeast Asian countries. Therefore, it will be difficult to obtain the support of all countries in the region, which will further worsen the regional security situation.

(3) The multilateral cooperation mechanism: The multilateral cooperation mode of the international security mechanism combines multilateralism with the concept of cooperative security, providing a feasible scheme for the construction of a security mechanism in Northeast Asia. A multilateral cooperation mode is the most reasonable choice for Northeast Asia, with both normative advisability and practical feasibility. As far as the normative dimension is concerned, the multilateral security cooperation mechanism is an inclusive rather than an exclusive mechanism. Within its institutional framework, it can effectively coordinate the interests of Northeast Asian countries based on equality. It can also solve regional security problems through dialogue and cooperation, enhance mutual trust, and realize common security based on the basic code of conduct for consultation and cooperation. In terms of the practical dimension, Northeast Asia is a place where the strategic interests of major powers converge. There are complicated and interrelated interest relations among countries. The relations need to be effectively coordinated within the institutional framework of multilateralism. This plan is also most likely to win the support of all parties under the current conditions. As both the collective security mechanism and the military alliance mechanism are infeasible in practice, the multilateral security cooperation mechanism is the only mode of security mechanism that can adapt to the existing security structure in Northeast Asia.

2.3.3.2 *Assumption and practice of a multilateral security cooperation mechanism in Northeast Asia*

As John Ruggie pointed out, due to the absence of institutional arrangements for multilateralism in security relations, the Asia-Pacific region has been unable to adapt to the fundamental changes that have taken place in global politics.[47] This defect is particularly prominent in Northeast Asia. A multilateral security cooperation mechanism is thus a necessary security mechanism in Northeast Asia. Northeast Asian countries have also put forward many ideas of regional security mechanisms based on the multilateral cooperation mode. The United States put forward a variety of security forms such as the "New Pacific Community," "Regional Security Organization," and "Northeast Asia Security Forum." Japan advocated the example of the "ASEAN Forum" in the form of a "Northeast Asia Forum." The ROK proposed the establishment of a "Northeast Asia Regional Forum" with the participation of six countries in Northeast Asia and advocated that at the initial stages, a triangular cooperation system should first be established with China, the United States, and the ROK as "minilateralism" model.[48] Russia also proposed the establishment of a conflict mediation center in Northeast Asia, a multilateral consultation mechanism, and a collective security system of six countries.

The exploration of constructing a multilateral security cooperation mechanism in Northeast Asian countries has begun. There are now quite a few multilateral cooperation or dialogue mechanisms available for Northeast Asian security. The official mechanisms at the government level include the Six-Party Talks on the DPRK nuclear issue and the cooperation mechanism with China, Japan, and the ROK within the framework of ASEAN Plus Three, namely, "10 + 3." Besides, the ASEAN Regional Forum (ARF), the East Asia Summit (EAS), and the Asian Cooperation Dialogue (ACD), which cover many countries in Northeast Asia, also provide institutional channels for dialogue and consultation. In addition, there are some non-governmental track II mechanisms playing an auxiliary role in the multilateral security consultation mechanism in Northeast

---

[47] John Ruggie, *Multilateralism Matters*, Translated by Su Changhe, *et al.* Hangzhou: Zhejiang People's Publishing House, 2003, p. 4.

[48] Sun Chunri, The ROK's expectation for the security mechanism in Northeast Asia in the next 15 Years from *"The ROK's National Strategy 2020." Journal of Contemporary Asia-Pacific Studies*, 2006, 11: 56.

Asia, such as the Council for Security Cooperation in the Asia Pacific (CSCAP), the Northeast Asia Cooperation Dialogue (NEACD), the Trilateral Forum on North Pacific Security, the China–US–Japan Trilateral Academic Seminar, the US–Japan–Russia Security Dialogue.

Among these multilateral cooperation or dialogue mechanisms, the Six-Party Talks on the DPRK nuclear issue is undoubtedly a core mechanism to promote multilateral security cooperation in Northeast Asia. If the Six-Party Talks mechanism in Beijing can operate smoothly in the long term, it will undoubtedly have a positive influence on the construction of the security mechanism in Northeast Asia. The lack of an institutionalized security structure in Northeast Asia requires a permanent security mechanism rather than a temporary one.[49] It can be said that the framework of the Six-Party Talks is not only the core mechanism to solve the DPRK nuclear issue but also the embryonic form of a multilateral security mechanism in Northeast Asia. If the DPRK nuclear issue can finally be properly resolved within the framework of the Six-Party Talks, this mechanism may spill over to other security issues in Northeast Asia, such as the establishment of a permanent peace mechanism for the Korean Peninsula and the promotion of security cooperation in the region. It can lay the foundation for a future institutionalized multilateral security mechanism in Northeast Asia.

2.3.4 The construction of a security mechanism in Northeast Asia

In Northeast Asia, a region with unresolved security dilemmas and complicated relations, building an effective regional security mechanism involves facing a series of problems in a long process. The construction of a regional security mechanism is both an objective process of historical evolution and an active process of rational design. The construction of the security mechanism in Northeast Asia cannot be separated from the conscious behavior of Northeast Asian countries as rational actors. Therefore, it is necessary to design a specific and feasible path to implement the concept of the security mechanism in Northeast Asia.

---

[49] Danish Institute for International Studies. *North Korea's Security Policy: Implications for Regional Security and International Export Control Regimes,* DIIS Report 2008: July 10, 2008, p. 31.

2.3.4.1 *Promoting governance through economy step by step*

David Mitrany once pointed out that "cooperation in a certain functional area would promote the change of cooperation attitude or expand the intention of cooperation from one area to other areas to carry out deeper cooperation in a larger scope."[50] The countries in the region are severely restricted by the regional security problems. Therefore, strengthening multilateral cooperation in the economic field and promoting regional political and security cooperation will become a rational choice in the process of constructing a security mechanism in Northeast Asia. Northeast Asian countries have complex and interlaced interdependence and are highly complementary in terms of capital, resources, technology, labor force, market, and other factors of production and economic structure. This has enlarged the space for regional economic cooperation and reduced any resistance. Subregional economic cooperation is also underway in the Yellow Sea–Bohai Sea Rim, the Sea of Japan Rim, and the Tumen River Basin. Especially after the global financial crisis in 2008, cooperation in maintaining financial security has become an important goal for Northeast Asian countries. This proves that there are far fewer obstacles to regional economic cooperation than regional security cooperation.

The current international relationships are no longer purely political and military relations but a complex system formed by intersecting politics, economy, military, society, and culture in a multi-dimensional way. Multilateral cooperation among Northeast Asian countries in the economic field can be gradually extended to non-traditional security fields such as energy security, ecological environment protection, and combating transnational crimes. Through exchanges and cooperation in these fields, trust will be established and a regional governance mechanism for non-traditional security governance will be built. Furthermore, cooperation in these areas will spill over to traditional security areas to enhance common interests and establish trust through dialogue, consultation, and cooperation. Through an all-round, multi-level, and cross-field cooperation network, we will expand consensus and promote the construction of security mechanisms in Northeast Asia.

---

[50] James Doherty, Robert Pfaltzgraff Jr., *Contending Theories of International Relations: A Comprehensive Survey.* Translated by Yan Xuetong, Chen Hanxi. World Affairs Press, 2003, p. 551.

The construction of the security mechanism in Northeast Asia should adhere to the principle of gradual and orderly progress. First of all, we should stagger the dialogue topics and areas of cooperation from easy to difficult. We should first start from those areas where the Northeast Asian countries have larger common interests, where it would be easy for them to reach consensus. Then, we should cultivate the habit of cooperation among countries and promote the development of security mechanisms. Secondly, the degree of institutionalization should be gradually promoted from low to high. There are differences between functional and institutional mechanisms in international systems. The security mechanism in Northeast Asia can start with a functional cooperation mechanism, continuously improve the level of institutionalization with the deepening of cooperation, and establish an institutional multilateral security cooperation mechanism with permanent systems. Finally, we should pay attention to the "progressive nature of time" and "hierarchy of space" in the process of constructing the security mechanism. For example, China and Russia jointly advocated the establishment of the Shanghai Cooperation Organization to strengthen the security cooperation against the three forces of terrorism, separatism, and extremism. China, Japan, and the ROK can first carry out economic and trade cooperation and promote the establishment of a free trade area. The Six-Party Talks on the DPRK nuclear issue can first develop into a functional security cooperation mechanism, and then gradually turn into an institutional security cooperation mechanism.

2.3.4.2 *Enhancing institutionalization by means of the framework of the Six-Party Talks*

The security mechanism is not like water without source. To build a security mechanism in Northeast Asia, we should not neglect the existing cooperative foundation and institutional arrangements. Instead, we should selectively rely on and utilize the existing foundation. The mechanism of the Six-Party Talks is currently the most feasible framework for multilateral security cooperation in Northeast Asia, within which China, the United States, Japan, Russia, the DPRK, and the ROK can collectively express and coordinate their security interests. Based on the existing mechanism of the Six-Party Talks, it is a viable way to construct a security mechanism in Northeast Asia by promoting development toward a universal multilateral security cooperation mechanism and improving institutionalization. At present, the Six-Party Talks in Beijing face many practical problems and dilemmas, and even the sustainability of the talks is being questioned. However, dialogue and consultation are the only effective ways of solving the peninsula issue.[51] The Six-Party Talks mechanism will play an irreplaceable role in solving the DPRK nuclear issue and maintaining peace and stability in Northeast Asia.

The Six-Party Talks mechanism is currently stagnant, yet the stagnation is not in line with the fundamental interests of all the countries concerned. To restart the talks, all parties concerned have already started active contact. China made it clear that the Six-Party Talks will balance the concerns of all parties and realize the denuclearization of the peninsula. It is hoped that all parties concerned will maintain contact and dialogue, continue to work to resolve their differences through negotiations, and strive for an early resumption of the Six-Party Talks.[52] From July 28 to 29, 2011, representatives of the DPRK and the United States held a bilateral meeting in New York to discuss the resumption of the long-stalled Six-Party Talks. From October 24 to 25, the two delegations held a second round of meetings in Geneva to discuss issues related to the resumption of the Six-Party Talks. Although the DPRK's two satellite rocket tests in 2012 and its third nuclear test in February 2013 further strained the security situation in Northeast Asia, the hope of a resumption of the Six-Party Talks is far from over. On June 19, 2013, the DPRK once again stated in the first strategic dialogue between China and the DPRK that it was willing to hold dialogue with relevant parties and participate in any form of talks, including the Six-Party Talks, hoping to resolve the nuclear issue peacefully through negotiations.[53] The DPRK–US game is still a real problem. It is quite possible to resume and restart the Six-Party Talks in Beijing with China's "shuttle diplomacy" and the progress of negotiations in the DPRK–US bilateral dialogue.

The current Six-Party Talks mechanism is still a functional regional security mechanism. It is only a temporary and informal negotiation mechanism set up by all parties concerned to solve the DPRK nuclear

---

[51] China's Position Paper for the 67th UN General Assembly, website of the Ministry of Foreign Affairs of the People's Republic of China, http://www.fmprc.gov.cn/chn/pds/wjb/zzjg/t970916.htm, July 8, 2015.
[52] The DPRK Willing to Restart Six-Party Talks, Hoping for Peaceful Resolution of Nuclear Issue, *People's Daily Online*, http://yn.people.com.cn/GB/news/world/n/2013/0620/c228495-18900563.html, June 20, 2013.
[53] *Ibid.*

issue, with a low degree of institutionalization. It is not a permanent body with a "legally binding relationship of rights and obligations" among member states.[54] The first step to building a security mechanism in Northeast Asia is to restart the stalled Six-Party Talks and make it a fixed mechanism. Based on properly resolving the DPRK nuclear issue, China will promote the institutionalization of the Six-Party Talks mechanism. Under this institutional framework, countries can hold regular consultations on regional security issues. They can gradually expand the scope of topics and initiate dialogue and cooperation on a wider range of regional security issues so that a true multilateral security cooperation mechanism will gradually be developed in Northeast Asia.

2.3.4.3 Giving full play to China and actively participating in the construction of a mechanism

China should become an active advocate, participant, and leader in the construction of the security mechanism in Northeast Asia, which is in line with its interests and current policies. Peace and security in Northeast Asia can provide a stable surrounding environment for China's own development. At the same time, a security mechanism in Northeast Asia based on win-win cooperation is in line with China's consistent foreign policy. China has always advocated that "countries in the region respect each other, increase mutual trust, seek common ground while putting aside differences, safeguard regional peace and stability, and settle disputes including those over territorial claims and maritime rights and interests through dialogue and friendly negotiation."[55] China's active participation in the construction of the security mechanism in Northeast Asia is conducive to the realization of its national security interests. In return, China will also play an essential and positive role in the construction of the security mechanism in Northeast Asia.

Strategic mutual trust among Northeast Asian countries is the basis for regional security cooperation. If China is to play its dual role in the construction of a regional security mechanism, the first step is to build

---

[54] Huang Fengzhi, Jin Xin, Review of the Six-Party Talks on the DPRK's Nuclear Issue, *Contemporary International Relations*, 2012, 12: 13.

[55] White Paper on *China's Peaceful Development*, the State Council Information Office of the People's Republic of China, http://www.scio.gov.cn/zxbd/nd/2011/Document/1006416/1006416.htm.

trust among countries and eliminate any worries about China's rise. As a regional power and advocate of regional security mechanisms, China will find it difficult to promote the construction of a multilateral security cooperation mechanism in Northeast Asia unless it can resolve the doubts of the countries in the region about itself. China should establish an image of a responsible big country. It should participate in international affairs with a more positive attitude and give full play to its role in providing regional public goods and dealing with regional security issues. It should take practical actions to dispel the doubts of the neighboring countries in Northeast Asia about itself. On regional non-traditional security issues, China should actively assume the responsibility of a big country to eliminate misunderstanding and enhance mutual trust. China should "continue to promote friendship and partnership with our neighbors, consolidate friendly relations and deepen mutually beneficial cooperation with them, and ensure that China's development will bring more benefits to our neighbors."[56] Only in this way can the influence of the "China threat" theory be dispelled and favorable conditions be created for the realization of national interests and the maintenance of regional security.

On the basis of building political mutual trust, China can join hands with other countries in the region to promote the construction of a multilateral security cooperation mechanism in Northeast Asia. At the present stage, China should make efforts in two aspects. The first is to strengthen economic cooperation with other countries in Northeast Asia to promote the construction of free trade areas and the process of regional integration. It should promote political development by way of economic development so as to promote the functional spillover of regional cooperation mechanisms. The second is to actively carry out diplomatic mediation, persuading relevant countries to return to the Six-Party Talks as soon as possible to promote the resumption and sound operation of the mechanism. Under the principles of dialogue, consultation, and seeking common ground while reserving differences, all parties are urged to reach a consensus on cooperation. With efforts of China and other countries, the security mechanism in Northeast Asia will be continuously improved, thus providing an institutional guarantee for promoting security cooperation in the region and safeguarding the security interests of all countries.

---

[56] Hu Jintao, Firmly March on the Path of Socialism with Chinese Characteristics and Strive to Complete the Building of a Moderately Prosperous Society in All Respects-Report to the Eighteenth National Congress of the Communist Party of China, *People's Daily*, November 18, 2012.

Chapter 3

Disputes Over Territorial Sovereignty and Maritime Rights and Interests in Northeast Asia and China's Strategy and Countermeasures

Countries in Northeast Asia are adjacent to each other on land and share seas. They have formed close contact and interdependent relations, but there are also disputes over the sovereignty of islands and maritime delimitation. Due to historical, legal, political, and economic reasons, disputes over the ownership of islands and maritime delimitation among countries in Northeast Asia have become very complicated, thereby affecting the development of relations among those countries. There are disputes over territorial sovereignty and maritime rights and interests between Russia and Japan, China and Japan, the ROK and Japan, and the DPRK and the ROK. This territorial sovereignty and the maritime delimitation disputes involve the political, economic, and security interests of all countries. In recent years, such disputes have become increasingly fierce, seriously affecting trust and cooperation among the countries and leading to instability and thereby regional conflicts. This has led to issues in observing international laws and norms, fully respecting history and reality, and fairly and reasonably settling disputes over territorial sovereignty and maritime rights and interests through diplomatic negotiations. China should design its diplomatic strategy from the point of view of a major country engaging with neighboring countries, make a long-term plan, actively deal with the situation in Northeast Asia, and properly solve the problems in this region. China should effectively safeguard its territorial sovereignty and maritime rights and interests in Northeast Asia, and at the same time try not to hinder regional cooperation. China should safeguard peace and stability in Northeast Asia and create a good regional and international environment to ensure its own peaceful development.

3.1 Disputes Over Territorial Sovereignty and Maritime Rights and Interests in Northeast Asia and Their Impact

Disputes over territorial sovereignty and maritime rights and interests in Northeast Asia are an important factor affecting the relations between the countries in that region and are a source of potential threat to regional peace and stability. Disputes over territorial sovereignty and maritime rights and interests in Northeast Asia mainly involve the following: the territorial dispute over four islands (called the Northern Territories in Japanese and the Southern Kurils in Russian) between Russia and Japan, disputes over Diaoyu Dao and the delimitation of the East China Sea between China and Japan, the territorial dispute over a set of islands (called Dokdo in Korean and Takeshima in Japanese) between the ROK and Japan, the dispute over the boundary between the ROK and the DPRK, and the disputes over the delimitation of the Yellow Sea and Suyan Rock between China and the ROK. These disputes are remnants of historical issues and involve the application of international law and international maritime law. These disputes have become regional hot-button issues affecting the relations between the respective countries.

3.1.1 Basic characteristics of disputes over territorial sovereignty and maritime rights and interests in Northeast Asia

The disputes over territorial sovereignty and maritime rights and interests in Northeast Asia cover almost every country in this region and are of a very sensitive nature. They involve the foreign policy, national security, domestic political situations, and media opinions of the relevant countries. At the same time, these disputes are also affected by interventions from outside Northeast Asia. The frequent occurrence of such interventions has exacerbated the complexity of the disputes.

In terms of the current situation, the disputes over territorial sovereignty and maritime rights and interests in Northeast Asia are quite difficult to resolve in a short period of time, except for the border dispute between China and Russia, which has been properly tackled. Therefore, it can be said that the current disputes have fallen into the dilemma of a zero-sum game. Judging from the development trend of the region, these disputes may affect or even dominate the security situation for a long period of time.

Based on the overall situation, the disputes over territorial sovereignty and maritime rights and interests in Northeast Asia are mainly characterized by the following features:

First of all, overt and covert disputes coexist. At present, most disputes over territorial sovereignty and maritime rights and interests in Northeast Asia have evolved into international disputes. Most of these disputes have become the overt hot-button topics, while the Yellow Sea delimitation dispute and the Suyan Rock dispute between China and the ROK are covert hot-button topics, which may turn into overt disputes at any time due to the intensification of various factors.

Secondly, cooperation and confrontation are intertwined. Disputes over territorial sovereignty and maritime rights and interests in Northeast Asia involve both factors of confrontation between the concerned countries in the disputed area and factors of dialogue and necessary cooperation between the countries. Take the dispute over Diaoyu Dao between China and Japan as an example. Since the collision of vessels between China and Japan in 2010, there have been frequent confrontations between Chinese and Japanese government vessels in the area. In 2012, China and Japan held the first maritime consultation, during which Diaoyu Dao was one of the core issues.[1] Based on an analysis of the Diaoyu Dao issue, both cooperation and confrontation are intertwined in the dispute, and there is a possibility of transformation from confrontation to cooperation and vice versa. The key facilitation factor is how China and Japan deal with this dispute.

Finally, intervention and counteraction can complicate a situation. A dispute comprises the relationship between the parties involved and the extraterritorial factors. At present, disputes have become more

---

[1] China and Japan Hold First Round of High-Level Consultations on Ocean Affairs, *Xinhua* Website, http://news,Xinhuanet.com/world/20L2-05/16/c_111968122.htm (received online on May 16, 2012).

complicated due to the involvement of external factors, especially the United States. It should be emphasized that many disputes in Northeast Asia originate from changes in international relations led by the United States after the World War II. It can be said that it is the United States' intervention to some extent that has caused disputes over territorial sovereignty and maritime rights and interests in Northeast Asia. In fact, the United States is one of the historical sources of disputes in Northeast Asia. The United States has been taking advantage of disputes by instigating continuous escalation and intensification of disputes to realize some control over these areas, thus gaining considerable strategic benefits. As long as the disputes continue, the US retains its military presence in Northeast Asia, and the intensification of the disputes only strengthens the regional hegemony of the US. As for the parties involved in the disputes, such as China and Russia, they are wary of US participation. US participation has not only caused more trouble for China, Russia, and other countries but has also turned the disputes into an important bargaining chip to contain China and Russia. Therefore, it will be more advantageous to effectively counter US intervention and participation in order to fairly and reasonably settle these disputes.

3.1.2 Political dilemma caused by disputes over territorial sovereignty and maritime rights and interests in Northeast Asia

The complexity and uncertainty of the *status quo* and causes of disputes over territorial sovereignty and maritime rights and interests in Northeast Asia have gradually evolved into political dilemmas, leading to the involvement of major power relations.

3.1.2.1 *Factors making disputes over territorial sovereignty and maritime rights and interests in Northeast Asia a political dilemma*

The inevitability of the political aspect in the disputes over territorial sovereignty and maritime rights and interests in Northeast Asia comes from the basic concepts of international relations as formed by western countries. For more than one hundred years, western countries controlled parts of Northeast Asian, due to which their concepts of nation-states, territory, and sovereignty have also taken root in Northeast Asian countries. Today, it is a fact that certain concepts of the Westphalian system have taken root in Asia, especially Northeast Asia.

The political issues caused by or leading to the disputes over territorial sovereignty and maritime rights and interests in Northeast Asia have gradually been uncovered due to internal pressure from the public, the media, some political organizations, and interest groups. The territorial disputes are zero-sum games, and the involved governments are unwilling to give in. At the same time, strong pressure from some domestic political interest groups, local governments, and media has forced governments to stick to relatively tough stances in these disputes.

Upon analyzing the external constraints, we can see that the participation of the United States in the disputes has, in fact, reduced the strategic space for other countries to deal with the disputes. With regard to the boat collision accident in Diaoyu Dao, when Chinese non-governmental activists and Japanese right-wing activists and politicians arrived in Diaoyu Dao in 2012, the US government made a statement that Article 5 of the Mutual Defense Treaty between the United States and Japan is applicable to the Diaoyu Dao issue. This shows that the United States will support Japan in case of any confrontation relating to this issue. In this sense, the United States fulfilled its obligations as an ally to Japan by providing a strong diplomatic and military response to China. At the same time, the US stance also stimulated Japanese right-wing forces to continue their political tirade on the Diaoyu Dao issue under the guise of US "protection" and put more pressure on the Japanese government. The Japanese government, under domestic pressure and due to the US statement offering diplomatic and military support, restricted its diplomatic activities in China, especially taking relatively moderate measures that can win the trust of China.

The emergence of the political angles in the disputes over territorial sovereignty and maritime jurisdiction in Northeast Asia has objectively intensified the regional arms race and caused tension in the regional security situation. The trend of the disputes becoming normalized will also affect the relations among countries, resulting in a serious lack of mutual trust and reducing the possibility of peaceful resolution. Such political dilemma has also led to further instability in the security situation in Northeast Asia, which is not conducive to necessary exchanges and cooperation, and has resulted in the gradual weakening of the efforts made by various countries to establish a regional security mechanism.

3.1.2.2 *Political dilemma caused by disputes over territorial sovereignty and maritime rights and interests in Northeast Asia*

After a concrete analysis, the political dilemma brought about by the disputes over territorial sovereignty and maritime rights and interests in Northeast Asia is explained in the following four situations.

Firstly, the disputes cannot be fundamentally resolved in a short period of time. Without using military means, it is difficult to use diplomatic negotiation to effectively allocate disputed islands and sea areas to one of the disputing countries. Even if the disputed islands are divided into two parts for each of the two sides in the disputes, the division of the exclusive economic zone around the islands is difficult to perform. At the same time, it is doubtful whether the governments and people of the concerned countries will agree with the modes for settling the disputes.

Even as the disputes are difficult to resolve in a short period of time, there are possibilities that they may turn into large-scale armed conflicts. Apart from the boundary dispute between the DPRK and the ROK, which has already caused armed clashes, the other disputes are very likely to become armed conflicts. Based on an analysis of the security situation in Northeast Asia after the Cold War, if these disputes turn into large-scale armed conflicts or even local wars, they will definitely damage the peace and stability of the entire Northeast Asian region and further affect cooperation of the concerned countries in many fields such as regional politics and trade.

Secondly, the disputes over territorial sovereignty and maritime rights and interests in Northeast Asia show obvious spillover effects. The disputes can spread to other regions and even the whole world. The political problems brought about by the disputes have resulted in mutual distrust among countries, which has further led to the lack of practical cooperation on both the regional and global levels, thus affecting regional integration and cooperation. As domestic public opinions may have vastly different expectations of the responses of various countries, the disputes may expand to the domestic level, which may affect the ruling party's position in the country and may also become a factor leading to social instability. If political issues are not effectively attended to and managed in a timely manner, they may continue to spread among the people of the concerned countries, aggravating the deterioration of the relations among the various countries.

Thirdly, disputes are greatly affected by external interference. As mentioned earlier, the role of the United States in the disputes is manifold. The United States is one of the causes for the emergence and worsening of most disputes in the region. During the Cold War period, the United States was responsible for the disputes over territorial sovereignty and maritime rights and interests between China and Japan, the DPRK and the ROK, and the ROK and Japan. In the post-Cold War era, US participation in the disputes has objectively intensified the disputes and caused tension in the security situation in the entire region.

Fourthly, disputes over territorial sovereignty and maritime rights and interests in Northeast Asia have new uncertainties. Because of the long-standing nature of the disputes, it is difficult to eliminate the political aspects in a short period of time. Although all countries actively advocate settling disputes through diplomatic means, they have not given up non-diplomatic means. For example, Japan has continuously strengthened its military deployment in the Southwest Islands, and one of its main purposes is to strengthen its actual control over Diaoyu Dao.

3.1.2.3 *The overall effects and prospects of the political dilemma caused by disputes over territorial sovereignty and maritime rights and interests in Northeast Asia*

Disputes over territorial sovereignty and maritime rights and interests have gradually evolved into one of the core political issues in Northeast Asia. The intensification of these disputes has seriously affected the political mutual trust and mutual relations among countries in Northeast Asia.

Since September 2012, Japan's so-called "nationalization" of Diaoyu Dao has sped up its dispute with China, bringing China–Japan relations to a new low. Apart from a handful of ministerial-level contacts on the Diaoyu Dao issue, diplomacy between the two countries was completely suspended. The then Vice Foreign Minister Zhang Zhijun pointed out that at all levels of contacts and consultations with the Japanese side, the Chinese side pointed out China's solemn position on the Diaoyu Dao issue and the steely resolve of the Chinese government to uphold China's territorial sovereignty. The Chinese government has urged the Japanese government to admit its mistake, mend its ways, and take concrete actions to properly handle the issue.[2] According to analysis of the Chinese government's stance, the resumption of China–Japan relations depends to a large extent on the Japanese government's attitude toward the Diaoyu Dao issue.

The disputes over territorial sovereignty and maritime rights and interests in Northeast Asia have gradually affected the security of Northeast Asia. The continuous intensification of the disputes has resulted in confrontations between the navies and maritime law enforcement forces of the concerned countries in the disputed sea areas. This has intensified the continuous tense security situation in the region. In the future evolution of disputes, effectively managing and controlling regional security will be a rational choice for easing regional security tensions and seeking political solutions to the disputes.

Training exercises of the Chinese navy in the Pacific region are a normal part of China's national defense construction. However, due to the low level of mutual trust between China and Japan, the normal training of the Chinese navy in the Pacific region has become one of the topics of contention between the two countries. When we analyze the intensifying dispute between China and Japan over Diaoyu Dao and the delimitation of the East China Sea, we can see that the Chinese navy's offshore training has become a reflection of the reality of regional security after "excessive" attention by the Japanese government and inappropriate media hype.

3.1.3 The impact of disputes over territorial sovereignty and maritime rights and interests in Northeast Asia on state-to-state relations

The disputes over territorial sovereignty and maritime rights and interests are important factors affecting the development of state-to-state relations. Improper tackling of the disputes may lead to conflicts and wars among the concerned countries as well as long-term tension and confrontations. However, due to historical and political reasons, disputes between neighboring countries are inevitable. The problem lies in how to rationally and

---

[2] A Record of Answers and Questions of Vice Foreign Minister Zhang Zhijun on the Diaoyu Islands Issue, website of the Ministry of Foreign Affairs of the People's Republic of China, http://www.fmprc.gov.cn/chn/gxh/tyb/zyxw/t982918.htm (received online on May 20, 2015).

calmly deal with the disputes so as to reduce their negative impact on state-to-state relations and avoid seriously affecting the development of state-to-state relations.

3.1.3.1 *Disputes over territorial sovereignty and maritime rights and interests in Northeast Asia as an important factor affecting the development of the state-to-state relations*

Disputes over territorial sovereignty and maritime rights and interests in Northeast Asia have an important impact on state-to-state relations, which manifests not only in the bilateral relations but also in multilateral relations. The most prominent impact in this regard have been on Russia–Japan relations, China–Japan relations, China–US relations, ROK–Japan relations, China–Japan–ROK trilateral relations, and China–Japan–US trilateral relations.

The territorial dispute over the four islands (called the Northern Territories in Japanese and the Southern Kurils in Russian) between Russia and Japan is a residual problem from the Soviet era. Due to the differences between Russia and Japan on the territory issue, the development of Russia–Japan relations has been seriously affected. Seventy years after the end of World War II, Russia and Japan have still not signed the post-war peace treaty due to this territorial dispute, which has put Russia–Japan relations in an abnormal state. This will greatly affect the trust and cooperation between Russia and Japan. In the early days of Russia's emergence after the fall of the Soviet Union, Japan, in order to exert pressure on Russia, applied the principle of "inseparable relation between politics and economy," stating that if Russia did not return the four northern islands, Japan would not provide economic aid and large-scale investment to Russia. Resolving the territorial issue has often become an important topic for the leaders of Russia and Japan to talk about in their meetings. However, due to differences in their positions, the territorial dispute has become an insurmountable obstacle in the development of the relations between the two countries.

The dispute between China and Japan over Diaoyu Dao and the delimitation of the East China Sea has seriously affected the development process of bilateral relations. At the same time, conflicts between the general public of the two countries over the disputes have gradually emerged.

Japan's right-wing forces have used the disputes to gain political capital, further intensifying the dispute. Therefore, one issue is finding effective measures at the levels of both government and the public to ease the disputes while maintaining bilateral relations between the two sides.

The frequent intervention of the US has in fact affected the development of China–US relations. China and the United States have a wide range of common interests in many areas in Northeast Asia and the world. However, the United States has deployed a large number of military forces in the areas neighboring China through its intervention in various disputes over territorial sovereignty and maritime rights and interests in Northeast Asia. For example, the United States deployed an anti-missile system in the western Pacific during the Diaoyu Dao issue between China and Japan in 2012,[3] which posed a substantial threat to China's national security. This makes it difficult for the United States to gain China's trust in regional security affairs and for the two countries to achieve strategic mutual trust and active cooperation in security affairs.

Whether China and the ROK can properly handle the Yellow Sea delimitation and the dispute over the Suyan Rock is an important issue facing the relations between the two countries and requires the joint efforts of the two countries. Over the past 20-odd years since the normalization of China–ROK relations, remarkable achievements have been made in the development of bilateral relations. However, there are also many problems in China–ROK relations. When China and the ROK are dealing with the disputes over the delimitation of the Yellow Sea and the Suyan Rock, they need to also tackle other problems cautiously and try not to be affected by outside factors.

The dispute between the ROK and Japan over a set of islands (called Dokdo in Korean and Takeshima in Japanese) has seriously affected the development of bilateral relations. In 2012, due to the intensification of conflict, the signing of the General Security of Military Information Agreement (GSOMIA) between the ROK and Japan was postponed, and Japan immediately announced the suspension of monetary cooperation between the two countries. To tackle the dispute over Dokdo, the ROK decided to set up a sovereignty monument on the islands. Obviously, the appearance of the present situation and even the repeated occurrences have brought no benefit to the normal development of ROK-Japan

---

[3] Daily Press Briefing. *Victoria Nuland*, August 23, 2012. http://www.state.gov/r/pa/prs/dpb/2012/08/196881.htm.

relations. Although the United States is actively coordinating between the two countries, the pressure due to historical issues and the territorial dispute still pose an insurmountable obstacle for future relations between the two countries.

The extent and evolution of the disputes over territorial sovereignty and maritime rights and interests in Northeast Asia have impacted US–Japan relations. The disputes have further promoted and strengthened US–Japan defense cooperation, leading to joint military exercises on a larger scale and a longer duration. However, the deeper issue is the fact that through the in-depth development of US–Japan defense cooperation, Japan needs to actively support US actions in Northeast Asia, the Asia-Pacific region, and even global affairs. In this way, Japan can become an important ally of the US in exercising the latter's regional and global hegemony. At the same time, when Japan has a diplomatic crisis or even military conflict with its neighbors, the space available for the US to make strategic choices is also narrowed.

As far as US–ROK relations are concerned, the US has deployed troops to the Korean Peninsula for a long time to strengthen the US–ROK military alliance. The US has also used many issues on the Korean Peninsula to its advantage, including the border dispute between the DPRK and the ROK and DPRK's nuclear issue. The United States also strengthened its control over the US–ROK military alliance, making the ROK more likely to take commands from the United States in security affairs in Northeast Asia. It is worth paying attention to the fact that although there have been many maritime military conflicts between the ROK and the DPRK, the US troops stationed in the ROK have not substantially intervened in the conflicts. However, if the US troops intervene, the conflict between the DPRK and the ROK may escalate into a larger-scale conflict or even a war. Therefore, in the future, the boundary dispute between the DPRK and the ROK will become one of the reasons for the strengthening of US–ROK relations.

From a multilateral perspective, China, Japan, and the ROK are all involved in disputes in this region. China, Japan, and the ROK should consider the following two issues: first, how to avoid the impact on the cooperation of the three countries caused by the intensification of the disputes in Northeast Asia; second, within the trilateral framework of China, Japan, and the ROK, through cooperation and mutual trust, the necessary preconditions need to be created for the effective response and final settlement of the disputes. In 1974, the ROK and Japan signed the continental shelf boundary agreement on the delimitation of the East China Sea. The delimitation of the East China Sea involves the maritime rights and interests of China, Japan, and the ROK. Without the participation of China, a coastal country of the East China Sea, the two countries unilaterally divided the East China Sea and ignored China's maritime rights and interests. This agreement is of course not recognized by China. Therefore, issues related to the future division of the exclusive economic zones in the East China Sea will need to be solved by China, Japan, and the ROK.

The Diaoyu Dao issue between China and Japan also involves trilateral relations between China, the United States, and Japan. It can be said that the United States bears the main responsibility for appearance of the Diaoyu Dao issue. The United States took advantage of the intensification of the Diaoyu Dao issue between China and Japan to gain strategic benefit, strengthen the US–Japan military alliance, and enhance its strategic advantage. In the Diaoyu Dao issue between China and Japan, the United States supported Japan in order to obtain Japan's strong support, in turn, to maintain hegemony in East Asia. The United States also used this to contain China's rise and implement its "Asia-Pacific rebalance" strategy. The influence of the United States on the settlement of the Diaoyu Dao issue and the delimitation of the East China Sea between China and Japan cannot be underestimated. Therefore, the development of trilateral relations between China, the United States, and Japan is extremely important to coordinate and resolve the disputes over territorial sovereignty and maritime rights and interests between China and Japan.

As far as the trilateral relations between the United States, Japan, and the ROK are concerned, the intensification and continuation of disputes over territorial sovereignty and maritime rights and interests in Northeast Asia will, to a certain extent, help the United States take the opportunity to ensure coordination and cooperation between the United States, Japan, and the ROK in many East Asian affairs. The continuation of such coordination and cooperation will help the United States maintain its hegemony and strategic advantages in Northeast Asia and even the entire Asia-Pacific region. However, if the intensification of disputes over territorial sovereignty and maritime rights and interests in Northeast Asia is beyond the control of the United States and its allies, and thus leads to even wider military conflicts and wars in the region, the United States may also involve itself in regional conflicts or wars due to the involvement of its allies.

3.1.3.2 Disputes over territorial sovereignty and maritime rights and interests in Northeast Asia casting a shadow over the development of future state-to-state relations

Due to the lack of a corresponding mechanism for controlling disputes over territorial sovereignty and maritime rights and interests in Northeast Asia and the complicated relations between regional powers, such disputes will have a negative impact on the future development of relations between countries in this region.

First of all, state-to-state relations and the security situation in Northeast Asia will become more complicated. Due to the long-standing disputes over territorial sovereignty and maritime rights and interests in Northeast Asia, countries lack strategic mutual trust, which will have a negative impact on mutually beneficial cooperation and regional integration among countries in the region. The existence of this non-benign trend makes it difficult to realize regional integration similar to the ASEAN or EU.

Secondly, the interaction between countries inside and outside Northeast Asia is complicated. This complication is mainly reflected in the disputes over territorial sovereignty and maritime rights and interests, which have resulted in both exclusion and cooperation among relevant countries. The Northeast Asian region shows two interwoven processes: The first process is the promotion and deepening of regional integration. China, Japan, and the ROK are striving to promote regional trade liberalization, realize connectivity, and facilitate the negotiation of a free trade agreement among the three countries. The second process is the continuous escalation of disputes over territorial sovereignty and maritime rights and interests in Northeast Asia, resulting in the regional insecurity in Northeast Asia. The lack of security mechanisms makes this insecurity more prominent, especially the various interventions of the United States in the disputes.

Finally, there is a trend of invalidating strategic relations among countries. After the end of the Cold War, China established a wide range of strategic relations with many neighboring countries, such as Japan and the ROK. As the disputes over territorial sovereignty and maritime rights and interests in Northeast Asia continue to have negative impacts on national strategic relations, these relations show a trend of hollowing out their contents and invalidating their functions. This is because these countries ignore or belittle China's national sovereignty and interests when they are involved in disputes over territorial sovereignty and maritime rights and interests, which directly damages the development of their strategic relations with China.

3.1.3.3 China's designation of the East China Sea Air Defense Identification Zone as a preventive mechanism for safeguarding territorial sovereignty and maritime rights and interests

On November 23, 2013, China's Ministry of National Defense issued the Statement by the Government of the People's Republic of China on Establishing the East China Sea Air Defense Identification Zone and the Announcement of the Aircraft Identification Rules for the East China Sea Air Defense Identification Zone of the People's Republic of China, announcing the establishment of an Air Defense Identification Zone (ADIZ) in the East China Sea. The former mainly deals with the basis and geographical scope for setting up the ADIZ in the East China Sea. The latter mainly deals with the main management rules for the ADIZ in the East China Sea. It also declares that the Ministry of National Defense of the People's Republic of China is the administrative organ of the East China Sea ADIZ and that these rules will come into force at 10 am November 23, 2013.[4] After the announcement of the establishment of the East China Sea ADIZ, China's Ministry of National Defense immediately began to manage the East China Sea ADIZ effectively.

According to the official explanation of China's Ministry of National Defense, the purpose of establishing the East China Sea ADIZ is "safeguarding China's national sovereignty and security of the territory and air space and maintaining flying orders. It is also a necessary measure for China to effectively exercise its right for self defense. It is not directed against any specific country or target, nor will it affect the freedom of

---

[4]Announcement of the Aircraft Identification Rules for the East China Sea Air Defense Identification Zone of the People's Republic of China, website of the Ministry of National Defense of the People's Republic of China, http://news.mod.gov.cn/headlines/2013-11/23/content_4476124.htm.

overflight in the relative airspace."⁵ In other words, China's designation of the East China Sea ADIZ is based on its own national sovereignty and security to maintain peace and stability in the East China Sea. Therefore, the East China Sea ADIZ shows that China has made a major international contribution and shouldered responsibility in the Northeast Asia region. Through the effective management of the East China Sea ADIZ by the Chinese Ministry of Defense, security can be ensured in the region. The Chinese government has made it clear that China's setup of the ADIZ is a justified act of self-defense. Besides, the East China Sea ADIZ is not a no-fly zone. The Chinese Ministry of National Defense clearly stated that "it is worth mentioning that China has always respected the freedom of flight enjoyed by all the countries in accordance with the international law. The establishment of the East China Sea ADIZ does not change the legal status of relevant air space and routine international flights will not be affected in anyway."⁶ China, as an independent sovereign state, will effectively manage the ADIZ and serve the international community in this manner.

China's setup of the East China Sea ADIZ will effectively safeguard its strategic space for national security as it will provide warning about aircraft that may pose a threat to China's national defense and take measures to deal with the threat. According to the Chinese Ministry of National Defense, "China's armed forces will adopt defensive emergency measures to respond to aircraft unwilling to cooperate in the identification or refuse to follow the instructions."⁷ Obviously, the specific measures taken by the East China Sea ADIZ are defensive in nature.

After the establishment of the East China Sea ADIZ, China's Defense Ministry began its monitoring and management. On November 28, 2013, the Air Force of the CPLA started conducting air patrols over the East China Sea ADIZ in a routine manner. During a patrol on November 29, 2013, the Chinese Air Force effectively identified foreign military aircraft

---

⁵Defense Ministry Spokesman Yang Yujun's Response to Questions of ADIZ at Regular Press Conference, the Ministry of National Defense of the People's Republic of China, http://news.mod.gov.cn/headHnes/2013-ll/23/content_4476146.htm.
⁶*Ibid.*
⁷Announcement of the Aircraft Identification Rules for the East China Sea Air Defense Identification Zone of the People's Republic of China, Ministry of National Defense of the People's Republic of China, http://news.mod.gov.cn/headlines/2013-ll/23/content_4476124.htm.

entering the East China Sea ADIZ. These aircraft included 2 batches of 2 US P-3 and EP-3 air scouts and 7 batches of 10 Japanese E-767, P-3, and F-15. The establishment of the ADIZ has thus been a success as it has made positive contributions to China's national security and the peace and stability of the entire region.

The establishment of the East China Sea ADIZ will enhance China's national defense capability to safeguard territorial sovereignty and maritime rights and interests. With the escalation of disputes in Northeast Asia, China is facing more severe and dangerous challenges. The establishment of the East China Sea ADIZ will provide China with the ability to influence the settlement of disputes over territorial sovereignty and maritime rights and interests in Northeast Asia.

First of all, the setup of the East China Sea ADIZ enables Chinese military forces to safeguard national security. The effective management of the East China Sea ADIZ will provide China with the necessary strategic initiative to deal with and control disputes over territorial sovereignty and maritime rights and interests in Northeast Asia.

Secondly, the setup of an ADIZ in the East China Sea enables China to take timely and effective measures in response to emergencies and conflicts. Due to the escalation and intensification of disputes over territorial sovereignty and maritime rights and interests in Northeast Asia, China faces the possibility of armed disputes and wars in the region, not just on land but on sea and in the air. For example, in early 2013, Japan passed a resolution to fire tracer bullets at China's patrol aircraft in the East China Sea.[8] The establishment of the ADIZ in the East China Sea can at least provide a useful measure for China to deal with such conflicts.

Finally, the setup of the East China Sea ADIZ also provides China with corresponding institutional preparations for its participation in crisis management. China's setup of the East China Sea ADIZ is also a preventive mechanism for effectively controlling disputes in Northeast Asia. While it provides strategic power to China, it also provides an opportunity for China to participate in the settlement of disputes in Northeast Asia and to carry out bilateral and multilateral dialogues and cooperation. The United States and Japan have clearly expressed their opposition to the establishment of the ADIZ in the East China Sea. However, they have not taken any aggressive action. The Chinese patrol of the ADIZ has not been

---

[8] A reply of Defense Minister for the question from Chinese Media: A flare will be issued to warn the intruder of the aircraft. Asahi Shinbun, January 15, 2013.

hindered by the US and Japanese forces. It can thus be claimed that the establishment of the ADIZ has provided favorable conditions for effective dialogue and cooperation among countries in the East China Sea.

3.2 China's Territorial Sovereignty and Maritime Rights and Interests in Northeast Asia and its Strategic Choice

Safeguarding China's territorial sovereignty and maritime rights and interests is a long-term task for which the goal is constantly expanding.[9] It has always been the basic principle of strategists to draw on advantages and avoid disadvantages. In handling disputes over islands and seas with neighboring countries in accordance with international law and norms, China can not only safeguard its own territorial sovereignty and maritime rights and interests but can also display and embody its image as a peaceful, friendly, and responsible power.

3.2.1 China's political and security interests in safeguarding national territorial sovereignty and maritime rights and interests

In Northeast Asia, China's territorial sovereignty and maritime rights and interests mainly involve the Diaoyu Dao issue in the East China Sea, the delimitation of the exclusive economic zone and submarine continental shelf in the East China Sea, the delimitation of the exclusive economic zone in the Yellow Sea, and the Suyan Rocks issue. The East China Sea and the Yellow Sea are China's coastal areas, which are not only rich in marine resources and seabed mineral resources but are also part of China's strategic passage to the Pacific Ocean. They are of great strategic significance to the national maritime security of eastern China. There are differences and disputes between China and Japan over Diaoyu Dao and the delimitation of the East China Sea, and between China and the ROK over Suyan Rocks and the delimitation of the Yellow Sea. Safeguarding China's national sovereignty, rights and interests, and exclusive rights

---

[9] Wang Yizhou (2003). *Global Politics and China's Foreign Policy*. Beijing: World Affairs Press, p. 240.

over development and utilization of the islands and exclusive economic zones in the East China Sea and the Yellow Sea is an important political and security issue for China.

3.2.1.1 Safeguarding China's maritime sovereignty and building the cornerstone of maritime strategy

China has a long coastline of about 18,000 kilometers and an island coastline of more than 14,000 kilometers, with a total length of more than 32,000 kilometers. According to the United Nations Convention on the Law of the Sea, China can claim an area of about 3 million square kilometers of ocean land, but this does not mean that it completely controls all the claimed ocean land. In the East China Sea, the delimitation of the exclusive economic zone and the Diaoyu Dao issue between China and Japan constitute major constraints for China. In addition, the Obama administration pursued a strategy of focusing on the Asia-Pacific region and used its alliance system to construct a three-layer island chain to contain China's strategic maneuver space at sea. It further aggravated China's long-standing situation of "having seas with no easy access to the ocean." Therefore, China's maritime strategy is actually the only way for China to move toward a new and broader international space. However, China's maritime strategy should be subordinated to the overall strategy of peaceful development so that issues can be considered in an all-round way.

China's overall maritime strategy was planned in the late 1980s, came into existence in the mid-1990s, and developed rapidly in the first decade of the 21st century. With the relaxation of the Cold War atmosphere in the late 1980s and the overall warming of China–Soviet relations, China gradually adjusted to a new strategy of "simultaneous development of land and sea." Since then, China began to plan its own 100-year "Blue-Water Strategy," which involved moving away from the ban on maritime trade with foreign countries that was followed during the Yuan, Ming, and Qing dynasties and also moving away from the 1970s strategy of fortress-like coastal defense with the army given more importance than the navy. Therefore, China's overall maritime strategy is to change its long-standing situation of "having seas with no easy access to the ocean" to the greatest extent and to provide sustained spatial support and resource guarantees by recovering and developing its "blue territory."

As an important treasure house of resources, a safety barrier, and a major transportation artery to the world, the South China Sea has become more and more prominent due to its strategic position in today's globalized economy. As an important component of China's overall maritime strategy, the formulation, implementation, and adjustment of the East China Sea strategy should be coordinated with and subordinated to the process of its overall ocean strategy.

China's East China Sea strategy is consistent with its overall ocean strategy, and the overall ocean strategy is consistent with its overall development strategy. China's ocean strategy can be divided into three stages. Before the end of the 20th century, during the "Yellow-Water Navy" stage, China's strategy in the East China Sea was mainly to pursue "offshore defense," passively driving away foreign ships from its 12-nautical-mile territorial sea. China's marine resource exploration was also concentrated in shallower offshore waters. In the first ten years of the 21st century, China's marine strategy entered the second stage, that is, the "Blue-Water Navy" stage. The strategy in the East China Sea was adjusted to the "active defense" posture. The fleet size of the Chinese navy was much larger and the navy moved far away, going as far as Somalia to safeguard national interests. At the same time, China's marine development technology is also rapidly improving and gradually advancing into deep-sea exploration. In the next 20 years, China's marine strategy will enter the third stage, that is, the "Deep-Blue Navy" stage. The East China Sea strategy will completely move away from the strategic containment of the first island chain. China's marine exploration has also progressed greatly. With the improvement of deep-sea exploration technology, China will be fully capable of independently developing deep-sea resources. Chinese warships will assume greater responsibility for international maritime security. Chinese merchant ships will sail in every corner of the world. China's influence will be recognized by the world and trusted by all peace-loving countries.

3.2.1.2 *Maintaining international order in Northeast Asia after World War II and preventing a revival of Japanese militarism*

Maritime territorial and development disputes in Northeast Asia are not only historical vestiges but also closely related to the ineffective settlement of post-war colonial and military issues and changes in the international situation since the Cold War. At present, some major territorial disputes include those between Russia and Japan over the four islands (called the Northern Territories in Japanese and the Southern Kurils in Russian), between Japan and the ROK over a set of islands (called Dokdo in Korean and Takeshima in Japanese), between China and Japan over Diaoyu Dao, and between China and Japan over the delimitation of the exclusive zone and continental shelf in the East China Sea. Since all these disputes involve Japan, ROK's media has resorted to calling Japan "a troublemaker in Northeast Asia."[10] When resolving maritime disputes and safeguarding its national maritime rights and interests, China must realize that the substantive issue behind these specific disputes is to ensure the legitimacy of the post-war Yalta order and the existing international order in East Asia. This is not only in China's national interest but also in the interests of all countries in East Asia. Therefore, China needs to combine the settlement of maritime territorial disputes with the grand historical proposition of guarding against the revival of Japanese militarism and consider the policy interaction between the two sides in this big context, instead of making compromises on major issues of right and wrong due to technological progress.

In November 2014, Shinzo Abe suddenly announced the dissolution of the House of Representatives and called for an election about two years in advance. On December 14 of the same year, Japan's 47th House of Representatives election was announced, and the Liberal Democratic Party won the election again, not unexpectedly. Japan's right-wing inclination was confirmed in the election. Abe's attempt to amend the constitution was also considered at the legislative level. Although the new parliament was unable to amend the constitution by a two-thirds majority, amending the peace clause of the constitution became the main axis of Japan's political life for some time. To ensure constitutional amendment, the Abe administration planned to use the majority seats of the Liberal Democratic Party in Japan's House of Representatives to legalize the "collective self-defense rights" before amending the constitution by amending a series of laws such as the Self-Defense Forces Law, the Law on Surrounding Events, the Law on International Peace and Cooperation (PKO Cooperation Law), and the Law on Ship Inspection. Japan intended to completely abandon its "exclusive defense" policy implemented after World War II and instead participate in international military operations

---

[10] The ROK's media call Japan a troublemaker in Northeast Asia and territorial disputes continue, Tencent.com, http://news.qq.com/a/20080716/002007.htm, July 16, 2008.

even when it is not attacked. The aim of these actions is to neutralize China's maritime threat over the Diaoyu Dao issue. The radical populist public opinion in Japan instigated by Abe will have a great impact on the Japanese government's long-term strategy as this issue is by no means one of purely internal affairs. China needs to realize that the politicians who stir up trouble, and the forces behind them, do not have the sincerity to reflect on and debate on international strategy and regional strategic situations. They only magnify individual issues and incite public opinion to exert pressure on the domestic political system and other countries at the same time. This phenomenon is particularly evident in the interaction between the Tokyo local government and the Democratic Party cabinet. The Chinese government must clearly show its opposition to such acts, which obviously arrogate the exclusive power of the central government but appear under the guise of nationalism and patriotism as it is in the fundamental interest of China.

3.2.1.3 *Separating sensitive and complex maritime disputes from the process of regional cooperation*

From 2000 to 2013, the proportion of the ROK's exports to China rose from 10.7% to 26.1%, and China became the ROK's largest offshore market. In 2014, direct investment of the ROK's enterprises in China increased by 29.8% year on year, reaching US$3.97 billion. The total bilateral trade between China and the ROK was likely to exceed US$300 billion in 2015. It will even exceed the total bilateral trade between China and Japan. Furthermore, bilateral trade and direct investment between China and Japan have both declined. According to statistics from the General Administration of Customs of the People's Republic of China (GACC), China–Japan trade in 2014 totaled US$310 billion, or about RMB1.92 trillion, down 1% year on year. China's exports to Japan fell by 1.4% and imports fell by 0.5%. From 1993 to 2003, Japan was China's largest foreign trade partner for ten consecutive years. However, in 2012, Japan fell to China's fifth-largest trading partner.[11] In 2014, Japan's direct investment in China decreased by 38.8% from the previous year to US$4.33 billion. This is a continuous decline after Japan's direct

---

[11] General Administration of Customs: Japan Declines to China's Fifth Trade Partner in 2012, http://finance.chinanews.com/cj/2013/01-10/4476603.shtml, January 10, 2013.

investment in China fell by 4% year on year in 2013, the most significant drop in 25 years.[12] The imbalance in economic and political relations among China, Japan, and the ROK has greatly affected the medium- and long-term prospects of the regional agenda and increased the uncertainty in the relations among the three countries. China's development still needs a clear and predictable process of regional integration. Therefore, China needs to consider how to divide regional economic cooperation and sensitive territorial disputes.

Can international strategic goals be equivalent to national core interests? The "simplicity" of global strategic objectives implies "the limited effectiveness of international strategies." The core interests of a country may always exist along with the nation-state, but a strategic plan is only reasonable within a time span of several decades. A country may have a large number of core interests. As far as these interests are concerned, it is not easy to judge which is more important. Many core interests require the country to invest a large number of resources in protecting them, and the formulation of the strategy means that the central government obtains legal authorization and makes a direction choice within a specified period for the investment of limited resources in the name of the country. In this sense, a correct strategy is consistent with the direction of safeguarding the country's core interests in the long run, but in its own life cycle, it will absolutely contradict the protection of some core interests. Core interests and strategic objectives cannot be equated in theory. In the face of widespread disputes over territorial sovereignty and maritime rights and interests in Northeast Asia, the question governments should answer in their policy thinking is not "whether territorial sovereignty integrity belongs to the core interests of the country" but "what is the relative position of the disputed territorial issues in the overall international strategy of the country." According to the magnitude of the threat and the judgment of emergencies, there is certainly room for revision of a country's strategic objectives.

Disputes over territorial sovereignty and maritime rights and interests often involve the interests of core countries. In the process of settling

---

[12] Jiang Ruiping (2014). Economic Mutual Benefit and Political Mutual Trust in China-Japan-ROK Cooperation, *Proceedings of the Conference on "Formation and Future of East Asian International Order- the 4th East Asian Community Forum,"* pp. 211, 208, quoted from Liu Jiangyong (2015). 'Abe Politics' and China-Japan-ROK Relations, *Northeast Asia Forum*, No. 3, 2015.

disputes, there will be a tendency to abandon compromise and encourage toughness. Sometimes, it becomes a centralized outlet for many outstanding issues, which increases the complexity of solving the problem. It is of fundamental interest to China to maintain its peaceful development strategy. Therefore, it is necessary to separate the sensitive disputes over territorial sovereignty and maritime rights and interests from the overall situation of peaceful development. This is China's attitude as a major country and its attempt to distinguish its foreign policy from Japan's so-called "nationalization" and Abe's conservative policy. China needs to be alert to the tendency of some countries to regard disputed territories as a tool to limit the growth of the influence of other countries.

3.2.2 China's economic interests in protecting national territorial sovereignty and maritime rights and interests

The 21st century has been called the ocean century. All countries in the world, especially the major ocean countries, have formulated or promulgated national ocean strategies and related legal systems, and are vigorously promoting the implementation of ocean development activities. To guarantee the supply of energy resources and ensure sustainable economic development, China must implement a strategy of marine development. Marine interests are related to China's national security, unification, and development. At the same time, China is a country with relatively unfavorable marine geography, its marine awareness is weak, and its marine laws and strategies are lagging. Therefore, China should take the Diaoyu Dao issue as an opportunity to actively promote the implementation of the Outline of the National Planning for Marine Development; formulate, revise, and improve relevant marine legal systems; and strengthen bilateral, regional, and international marine cooperation in order to safeguard its marine rights and interests.

3.2.2.1 *The vigorous development of China's marine economy*

With the implementation of the marine development and marine power strategy, China's maritime economy has made great progress. The total output value of the marine economy rose from RMB285.522 billion in 1996 to RMB2492.9 billion in 2007, and its share of GDP also rose from

1.9% to 10.11%. It was predicted that China's marine economy will exceed RMB12687.9 billion by the end of 2015.[13] China has formed an export-oriented marine economic system with marine fishery, coastal tourism, marine oil and gas, marine transportation, marine shipping, marine salt, seawater utilization, and marine biopharmaceuticals being the main industries. In 2004, China's total export of seafood ranked first in the world and its export earning capacity ranked first in large agricultural exports. China's mariculture industry has ranked first in the world for 19 years in a row, and the output of the marine salt industry has ranked first in the world for many years as well, with the shipping industry accounting for more than 23% of the world market share.[14] China has formed four major marine economic circles, involving the Bohai Sea, the Yangtze River Delta, the Pearl River Delta, and the Beibu Gulf. Five national economic zones have been established with approval from the central government: the Shandong Peninsula Blue Economic Zone, Zhejiang Ocean Economic Development Demonstration Zone, Guangdong Marine Economy Comprehensive Experimental Zone, Marine Functional Zone, and Fujian Straits Blue Economy Zone.

The increasing prosperity of the marine economy is reflected not only in its contribution to GDP but also in its contribution to China's economic and industrial restructuring and sustainable development. After 30 years of accumulation and development, China's marine economy has moved from offshore to the high sea and from the coast to the ocean. The proportion of traditional marine farming, fishing, marine transportation, and marine industry is reasonable and has achieved considerable international competitiveness. With the vigorous development of the global marine industry, the upgrading of the structure and competitiveness of the marine industry has become an important part of the long-term development plan of China's national economy and a core component of China's sustainable development strategy.

In order to ensure sustainable development of the marine economy, China has issued a series of documents including the Outline of the National Planning for Marine Development, Outline of the National Planning for Development of Marine Economy, and Outline of the

---

[13] Luo Peng, Bai Fuchen and Zhang Li (2009). The forecast of China's marine economic prospects in China, *Fishery Economic Research*, No. 2.

[14] La Quanheng (2014). Study on the development strategy of China's marine economy, *China National Conditions and Strength*, No. 12, 2014.

National Planning for the Marine Development through Science and Technology (2008–2015). In a report to the 18th National Congress of the CPC, concepts like "Five-in-One New Pattern" (all-round economic, political, cultural, social, and ecological progress) and "maritime power" were clearly put forward. President Xi Jinping wrote in the preface to *Ocean: Zhejiang's Future — Strategic Research on Accelerating the Marine Economic Development* that he had worked in Fujian for a long time, and he was deeply impressed by the ocean and had strong feelings for it. Developing the marine economy was one of his long-term goals.[15]

After 30 years of exploration, China established a complete and systematic approach to the opening up of its marine economy, including the research and development of marine technology, protection of the marine environment, and realization of marine security. The development of the marine economy put forward new and clear requirements for the diplomatic work of the Chinese government, that is, to ensure harmony between the development of the marine economy and regional marine order and provide a stable external environment for sustainable development of the marine economy. Therefore, the Chinese government has clearly defined the basic policies of adjusting the marine economy structure to highlight the key points and vigorously develop the pillar industries while taking into account the overall consideration of marine economic development and national defense construction to ensure the national defense security.[16]

3.2.2.2 Eliminating the unilateral view of maritime rights and interests through attractive regional economic cooperation agendas

A marine economy is an economical form with obvious openness. Its long-term development should be based on consensus and cooperation of all countries around the particular body of water. Although there may be no breakthrough in solving differences in territorial sovereignty and

---

[15] Cui Wanglai (2015). Xi Jinping's ideology on oceans, *Journal of Zhejiang Ocean University* (Humanities Edition), No. 2.

[16] State Council and State Oceanic Administration. Outline of the National Planning for Marine Economic Development. http://www.cme.gov.cn/gh/gy.htm (received online on July 20, 2015).

allocation of maritime rights and interests among countries in the short term, there has been a universal demand for Northeast Asian countries to actively develop marine economies. Countries need to adopt new points of interest so that cooperation can be realized in a way acceptable to all parties. A stronger regional economic cooperation agenda is essential. However, one obvious feature of the current regional political conflicts is that economic matters are often regarded as pressure tools to force one side to concede. Japan's wavering over the China–Japan–ROK FTA and TPP negotiations signals its departure from the process of regional integration in Northeast Asia. People used to describe the situation in Northeast Asia as "hot economics, cold politics," but now there are precursors of "cold politics, cold economics." This means that in the presence of a large number of interference factors, the process of regional economic cooperation has begun to show signs of negative development. If this trend is not reversed, it may become a serious problem and eventually lead to stagnation or even retrogression of promising regional marine economic cooperation. Of course, the regionalization we advocate is not the traditional regionalization involving "external exclusiveness."[17] It is a new regionalism that is open to cooperation. This new regionalism framework will not affect the traditional alliance relationship between disputing parties. It only means that Northeast Asian countries will have closer cooperation and better mutual recognition on functional issues, including marine economic cooperation and development. The historical development of Northeast Asia is entirely different from that of Europe. Its regionalization mode only needs to change "the development model that used to be dominated by unilateral independent actions."[18] It does not mean that all countries should establish a regional organization with an extremely large range and power to manage the behaviors of all countries, nor does it mean that regionalization development involves sacrificing the sovereignty requirements of all countries. The process of economic cooperation in Northeast Asia can aim at providing a good external environment for settling marine economic cooperation issues of common interest to all countries and making preparations for relevant negotiations. At present, the low level of institutionalized cooperation among Northeast

---

[17] Qiu Shengyan and Gu Lina (2007). Discrimination of the concepts of Dodson doctrine, regionalism and bilateral doctrine, *Economic Review Journal*, 2007(10).

[18] Wang Shengjin (2007). The development trend and path choice of Northeast Asian Regional Economic Cooperation, *Journal of Social Sciences of Jilin University*, No. 7.

Asian countries shows that the problem faced by regionalization is not the spillover of technical cooperation to the political field, but the problem that political problems hinder the spillover effect. Reversing this trend requires that problems in different areas be treated and dealt with separately. Various regional and subregional systems and forms of dialogue may seem messy, but in fact, they have actively promoted the development of regional cooperation.

3.2.3 China's strategic choice for safeguarding national territorial sovereignty and maritime rights and interests

In the 21st century, only when the territorial issue is truly embedded in China's international strategic framework can we solve the current difficulties China is facing. In order to achieve this, we need to realize the actual use of China's territorial and maritime strategy from two aspects so as to turn it from an abstract concept into realistic policy action.

3.2.3.1 *Strategic coordination between safeguarding territorial sovereignty and maritime rights and interests and China's peaceful development*

Safeguarding China's territorial sovereignty and maritime rights and interests is of utmost importance to China. However, it will not be the whole content of China's Northeast Asia diplomatic strategy and policy. Under the general policy of peaceful development, one is required to balance sovereign issues and peaceful development.

First of all, from the perspective of goal selection, on the issue of territorial disputes in Northeast Asia, China hopes to achieve the two goals of maintaining peace in the region and defending national sovereignty and territorial integrity at the same time. However, ultimately China needs to establish a core goal in its multi-objective structure. This goal has absolute priority in practice and is the primary goal of the entire strategic system. China needs to make a time-bound judgment as to whether worsening territorial disputes will pose heavy external pressure in the next 5 to 10 years to the extent that it needs to revise its original strategic framework.

To find an answer, two issues need to be clarified. First, what are the original strategic core objectives? Second, can territorial disputes be resolved within the original strategic framework? In December 2005, the State Council Information Office of the People's Republic of China (SCIO) published a white paper titled *China's Peaceful Development*, which explains the basic strategy from five aspects. Firstly, peaceful development is the inevitable way for China's modernization. Secondly, China will promote world peace through its own development. Thirdly, China will rely on itself and achieve development through reform and innovation. Fourthly, China will achieve mutually beneficial common development with other countries. Fifthly, China will build a harmonious world marked by sustained peace and common prosperity. Within the basic strategic framework of peaceful development, maintaining peace in the surrounding areas is not only a condition and means to achieve sustainable economic and social development in China but also constitutes a strategic goal as important as peace. The essence of the peaceful development strategy is still a development strategy. The strategy implies two basic prerequisites. One is that China's development level is still insufficient. The other is that China's rapid development cycle is not yet over, and there is still great room for development. The emphasis on the goal of peace is not intended to ignore the potential risks in the international environment and the unstable factors in the surrounding environment, including territorial disputes. Instead, after China realizes the potential risks, it will concentrate on changing its fragile *status quo* within a period of time so as to enhance its ability to withstand dangerous situations that may occur in the future. The famous strategy of Goujian, King of Yue state during the Spring and Autumn Period and Warring State Period (770–221 BC), outlined in *Zuozhuan: The First Year of Aigong*, is still thought-provoking: "Yue state used ten years for rehabilitating and another ten years for educating its people and training its soldiers. Twenty years later, Yue state defeated Wu state and turned the palace of Wu state into a marsh." The twenty years of peace were not without threats and challenges from outside. The Wu state's excesses and arrogant insults have been recorded in various documents of the Spring and Autumn Period. Yue state paid a high price for development in those 20 years. If we regard 20 years as a strategic cycle for Yue, then during this period Yue obviously severely limited the scope of application of its policy measures, and all other needs except "rehabilitation" and "education" were artificially suppressed, although these needs were reasonable and necessary in themselves.

Then, within a strategic framework of peaceful development, is China doomed to do nothing on the disputed territory issues? China of course needs to do something, but in a limited way. On the one hand, the military and diplomatic fields are themselves components of peaceful development. Today, when China's overall national strength and international influence have greatly improved, it can invest more in safeguarding national security. China has the ability to safeguard national territorial integrity and cope with emergencies. On the other hand, the strategy of peaceful development limits the direction of the strategic resources and the scope of policy choices. Territorial disputes are especially important. The only way to completely resolve the disputes is to change the *status quo* of the land and ocean in dispute. The probability of success in resolving territorial disputes through negotiation is extremely small. In fact, China can strengthen the inclination and speed of resources in this field within the framework of the current strategy and lay a solid foundation for thorough future changes. However, problems of what the future changes are and how to realize them can only be clear after the strategic objectives are completely revised.

Secondly, on the issue of modifying strategic objectives, economic development, international image enhancement, and territorial recovery as well are the core interests of the country. Therefore, it is difficult to simply compare which is more important than others. It is also difficult to simply conclude the appeal to the complete change of the *status quo* is irrational or incorrect. With regard to the disputes on Diaoyu Dao, the East China Sea, and other issues, there is a chorus of voices not only from the public but also from strategy designing and implementing departments. This leads to a very real problem: Strategic objectives are inherently cyclical and strategic adjustments will always occur. So, what kind of modifications and adjustments are reasonable? Traditional international strategic research always takes strategic adjustments as the only feedback processes to "external environment," viewing changes in the external environment as the root of adjustments. Such thinking runs counter to the concept of classic strategic management. According to R. E. White's point of view, the transformation of strategic decision-making starts from the cognitive reorganization and adjustment of the dialogue process and functions of the strategic management system (including informal organizations).[19] With the Diaoyu Dao and East China Sea issues

---

[19] Chakravarthy, B.F. and White, R.E. (2002). Strategy process: Forming and implementing and changing strategies. *Handbook of Strategy and Management*, Sage Publications.

seriously impacting national sentiment, the domestic strategic dialogues should brook no delay. At present, there is no lack of attention or emotional expression in China, but these expressions, carried out by media, are oriented to stimulate enthusiasm rather than solve problems, to exert pressure instead of shouldering any responsibility. A full and rational dialogue can not only ease social anxieties, making clear the strategic expectations and condensing the national consensus, but can also provide a platform for discussion on specific policies. If we are going to change our policy on the issue of Diaoyu Dao, what changes will happen in the international environment? What is the possibility of external military interference? Do our national defense departments have any pre-arranged planning? Are there any problems in the distribution and application of the military force? Can these problems be solved through the coordination of different departments? What is the worst expectation of the foreign affairs departments? What are the possible impacts on the economy brought about by the territory disputes? How will the government respond to appeals from the general public? All these propositions are vital to the overall strategic development in the future and the answers to these questions can only come from a high-level, all-around, sustainable, and responsible strategic dialogue system. So, whether China is going to adjust its fixed strategy or not and whether the possible adjustments are fine-tuning or total revision, we need to answer the above-mentioned questions first. Otherwise, China will be performing blind actions.

Finally, there is the cost of the strategy. To examine whether a grand strategy concerning the future development of a country is mature or not depends not only on the reasonableness of the goals and the applicability in practice but also on the cost. We must attach great importance to the study of the strategic cost, identifying the strategic value brought forth by the strategic cost and comprehensively evaluating strategic capabilities, to form a deep understanding and high recognition of the national strategy.

3.2.3.2 *Safeguarding territorial sovereignty and maritime rights and interests: from technical negotiations to strategic negotiations*

From the perspective of its development stage, the Northeast Asian regional cooperation has now basically realized the scale of the regional economy but without a systematic political cooperation relationship. Under such circumstances, it is unrealistic to expect a "package" solution to the issues of territorial jurisdiction and maritime delimitation that China is facing. For complex territorial and maritime disputes and ocean development issues, there are usually two solutions. The first is to refer to Joseph Nye's "key spillover" program and try to reach a "package" agreement on the issue politically, so as to promote a thorough solution of territorial and maritime issues based on joint development and political consultation. Second, drawing lessons from the research results of David Mitrany and Ernst Haas, one can promote technical or non-political cooperations between governments or non-governmental organizations in basic but complicated legal, historical, and political fields, reach basic consensus, and consolidate the legal basis of relevant issues so as to slowly push forward the basic technical negotiations to higher-level ones. As a matter of fact, the two solutions of the settlement are not mutually exclusive. In view of the complicated historical and practical disputes in Northeast Asia, it is very difficult to directly transition the settlement of territorial and maritime issues to political coordination. Therefore, the establishment of a network of technical or non-political mechanisms is a necessary intermediate stage in the construction of relevant working mechanisms.

According to Mitrany's network theory of technical working mechanisms, political issues always contain a lot of technical content. Although the solutions to these problems cannot be said to have nothing to do with ideology or nationalism, they rely more on professionals to negotiate and find long-term solutions.[20] Haas further explained that in today's increasingly regulated society, sensitive political issues would have more and more complicated details. For example, territorial and maritime issues involve many details such as international law, archaeology, economic cooperation and development, and politics. All of these require a lot of painstaking discussions. Some of these tasks need to be solved through technical, bureaucratic consultations in various countries, while many need to be completed by non-governmental social organizations. The deepening of these negotiations will push the discussions to new levels, and the corresponding consensus and mutual understanding will lead to

---

[20]Thompson, K.W. (1980). *Master of International Thought: Major Twentieth-Century Theorists and the World Crisis*. Baton Rouge: Louisiana State University Press.

higher-level negotiations.[21] The following issues need to be considered under the current conditions: How to activate scattered technical cooperation in different fields? How to make these non-political cooperation mechanisms form an institutional network? How to accelerate further development of negotiations on sensitive issues? Based on the current situation, what is most suitable for China and what China can do to break the current deadlock is to act as an active advocate and practitioner of the negotiations on these issues in Northeast Asia. In order to achieve this goal, China needs to make progress in the following areas.

First of all, we will effectively promote non-governmental communication, including dialogue between academia and social organizations. Broadly speaking, regional cooperation includes "formal or informal continuous cooperation"[22] by non-governmental organizations or private institutions. Now, the civil pressure on the territorial and maritime issues in China and other countries is unilateral. Many contradictions are not substantive but are based on prejudice and misunderstanding. The purpose of exchanging data and information with each other is not to persuade the other party or accept the other party's position, but to establish communication habits, cultivate transnational social communication channels, and establish a mutually respectful identity. This kind of long-term work often cannot directly provide solutions to territorial and maritime problems. Still, it can effectively prevent negative factors from rapidly expanding into social pressure and establish the necessary easy atmosphere.

Secondly, one can establish a stable bilateral working procedure. If there are stable working procedures and "common standards," a stable cooperation mechanism is set up, and a smooth diplomatic channel capable of quickly transmitting the views of both sides is established, then the communication mechanism will play an important role in finding solutions. The China–Japan–ROK Cooperation Action Plan adopted at the China–Japan–ROK Summit in 2008 has already demonstrated the important value of establishing bilateral and multilateral working procedures. Only when the political will of all countries is dependent on the information, judgment, and channels of professional departments will the statesmen seek direct involvement in territorial and maritime disputes with a

---

[21] Ernst, B. H. (1961). International integration: The European and the universal process. *International Organization*, 15(3), 372.

[22] Mark, A. and Ravenhil, J. (eds.) (1995). *Pacific Cooperation: Building Economic and Security in the Asia-Pacific Region*, Boulder: Westview Press, p. 158.

view to solve them. Official cooperation at the technical level can also deepen the interdependence of Northeast Asian countries and cultivate national elites who understand and are familiar with regionalization and stable transnational governmental ties. If given enough time, transnational mechanisms can even be mutually beneficial, assuming a neutral attitude in order to reduce disputes. Of course, it takes time for government departments of various countries to establish such a mature working mechanism. In this process, what needs to be handled carefully is how to prevent the intergovernmental cooperation mechanism and working procedures from being corrupted by political turmoil.

Finally, the continuity of strategic planning and policy practice should be maintained. China's rise has become one of the most important international political phenomena of the 21st century. This rise makes China's communication and collision with the external environment more frequent. Continuing the momentum of its rapid development and improving its international status have posed a great challenge to China's international strategic planning and practical ability. Facing a complex and changeable international environment and major diplomatic challenges, China needs to establish an overall strategic framework and propose solutions to sensitive issues, including territorial sovereignty and maritime rights and interests within the overall framework. Any thinking that attempts to solve the problem separately from the overall framework, or that hopes to achieve success in a short period of time and ignores the long-term development plan, is against strategic thinking and should be avoided by China's foreign affairs department.

3.3 China's Strategy and Countermeasures to Resolve the Diaoyu Dao Issue Between China and Japan

The Diaoyu Dao issue is one of the most sensitive and complicated issues between China and Japan. It has an important impact on China–Japan relations and peace and stability in Northeast Asia. The dispute between China and Japan over Diaoyu Dao is a long-standing historical issue. It involves complicated political, historical, legal, economic, and security issues. According to the principles of international law, it is the rational choice for both China and Japan to respect history and reality and peacefully settle the dispute over Diaoyu Dao through diplomatic negotiations.

According to the white paper *Diaoyu Dao, an Inherent Territory of China* released by the State Council Information Office of the People's Republic of China in September 2012, Diaoyu Dao and its affiliated islands are an inseparable part of the Chinese territory. Diaoyu Dao is China's inherent territory in historical, geographical and legal terms, and China enjoys indisputable sovereignty over Diaoyu Dao. Japan's occupation of Diaoyu Dao during the Sino-Japanese War in 1895 is illegal and invalid. After World War II, Diaoyu Dao was returned to China in accordance with such international legal documents as the Cairo Declaration and the Potsdam Proclamation. No matter what unilateral step Japan takes over Diaoyu Dao, it will not change the fact that Diaoyu Dao belongs to China. For quite some time, Japan has repeatedly stirred up trouble on the issue of Diaoyu Dao. The Japanese government announced the "purchase" of Diaoyu Dao and its affiliated Nanxiao Dao and Beixiao Dao, and the implementation of so-called "nationalization." This is a move that grossly violates China's territorial sovereignty and seriously tramples on historical fact and international jurisprudence.

3.3.1 China's strategic choice to resolve the dispute over Diaoyu Dao between China and Japan

After the dispute over Diaoyu Dao occurred, Japan built a complete ocean strategy and ocean management system and sought political support through an alliance system in the international arena. China should also speed up the improvement of corresponding marine legislation to ensure China's territorial sovereignty and marine rights and interests.

3.3.1.1 *The path of international law to solve the dispute*

Up to now, disputes over island sovereignty have mainly been settled through international arbitration and international judicial procedures. Arbitration is one of the important methods for peaceful settlement of maritime disputes stipulated in the United Nations Convention on the Law of the Sea. It is also a compulsory procedure that the parties to the dispute can choose at will. The International Court of Justice is the most important international judicial organ. The International Court of Justice plays an irreplaceable role in dealing with and solving many legal problems faced by the international community and in promoting the process of the international rule of law. Also belonging to the international judicial process is the International Tribunal for the Law of the Sea, which was established in 1996 under the United Nations Convention on the Law of the Sea. It is a body specializing in maritime disputes. It has its own characteristics in jurisdiction and procedures and is also helpful to supplement the deficiencies of some functions of the International Court of Justice. According to the principles of international law, it is undoubtedly an important body to coordinate and arbitrate the Diaoyu Dao issue between China and Japan through the International Court of Justice.

3.3.1.2 *Strengthening China's marine legislation and enforcement*

In September 2012, the Chinese government, following the Law of Territorial Sea and the Contiguous Zone of the People's Republic of China, demarcated and announced the baseline of the territorial sea of Diaoyu Dao and its affiliated islands. The Chinese government also vowed to continue to promulgate relevant laws and regulations to improve the territorial sea system further. This is of great significance in speeding up the improvement of China's marine policy and legal system, clarifying the limits of the sea areas under China's jurisdiction, and clarifying the rights and obligations of China's maritime power to enforce the law in Diaoyu Dao and its affiliated sea areas. In accordance with the UNCLOS and relevant provisions of international law, the Chinese government has submitted the relevant coordinates and charts of the Diaoyu Dao territorial sea baseline to the Secretary-General of the United Nations. This will provide a legal basis for China to manage the Diaoyu Dao waters in accordance with domestic laws and relevant international laws. It can be said that this is a new balance rebuilt by China and Japan on the Diaoyu Dao issue.

Regarding the formulation of the basic ocean law, it has already been covered in the *Agenda of China Sea in the 21st Century* (1996).[23] As a comprehensive basic law regulating ocean issues, the law should specify the objectives, principles, and specific measures of ocean development and management. This is undoubtedly of great significance to mobilize the efforts of the whole country, to improve the marine management system, and to realize the desire to build a powerful oceanic country. Since

---

[23] State Oceanic Administration (1996). *Agenda of China Sea in the 21st Century*. Beijing: China Ocean Press, p. 39.

the promulgation and implementation of the Law on the Exclusive Economic Zone and the Continental Shelf of the People's Republic of China in 1998, no corresponding supporting regulations and detailed implementation rules have been formulated. In order to deal with maritime conflicts, including delimitation disputes, it is necessary to formulate and refine the corresponding regulations as soon as possible. At the same time, consideration should be given to the formulation of new laws and regulations for ocean affairs on the basis of the basic law of the sea, including coastal zone management law and maritime safety law, among which the maritime safety law should cover maritime territorial safety, marine resources safety, maritime traffic safety, marine environment safety, etc., in order to safeguard national security and ensure marine rights and interests.[24]

Whether it is the implementation of the marine development strategy or the Planning Outline, a strong marine law enforcement team is needed. Due to the presence of multiple departments, compartmentalization, and lack of unified coordination of China's ocean affairs management, the integration of maritime rights enforcement forces in the sea-related departments should be strengthened. The practices and experiences of the ROK can be used for reference, including the allocation of corresponding facilities, regular training of law enforcement personnel, and the formation of coast guard units in order to strengthen maritime law enforcement forces and safeguard China's ocean rights and interests.

3.3.1.3 *Strengthening the national defense forces and accelerating navy construction*

Japan's right-leaning trend is one of the greatest challenges to China's peripheral diplomacy in the 21st century and to the Yalta agreement. Japan's right-leaning trend and its move to strengthen its forces are not temporary fluctuations of its policy but part of a consistent and established national policy. Even if there is a change of government, the right-leaning trend can only vary in degree. As for China, it must clearly realize that it is impossible to solve the Diaoyu Dao issue solely through consultation and compromise. At present, "China has maintained routine presence and

---

[24] It's Urgent to Formulate a Marine Security Strategy, *China Ocean News*, March 12, 2008.

exercised jurisdiction in the waters of Diaoyu Dao" through marine surveillance vessels.[25] However, China must consider the possibility of a sudden worsening of the Diaoyu Dao issue and a military conflict, so it has to be well prepared. China will not give up its diplomatic efforts, but it must develop its military power vigorously. China should counter Japan's hostile attitude with the modernization of its military, curb Japan's military attempt to challenge the Yalta system with the promotion of military deterrence, and prevent Japan from taking risks on the Diaoyu Dao issue with practical and effective show of naval force and occupation of the islands. Chairman Mao Zedong once pointed out, "If we seek peace through struggle, peace will prevail; if we seek peace through compromise, and peace will perish." The enhancement of China's national defense force, especially its naval capability of containment, is not an obstacle to diplomatic negotiations on Diaoyu Dao, but seems to be a necessary tool for Japan to sit at the negotiation table with a rational mind.

From the perspective of military diplomacy, the application of China's military tools should achieve the following goals. Firstly, China's navy must have practical deterrent and intervention capabilities. Secondly, China's national defense forces need to make Japan and its allies realize that the Chinese government's will to defend its sovereignty over Diaoyu Dao is firm and cannot be challenged. Finally, the aim of the Chinese navy's actions is not to stimulate further deterioration of China–Japan relations but to force Japan to return to a rational position.

3.3.2 China's basic countermeasures for resolving the China–Japan dispute over Diaoyu Dao

The Diaoyu Dao issue between China and Japan is a historical issue as well as a practical one. Diaoyu Dao is China's inherent territory. However, effectively safeguarding China's territorial sovereignty over Diaoyu Dao, effectively controlling and properly resolving the Diaoyu Dao issue, and avoiding further tensions and conflicts between China and Japan are the major challenges China is facing. According to historical, political, and legal causes for the Diaoyu Dao issue, China must adopt

---

[25] State Council Information Office, the People's Republic of China (2012). *Diaoyu Dao, an Inherent Territory of China*, http://www.gov.cn/jrzg/2012-09/25/content_2232710.htm, September 25, 2012.

comprehensive policies and effectively deal with the issue. From the perspective of diplomatic solutions, China can choose a path and means based on mainly international laws and systems, political wisdom, legal advantages, and the moral high ground.

3.3.2.1 *Strengthening sovereignty and peacefully settling the disputes*

China has long adhered to the principle of "shelving differences and seeking joint development on the basis of acknowledging China's sovereignty." With the continuous escalation of the Diaoyu Dao issue, it is now necessary for China to put forward its best national strategies for marine disputes and principles to solve the dispute. These strategies and principles reflect China's national interests, tally with the actual situation, and demonstrate the national consensus of China. These strategies and principles emphasize the existence of China's sovereignty, promote bilateral negotiations, and develop and utilize ocean resources in a rational way.[26]

At the same time, the core of China's national strategy is to develop its economy. Therefore, diplomatic strategy and ocean strategy should serve this central task. Maritime delimitation and island sovereignty disputes are very important in a practical sense. They are related to the vital interests of a country, and every inch of land should be fought for. However, in the framework of the overall objective, it is necessary to avoid direct conflicts in order to maintain a peaceful and stable region and environment. In order to strive for a peaceful and stable environment for development, we must neither give up our claim to disputed sea areas and islands nor use force randomly. We should make full use of all kinds of "soft power," such as prestige, diplomatic tactics and skills, and cultural appeal, to deal with large and small maritime frictions and challenges in line with China's cultural tradition and diplomatic policy. We should seize the opportunity to use various international occasions to reiterate China's claims and regularly send maritime forces to patrol disputed waters and islands to enforce China's jurisdiction. At the same time, we will

---

[26] Professor Zhang Xinbao's speech at the symposium on the United Nations Convention on the Law of the Sea was quoted from Wang Xiuwei (2012). Legal thinking on China's ocean dispute settlement: A summary of the symposium on the United Nations Convention on the Law of the Sea, *China Legal Science*, 2012(6).

strengthen the modernization of the navy to protect our marine rights and interests, and effectively deter and restrain potential trouble. However, we should not forget the old Chinese adage that "the best way is to foil the enemy's plans, the next best is to use diplomacy, the following is to attack the enemy's forces, and the least desirable way is to assault the enemy's cities."

3.3.2.2 Carrying out cooperation between the Chinese mainland and Hong Kong SAR, Macao SAR, and the Taiwan region in safeguarding sovereignty over Diaoyu Dao

China's Taiwan region is an aspect that cannot be ignored in resolving the Diaoyu Dao issue. It is necessary to consider and give full play to the Taiwan region's positive role in resolving the Diaoyu Dao issue. In the white paper *Diaoyu Dao, an Inherent Territory of China*, China clearly points out that "Diaoyu Dao has been an inherent territory of China since ancient times. This is the common position of the entire Chinese nation."[27] Moreover, the Taiwan region has a common or similar position on the issue of the island's sovereignty dispute. People in Taiwan have always opposed Japan's attempt to grab Diaoyu Dao. Some scholars in the Taiwan region have done a lot of admirable work on how to safeguard the maritime rights and interests of the Chinese nation. While appreciating the Taiwan region's role in the Diaoyu Dao issue, China must also carefully and comprehensively evaluate the manner of sorting out the issue, what steps and measures to take, what benefits and negative effects it may have on the settlement of other disputes, and what impact it can have on cross-strait relations.

Hong Kong SAR civilians have always played a very special role in defending the Diaoyu Dao territory and have rich experience in "safeguarding Diaoyu Dao." The escalation of the Diaoyu Dao issue has created a potential opportunity for cooperation between the Chinese mainland, the Taiwan region, and Hong Kong SAR, and has given Chinese people at home and abroad an incentive to unite. Full attention

---

[27] State Council Information Office of the People's Republic of China (September 2012). *Diaoyu Dao, an Inherent Territory of China*, http://www.gov.cn/jrzg/2012-09/25/Content_2232710.htm.

should be paid to the effective cooperation between the Chinese mainland, the Taiwan region, and Hong Kong SAR on the Diaoyu Dao issue, including holding regular academic conferences to discuss the issue and coordination and cooperation among non-governmental activists.

3.3.2.3 Strengthening the publicity of opinions at home and abroad and taking the high ground in legal and moral principles

Japan's plot to steal Diaoyu Dao is a serious challenge to the post-war international order and a blatant denial of the victory of World War II. We should make full use of historical and legal evidence, strive for recognition of public opinion in the international community, and occupy a higher legal and moral position. On September 25, 2012, China published a white paper entitled *Diaoyu Dao, an inherent Territory of China*, which comprehensively and systematically expounded the position of the Chinese government on the Diaoyu Dao issue. We should take this as a benchmark and publicize such opinions at home and abroad.[28] Japan frequently and arbitrarily takes unilateral actions on Diaoyu Dao. It refuses to recognize the objective existence of the Diaoyu Dao issue, ignores the obligations of the UN Charter and the UN Convention on the Law of the Sea, and refuses to sit down with China for negotiations. It forces China to take corresponding countermeasures, thus escalating the conflict between the two sides over the Diaoyu Dao issue on both official and private levels. It can be predicted that if Japan continues to stick to its erroneous position and does not recognize the objective existence of the Diaoyu Dao issue, it will not be possible to resolve the issue through negotiations with China, and the conflict between the two sides will not cease. China will be forced to take action and wage counterattacks against Japan. Japan must bear national responsibility for such a situation and its possible consequences. Therefore, it is a more rational choice to face up to reality, respect history and facts, abide by the UN Charter's obligation to settle disputes peacefully, earnestly implement the UN Convention on

---

[28] Wang Xiuwei (2012). Legal thinking on settling China's maritime boundary disputes: A summary of the symposium on the United Nations Convention on the Law of the Sea, *China Legal Science*, 2012(6).

the law of the Sea's obligations regarding transitional arrangements and restraint from unilateral actions, and seek peaceful methods to resolve differences and effectively control disputes.

3.4 China's Strategy and Countermeasures for Resolving the China–Japan Disputes Over Maritime Rights and Interests in the East China Sea

The maritime rights dispute between China and Japan mainly refers to the delimitation of the exclusive economic zone between the two sides in the East China Sea. The exclusive economic zones of China and Japan overlap on the East China Sea. China and Japan have big differences on how to divide the exclusive economic zones of the East China Sea. According to the UN Convention on the Law of the Sea, China advocates the delimitation of the exclusive economic zone between China and Japan based on the principle of the natural extension of the mainland on the seabed. The Japanese government adheres to the principle of the equidistant median line. Because the East China Sea has important economic, resource, transportation, security, and strategic values, it is difficult for China and Japan to resolve this dispute.

3.4.1 An international law basis for resolving the China–Japan disputes over maritime rights and interests in the East China Sea

The dispute between China and Japan over the delimitation of the East China Sea first involves the interpretation and application of the UNCLOS. Considering the complexity of the delimitation of the exclusive economic zone, the UNCLOS provides two ways to solve the problem, namely, the principle of fairness and the principle of the equidistant medium line. This dispute between China and Japan stems from differences in the application and interpretation of the UNCLOS.

In the process of drafting the UNCLOS, there were big differences in the delimitation method of the exclusive economic zone. In principle, two opposing voices have emerged in the delimitation of exclusive economic zones between neighboring countries or countries in opposite direction. The first advocates delimitation according to the "principle of fairness" and the other advocates delimitation according to the "principle of the equidistant median line." These two opposing voices reflect the status of each sovereign country in pursuit of maximum national benefit. "The group of countries that adhere to the 'principle of fairness' as the demarcation standard believes that the 'equidistance rule' has become a rule of international law and lacks legal certainty. They cite the 1969 adjudication of the International Court of Justice in the North Sea Continental Shelf case to reinforce this conclusion." However, the "equidistance" group has extensively quoted state practice to prove the fairness of the equidistance method and criticized the "principle of fairness" as the "principle without principle." Once a dispute arises, there will be no uniform standard for fairness among all parties.[29] In order to obtain maximum recognition among the involved parties, in 1982, the UNCLOS adopted a compromise and vague expressions on many issues. Therefore, the final specific rules for delimitation of exclusive economic zones and the continental shelf have become a product of mutual compromise.

The eclectic expression of "fair settlement" can be interpreted as fairness of results or fairness of means. It caters to the countries that advocate the "principle of fairness" and the countries that advocate "equal distance and equal distribution." Due to the vagueness in the terms of "fair settlement," it has become a legal expression acceptable to all countries. The gap created by the system in pursuit of universal applicability has led to a tendency of each claimant country to maximize its own rights and interests in the legal understanding of the specific application. This has also laid a difficult-to-clarify discourse symbol crisis for all parties to the dispute in the future.

Judging from the current practical problems in the dispute over the delimitation of the East China Sea, it is a clear case of "one law, two interpretations" based on the UNCLOS documents, and China and Japan have been unable to reach legal and political consensus. In order to gain national interest in the zero-sum game to the maximum extent, each country accepts the principle of fairness as the most favorable division method for itself and interprets the proposal of the other party as

---

[29] Li Huiling (2005). *The Continental Shelf Dispute of China-Japan in East China Sea and the Prospect under International Law*, Shaanxi Normal University, Master Thesis, p. 12.

contrary to the principle of fairness. This has become an important reason why sea law is not effective in solving specific problems. If each party to the dispute believes that it has an absolute moral and legal basis, then the conflict brought about by this concept will be more difficult to reconcile.

Japan believes that the Okinawa Trough, with a depth of 2,700 meters, is only an accidental depression of the continental shelf in the East China Sea. The real continental shelf in the East China Sea is located in the Mariana Trough, with a depth of 11,035 meters, west of the Japanese archipelago and at the junction of the Pacific and Eurasian plates. Therefore, according to Japan, China and Japan, as two countries in opposite directions and with a common continental shelf, should stipulate the following in accordance with articles 74 and 83, paragraph 1, of the UNCLOS: "the delimitation of the exclusive economic zones of countries with opposite coasts or neighboring countries shall be determined by agreement on the basis of international law referred to in article 38 of the statute of the international court of justice, so as to achieve a fair solution."[30] This fairness mainly refers to the average division of sea area through the principle of "equidistant median line."

However, it is worth noting that the dividing method of "equidistant offline" is only ideal when the coasts of the two opposite countries are straight. In reality, the coastlines between a vast majority of countries are uneven. On the delimitation of the continental shelf between Germany and the Netherlands, and Germany and Denmark in the North Sea, the presiding judge ruled on the median line method in his judgment. The equidistant method is not a mandatory rule of customary law. In the case of the North Sea, it would be unfair to simply demarcate the boundary according to the equidistant method regardless of the geographical environment, thus resulting in simplification on the surface. Therefore, Germany has no obligation to accept the equidistance rule. Delimitation means to "adopt an agreement, in accordance with the principle of fairness, and taking into account all relevant circumstances so that each country can obtain as much as possible all parts of the continental shelf that constitute the natural extension of its land territory,

---

[30] The 1982 United Nations Convention on the Law of the Sea, website of the East China Sea Branch of the State Oceanic Administration, http://www.eastsea.gov.cn/Module/Show,aspx? Id=1452 (received online on July 20, 2015).

and not encroach on the natural extension of another country's land territory."[31]

China maintains that although China and Japan are facing each other as coastal countries, they do not share continental shelves due to the barrier of the Okinawa Trough. Therefore, in the delimitation of the exclusive economic zone in the East China Sea, the principle of "natural extension of the continental shelf" should be adopted in accordance with Article 76, Paragraph 5, of the UNCLOS,[32] and China's marine rights and interests should be extended to the Okinawa Trough. In addition, China believes that the coastline on the Chinese side (including Taiwan region) is 748 kilometers long in the demarcated sea area, while the coastline of Japan's Ryukyu Islands facing the East China Sea is 415 kilometers long,[33] with a ratio of 1.8:1. According to the international legal precedent of the 1984 Gulf of Maine case, although the ratio of coastline length between the United States and Canada is only 1.32:1, the International Court of Justice still believed that this difference was of "undeniable importance. This provided a legal basis for the amendment of the third-step equivalence distance line," and thus the final amendment of the intermediate line was adjusted in favor of the United States.[34] Therefore, it is certain that even if the division method of the median line is finally submitted to the UN Ocean Court, it will not completely divide the disputed sea area evenly, but will provide a revision based on the proportion of coastline length.

---

[31] The Teaching Center of Law Experimental Practice of Renmin University of China: North Sea Continental Shelf Case-Principle of Delimitation of Continental Shelf, http://www.law.ruc.edu.cn/lab/ShowArticle.asp?ArticleID=16448 (received online on July 20, 2015).

[32] The article of the Convention stipulates the following: "The fixed points comprising the line of the outer limits of the continental shelf on the seabed, drawn in accordance with paragraph 4 (a)(i) and (ii), either shall not exceed 350 nautical miles from the baselines from which the breadth of the territorial sea is measured or shall not exceed 100 nautical miles from the 2,500 metre isobath, which is a line connecting the depth of 2,500 metres."

[33] Gao Jianjun (2006). China-Japan dispute over demarcation of East China Sea from the perspective of International Law: Also on irrationality of Japan's proposition, *Global Legal Review*, 2006(6).

[34] The Teaching Center of Law Experimental Practice of Renmin University of China: Maritime Region Delimitation in Gulf of Maine: Single Maritime Delimitation, http://www.law.ruc.edu.cn/lab/ShowArticle.asp? ArticleIID=16449 (received online on July 20, 2015).

3.4.2 China's strategic thinking on resolving China–Japan disputes over maritime rights and interests in the East China Sea

China and Japan are important neighbors, and both are powers in Northeast Asia. The demarcation of the East China Sea reflects the structural conflict between China and Japan. Therefore, we should not only consider and plan from the perspective of international law but also China's grand strategy, so as to achieve overall consideration and comprehensive implementation. In terms of strategy, China's policy choice in the dispute over maritime rights and interests between China and Japan in the East China Sea should be subordinated to its overall maritime strategy, which should be planned with the aim of peaceful development. At present, China and Japan cannot find a mutually acceptable solution to the delimitation of the East China Sea in the short term. An acceptable solution will weaken the negative impact of the dispute on China–Japan relations. The urgency and importance of replacing the original thorny issue with new topics of cooperation and revenue expectations is also a customary way for international political functionalism to solve regional cooperation problems.

3.4.2.1 *Embedding ocean strategy into national grand strategy*

There is an irrefutable truth in Chinese chess culture: "Great wise men follow trends, and great fools seek one success." The East China Sea should be regarded as part of the marine strategy and the marine strategy as part of the overall strategy. The formulation of all strategies should be subject to the long-term, multi-level, and wide-range overall strategic deployment of China's rise.

Security and economic benefits are the primary interests pursued by a country. The dispute between China and Japan over the delimitation of the East China Sea includes both maritime delimitation and disputes over seabed oil and gas resources. It concerns not only China's national security interests but also its national economic interests. The dispute in the East China Sea has interwoven the issues of traditional territorial sea security and marine energy development, making it impossible for any single policy tool to achieve its objectives fully. For example, maritime delimitation disputes focus on the factual control of the territorial sea and exclusive economic zone, while the competition for marine energy development pays more attention to attaining an equal proportion of oil and gas resources. The "Emery Report" mentioned that there is a huge oil storage basin on the continental shelf in the East China Sea. It is located at the point where the line between China and Japan is equidistant. However, oil and gas resources are different from solid mineral resources, which are in a liquid state in the seabed oil basin. Under the "straw effect," the key to the problem becomes the competition between China and Japan in terms of marine exploitation capacity. Therefore, which policy tool or strategy choice is more appropriate can only be decided according to the actual situation.

Safeguarding China's maritime rights and interests is a necessary part of China's peaceful development strategy and it needs to be incorporated into China's long-term and overall development strategy. The path of China's peaceful development is not only a long and complicated process with vested interests in the international community but also a process of gradually approaching from the semi-core region to the core region of the international system. Therefore, the process of China's peaceful development should be regarded as a big game of interest. The deep-seated structural contradiction behind the maritime rights dispute between China and Japan requires us to not only believe that "time and history are on China's side" but also maintain sufficient restrain, to deal with the situation in an all-round way, plan for the overall situation, and to focus on the long term. As an important part of the country's overall development strategy, China's marine strategy aims to promote the orderly implementation of the overall strategic plan. The subordinate position of China's maritime strategy to the strategy of peaceful development also determines that China should adopt a more flexible and pragmatic attitude in negotiations with Japan.

3.4.2.2 Adhering to a pragmatic and flexible mutually beneficial cooperative strategy in the China–Japan dispute of maritime rights and interests

As a developing major power, China has undergone a highly unbalanced and long-term development, and it has to respond to many specific and complex challenges at home and abroad. A relatively peaceful and stable international environment is of considerable significance to China's sustainable development. The structural balance of power between China and Japan is difficult to change in the short term. Moreover, the trilateral power structure between China, the United States, and Japan is far from being conducive to China, and it is hard to imagine a negotiation result that is hugely beneficial to either side. Behind the dilemma of the current China–Japan maritime rights and interests dispute is a stalemate in power balance. China should have a lot of confidence based on its historical track record. Prudence and patience are the most precious assets for a country that is rising.

We should also realize that Japan is still a regional power in the political and economic fields, and the US–Japan alliance still has superiority power compared to China, which means that the China–Japan dispute in the East China Sea cannot reach a favorable outcome for China in the short term. A wise and prudent negotiation strategy should be phased. China should pay attention to the substantive results achieved in each phase and seek to realize its national marine rights and interests through joint development.

On the issue of joint exploitation of oil and gas resources in the East China Sea, both China and Japan have the capacity to exploit marine oil on a large scale. Realizing cooperative exploitation has become the key for both countries to resolve the development deadlock and achieve mutual benefit. After World War II, the North Sea cooperation model of European countries was used as a reference in the East China Sea. However, the submarine topography in the North Sea region is more complicated than that in the East China Sea and Norway's open sea has deep trenches. Under the premise of mutual political understanding and trust among countries surrounding the North Sea, not only has the border demarcation problem been solved but "North Sea Brent crude oil" jointly produced by the five North Sea countries has also gained the second-largest share, which affects the international crude oil futures price more than West Texas light crude oil from the United States.

In June 2008, China and Japan reached a historic China–Japan Consensus of Principles on the East China Sea Issue, which divides 2,700 square kilometers of common development zone in the waters 30 degrees north latitude and 126 degrees east longitude. Although this is a small step in the history of China–Japan maritime cooperation, it is undoubtedly a big step in the history of building a strategic and mutually beneficial relationship between China and Japan. If peace, stability, and cooperation in the East China Sea can be achieved through "win-win cooperation," Northeast Asia may form its own "North Sea Brent Cooperation Model."

3.4.2.3 Shifting the focus of relations among the regional countries through the Belt and Road Initiative

In September and October 2013, President Xi Jinping successively established initiatives to build the Silk Road Economic Belt and the 21st Century Maritime Silk Road. At present, the Belt and Road Initiative construction has won wide recognition and support from all countries across the world. In essence, the Belt and Road Initiative will transform border areas between countries from "marginal areas" within a country to "core areas" with development potential, enhance their spatial accessibility and power, and achieve the goal of mutual benefits for multiple parties.[35] Although Japan has refused to join the Belt and Road Initiative at present, as long as the strategic layout of the Belt and Road Initiative is formed in the region around East Asia, Japan must face huge economic opportunities and the challenge of missing opportunities after its refusal. Therefore, in this sense, Japan's attitude toward the Belt and Road Initiative is essentially opportunistic rather than rigid. As long as Japan recognizes the possibility of the two countries benefiting from the Belt and Road Initiative, it will give up its provocative attitude toward maritime rights and interests based on realistic considerations and seek active cooperation with the Chinese government. This enables the Northeast Asian region to solve disputes and develop together.

With the implementation of the Belt and Road Initiative, China can break the political and security deadlock between China and Japan through subregional economic cooperation. By promoting regional economic integration in Northeast Asia, Japan's political right deviation and its path to military power are restricted within a multilateral framework covering all countries in Northeast Asia. China's northeast region has established close economic ties with Japan. Through this subregional cooperation, we can change our focus, increase the points of agreement,

---

[35] Liu Sisi (2014). Belt and road: New paths in research on theories of cross border subregional cooperation, *South Asian Studies*, 2014(2).

and introduce China–Japan relations into the development of "mutually beneficial cooperation." This will ease the current political dilemma facing China and Japan, make the maritime dispute between China and Japan lose its original security connotation, enhance the spillover function of the China–Japan regional cooperation network system, and lay a foundation for a reasonable solution to the maritime rights dispute between China and Japan.

Chapter 4

Energy Security in Northeast Asia and China's Energy Cooperation Policy

With the development of economic globalization, energy production, transportation, supply, and consumption are increasingly becoming international. National energy security is now closely linked with the regional and global energy environment. Energy security in this era is different from that of any period in human history and has acquired new connotations. The economic prosperity and development of the countries in Northeast Asia has made it an irreversible trend of the times to maintain peace and stability, promote development and prosperity, and achieve mutual benefit and mutual beneficial results. The continuously improving regional environment has injected a strong impetus into all-round cooperation among countries. However, affected by the long-standing problems left over from the Cold War and territorial issues, the countries in Northeast Asia are still in a state of "doing things in its own way" in the field of energy security, and the energy cooperation in Northeast Asia is still at the primary stage of development. The Belt and Road Initiative put forward by the Chinese government has created a new platform for cooperation in the Tumen River region and even the entire Northeast Asian region. Energy projects can determine the future development direction of cooperation, creating the necessary objective environment for improving regional energy security and transportation infrastructure. Whether Northeast Asian countries can find a convergence of interests in energy cooperation at this new historical starting point remains to be seen.

4.1 Energy Security Situation and Energy Strategy of the Northeast Asian Countries

China, Japan, and the ROK in Northeast Asia are big energy-consuming countries, but their energy resources are very scarce. At present, oil and gas imports in Northeast Asia mainly come from the Middle East, relying on sea transportation through the Strait of Hormuz and the Strait of Malacca, which poses great security risks. Russia, which is part of Northeast Asia, is a major energy producer and exporter in the world. However, Russia's energy export capacity to the Northeast Asian countries is very limited, and it cannot become a major supplier of regional energy markets. There is no stable energy cooperation mechanism in Northeast Asia. With the rapid economic development of the countries in Northeast Asia, the energy consumption and import scale will continue to increase, causing a complicated energy security situation in the region.

According to BP's 2014 World Energy Statistics Yearbook, China is the world's largest energy consumer. The oil consumption in 2013 was 507.4 million tons, ranking second in the world. The natural gas consumption was 145.5 million tons of oil equivalent, ranking fourth in the world. The coal consumption was 1.9253 billion tons of oil equivalent, ranking first in the world, and the total energy consumption ranked first in the world.[1] China's net oil imports reached 341.7 million tons in 2013. Japan is a traditional energy importer, with 223.7 million tons of oil imported in 2013. The ROK is 100% dependent on imported oil, with 108.4 million tons of oil imported in 2013. In 2013, China, Japan, and the ROK accounted for 19.7% of the world's oil consumption and 59% of the total oil consumption in the Asia-Pacific region. Japan, the ROK, and China's Taiwan region are the most important liquefied natural gas (LNG) markets in the Asia-Pacific region and the world. After the financial crisis broke out in 2008, Russia's energy exports began to tilt toward countries in Northeast Asia. After the Ukraine crisis, the West imposed comprehensive sanctions on Russia. Due to the need for economic security, the focus of Russia's energy development strategy began to shift to the Asia-Pacific

---

[1] BP. *BP Statistics Review of World Energy 2014*, June 2014. http://www.bp.com/con-tent/dam/bp/pdf/Energy-economics/statistical-review-2014/BP-statistical-review-of-world-energy-2014-full-report.pdf.

region, and energy cooperation between Russia and countries in Northeast Asia grew.

4.1.1 Russia's energy security situation and energy strategy

After the global financial and economic crisis in 2008, great changes have taken place in the global energy market and energy pattern, with Europe's economy shrinking and energy consumption declining. The Asia-Pacific region had sustained economic development. Northeast Asia became the most dynamic region in the world. The world energy consumption market turned to the Asia-Pacific region. At this time, Russia faced a major economic impact due to the complicated energy situation at home and abroad. For Russia, the European energy security environment became more and more complex. All the external factors that affect energy exports were sending negative signals to Russia: the decline in demand, the price formation mechanism, and the diversified adjustment of EU countries' energy policies. Russia's energy security situation urgently called for the establishment of a diversified energy export market.

Europe is Russia's traditional energy market. Since 2000, Russia had been committed to opening up new oil and gas pipelines to Europe. Due to the impact of the Ukrainian crisis, Russia decided to abandon the South Stream natural gas pipeline construction plan, which has had a huge impact on Russia's existing energy strategy. However, expanding oil and gas exports with Türkiye cannot offset the losses in the European market. Türkiye has been seeking to join the EU for many years, making the relationship between Russia and Türkiye more uncertain. Russia has regarded Türkiye as its sales market and transit country, which is not optimistic in terms of market size and political risk assessment. Under the multiple pressures of falling oil prices worldwide, devaluation of the ruble, and western sanctions, Russia's oil and gas exports to Europe faced increased political risks. Coupled with the EU sanctions on Russia, Russian energy companies were facing difficulties in both capital and technology.

Crazy fluctuations in international energy prices posed a great threat to Russia's energy security. For Russia, a big country that relies heavily on energy exports, energy price security is a complex concept. High oil prices caused by price fluctuations are as bad for Russia's economic development as low oil prices. The reason is that Russia's energy security is not a simple economic indicator, nor is it the simple income from energy transactions.

It is the sign to show whether Russia's economic security and economic structure are arranged in the right way. Before the US subprime mortgage crisis broke out, international oil prices basically maintained an upward trend for ten years. OPEC's oil price package hit the record high of US$140.73 per barrel on July 3, 2008. The sharp rise in oil prices enabled Russia to obtain a real energy price dividend and overcome the economic and social crisis caused by the disintegration of the Soviet Union and economic transformation. From 2004 to 2008, Russia's GDP growth was 7.1%, 6.4%, 6.8%, 8.1%, and 6.0%, respectively. The government's fiscal revenue grew exponentially, the purchasing power of the people greatly increased, and investment and consumption in the economic field increased rapidly. However, the rise in international oil prices also had some negative effects on Russia's economy, posing a threat to its sustainable and stable development. Firstly, the rise in oil prices led to an increase in the prices of domestic production factors and commodities, triggering inflation. With the economic recovery, the inflation problem in Russia was not effectively controlled. Secondly, during the period of rising international oil prices, the energy sector expanded rapidly, the reallocation of production factors in the domestic economic structure could not be completed in a short period of time, and a balanced development of various production sectors was not established. Thirdly, the increase in the country's foreign exchange income led to an appreciation of the ruble, which reduced the competitiveness of Russia's manufacturing industry, with imported products flooding the Russian market, and nearly one-third of the goods in Russia's consumption system needing to be imported from foreign countries. Fourthly, the huge profits brought about by high international oil prices caused inefficient development of Russia's economic production. Contradictions among all social strata are increasing. The high oil prices didn't bring about real economic development to Russia. When the financial crisis broke out in 2008, Russia's GDP immediately showed a negative growth of 1.3% in the fourth quarter of that year and remained negative throughout 2009. Although it maintained a 3–5% growth rate from 2010 to 2013, it still did not return to its pre-crisis development level.

The international energy price dropped sharply in 2014, and the Russian ruble fell sharply due to the energy market and geopolitical factors. The risk of inflation in Russia was accelerating, which led to an overall rise in prices. The fragility of Russia's economy was fully exposed. According to data released by the International Monetary Fund, Russia's

GDP fell by 3.7% in the 2015.[2] This was the first time in nearly five years that Russia's economy was facing negative growth. One of the main reasons for Russia's recession was the decline in international oil prices and the "linkage" between oil prices and the ruble exchange rate. In the 2014 fiscal budget of the Russian Federation, oil and gas exports were Russia's main source of foreign exchange revenue and budget funds, accounting for 48% of the total fiscal revenue. To a large extent, the ruble was equivalent to petroleum currencies. Due to a lack of confidence in Russia's overall economic situation, a large amount of foreign capital fled the Russian market, and the Russian ruble exchange rate continuously hit a record low, falling by about 60% against the US dollar in 2014. As far as Russia's real economic structure was concerned, international oil prices bottoming out had a decisive impact on Russia's economic prospects. Relying on other domestic industries to compensate for energy industry losses was unlikely to reverse the economic situation. Moreover, Russia's domestic fuel and energy complex had problems such as aging equipment, relatively backward science and technology, regions with unbalanced investment, and the need to focus on developing energy-saving technologies and deep processing of primary energy resources. In terms of energy exports, Russia's traditional energy market, especially the EU, grew slowly or even stagnated. Competition in key global energy markets was fierce, energy markets were extremely unstable, globalization of resources was making a transition to regional self-sufficiency, and energy prices fluctuated dramatically.[3] Based on these problems, Russia's energy strategy underwent major adjustments.

In 2010, the Russian government adjusted the Natural Gas Development Plan in Eastern Russia issued in 2007 and the Overall Layout Plan of Electric Energy Facilities Before 2020 issued in 2008, extending the planning period to 2030 and continuing various strategic indicators and priority development directions. In 2011, Russia formulated the Overall Development Plan of the Natural Gas Industry by 2030, the Overall Development Plan of the Russian Oil Industry by 2020, the Overall Development Plan of the Russian Coal Industry by 2030, and

---

[2] International Monetary Fund, *World Economic Outlook Database, April 2016*, April 12, 2016, http://www.imf.org/external/pubs/ft/weo/2016/01/weodata/index.aspx.
[3] Report of Russian Academy of Science (on long term development of Russian gas industry). http://www.energystrategy.ru/ab...ins/source/Bushuev_ES-2035-17.02.14.pdf.

Comprehensive Development Plan of Electric Energy in the Far Eastern Federal District of Russia by 2025. These energy development plans all defined the energy market in Northeast Asia as an important direction for Russia's energy export in the future and proposed to develop resources in eastern Russia. Russia began to promote energy cooperation with China, Japan, the ROK, and other major energy-consuming countries. Since energy projects are long-term strategic investments, Russia's energy cooperation with Northeast Asian countries is mostly at the stage of project negotiation and infrastructure construction, and the specific trade cooperation indicators cannot be compared with those of Europe. However, the China–Russia oil pipeline project has become a landmark strategic move, marking the fact that Russia's diversified energy strategy has entered the Asia-Pacific development stage. Countries in Northeast Asia will become Russia's most direct and geographically advantageous partners.

In 2014, the Russian Energy Strategy Research Institute formulated a draft of Russia's Energy Development Strategy by 2035 and submitted it to the Ministry of Energy for consideration. If the draft is implemented, energy development in eastern Russia and energy cooperation in the Asia-Pacific region will enter a new all-round development stage. The draft of Russia's Energy Development Strategy by 2035 proposes that the national energy policy be changed from a resource-based material type to a resource-based innovation type. The focus of Russia's energy strategy will no longer be the increase of quantity, but the quality of the energy consumption structure, such as improving energy services, developing energy-saving technologies, and developing high value-added industries such as electricity and petrochemicals.

For the Russian economy, the fuel energy complex is no longer a "blood supplier" or an "engine," but the condition for the infrastructure development, the guarantee of energy integration and comprehensive development of energy in various regions, and finally the supporter of the establishment of energy clusters and the realization of electrification in the country. Meanwhile, Russia is focusing on realizing the infrastructure synergy effect of fuel–energy complex in energy investment and innovation and the diversification of LNG production and energy exports (in the east). Professor Stapran (Н. Стапран) of Moscow Institute of International Relations stated that "according to the data available, the Asia-Pacific region will become the locomotive driving the growth of world demand for oil and natural gas by 2020. Once the center of gravity shifts from the west to the east, hydrocarbon compound suppliers will fully seize the Asian continent."[4] The draft of *Russia's* Energy Development Strategy by 2035 sets the Asia-Pacific region as the priority direction for Russia's foreign energy strategy in the next 20 years. It has set development goals and tasks for the construction of energy bases in eastern Russia and the establishment of an energy export network oriented toward Northeast Asia. In 2015, the G7 decided to continue to impose sanctions on Russia due to which Russia will not be able to obtain funds and technology from western countries. Russia needs Northeast Asian countries, especially China, the ROK, and Japan, which have financial and technological advantages, to participate in energy development in the east. In the process of implementing Russia's national energy strategy, the cooperation of Northeast Asian countries has become indispensable. Promoting energy cooperation in Northeast Asia has become the key to ensuring Russia's energy security and realizing Russia's energy development strategy.

4.1.2 Japan's energy security situation and energy strategy

Japan is a country with extremely poor oil and gas resources. Due to its low energy self-sufficiency, the energy security situation is very fragile. According to BP Statistics Review of World Energy 2014, the imbalance in Japan's energy reserves, production, and consumption is very serious. Japan's oil, natural gas, and coal resources are almost negligible for its economic scale. Its oil and natural gas resources are completely imported, and its coal output is less than 1% of its consumption. After the Fukushima nuclear accident, almost all production in Japan's nuclear system ceased. Compared with 2012, Japan's nuclear energy decreased by 18.6% in 2013 (see Table 4.1).

Solving the contradiction between the shortage of energy resources and energy consumption has always been the aim of the Japanese government in terms of adjusting its energy structure. In 1973, oil accounted for 75.5% of Japan's primary energy supply. As Japan accelerated the utilization of nuclear power, natural gas, and coal and the development of new energy sources, in 2009, the proportion of oil in the primary energy supply

---

[4] Russia is exporting energy to Asia. http://russiancouncil.ru/inner/?id4=3016#top.

Table 4.1. Energy production, consumption, and reserve in Japan in 2013.

Item	Petroleum	Natural gas	Coal	Nuclear energy	New energy
Reserve	—	—	337 million tons	—	—
Production	—	—	700,000 tons of oil equivalent	—	—
Consumption	208.9 million tons	116.9 billion cubic meters	129 million tons of oil equivalent	3.3 million tons of oil equivalent	9.4 million tons of oil equivalent
Proportion of world consumption	5.0%	3.5%	3.4%	0.6%	3.4%
Annual growth	−3.8%	0.2%	3.6%	−18.6%	15.9%

Source: BP Statistics Review of World Energy 2014, June 2014. http://www.bp.com/cont-ent/dam/bp/pdf/energy-economics/statistics-review-2014/bp-statistics-review-of-world-energy-2014-full-report,pdf.

decreased to 42.1%, and the proportion of coal (21.0%), natural gas (19.0%), and nuclear power (11.5%) as alternative energy sources for oil continued to increase, gradually diversifying its energy supply. After the earthquake in Japan and the Fukushima Daiichi nuclear power plant accident, the proportion of nuclear power decreased. In 2013, the proportion of oil in the primary energy supply was 45.6%, coal 26.0%, natural gas 22%, and nuclear power down to 0.85%.

Due to the effective implementation of energy-saving measures and the comprehensive influence of economic growth factors, Japan's energy consumption growth is relatively slow. Japan's oil consumption dropped year by year, to 209 million tons in 2013, with an annual growth rate of −3.8%. Total primary energy consumption increased from 360 million tons in 1980 to 520 million tons in 2007, with an average annual growth rate of only 1.6%. In 2010, the consumption hit 500 million tons of oil equivalent. From 2003 to 2013, the world's oil consumption increased by 13.9%, but Japan's oil consumption increased by −16.7%, from 5.456 million barrels per day in 2003 to 4.551 million barrels per day in 2013.[5] As a result, Japan's share of global oil imports is declining. However, Japan's natural gas consumption has been on the rise, increasing 27.8 times (from 3.4 billion cubic meters to 94.5 billion cubic meters) from 1970 to 2010. Japan's natural gas consumption increased to 116.9 billion cubic meters in 2013,[6] and Japan's absolute imports of LNG will increase in the future. However, Japan's relative market share will decrease because the import volume of other countries is growing faster than that of Japan. Japan is quite different from the United States and Europe in its use of natural gas. Japan can only import natural gas in the form of LNG, and mainly uses that to generate power to meet concentrated demands and to supply to urban gas companies of a certain scale. Japan has formed a unique infrastructure development pattern, that is, to build LNG bases in regions with natural gas demand, and then transport them from the bases with pipelines as needed.

Japan is the world's largest importer of coal. Japan's coal imports exceeded its domestic coal production in 1970, exceeded 100 million tons in 1988, and reached 190 million tons in 2012, exceeding 99% of Japan's total coal consumption and accounting for 24% of the world's coal trade. That number included 60 million tons of coking coal imported mainly from Australia, Canada, the United States, China, Russia, and South Africa and 90 million tons of thermal coal imported mainly from Australia, China, the United States, South Africa, Canada, and Russia.

Although uranium for nuclear power in Japan is also imported from abroad, it is a "quasi-domestic energy" with less dependence due to its high energy density and easy storage, and the used fuel can be reused as fuel through secondary treatment. According to Japan's comprehensive energy statistics, its energy self-sufficiency rate was 18% in 2008 and 7% in 2009. After the nuclear leak accident, Japan's nuclear energy supply rate greatly decreased.

In order to ensure the safety of energy supply, Japan has implemented a strategy of diversification of energy supply. Due to the expansion of Japan's economy, the growth rate of its energy consumption is higher than the growth of its GDP. The development of the residential industry and commerce rapidly increases the consumption of civil energy. Japan has

---

[5] BP. *BP Statistics Review of World Energy 2014*, June 2014. http://www.bp.com/con-tent/dam/bp/pdf/Energy-economics/statistical-review-2014/BP-statistical-review-of-world-energy-2014-full-report.pdf.
[6] *Ibid.*

launched an active energy policy to reduce energy consumption while the economy grows, improve the energy utilization efficiency of the industrial sector, promote the development of energy-saving industries, and control the energy consumption of the transportation sector.

The diversification strategy and energy conservation policy are the core values of Japan's energy policy. To ensure the security of the domestic energy supply, Japan gradually diversified the domestic energy supply and constantly adjusts its policy according to the different needs of different periods. After World War II, in order to meet the needs of post-war reconstruction, Japan gave priority to ensuring the increase of coal production by providing the necessary labor, capital, and materials, and realizing economic revival through an integrated coal production system.

After the arrival of the period of high economic growth (1962–1972), Japan shifted its energy supply from coal to oil and implemented the "oil-based, coal-supplemented" policy. In 1962, oil surpassed coal as the first category of energy supply. Japan then established the industrial structure of coal to ensure a stable supply of oil and adhere to the principle of purifying and processing imported oil at the place of consumption. The government supervised the oil-processing capacity and oil production plan. The world's first oil crisis occurred in 1973, which had a great impact on Japan, whose dependence on oil exceeded 70%. In order to cope with the crisis, the Japanese government set up an "emergency headquarters to stabilize national life." The Japanese Cabinet approved the Outline of Emergency Oil Countermeasures, formulated Law on Optimization of Oil Supply and Demand and the Law on Emergency Measures to Stabilize National Life, and launched a large-scale campaign to reduce energy consumption. In 1974, the United States, Japan, and other major oil-consuming countries formed the "Energy Coordination Group" and the "International Energy Agency" (IEA), and passed the International Energy Program Agreement (IEP), which stipulated the establishment of emergency oil reserves. The agreement required all countries to have no less than 90 days of net oil imports in the previous year and set out urgent measures to reduce oil consumption. After the oil crisis, Japan attached great importance to energy supply, regarded safeguarding supply as an extremely important policy for the country's future development, and took necessary measures to reduce dependence on oil and diversify energy sources, ensuring a stable supply of oil, promoting energy conservation, and researching and developing new energy sources. The research and development of new energy sources was regarded as a long-term task.

After the second oil crisis, Japan optimized its energy supply structure while ensuring a stable energy supply. The goal of "alternative energy supply" was set in 1980 through the Alternative Energy Law. In order to promote the all-round development of oil alternative energy technology, an administrative agency called the New Energy and Industrial Technology Development Organization (NEDO) was established. At the same time, the energy conservation legislation was further strengthened and a comprehensive energy conservation policy was promoted. In 1979, the Law on Rational Use of Energy (Energy Conservation Law) was enacted to promote overall energy conservation in the fields of construction and machinery. The "Moonlight Plan" was launched in 1978 to improve energy conversion efficiency and develop energy recovery and utilization technologies. The government subsidized the research and promotion of energy-saving technologies, reaching a world-class level of energy efficiency.

Japan attaches great importance to improving laws and implementing long-term and comprehensive plans and measures. In October 2003, the Japanese government put forward the "basic energy plan." The first revision was made in March 2007, mainly to deal with global warming, expand the development of new energy sources, actively promote nuclear power, ensure a stable supply of oil and other energy sources, and strengthen energy conservation. In June 2010, Japan carried out the second revision. Its main contents include the following:

Firstly, Japan adjusted and optimized the energy structure and vigorously developed and utilized renewable energy. Japan's renewable energy technology has reached a high level and the government has been promoting the development of new energy sources, such as solar energy, wind energy, and biomass energy. The Japanese government has also developed and promoted clean energy vehicles and fuel cells as "innovative high-performance energy utilization technologies" that help expand new energy sources. They help to diversify energy sources and prevent global warming. Renewable energy, represented by solar cells, has great development potential and will promote economic development. It can also bring into play the independent creativity of various regions, and even citizens can participate in the energy supply. At present, there are still problems with unstable power generation and high cost, which need further development of battery and other technologies.

Secondly, Japan established an oil reserve system. At a meeting of oil-consuming countries held in February 1974, at the initiative of the

United States, major oil-consuming countries including Japan established the "Energy Coordination Group (ECG)" and in the same year passed the International Energy Plan Agreement (IEP) and established the "IEA" under the Organization for Economic Cooperation and Development (OECD). To strengthen the energy self-sufficiency and emergency response capability of member countries, the International Energy Plan (IEP) required member countries to maintain oil reserves equivalent to their net imports of 90 days in the previous year and established an emergency oil-sharing mechanism including consumption reduction measures. In the 1970s, there were two oil crises, which the IEA member countries tackled and increased the oil reserves. In the 1980s, the national reserves adopted by Japan and other countries and the public oil reserves, such as the association reserves adopted by Germany and France, were further strengthened. As of the end of 2010, IEA member countries (only net importers) had an average of 146 days of net imported oil reserves.

Before the big earthquake in Japan and the Fukushima Daiichi nuclear power plant leakage accident, Japan has been wanting to establish an energy society with decreasing dependence on "nuclear energy," hoping to ensure a stable supply of energy and solve environmental protection problems as well. After the earthquake in Japan, the Japanese Minister of Economy and Industry Kaeda said that the accident had shaken the foundation of Japan's energy policy. In order to study the basic direction of energy policy, Japan held an "expert meeting on future energy policy" on May 12, 2011. At the G8 Deauville Summit held on May 26–27, 2011, then Japanese Prime Minister Naoto Kan made a speech on the energy policy, pointing out that Japan should develop another two pillars of "natural gas energy" and "energy conservation" based on the two existing pillars of "nuclear energy" and "fossil energy" for the future.

Since then, Japan's energy strategy has undergone another transformation, which is reflected in the following aspects: The first is that the economy and society will get rid of the dependence on nuclear power and strictly abide by the 40-year restriction on the operation of existing nuclear facilities. The operation of existing nuclear facilities must be confirmed by the Nuclear Regulatory Commission. In addition, it is proposed not to build or expand nuclear power plants. The second is to complete the clean energy revolution. Japan wants to make clean energy its main power source, relying on technological innovation and policy guidance to promote the clean energy revolution. Japan has formulated a series of specific quantitative indicators. In terms of electricity and energy saving, Japan wants to realize the goal of reducing electricity consumption by more than 110 billion kwh and energy consumption by more than 72 million tons of oil equivalent by 2030 compared with 2010 through equipment renewal, technological revolution, research and development of new heat insulation materials, intelligent energy saving, renewable energy utilization, and other means. The third is to ensure a stable supply of energy. At present, stable and cheap fossil fuel is important for Japan's economy and society, and the importance of coal-fired power generation is increasing day by day. With the promotion of clean energy, the consumption of fossil fuels will be reduced. In terms of thermal power generation, Japan has the most advanced high-level environmental protection technology. Therefore, Japan needs to formulate a strategy that combines the promotion of international technology with economic growth. The fourth is to amend the Mining Law. The mining laws and regulations enacted shortly after World War II caused disorderly resource exploration activities. In order to ensure the rational management of domestic resources, Japan made the first amendment to Mining Law enacted in 1950. On January 21, 2012, amendments to Japan's Mining Law came into effect. The amendment to Mining Law added criteria to apply for mining rights and established a new procedure for the same.

Japan's energy policy pays more attention to energy cooperation with regional countries and proposes an "innovative energy environment strategy," focusing on the development of new energy sources. Japan's Ministry of Economy, Trade, and Industry put forward in its Energy Supply and Demand Outlook 2030 that Japan's energy security strategy must be based on the growth of energy demand in Asia. Japan should establish a long-term energy cooperation mechanism with Asian countries to promote the transformation of Japan's energy strategy from "one country" to "the whole region." Japan believes that China is the largest demand country with the fastest growth in energy demand and China's energy demand has already posed great competitive pressure on Japan. Yet Japan also thinks that if the competition between the two major energy-consuming countries is too fierce, then Japan will have little choice when faced with the pressure from the energy exporting countries united as group, and this will be favorable to its won energy strategy. It is from this perspective that Japan also actively advocates multilateral energy cooperation with neighboring energy-consuming countries in order to better deal with energy suppliers.

4.1.3 The ROK's energy security situation and energy strategy

The ROK is a country with very poor oil and gas resources. Its energy consumption mainly depends on imports, and its dependence on international oil and natural gas is very high. There is a huge gap between the reserves, production, and actual consumption of oil, natural gas, coal, and nuclear energy in the ROK (see Table 4.2).

Since the late 1980s, the ROK's energy consumption growth rate has increased significantly. The ROK's primary energy consumption increased from 38 million tons of oil equivalent in 1980 to 270 million tons of oil equivalent in 2012, ranking eighth in the world. The ROK's energy consumption mainly depends on oil, coal, and natural gas. From 1980 to 2012, the consumption of oil increased from 2.41 billion tons to 10.88 billion tons, but the share of oil in energy consumption decreased from 61.1% to 40.1% and decreased by another 40 million tons in 2013. In 2014, the ROK ranked ninth in the world in oil consumption. Coal consumption increased from 13.2 million tons of oil equivalent to 81.6 million tons of oil equivalent, but its share also decreased. The

Table 4.2. Energy production, consumption, and reserves in the ROK in 2013.

Item	Petroleum	Natural gas	Coal	Nuclear energy	New energy
Reserves	—	—	126 million tons	—	—
Production	—	—	800,000 tons of oil equivalent	—	—
Consumption	108.4 million tons	52.5 billion cubic meters	81.9 million tons of oil equivalent	31.4 million tons of oil equivalent	1 million tons of oil equivalent
Proportion of world consumption	2.6%	1.6%	2.1%	5.6%	0.4%
Annual rate of growth	<0.05%	4.9%	1.4%	−7.4%	18.1%

Source: BP Statistics Review of World Energy 2014, June 2014, http://www.bp.com/cont-ent/dam/bp/pdf/energy-economics/statistics-review-2014/bp-statistics-review-of-world-energy-2014-full-report.pdf.

decrease in coal consumption was mainly due to strict environmental control and higher production costs. Most of the reduction in oil and coal consumption was replaced by LNG. The ROK started to consume natural gas only in 1986. After that, the consumption rapidly expanded from 3.4 billion cubic meters in 1990 to 52.5 billion cubic meters in 2013. The sharp increase in LNG was mainly due to environmental protection considerations. In addition, the consumption of nuclear energy also increased and the consumption of hydropower decreased since 1990.

The huge gap between energy consumption and production in the ROK is mainly made up of imports. Since 1990, the ROK's oil imports have increased year by year, reaching 1.38 million barrels per day in 1991 and 2.46 million barrels per day in 2013, ranking fifth in the world in crude oil imports. 87% of the ROK's oil imports come from the Middle East and 12% from Asian countries. The ROK's natural gas depends entirely on imported LNG. In 2013, the ROK imported 54.2 billion cubic meters of LNG, including 18.3 billion cubic meters from Qatar, 7.7 billion cubic meters from Indonesia, 5.9 billion cubic meters from Oman, and 4.9 billion cubic meters from Yemen. Besides, the ROK has imported more than 80 million tons of coal annually, making it the world's most important importer of power coal.

The ROK's main sources of energy are anthracite, oil, natural gas, and hydropower, but its fossil resources and exploitable hydropower resources for power generation are scarce, and energy supply is almost entirely dependent on imports. In order to achieve a stable energy supply, the ROK government has been actively promoting the development of domestic natural gas and other resources, as well as overseas resource development and diversification of energy-importing countries. While promoting the efficient use of energy, the ROK has also been promoting the development of renewable energy in recent years. According to the Basic Law for Energy promulgated in March 2006, a long-term energy strategy was to be formulated every five years within 20 years, namely, the Basic Strategic Plan of National Energy. In August 2008, at the third meeting of the National Energy Commission chaired by the president, the first national basic energy plan after the Basic Law for Energy was adopted. In this plan, the ROK's development goal by 2030 was proposed, that is, to greatly expand nuclear power generation and renewable energy.

The goals of the national energy basic plan include decreasing the unit energy consumption by 46%, that is, from the current 0.341TOE per US$1,000 of GDP to 0.185TOE per US$1,000 of GDP by 2030. By 2030, the proportion of fossil energy including oil (primary energy) will be reduced from the current 83% to 61%, the proportion of renewable energy will be increased by 4.6 times, that is, from the current 2.4% to 11%, and the proportion of nuclear power will be increased from the current 14.9% to 27.8%. Another goal is to increase the research and development budget for "clean technology" and other energy technologies, promote the selection, development, and introduction of key technologies, and increase the rate of independent development of oil and natural gas from the current 4.2% to 40% by 2030.

The Ministry of Commerce, Industry, and Energy (MOCIE) is the administrative agency of the ROK's energy and mineral policies and manages its major energy companies. It includes the Energy and Resources Policy Bureau, the Nuclear Energy Industry Bureau, and the Electricity Industry Committee. The ROK's energy policy is mainly manifested in the following aspects:

The first aspect is to increase the proportion of natural gas, nuclear energy, and other renewable energy. The ROK government has taken many measures to decentralize the energy supply structure. The first measure is to promote the use of natural gas. The ROK has further promoted the development of the natural gas industry through the use of technologies such as combined cycle power generation, natural gas refrigeration, and compressed natural gas power vehicles. In the late 1990s, the government announced a natural gas industry reform plan. It introduced a competition mechanism in the natural gas market and gradually opened up the import business of LNG. The second measure is to encourage the development of nuclear energy. The ROK's energy policy regards nuclear energy as the main source of electricity. The ROK's Ministry of Science and Technology is solely responsible for nuclear energy research and development, nuclear energy safety, and nuclear energy protection. The ROK has been building nuclear power plants since the 1970s and began a 10-year technology transfer program with Westinghouse Electric Corporation in 1987 to achieve technological autonomy. Now, the ROK has achieved 95% technical autonomy in the whole field from the design to the construction of nuclear power plants. A total of 20 nuclear power plants have been built with ROK's own nuclear technology. After the earthquake in Japan, the ROK Chief Minister of Knowledge Economy Choi Joong-Kyung issued a special statement saying that the ROK would not abandon its nuclear power generation plan and that nuclear power would account for 59% of the electricity generation market by 2030. In terms of nuclear power generation, the utilization rate of Japanese facilities is 63.3% and that of the ROK's facilities has reached 91.1%, making it possible to use nuclear power more economically. In December 2009, the ROK defeated rivals such as France, the United States, and Japan and won an export contract for nuclear power plants worth at least US$20 billion from the United Arab Emirates, thus becoming the sixth country in the world to "export" nuclear power plants. The final measure is to increase the ratio of other renewable energy sources. The ROK government established a research and development and promotion plan for new and renewable energy technologies in 2003 and formulated detailed plans and targets year by year. In order to develop new and renewable energy technologies, the government has chosen three major areas with market development potential, hydrogen fuel cells, photovoltaic energy, and wind power, and has concentrated its funding in these areas. For the electricity generated by the five new renewable energy sources — solar energy, wind energy, small hydraulic power, landfill gas, and waste incineration heat energy — the ROK government provides subsidies for the difference between the power generation cost and the average market electricity price for five years. The plan aims to further improve the ROK's generating capacity of the new renewable energy. In order to promote the use of new renewable energy, the ROK Ministry of Trade, Industry, and Energy also launched a renewable energy demonstration plan, selecting specific locations to establish "green villages" to demonstrate the use of various new renewable energy sources for manufacturers to research and develop. In order to further support the development of renewable energy sources such as solar power generation and wind power generation, the government formulated a five-year related budget in 2008. The government's related budget for the development of renewable energy sources totaled 4.4 trillion Korean won, more than twice the amount set aside by former President Rohm Moo-hyun. Although much effort has been made, the ratio of renewable energy in South Korea is far lower than that in developed countries. The proportion of renewable energy in total power generation increased from 2.43% in 2008 to 2.61% in 2010, with an average annual growth rate of only 0.06 percentage points in three years.

The second aspect is to pay attention to energy conservation and environmental protection. The ROK mainly promotes the improvement of energy efficiency by adopting energy-saving campaigns and adjusting the proportion of energy prices. For example, after the first oil crisis in 1973, the ROK government launched an energy conservation campaign by establishing the Energy Consumption Promotion Committee. In the 1980s, the energy conservation movement grew further. In the industrial sector, the goal was to establish an energy-efficient structure, and the petroleum fund was used to replace outdated equipment with high-efficiency equipment. At the same time, technical guidance was given by energy management agencies to promote the establishment of a "long-term energy unit reduction plan" and to determine the amount of energy needed for unit production of major industrial species. In the 1990s, the ROK established the National Energy Conservation Promotion Committee with the Prime Minister as its chairman, raising the energy conservation campaign to a new level. To carry out national energy conservation activities, expand investment in energy conservation facilities, invigorate energy technology development, improve the energy utilization rate, and transform the economic and social structure to a low-energy consumption type, the ROK also adjusted its energy price comparison system and transformed its industrial structure. In addition, the ROK government carried out energy price reform, reformed the energy price comparison system, and promoted energy conservation and transformation to a low-energy consumption industry through rationalization of the energy price level. According to the requirements of the Kyoto Protocol, the ROK government strove to develop energy-saving technologies and reduce greenhouse gas emissions. The measures taken included introducing energy conservation, improving energy efficiency, increasing the proportion of clean energy such as nuclear power and natural gas in energy consumption, actively developing new and renewable energy technologies, and formulating an environment-friendly and low-carbon energy system throughout the country.

 The third aspect is to increase oil reserves. The oil reserve system of the ROK consists of national reserves and private reserves. The ROK government established the Korean National Oil Corporation in 1979, which is responsible for the construction, management, and operation of reserve bases and reserve oil. The national reserve is the core of the strategic petroleum reserve. In 1980, the ROK government set the oil reserve for 60 days of domestic consumption. In 1993, the government formally established a private oil reserve system, stipulating that private oil companies should maintain 30 to 60 days of oil reserves, mainly undertaken by 5 refineries, 2 LPG importers, 17 oil importers, and 5 petrochemical enterprises. In 1995, the ROK added seven more oil reserve bases, making the oil reserve reach the domestic consumption target of 60 days in 2006.

The ROK's national oil reserves remain at the level equivalent to the oil consumption of 106 days.

The ROK government's funds for oil reserves mainly come from the surtax on oil imports. The ROK law requires importers to pay a surtax of 13 Korean won to the government for every liter of oil or petroleum-processed products imported, but the import of emergency reserves is exempt from tax. Additional tax revenue is used to set up an "oil price buffer reserve fund" to deal with oil price fluctuations and oil supply disruptions. In addition, insufficient funds are supplemented by financial allocations or bank loans. With the sharp rise in oil prices and the interruption of oil supply, the government will set a target price for oil products. Oil-processing enterprises must supply oil products to the market at this price. The government will use the Oil Price Buffer Reserve Fund to compensate for oil-processing enterprises.

4.1.4 The energy security situation and energy strategy of Mongolia and the DPRK

As a landlocked country, Mongolia borders Russia in the north and China in the east, south, and west. The land boundary line between China and Mongolia is 4,710 kilometers long. In 2013, Mongolia's GDP was US$11.52 billion, up 11.7% year on year. Mongolia's energy production is dominated by coal. The total primary energy production in 2012 was about 26.18 million tons of standard coal, of which raw coal, crude oil, and biofuel accounted for 96.5%, 2.7%, and 0.8%, respectively. 94% of the raw coal output and 98% of the crude oil output are exported, and the national energy consumption is only 5.63 million tons of standard coal.[7] Mongolia is rich in oil resources, mainly in the Dornogovi, Dornod, and Tuv provinces, where there are more than ten large oil fields. Comparatively speaking, Mongolia does not have much oil resources. Still, experts predict from a geological point of view that there are about 400 million tons of oil reserves in Zuun Bayan and Tsagan Els in eastern Mongolia.[8]

---

[7] Overview of Mongolia's Energy and Electric Power Industry, National Transmission and Distribution Technology Cooperation Network, http://www.eptc.org.cn/news/international dynamics/20140902/15642.html, September 2, 2014.

[8] Guo Ming. Charm of Mongolia's Mineral Resources. *China Land and Resources News*, July 27, 2004.

In 2010, the installed capacity of power generation in Mongolia was about 832,000 kilowatts, almost all of which was attributed to coal. In 2012, this country generated 4.816 billion kwh of electricity, imported 366 million kwh, exported 21 million kwh, and supplied 5.161 billion kwh domestically.[9] The relatively low level of energy consumption and abundant coal resources make Mongolia's energy security situation, which is relatively sparsely populated, obviously different from that of other Northeast Asian countries.

Since the 1990s, Mongolia has begun to carry out privatization reform. After more than 20 years of development, Mongolia's economy began to recover and showed a rapid growth trend. Mongolia's greatest competitive advantage lies in the abundant mineral resources in its territory, with good economic growth prospects and a high degree of marketization. The Mongolian government implements the strategy of "rejuvenating the country through mining," and the national economy is developing rapidly under the impetus of mining development. In 2012, Mongolia's GDP grew by 12.3%, making it one of the fastest-growing economies in the world. Mining also became the sector that attracted the most foreign investment in the country. According to the Global Competitiveness Report 2012–2013, Mongolia ranks 93rd among the 144 most competitive countries and regions in the world. In order to change the economic development trend of extensive raw material export, the Mongolian government is further promoting foreign investment. It does not support direct export of raw ore resources; instead, it encourages foreign investment to set up factories in Mongolia and develops industries such as semi-processing and deep processing of mineral products so as to improve the domestic industrial chain. At present, some foreign enterprises hope to invest in Mongolia to set up power plants, consume coal resources locally, and export electricity to other countries. However, the Mongolian government's policy toward foreign investment is unstable and has been suffering from complaints. The Foreign Investment Law enacted in 2008 requires all foreign investors to register with Mongolia's Foreign Investment and Foreign Trade Agency (FIFTA), raising the minimum capital for foreign investment from US$1,000 to US$100,000. In 2012, Mongolia's parliament revised the Foreign Investment Law again to restrict foreign investment in the country's three strategic industries of mining, finance, and communications. In

---

[9] International Monetary Fund, *World Economic Outlook Database, April 2016*, April 12, 2016, http://www.imf.org/external/pubs/ft/weo/2016/01/weodata/index.aspx.

these three strategic industries, if the proportion of foreign investment exceeds 49% and the investment exceeds 100 billion Mongolian tugriks (about US$60 million), the government must submit it to the parliament for decisions. Therefore, from the practical point of view, the factors restricting Mongolia's energy export are both the objective factors in the external market and the factors in the internal market, such as simple export market and weak infrastructure, unstable foreign investment policies and laws, poor investment environment, strict environmental protection policies, large exchange rate fluctuations, and relatively strong local privileges. The latter is an important reason for many foreign enterprises to suffer setbacks in their investment in Mongolia. But on the whole, Mongolia's investment in and development of energy and mineral resources and bilateral trade are entering a new period of strategic opportunities. The development of Mongolia's coal and oil resources, the coal chemical industry market, the electricity market, clean energy sources such as wind energy and solar energy, and infrastructure construction will be key areas of and directions for Mongolia's investment in the next five years. The direct export of energy minerals and the comprehensive utilization of local conversion will be the new forms of Mongolia's energy development in the future.

The DPRK is a country that is very short in energy resources. There are no oil and natural gas resources. The production of energy mainly involves coal and hydropower. The DPRK's proven coal reserves are 14.74 billion tons, of which 11.74 billion tons are anthracite and 3 billion tons are lignite, and the recoverable reserves under the current technical conditions are about 7.9 billion tons.[10] Anthracite is mainly produced in South Pyongan Province and North Pyongan Province and bituminous coal is mainly distributed in North Hamgyong Province and South Hamgyong Province. According to the regional division, the DPRK has four major coalfields, namely, the northern part of South Pyongan, the southern part of South Pyongan, the northern part of North Hamgyong, and the southern part of South Hamgyong. At present, there are more than 100 coal mines at the central level in the DPRK, including more than 70 anthracite mines, more than 30 anthracite mines, and more than 500 small and medium-sized coal mines at the local level. In the south of South Pyongan, there is an area of 80 kilometers extending to the west and

---

[10] BP. *BP Statistical Review of World Energy 2014*, http://www.bp.com/content/dam/bp/pdf/Energy-economics/statistical-review-2014/BP-statistical-review-of-world-energy-2014-full-report.pdf, June 2014.

east with Pyongyang as the center and this are is rich in anthracite. The largest coal mines in the north are Aoji Coal Mine in Undokgun, Obong in Musan County, and Hoeryŏng in Hoeryŏng city. The Anju coal mine has seven ledges, each with a thickness of 25 meters. It is rich in the brown coal with the calorific value of over 5,300 kcal and the annual output is 7 million tons. It is the largest coal mine in the DPRK. In addition, the DPRK has more than 650 small and medium-sized hydropower stations, generating 145 billion kwh of electricity annually.

After the disintegration of the Soviet Union, the DPRK lost the opportunity to import oil and electric power equipment from the Soviet Union at low prices, thus leading to a complete stagnation in its industrial and agricultural production. Since oil-based energy resources were gradually cut off, the DPRK's highly mechanized agriculture was completely paralyzed in the 1970s. Fertilizer production plummeted due to the shortages of raw materials and electricity. The international blockade has cut off the import of chemical fertilizers and gradually turned the energy crisis into a food crisis, which has become the most serious problem that directly threatens national security. Moreover, the shortage of energy has also led to a decline in the level of electricity production in the DPRK. The DPRK produced 28.1 billion kwh of electricity annually in 1975 and set a record high of 29.2 billion kwh in 1989. Since then, it has dropped for ten consecutive years. By 1998, the DPRK had only 17 billion kwh of electricity.[11] In fact, the main reason for the DPRK's poverty and backwardness lies in the shortage of energy resources. The DPRK's Sinuiju–Pyongyang railway was electrified as early as 1964, while Northeast China did not have an electrified railway line until 2000. At the end of 1978, China had a population of 962.59 million, with a power generation capacity of 256.6 billion degrees at 266.6 degrees per capita. In 1970, the DPRK's per capita generating power reached 1,184 degrees, reaching the level of primary developed countries at that time.[12] With the disintegration of the Soviet Union, Russia completely changed its policy toward the DPRK and cut off all energy relations with the DPRK. In this period, many remote areas in the DPRK could only supply electricity for about one hour a day. And because the voltage was very unstable, motors were difficult to rotate, precision electronic equipment was often burned down, many

---

[11] Mei Xinyu, Inspiration from the DPRK's Energy Problem. *China SOE*, 2014, 11, p. 54.
[12] *Ibid.*

modern factories had to become manual workshops, and transportation was also seriously affected.

Since the 1990s, the DPRK government has implemented a hydropower strategy to solve the problem of insufficient energy supply. After years of efforts, the DPRK's energy consumption structure, which relied solely on fossil energy, greatly improved, and its dependence on oil has greatly decreased. A series of hydropower stations have been built in the DPRK, including Huichon, Ryesong-gang, and Orang-chon. These hydropower stations have been put into full production. According to a report by the DPRK's *Rodong Sinmun* (Workers' Newspaper) on November 25, 2013, several large hydropower stations in South Hamgyong Province can exceed their power production tasks every month. In addition, the DPRK also changed its oil-fired power station to a coal-fired power station, aiding the energy and power industry in its recover. In recent years, the major cities in the DPRK have begun lighting up at night. Based on the energy production, Pyongyang and other cities have been able to build commercial services and amusement facilities in the past two years that consume a lot of electricity. With the addition of electricity imported from China, the DPRK's electricity supply has greatly improved. In 2014, the DPRK and Russia reached a trade agreement settled in rubles, and Russia proposed to promote the construction of a power network connecting Russia's Far East and the Korean Peninsula.

4.2 Energy Cooperation and Competition between Countries in Northeast Asia

Due to the rapid economic development in Northeast Asia, the region has become the world's most important energy consumption center. Countries in Northeast Asia have complementary energy resources. Energy cooperation is continuously developing. At the same time, there is fierce competition in the energy market. On the one hand, as Northeast Asian countries have common interests in developing regional energy cooperation and ensuring their own energy security, the energy cooperation among countries is continuously expanding. It includes cooperation between energy resource countries and energy importing countries. On the other hand, China, Japan, and the ROK are all highly dependent on energy imports for their economic development. The convergence of energy import channels easily leads to competition among the three countries in the international energy market. At present, the energy competition among China, Japan, and the ROK is mainly focused on Russia's Far East and Siberia, the Caspian Sea, and Africa. The energy competition may enter a benign track through bilateral and multilateral coordination, thus promoting the stability of the energy market in Northeast Asia and the energy security of all countries. If this vicious energy competition continues, it will also restrict the stable economic development of Northeast Asian countries and the common prosperity of the whole region.

4.2.1 Energy cooperation among countries in Northeast Asia

Countries in Northeast Asia are actively cooperating in energy infrastructure construction. The construction of energy infrastructure is the basis for regional energy cooperation. Comprehensive cooperation in the field of energy infrastructure construction can promote extensive cooperation in energy development, transportation, processing, and other related industrial chains throughout the region. Energy infrastructure generally includes the establishment and construction of energy transportation systems, railways, pipelines, power grids, and the infrastructure needed for upstream energy development and downstream processing. In recent years, countries in Northeast Asia have launched comprehensive cooperation in the fields of logistics and transportation systems, electric power transportation systems, and oil and gas pipeline systems, and have achieved great economic benefits.

Power cooperation is the first energy cooperation project launched in Northeast Asia. China's ultra-high-voltage, the smart grid equipment manufacturing and test technology have reached the advanced world level. It has built and operated the world's largest ultra-high-voltage and electricity transmission system, ultra-high-voltage and electricity transmission lines, and smart electricity grids. China has formed a complete system of electrical equipment industry chain and manufacturing system and is very active in the global cooperation. During the 20 years of power cooperation between China and Russia, the electricity trade volume between the two countries reached 13.639 billion kwh, saving 4.6381 million tons of coal and 12.9572 million tons of carbon dioxide.[13] However,

---

[13] 22 years of Sino-Russian power cooperation, 13.6 billion kilowatt-hours of Russian power have been imported, China News Website. http://finance.chinanews.com/ny/2014/10-23/6709116.shtml, October 23, 2014.

after the signing of China–ROK Free Trade Agreement (FTA), Korea Electric Power Corporation and China Huaneng Group signed a Memorandum of Understanding on Project Cooperation, a Memorandum of Understanding on Strategic Cooperation in Scientific Research, and a Memorandum of Understanding on Cooperation in Technical Joint Research. China Huaneng Group and Korea Electric Power Corporation will give full play to their respective advantages, actively promote the cooperative development of domestic and overseas electric power projects, strengthen communication and exchange in enterprise strategy, management, market, science and technology, environmental protection, and personnel training, and carry out cooperative research. The Russia–DPRK energy bridge project is also being discussed by the two governments. In the first phase of the project, energy infrastructure and 110-kilowatt power transmission lines will be built between Russia's coastal border area and the DPRK's Rason Free Economic Zone. The Rason Free Economic Zone had a power grid load of 30,000 kilowatts in 2014, and its power grid load will rise to about 600,000 kilowatts by 2025. In order to meet the power demand for future power growth, the Russian contractor will build a new high-voltage transmission line under the framework of the energy bridge project. The ROK was also interested in cooperating with the DPRK to introduce Russian power resources into the country. However, due to the complicated and changeable inter-Korean relations, this cooperation has not been implemented. The Rajin-Khasan Logistics Project was one of the main parts of the ROK-Russia Joint Statement issued in 2013. It is an important logistics infrastructure project for Russia and the DPRK to realize coal cooperation. The DPRK here is right according to the Chinese source book. It is of great significance for the Korean Peninsula to enter the Eurasia logistics transportation system. However, at present, the railway cannot be realized due to the issues in the Korean Peninsula.

Cooperative infrastructure construction in the fields of oil and natural gas is important in Northeast Asia. China, Japan, the ROK, and the DPRK are energy-consuming countries, while Russia is a major energy producer and exporter. Although these four countries have interests in the field of energy, they have not formed an effective cooperation mechanism.

China–Russia cooperation in the field of oil and gas is of strategic significance in Northeast Asia. In the process of China–Russia oil and gas cooperation, the oil and gas transportation infrastructure in Northeast Asia has been continuously improved, and the related energy trade system and financial system have gradually realized regionalization and internationalization. In 2009, China and Russia reached a long-term oil pipeline trade agreement worth US$25 billion for 15 million tons of crude oil annually. The China–Russia crude oil pipeline was officially put into operation in 2011. In 2012, the crude oil trade between China and Russia topped 22 million tons. The "oil-for-credit" deal in 2009 started a new era of China–Russia energy cooperation. The implementation of the agreement not only improved the stability of Russia's oil supply to China but also facilitated the development of promising oil and gas fields in East Siberia and the Far East.[14] In 2014, China and Russia signed the China–Russia East Route Natural Gas Supply Purchase and Sale Contract. Natural gas cooperation has become another important milestone in their energy cooperation involving the development of the Chayanda Gas Field in the Republic of Sakha (Yakutia) and the expansion of the Kovykta Gas Field into an integrated complex, providing natural gas export sources for the Siberia pipeline. The Power of Siberia pipeline started its construction in 2014 and stretches across the Irkutsk region and the Amur region in the Russian Far East before reaching the border city of Blagoveshchensk. The first phase of the project is about 3,200 kilometers and the second phase is 800 kilometers, with a designed annual gas transmission capacity of 61 billion cubic meters.[15] The implementation of the China–Russia oil and gas pipeline project not only guarantees the energy security of the two countries and promotes the diversified development of the two countries' energy resources but also creates a new type of international energy cooperation mode, which will have an important impact on the development of future energy cooperation in Northeast Asia.

Although Russia and Japan have not established large oil and gas pipelines, Japan's large investment in Russia has also promoted the improvement of energy development infrastructure in Eastern Russia. Japan is an economically developed country in Northeast Asia and an important energy importer. Russia actively attracts Japan's investment in its energy sector while exporting oil and LNG to Japan. Japan promotes participation of its enterprises in energy development in Russia's Siberia and the Far East through government aid and low-interest loans. Japan is an important investor in Russia's Sakhalin-1 and Sakhalin-2 projects. Among them, Sakhalin-2 project is an LNG project established by

---

[14] Russia and China cooperation in oil industry. *Oil and Oil Exploration* 2009(78): 1011.
[15] Siberia Power natural gas transportation system. http://www.gazprom.ru/about/production/projects/pipelines/ykv, EB/OL, November 23, 2014

Sakhalin Energy Company and Japan's Tokyo Gas Company, Tokyo Electric Power Company, Kyushu Electric Power Company, Hiroshima Gas Company, and Kyoto Electric Power Company. The contract period is more than 20 years, and the total annual supply is about 4 million tons. Japan's Mitsui Products Co., Ltd. and Mitsubishi Commercial Co., Ltd. will acquire 12.5% and 10% of the shares of the project, respectively, and the operator of the project is Sakhalin Energy Company. The volumes of produced LNG were 9.6 million tons in 2010, 10.7 million tons in 2011, 10.9 million tons in 2012, and 9.75 million tons in 2013.[16] A third production line has also been planned. Moreover, in 2013, Japan's INPEX Holdings Inc. and Rosneft Oil signed an agreement to jointly develop the Magadan-2 and Magadan-3 oil fields, and Japan acquired 1/3 of the shares in the two oil fields. Among them, Magadan-2 has proven to store 2.45 billion barrels of oil and Magadan-3 has 950 million barrels. This agreement will have a positive impact on Russian–Japanese cooperation in energy development technology in alpine regions.

The cooperation between Russia and Japan in the field of LNG has not only enabled Russia's LNG to smoothly enter the energy market in Northeast Asia but has also made Sakhalin into a new LNG production base in Northeast Asia. After the Fukushima nuclear accident, Japan closed its nuclear power plants nationwide in 2011, requiring a large amount of imported LNG, thus expanding Russia–Japan cooperation. The data from the BP Review of World Energy Statistics 2013 show that more than 76% of Russia's LNG exports went to Japan in 2012. Japan's LNG import was only 70 million tons in 2010, rising to 78.5 million tons in 2011 and 87.3 million tons in 2012, an increase of nearly 25% in two years. During the same period, the total value of LNG increased by more than 70%, from about 3.5 trillion Japanese yen in 2010 to 6 trillion Japanese yen in 2012. Japan's LNG import price increased by about 55% on average, from about US$11 per million British thermal unit (BTU) in 2010 to about US$17 per million British thermal unit (BTU) in 2012. Japan's trade deficit in 2012 was about 6.9 trillion Japanese yen, most of which came from LNG imports.[17] In the energy cooperation between Russia and Japan, both sides have taken what they need and have achieved

---

[16] Liu Tao, Research on Russia's Asia-Pacific Energy Strategy in the Early 21st Century, Doctoral Dissertation, Jilin University, 2015, p. 84.
[17] Shoichi Ito, TPP Changes Energy Pattern in Northeast Asia. *Chinese Entrepreneur*, No. 8, 2013, pp. 40–41.

positive results. Judging from the current situation, Russia is more inclined to seize Japan's huge liquefied gas consumption market, while Japan has a more diversified energy import scheme due to rising shale gas production in the United States. Against the background of the escalating crisis in Ukraine, Japan has made clear its position and follows the US line of escalating sanctions against Russia, which will inevitably have a negative impact on future energy cooperation between the two countries.

Russia and the ROK have maintained good political, economic, and diplomatic relations. It is the common vision of Russia, the DPRK, and the ROK to establish and improve the energy transportation infrastructure across the Korean Peninsula. In 2010, Russia and the ROK reached an agreement on gas transmission to the ROK. In 2011, a road map for pipeline construction was determined.[18] The two sides hoped to push forward the natural gas pipeline project through the DPRK to transport the natural gas produced in Russia's Siberia to the ROK. In 2014, the ROK put forward the Eurasia Plan for the development of a unified Eurasian economic circle on the basis of promoting trust in the Korean Peninsula and Northeast Asia. One of the core development programs is the construction of the Eurasia Energy Network. The starting point of the Eurasia Plan is to naturally integrate the DPRK into the regional economic cooperation network by building railways, natural gas pipelines, and oil pipelines connected with Russia. However, tensions in the Korean Peninsula and the DPRK nuclear issue have always been major obstacles to the trilateral energy cooperation between Russia, the ROK, and the DPRK. Now, the energy cooperation between Russia and the ROK needs to solve two important problems: first, the economic profitability goal of energy cooperation; second, joint cooperation involving the DPRK to improve the energy security situation in the Korean Peninsula and safeguard peace and stability in the region.

4.2.2 Energy competition among countries in Northeast Asia

In Northeast Asia, there are large energy consumers as well as significant energy producers and exporters in the world. China, Japan, and the ROK are major energy consumers, while Russia is a major energy exporter in

---

[18] Russia and the ROK have reached agreement on natural gas. http://www.gazprom.ru/press/news/2012/february/article130054/, February 20, 2012.

the world. In recent years, Russia has actively explored the energy market in the Asia-Pacific region and promoted energy cooperation with countries in Northeast Asia. China, Japan, and the ROK are the world's three major energy consumers, and their economic development is highly dependent on energy imports. The convergence of energy import channels among China, Japan, and the ROK objectively enables the three countries to form a certain competitive relationship in the international energy market.

Since 2000, the economy in Northeast Asia has continued to grow at a high speed, and the energy demand in the region has increased dramatically. The sustainable economic growth of China and the ROK has caused the energy import of the two countries to reach a new high in recent years. Japan's dependence on imported energy has also reached a historical peak due to the shutdown of nuclear power plants. According to the forecast of the IEA, the energy demand in Northeast Asia will maintain a high growth of 8–10% in the next 20 years. China's demand for major energy sources such as oil and coal will more than double the current level by 2030, when it will surpass the United States as the world's largest energy consumer. To ensure their own energy security, other countries are actively expanding their energy import channels and promoting diversification of energy import sources. In view of the continuing turmoil in the security situation in the Middle East region, China, Japan, and the ROK have gradually reduced their dependence on oil supply from the Middle East and have instead spread their sources of oil imports to Russia, Central Asia, Africa, and Central and South America. Decentralization of energy import sources has become an important part of the energy security strategies of various countries, but it has also directly triggered fierce competition among Northeast Asian countries in expanding energy import sources and channels. The sheer direct consequence of this competition is the formation of the "Asian premium." Due to the lack of a protection mechanism for common interests, Asia's oil-consuming countries have to pay US$5 billion to US$10 billion more to oil-producing countries each year. Thus, the three major energy-importing countries of China, Japan, and the ROK have to bear the heavy "Asian premium." However, China has become the main and direct victim of the premium phenomenon since it has not yet established a perfect oil reserve mechanism. Only Russia has abundant energy resources in Northeast Asia, where Eastern Siberia and the Far East have abundant oil and gas reserves and great development potential. At present, Russia is the world's second-largest crude oil producer and the largest natural gas producer. Due to the geographical closeness, China, Japan, the ROK, and other major energy-demanding countries are competitively pursuing their energy strategies. In Northeast Asia, Russia has become the energy supplier with several bilateral energy agreements competing with each other. The competition between China and Japan in the field of energy is most intense. During the competition between China and Japan for the construction of Russia's oil pipeline, the project plan changed again and again and Russia's energy export and development projects were delayed repeatedly. At the same time, under the pressure of excessive energy competition between China and Japan, Russia's attitude wavered, which eventually affected the interest of all parties concerned and restricted the healthy development of energy cooperation in Northeast Asia. The dispute between China and Japan over oil and gas fields in the East China Sea is ongoing. In September 2005, a report released by Japan's Self-Defense Forces predicted three possibilities of China–Japan conflict, one of which was due to the growing competitive relations between the two countries for energy. Although the energy forum, in which officials, scholars, and entrepreneurs of the two countries participate, plays an active role in easing the energy competition, it cannot fundamentally change the competition between China and Japan in the energy field.

Energy competition among Northeast Asian countries is not only a competition for energy resources among energy-consuming countries, but also a direct competition between consuming countries and Russia as an energy producing country. The competition contains complicated geopolitical factors. The agreements on oil and natural gas pipelines between China and Russia in 2009 and 2014 temporarily ended the China–Japan pipeline dispute, but a cooperation pattern in Northeast Asia has not been formed as a result. The right-leaning deviation in Japanese politics, the existence of the Japan–US alliance, and the special geopolitical interests of the United States in Northeast Asia have become veiled but influential negative factors that affect the energy cooperation of regional countries. Moreover, after the Ukraine crisis, Japan took part in western sanctions against Russia and implemented a right-leaning policy toward Northeast Asian countries, which to some extent led to serious antagonism between Japan and Russia, China, and the ROK, due to which regional energy cooperation was almost at a standstill. In fact, geopolitical factors have been affecting energy cooperation in Northeast Asia. After China and Russia reached a natural gas deal, China had a great advantage over Japan in energy. However, Japan also needs Russia's energy supply, but it must do its best to dispel some concerns from its ally, the United States. The Japanese government is a partner of Rosneft's energy joint venture in the Far East called "Sakhalin-1." In the "Sakhalin-2" project, Mitsui and Mitsubishi have 12.5% and 10% shares, respectively. Although the company itself has not been sanctioned, the US sanctions do target Igor Sechin, chief executive of Rosneft. In addition, Japan relies on the supply of natural gas from the "Sakhalin-2" gas field, which makes it the likely first victim if the United States strengthens its sanctions against Russia. Since the Sakhalin project began to generate revenue in 2009, the project has been a stable source of LNG in Japan. Due to Japan's investment in Russian projects as well as the strong demand for fossil fuels after the nuclear power plant accident in 2011, it is difficult for Japan to stay isolated in the current energy situation. Moreover, compared with the early 21st century, Russia's expectation of economic development in Northeast Asia has been greatly raised. If Japanese enterprises hesitate in their energy cooperation with Russia, Russia will have to turn to other Northeast Asian countries. With the limited energy production capacity in Russia's Far East, Japan's energy supply cannot be fully met. However, the alliance with the United States makes it difficult for Japan to cooperate with Russia without reservation. Japan's condemnation of Russia in the Ukraine crisis directly reflects its compliance with the United States.

Besides, the outbreak of the financial crisis and the Ukraine crisis in 2008 prompted the China–Russia energy cooperation. However, due to the asymmetric economic strength and influence of the two countries, it was difficult for China and Russia to realize complementarity and compatibility of the energy interests. First of all, China has a foreign exchange reserve of more than US$3 trillion and has great financial strength. Although Russia has a foreign exchange reserve of more than US$500 billion and a large oil and gas reserve fund, due to the drastic fluctuation of international oil prices, the ruble exchange rate is extremely unstable. Therefore, Russia is very cautious in the use of the existing foreign exchange and oil and gas reserve fund despite its strong desire for the development of energy resources in the eastern part of the country. Therefore, Russia hopes to make use of Chinese funds but worries about overreliance on China. Although the two countries are naturally complementary in their energy resources, Russia worries about the gains and losses in regional energy cooperation, which lead to policy differences between the two countries in regional energy cooperation, as Russia strives to offset China's financial advantages. Russia hopes to maintain the "one-to-many" umbrella-shaped cooperation pattern in Northeast Asia and maintain its central position. In fact, this pattern is not conducive to Russia. During the Ukraine crisis, the fall in international oil prices seriously endangered Russia's energy and economic security. The absence of a regional cooperation mechanism exposed Russia to the crisis.

In short, energy security is very fragile for all countries in Northeast Asia. The energy security of energy-demanding countries like China, Japan, and the ROK depends on the improvement of the regional energy security. The energy and economic security of Russia as an energy-producing country also depends on the coordinated development and common prosperity of the region. What is more noteworthy is that due to the low interdependence of energy resources and fierce competition, Northeast Asian countries attach more importance to energy cooperation with foreign energy suppliers than to mutual cooperation among countries in the region, which will affect further develop in the region. Energy competition among energy-consuming countries in Northeast Asia may cause changes in the international energy pattern, thus bringing fluctuations to the international energy market. Due to the fierce competition among China, Japan, and the ROK, the monopoly interests of large western oil companies have been challenged. This has urged Russia's energy strategy to shift its focus to the Asia-Pacific region, thus challenging the monopoly of oil-exporting organizations in the west. Changes in geopolitical and economic forces caused by energy supply and demand, as well as new influencing factors such as fluctuations in international oil prices, will have a profound impact on the traditional energy pattern and its power distribution, thus triggering conflicts at the global and regional levels and creating new energy security issues. At present, the degree of dependence on trade among Northeast Asian countries is continuously increasing. Although it is still lower than that of the EU and North American Free Trade Area (NAFTA), it has increased compared to earlier times. The close economic relations between Northeast Asian countries make it necessary for all parties to strengthen cooperation. Damage to any party will inevitably negative impacts on both parties. Interdependence will enable countries to form a community, while vicious competition will harm the interests of all countries.

4.2.3 Problems in energy cooperation in Northeast Asia

There is still a big gap in energy cooperation in Northeast Asia involving both economic and political factors. Efforts to overcome these negative factors and actively promote energy cooperation in Northeast Asia will be in line with the common interests of all countries in the region.

First of all, geopolitical factors have a negative impact on Northeast Asia. The Cold War is over, but the shadow of the Cold War has not been removed. The situation in the Korean Peninsula is very tense due to long-term confrontation between the DPRK and the ROK, which has had an important impact on energy cooperation in Northeast Asia. Since 2000, Russia has actively promoted energy cooperation projects with the Korean Peninsula, including oil and gas pipeline projects and power grid connection projects, but so far, no substantial progress has been made.

Northeast Asia is undergoing an important transition period in the international system. China's comprehensive strength is continuously increasing. Japan seeks to become a political power, as it amends the pacifist constitution and lifts the ban on collective self-defense. The United States has continuously strengthened its bilateral military alliance with Japan and the ROK and strengthened its forward military deployment in Northeast Asia. Disputes over territorial sovereignty and maritime rights and interests among countries in Northeast Asia also reflect this structural contradiction and conflict. The new changes in the situation in Northeast Asia have deepened the security dilemma among the major powers and will inevitably have an important impact on the energy cooperation among the countries in the region.

Secondly, all the countries in Northeast Asia have established their own energy security systems, but they lack the necessary contact and communication with each other. There is no effective energy strategic reserve, no early warning system, no emergency response mechanism to deal with an energy crisis, and no necessary anti-risk capability in Northeast Asia. Due to the lack of a mature regional cooperation mechanism and effective energy coordination, the energy security interests of the countries in the region cannot be integrated. The lack of a perfect market mechanism and infrastructure for energy transactions among countries has led to a low level of integration in the energy market, making the idea of multilateral energy cooperation in Northeast Asia impossible to realize. Since there is no effective energy cooperation mechanism in Northeast Asia, different bilateral energy cooperation organizations compete with each other and competitions overtakes cooperation. This makes it impossible for countries to communicate and coordinate to solve problems arising from the exploration of resources, which is not conducive to mutually beneficial cooperation.

Finally, various unfavorable factors in Russia have also directly affected energy cooperation in Northeast Asia. Russia is a major energy supplier in Northeast Asia. Due to imperfect laws and regulations and relatively backward infrastructure, energy cooperation in Northeast Asia is greatly restricted.

At present, Russia's foreign energy cooperation laws and regulations are not perfect. Due to the absence of laws and regulations, any product-sharing agreement implemented in energy cooperation will lack legal protection. At present, Russia's energy-related laws and regulations are being constantly revised and improved as they lack stability, systematicness, and integrity. The examination and approval system for project management in Russia's central and local governments is rather complicated, which has become a major obstacle to investment in energy projects in Russia. Investment projects need to be approved step by step from the local government to the federal government, and even after the approval, the contract has to go through a long period of preparation and negotiation. Especially in joint ventures with Russian enterprises, the problem of distribution of profits and taxes among the federal and state governments and enterprises is tedious. Moreover, Russia imposes heavy taxes on foreign-funded enterprises, making it difficult for investors. Take Russia's Far East as an example: Although foreign-funded enterprises can enjoy certain preferential policies according to the Foreign Investment Law, these preferential policies are often offset by heavy taxes in the implementation process. Foreign capital and joint ventures need to pay more than 20 kinds of taxes, such as value-added tax, profit tax, transportation tax, sales tax, and public security tax, which often account for about 80% of the profits of enterprises. Under Russia's current tax system, investments in energy fields such as oil and gas have become unprofitable. According to calculations by Continental Resources Inc. of the United States, when Brent oil price is US$140 per ton, the after-tax price of crude oil of the same quality invested and produced in Russia is actually only equivalent to US$76, that is to say, the tax accounts for more than 45% of the oil price. This tax system is undoubtedly unattractive to foreign investment, which has seriously affected the enthusiasm of foreign enterprises to invest in Russian oil and gas exploration and development. Russia's oil and gas resources that are open to foreign investment are basically new oil and gas exploration areas with poor infrastructure. Foreign enterprises need to not only invest a large amount of money in infrastructure construction but must also continuously coordinate with Russia's local and federal authorities on the planning and construction of oil and gas export pipelines. In the past ten years, the Russian government's energy policy has been to increase state control over the energy industry and restrict foreign investment in the energy field. These factors add up to a situation that restricts the development of regional energy cooperation. According to Russia's Anti-Monopoly Law and Strategic Investment Law, pre-examination and supervision must be carried out for foreign investors who purchase strategic energy resources or oil and gas field development rights, especially for foreign investors who hold more than 50% of the shares. Due to the lack of basic standards, the Russian government can always prevent acquisitions on the grounds of "unpopularity" through various procedural mechanisms. This has led to an increase in the entry threshold for foreign investors to exploit their underground resources, and increased difficulty and risks for foreign enterprises to enter the Russian oil and gas development field.

4.3 China's Strategies and Policies for Energy Cooperation in Northeast Asia

Northeast Asia has diversified energy patterns. There are major energy producers and exporters as well as major energy consumers and importers. Strengthening energy cooperation among countries in Northeast Asia, and jointly dealing with energy security risks and challenges, is the only way to ensure energy security. China is a major energy consumer in Northeast Asia. It is an important part of China's energy strategy and policy to carry out energy cooperation in Northeast Asia, maintain energy security, promote the construction of energy cooperation mechanisms, and protect and support foreign investment and cooperation with Chinese energy enterprises.

4.3.1 China's energy security situation

China is the largest energy consumer and an important energy producer in Northeast Asia. In Northeast Asian countries, the asymmetry of China's energy resources endowment and energy consumption structure makes it stand out in the regional energy security. Broadly speaking, the main threat to China's energy security lies in the contradiction between the supply and demand and the destruction of the ecological environment caused by energy consumption. However, in a narrow sense, the essence of China's energy security threat is the problem of how to ensure China's sufficient, safe, and stable supply of oil and gas resources.[19] At present, China's oil and gas supply problem is prominent. Due to the increasing dependence on imported oil and gas resources, China's energy security will be more and more affected by changes in the oil and gas supply and prices in the international market, thus making the overall energy security situation in Northeast Asia even more complicated.

Firstly, there is an asymmetry between the rapid growth in China's energy consumption and its poor energy production capacity. From 1978 to 2014, China's total annual energy consumption volume increased from 570 million tons of standard coal to 4.26 billion tons of standard coal, an increase of 6.5 times. Energy shortages involving electricity, coal shortage, oil, and gas occur from time to time. Since the 1980s, the storage–production ratio of traditional fossil energy has been on a downward trend. By the end of 2013, the storage–production ratios of oil, natural gas, and coal were 11, 29, and 31 years, respectively. Energy consumption has been excessively dependent on coal for a long time, and structural problems are difficult to improve. Since 1978, the proportion of coal in the energy consumption structure has remained around 70%. In 2013, coal consumption was close to 3.6 billion tons, exceeding 50% of the world's total coal consumption. Coal-fired power generation accounts for 78% of the country's total power generation. In contrast, natural gas and non-fossil clean energy supplies, including nuclear power, hydropower, wind power, and photovoltaic power generation, accounted for only 5% and 9.6% of energy consumption in 2013, respectively.[20]

Secondly, China's energy consumption in Northeast Asia has caused the most serious environmental pollution. 85% of China's sulfur dioxide emission, 67% of nitrogen oxide emission, 70% of soot emission, and 80% of carbon dioxide emissions come from coal combustion.[21] Society

---

[19] Xia Yishan, *Research on China's International Energy Development Strategy*, Beijing: World Knowledge Publishing House, 2009, pp. 172–173.
[20] Research Center for Energy Security and National Development, National Development Research Institute, Peking University (authors: Wang Min, Xu Jintao, and Huang Zhuo). Research and Suggestions on China's Energy System Reform, Guangming Daily, June 10, 2015, 16th Edition.
[21] *Ibid.*

has paid a high price for the environmental pollution caused by energy consumption, which has become the biggest problem facing China's current energy development. In 2014, "controlling the excessive growth of energy consumption" was for the first time placed in the top ten tasks of China's national energy administration, which shows the urgency of resolving China's extensive energy use and prominent structural contradictions. At present, China's GDP energy consumption is 1.8 times higher than the world average. The huge contradiction between the energy reserves and energy consumption shows that the overall constraint on China's energy development comes not from low reserves but from low energy utilization efficiency caused by the rather extensive economic development pattern. The proportion of China's coal in total energy consumption is too high, while the proportion of natural gas and non-fossil energy is too low. According to China's Climate Change Plan (2014–2020), China's economic growth rate in 2014 was 7.4%, and the intensity of carbon dioxide emissions should have been 4%, which had already reached 5% in the first half of 2014. Energy consumption per unit GDP was originally planned to be 3.9%; however, in only six months, it reached 4.2%.[22] Besides, the severe administrative monopoly and price control in China's energy market have not only seriously hindered the efficient use of scarce energy resources, and the realization of energy conservation and emission reduction targets, but have also become a plague affecting economic growth.

The Chinese government has strictly controlled energy consumption in Beijing, Tianjin, Hebei, the Yangtze River Delta, the Pearl River Delta, and other regions by controlling the overall measures of energy consumption, such as changing coal to gas and coal to electricity. The Chinese government has closed small boilers, promoted cogeneration of heat and power, banned the construction of thermal power plants, moved high-energy-consuming industries to the west region, and implemented step-by-step electricity prices for high energy consumption. It aims to achieve the goals of closing plants of backward production capacity by substituting with clean energy. Since 2010, although the energy consumption per unit of GDP has decreased, the economic growth in these regions has slowed down due to environmental governance, which has also increased

---

[22] Xie Zhenhua, The 12th Five-Year Plan Carbon Intensity Reduction Target Can Be Achieved, http://en.chinagate.cn/news/2014-09/19/content_33557014.htm, received online on August 20, 2015.

the energy costs in these regions, thus causing the overall economic growth rate in China to decline. The ratio between China's GDP growth and primary energy consumption growth in the past 30 years has been about 1:0.6, but it has changed to 1:0.5 in the past ten years and is expected to further change to 1:0.4 in the next ten years.[23] The decline in the growth rate of China's energy demand has also had an impact on the energy demand in Northeast Asia. In the past ten years, China's energy consumption has increased by 40–60% of the increase in global energy consumption, with a maximum of nearly 80%. The decline in China's energy demand will inevitably lead to a slowdown in the growth of energy demand in Northeast Asia unless other Northeast Asian countries have substantial growth and exceptional performance in energy demand.

Thirdly, China faces serious risks to its oil and gas import. Due to the huge energy demand and imperfect strategic reserve mechanism, China has the highest energy import risk index among the countries in Northeast Asia. At the beginning of the 21st century, the proportion of China's oil imports from the Middle East and Africa was as high as 70%. After the establishment of the energy cooperation relationship with Central Asia and Russia, China's dependence on Middle East crude oil was still 51.85% in 2013, although its dependence on the oil from the Middle East and Africa decreased somewhat.[24] The ethnic and religious conflicts between and within countries in the Middle East and Africa are very complicated, and the political and economic situation has been in a state of constant turmoil. After World War II, there have been 15 oil outages in the international oil market, of which 13 occurred in this region. Moreover, China's oil imports are mainly from countries such as Saudi Arabia, Iran, Angola, Oman, Yemen, and Sudan, all of which are defined by the United States as "problem countries." The complex security situation and continuous turmoil in the Middle East region have made the energy security situation in the Middle East very fragile, while Iran and Sudan have been subject to economic sanctions by the United States. The economic sanctions imposed on Russia by western countries will also have a certain impact on China–Russia energy cooperation, and the economic risks of China's energy investment in these countries will also increase. The

---

[23] Lin Boqiang, Pursuing Higher-Quality Energy Consumption, *People's Daily*, January 27, 2014, 23rd Edition.
[24] 2013 Asian Oil Market Analysis: Crude Oil Imports Highly Depend on the Middle East. *China Energy News*, February 6, 2014. http://www.oilone.cn/1402/26/1402261056195.html.

stability of the oil supply has not fundamentally improved due to the increasing diversification of energy import channels.

Fourthly, there is an asymmetry between China's position in the international energy structure and its status as a major energy consumer. China did not have the right to speak for its own interests in international energy pricing. Due to the huge demand, the energy market in Northeast Asia has become a key factor in Asia's energy premium, while China, as the largest demander, has played a very limited role in stabilizing energy prices. China's market of domestic crude oil futures is underdeveloped, the strategic reserves of oil and natural gas have not yet been fully established, and its international influence is very limited. At present, oil and gas trade in China is mostly carried out in the form of spot transactions. International hot money often uses the International Oil Futures Trading Center to pull up international oil prices before China buys oil, forcing China to encounter the price trap of buying high and selling low.[25]

China also faces competitive pressure from other energy-importing countries such as Japan and the ROK. China, Japan, and the ROK have many similarities in their energy situation. They are all major energy-consuming countries in the world, and their energy security situation is not optimistic. In recent years, all countries have begun to implement the strategy of diversifying energy imports and actively carry out energy diplomacy in Africa, Russia, Central Asia, and Latin America, forming a fiercely competitive relationship. After the wars in Afghanistan, Iraq, and Libya, US military influence expanded from the Middle East to the world. All major oil- and gas-producing areas except Russia are under the control of the United States, whose leading position in the international energy pattern is constantly strengthening. In 2015, the G7 Summit decided to continue the sanctions on Russia. This not only threatens Russia's energy security but has negatively impacts China's energy security situation.

4.3.2 Strategies and measures for promoting energy cooperation in Northeast Asia

On November 8, 2014, Chinese President Xi Jinping announced that China would invest US$40 billion to establish the Silk Road Fund to provide investment and financing support for infrastructure, resource

---

[25] Ni Jianmin, *National Energy Security Report*, Beijing: People's Publishing House, 2005, p. 402.

development, industrial cooperation, and other connectivity-related projects along the Belt and Road. As one of the core themes of the Silk Road, energy cooperation will receive more financial support. The Vision and Actions on Jointly Building a Silk Road Economic Belt and a 21st Century Maritime Silk Road, issued in March 2015, proposes that China will give full play to the comparative advantages of various regions in the country, implement a more proactive opening strategy, strengthen the interactive cooperation between East and West, and comprehensively enhance the level of open economy. It is beneficial to Russia, China, the ROK, and Mongolia to promote regional energy cooperation and transportation facilitation in Northeast Asia. The driving effects of the Asian Infrastructure Investment Bank and Silk Road Fund on energy development, industrial investment, and transportation logistics in Northeast Asia will definitely break the status quo of "isolated islands" one by one in the region, and will have a positive impact on the energy industrial structure layout and energy cooperation of various countries in Northeast Asia.

Firstly, China should expand cooperation space in the fields of oil, natural gas, and electricity. At present, the trade volume of oil and gas among the countries in Northeast Asia is very limited, and there is still a lot of room for the development of energy trade in the region. China's economy ranks second in the world, and it has a large trading volume in the major energy exchange centers in the world. More than 30% of transactions on the London Metal Exchange and the London International Petroleum Exchange are related to China. Russia, as a world energy exporter, also occupies a huge share of the international energy trading center. In 2013, the Shanghai International Energy Exchange successfully registered in the Shanghai Free Trade Zone. The establishment of the Northeast Asia Energy Free Trade Area as a platform to undertake international crude oil futures will bring obvious benefits to both energy-exporting and -importing countries in the region. Although Russia is a major exporter of energy, its oil refining capacity is insufficient and its energy exports are mostly in the simple form of crude oil. However, Japan and the ROK in Northeast Asia have advanced oil refining technology and sufficient production capacity. If the oil from Russia can be further processed by Japan and the ROK, it can obtain a higher added value. However, since oil and natural gas are non-renewable energy, most OPEC members impose high export tariffs on energy products. And with the rising world energy prices, energy export tariffs are also rising. In response to this situation, through the integration of the energy market in Northeast Asia, member countries are urged to gradually reduce import and export tariffs on energy products and eventually form a free trade area for energy products. This will not only make full use of the resources and technological advantages of the member countries complementarily and carry out in-depth integration of upstream and downstream resources in the energy industry chain but will also bring about sustained prosperity of the energy industry in the region.

China, Japan, the ROK, and other countries in Northeast Asia are major oil importers. In order to cope with the possible energy shortage, all countries have established their own oil emergency reserve systems. China has just established a strategic oil reserve system, and the oil reserve base is in the initial stage of construction. Unlike Japan and the ROK, China is not a member country of the IEA. As each country has its own policies on oil reserves, the scale of regional oil reserves is small and the flexibility to deal with the energy crisis is insufficient. Therefore, it is necessary to integrate the reserve resources of various countries, improve communication and coordination among various countries, and finally form a unified regional oil reserve mechanism. In terms of concrete implementation, we can make full use of the geographical advantages of being close to Russia, Central Asia, and other major energy-producing areas, and learn from the relatively mature oil reserve experience of Japan and the ROK to establish a common energy reserve mechanism in Northeast Asia. First of all, all countries need to set up a unified oil reserve organization, jointly formulate reserve rules and relevant laws, and jointly invest, manage, and operate oil reserves. The reserve base can be selected at sea or near the border. Moreover, in the long run, it can also attract OPEC and other oil-producing countries to build crude oil transfer and storage facilities in Northeast Asia.

Apart from the oil and gas field, there is also much room for integration in Northeast Asia's electricity market. Russia has the largest electric power system in Europe and is the fourth largest in the world, especially in Siberia and the Far East of Russia, which are rich in fuel and power resources. Most of the large-scale power plants and hydropower stations are concentrated in this region. Countries in Northeast Asia can strengthen cooperation with Russia in the fields of electricity trade, ultra-high-voltage transmission technology, power grid construction, etc., to promote the development of electricity investment and trade in Northeast Asia. Only Russia, China, and Mongolia have power grid connections, and the potential transnational power grids in the future can include all countries in the region: Russia–Japan, Russia–China–ROK, Russia's Siberia–Mongolia–China, and Russia's Far East–DPRK–ROK. In the process of building Northeast Asia's electricity market, it is necessary for all countries to strengthen mutual communication and coordination, establish a power information-sharing mechanism, and bring about the convergence of power development and market demand. Through the signing of power cooperation framework agreements and long-term cooperation agreements, they can jointly negotiate the problems arising from power cooperation and formulate solutions and measures to ensure regional power energy security.

In order to realize the goal of energy market liberalization and integration in Northeast Asia, the countries in this region should make plans, establish energy exchanges, and promote energy futures commodities in Northeast Asia so as to gain certain pricing power in the international energy market and finally form a unified energy market covering the entire Northeast Asia region.

Secondly, in light of the Belt and Road Initiative, cooperation in the field of energy and maritime transportation will be carried out. China, Japan, the ROK, and other countries in Northeast Asia mainly import oil by sea. The process is relatively simple, and the transportation route is fixed. About 85% of China, Japan, and the ROKS's imported oil has to be transported through the Strait of Malacca. Therefore, the openness of the relevant sea areas is of considerable significance to the energy security of Northeast Asian countries. To maintain the safety of energy transportation, China, Japan, and the ROK can abandon Malacca and open up new energy transportation channels to minimize the risks through diversified energy supply and transportation channels. At present, there are mainly three new transportation routes available to Northeast Asian countries. One is Thailand's plan to build the Kra Canal. After the canal is completed, large oil tankers can bypass the Malacca Strait and enter the Gulf of Thailand directly from the Andaman Sea. In this way, the voyage can be shortened by 700 miles, and the one-way transportation cost of large oil tankers can be reduced by £180,000 pounds. The scale of investment in this project is estimated at US$25 billion. The Thai government has been striving for the introduction of foreign capital for joint construction. Both China and Japan have expressed a strong interest in this project. The second is the China–Myanmar oil pipeline. It can directly connect China with oil-producing areas in the Middle East. After passing through the

Indian Ocean, Middle East oil will flow directly from Myanmar to Yunnan, China, thus avoiding the potential risk of China's overreliance on the Malacca Strait for oil transportation. The third is the China–Kazakhstan oil pipeline. China has signed a framework agreement with Kazakhstan to carry out comprehensive cooperation in the oil and gas field. The focus of the cooperation is to jointly build a 3,088-kilometer oil pipeline from Atyrau in the west of Kazakhstan to Alashankou in Xinjiang, China. The completed pipeline can directly transport oil resources from Kazakhstan, Turkmenistan, and other Central Asian countries to China and other East Asian countries. It is also an important transportation route for Russia to supply oil to East Asia.

Thirdly, China should promote cooperation in energy conservation, new energy, and environmental protection in Northeast Asia. Over the years, Japan and the ROK have actively carried out energy-saving activities and have advanced energy-saving technologies. The two countries have complete laws and accumulated rich experience on issues related to energy conservation and environmental protection. Due to the rapid development of China's economy, the technical level of energy conservation and environmental protection needs to be upgraded. If Japan and the ROK can share their technology and experience with other countries in the region such as China, the pressure of the regional energy crisis can be reduced. Energy conservation training programs between China and Japan, and Japan's ODA loans to support China's development of energy conservation technology projects, have achieved gratifying economic and social benefits in this field. The two countries also have great room for cooperation in the development and utilization of new energy resources. Japan has accelerated the development and utilization of renewable energy technologies, including wind energy, solar energy, thermoelectric power generation, bioenergy, and geothermal utilization technologies, through the launch of the "Sunshine Project" and the "New Sunshine Project." Solar energy technology has entered the stage of large-scale utilization. At the same time, Japan is also actively carrying out research on cutting-edge technologies for power generation using tidal sand, waves, and garbage. China has abundant reserves of wind energy and solar energy, but its utilization efficiency is still relatively low. China can make full use of this opportunity to learn from Japan on the development and utilization of new energy resources and learn from Japan's mature experience. Through the development and utilization of new energy technologies, the dependence of various countries on traditional energy sources such as oil and natural gas will be reduced, and competition in energy consumption among Northeast Asian countries will be reduced.

Carbon emission reduction and environmental protection are also important platforms for countries in Northeast Asia to carry out energy cooperation. According to the Copenhagen Accord, Japan and the ROK, as developed countries, have heavy obligations to reduce greenhouse gas emissions. Countries in Northeast Asia can conduct complementary trade on carbon emission targets. As a developing country, China has relatively less pressure to reduce its carbon emissions, and the Kyoto Protocol stipulates that developed countries can fulfill their own emission reduction targets by helping developing countries implement emission reduction projects. According to incomplete statistics, the cost of emission reduction in developed countries is often 5–20 times higher than that in developing countries. Developed countries in Northeast Asia like Japan and the ROK can help China build emission reduction projects. By providing capital and technology to China to improve its energy utilization efficiency and sustainable development capacity, they can fulfill their emission reduction obligations under the Kyoto Protocol. This will save much more cost than if they complete the same emission reduction targets at home. This will also become a new way for China, Japan, and the ROK to cooperate.

4.3.3 The vision of establishing an energy cooperation mechanism in Northeast Asia

At present, energy cooperation in Northeast Asia is still promoted by the business and academic circles. Through forums such as the International Conference on Northeast Asian Natural Gas Pipelines, energy concerns of various countries are being discussed. But there is no formal communication and coordination mechanism at the official level. In the future, energy cooperation in Northeast Asia should focus on building subregional organizations or government-level institutions for multilateral energy policy cooperation. For China, Japan, the ROK, and other energy-demanding countries to maintain their own energy security, it is far from enough to rely solely on one country's energy strategy. Only through the establishment of a regional energy cooperation mechanism can energy-demanding countries be guaranteed energy security. As the largest energy demander and exporter in Northeast Asia, respectively, China and Russia should cooperate to play a greater role in promoting energy system cooperation in Northeast Asia.

Firstly, institutional cooperation in the energy field in Northeast Asia should be promoted. For Northeast Asian countries, the laws, regulations, policies, cross-border investments, and coordination of cross-border transportation are still new issues. The establishment of regional cooperation organizations needs to draw on experience from the Energy Charter. The charter is a mature multilateral cooperation mechanism. It aims to establish a stable and predictable investment environment by strengthening intergovernmental dialogue and cooperation in the fields of trade, investment, transportation, and improving energy efficiency. The charter is open, transparent, and non-discriminatory. The establishment of the Northeast Asia Energy Cooperation Organization should draw on the relevant legal framework of the Energy Charter. A government-level Working Committee should be established first, with regular meetings of senior officials meetings and various specific cooperation projects. By referring to the successful experience of the European Coal and Steel Community and the European Atomic Energy Community, countries in Northeast Asia should promote the formulation of a Charter of the Northeast Asian Energy Community which is binding. We should specifically formulate the aims, principles, membership, rights, and obligations of the Northeast Asian Energy Cooperation Organization. We should design the organizational structure, terms of reference, procedures for activities, implementation of resolutions, and monitoring mechanisms. We should work out the trade terms, investment measures, competition policies, technology transfer, investment promotion, and protection terms. And finally, we should establish ways for dispute settlement and other miscellaneous provisions. The principles and the purposes of the Northeast Asian Regional Energy Cooperation Organization are to promote long-term energy cooperation, maintain regional energy security, contribute to the promotion of economic growth, employment, and improvement of living standards of the member countries, and finally promote the process of the integration of the Northeast Asian region.

The member countries of the Northeast Asia Regional Energy Cooperation Organization should follow the following principles: (1) The principle of mutual benefit: Starting from ensuring the energy security of the entire region of Northeast Asia, the member countries should coordinate their energy policies, cultivate their self-sufficiency in oil supply in the region, reduce their dependence on external oil imports through long-term cooperation among members, jointly establish regional strategic oil reserves and emergency mechanisms, and construct market mechanisms such as oil futures and transit transport channels for energy products to safeguard the common interests of the members of the organization. (2) The principle of complementarity: We should make full use of the respective advantages of each member state in the field of energy, complement each other's advantages, and ensure mutual benefits. For example, we can jointly study and formulate preferential tax policies to promote energy efficiency, formulate a unified oil and gas development plan for the region, cooperate in the development and utilization of renewable energy resources, jointly establish research and development and application projects of new energy technologies, and jointly develop civil nuclear power safety technologies. (3) The principle of cooperation on an equal footing: This requires member states to conduct extensive cooperation in the energy field on a fair and voluntary basis, for example, jointly establish an energy market data-sharing platform and an energy transaction negotiation system, develop relations with organizations of oil-producing countries and other oil-consuming countries, and jointly protect the safety of international energy transportation routes. (4) The principle of open regionalism: This means that membership is open to all, not just limited to Northeast Asian countries, and other non-regional countries, once ready, can be accepted. Finally, through the exemplary role of the energy community, regional integration in Northeast Asia can be promoted.

The specific contents of the cooperation of the Northeast Asian Energy Community should be as follows: a unified regional oil reserve and the emergency response mechanism, a regional oil futures market, a preferential oil transit and transport mechanism, a unified preferential energy-saving tax measure within the region, a regional LNG development plan, joint cooperation in the development and utilization of renewable new energy resources, joint protection of international energy transportation routes and cooperation in the field of environmental protection, establishment of the Northeast Asian Energy Cooperation Forum and the Northeast Asian energy information-sharing mechanism. The rapid development of China's economy has enabled China to play an active role in promoting institutional cooperation in energy cooperation. In regional energy institutional cooperation, the principle of mutual benefit and all-round regional cooperation should be promoted.

Secondly, the formation of a joint energy database in Northeast Asia will be promoted. Providing accurate and timely information to the market can increase the transparency of the market, which is conducive to grasping the appropriate balance between supply and demand and suppressing excessive fluctuations in energy prices. Information sharing of basic economic indicators of supply and demand is very important. At present, Northeast Asian countries are actively participating in the construction of the Joint Oil Data Initiative (JODI) with the International Energy Forum (IEF), the United Nations Statistics Department (UNSD), Asia Pacific Economic Cooperation (APEC), IEA, Organization of the Petroleum Exporting Countries (OPEC), and other institutions. In March 2010, at a ministerial meeting of the IEF held in Cancun, all parties reached an agreement on collecting relevant data needed for oil supply and demand data, natural gas supply and demand data, with plans to expand the upstream development of oil and natural gas and the downstream refining capacity in an effort to realize the formal operation of a joint oil database. At the G20 summit held in Seoul in November 2010 and the special ministerial meeting of the IEF held in Riyadh in February 2011, all parties made every effort to improve the data further and decided on policies to enhance timeliness and credibility. Therefore, the establishment of a joint energy database including oil, natural gas, coal, and renewable energy in Northeast Asia is an important direction for future cooperation.

Thirdly, the establishment of an energy investment protection and cooperation mechanism is very important. Energy is a capital-intensive industry, and abundant capital is a necessary condition to integrate the upstream and downstream industries of the energy value chain. At the same time, the energy industry investment has the characteristics of being strategic, long-term, and continuous and is extremely vulnerable to the influence of the local political and economic change, so the investment risk is relatively higher. This requires that energy investment cooperation must be based on a framework of high political mutual trust and security. Thus, Northeast Asian countries can consider setting up an energy development bank in Northeast Asia to attract social and government investment and link the interests of all parties.

After the Ukraine crisis broke out, western sanctions against Russia had a significant impact on the international financing of the global energy industry. Since Putin came into power, Russia has been continuously tightening and restricting the share of foreign investors in the field of natural resources. Few foreign companies can hold controlling shares in related fields, especially in oil and gas and mineral projects that Russia considers of strategic significance. As a result of the sanctions, Russia has changed its strict control rules over upstream energy development projects. In 2015, Russian Deputy Prime Minister Arkady Dvorkovich publicly expressed at the Krasnoyarsk Economic Forum in Siberia that Chinese investors are welcome to enter the strategic oil and gas sector, which highlights Russia's urgent need for great foreign investment in developing strategic energy reserves. Western sanctions against Russia have deprived the country's major energy companies of the right to cheap loans and advanced technology, forcing Russia to strengthen ties with Asia. Dvorkovich's speech shows that the relationship between Russia and China is undergoing substantial changes. However, Russia's strategy of turning to the east has not been fully implemented, and the scale of change is also inconsistent with the actual development of Russia. Among China's overseas investments, China's investment in Russia is far less than that of Western countries. China must promote the construction of an energy investment mechanism from the perspective of regional cooperation, seize the possible opportunities to establish a "regional sharing" mechanism instead of focusing on a certain specific project and thinking only of the profits of the two parties in the project. Both the AIIB and the New Development Bank can play an effective role in this field.

Fourthly, the establishment of a protection mechanism for overseas investment and cooperation of energy enterprises is imperative. As the energy industry is often an important economic lifeline of a country, the unstable political situation in a country will often lead to changes in the country's energy industry policies, which will bring great risks to the investment of Chinese enterprises. There is a high degree of uncertainty in this kind of risk, and general insurance companies will not guarantee it. Therefore, the government should give risk management support to overseas energy investment. In this regard, we can learn from the experience of developed countries and establish overseas risk exploration funds to provide risk protection for domestic enterprises to explore the energy market overseas and increase support services for foreign cooperation of energy enterprises. In order to ensure China's energy security, the government should encourage energy enterprises to cooperate with foreign countries actively. Through supportive policies, laws, and funds, we will do a good job of serving the overseas mergers and investments of large energy enterprises in our country. Russia intends to give full play to the resource advantages of the Far East, develop the industrial chain related to oil and natural gas, improve the deep processing capability of oil and natural gas products, and give investors a large number of preferential policies. The

Chinese government should support enterprises to participate in Russia's energy exploration and enhance their ability to resist political and economic risks abroad. The most attractive investment areas for the new round of Far East development are in energy resources, transportation, and oil and gas processing, requiring huge investments and taking certain risks. We must jointly determine the price of oil and gas, reduce the transaction cost of oil and gas, and ensure the safe supply of energy by participating in upstream management. With the enhancement of China's economic strength, investment should be gradually increased to raise the proportion of "stock right oil" obtained in Russia. In this process, it is necessary to jointly establish a venture capital management fund for cooperative enterprises with Russia to provide risk management and financial support for enterprises. In particular, energy exploration projects need large investments while carrying high risks, which will limit the enthusiasm of enterprises for investment. Therefore, through the support and compensation of special exploration funds from the cooperation fund, the investment scope of enterprises can be expanded. In addition, the role of export credit insurance should be further developed to provide risk control and short-term financing services for strategic overseas energy investment projects to make up for the shortage of commercial insurance and loans.

At the same time, China should improve the relevant laws and regulations for overseas investment as soon as possible. The approval and management of overseas investments in China are carried out by different departments. This multi-department management has resulted in numerous approval links and low efficiency of overseas investment projects. In order to promote the overseas investment of energy enterprises, it is necessary to speed up the fundamental reform of the overseas investment approval system, reduce the approval level, simplify the approval process, and create a fair, just, and open investment mechanism and environment for the overseas investment of enterprises. In addition, the State-owned Assets Supervision and Administration Commission of the State Council (SASAC) and other management agencies of state-owned energy enterprises should work closely with foreign economic cooperation departments to give state-owned energy enterprises greater autonomy in overseas investment so as to organically combine the government's macro guidance with the prudent decision-making of enterprises. It is also necessary to strengthen information collection and research on forecasting the development trend of overseas energy markets and to establish and perfect an international energy market information system. At present, the incomplete information about the international energy market, especially the lack of investment information data in some emerging energy markets, has seriously restricted the pace of growth of China's enterprises in developing emerging energy markets. Therefore, the collection, sorting, and sharing of information on emerging energy markets in Central Asia and Africa should be strengthened. In addition, it is also necessary to track and monitor the macro and microeconomic environment, as well as the social and political situation of overseas markets, to build a comprehensive international energy industry investment database, and to collect and sort out the basic statistical information of overseas energy markets. Through reliable information dissemination agencies and channels, overseas investment enterprises are provided with information on the place where they invest in the energy, the market structure, investment policies, and relevant laws and regulations so as to ease the process of cooperation.

Chapter 5

Economic and Trade Relations in Northeast Asia and China's Regional Cooperation Policy

Trade and investment facilitation and liberalization are the key processes of regional economic cooperation. Since the early 1990s, economic relations among the countries in Northeast Asia have become increasingly close. However, the development of trade and investment facilitation and liberalization is still slow. Since the end of the 20th century, China, Japan, and the ROK have instituted free trade areas, cooperation mechanisms, and some trade and investment liberalization and facilitation measures, which have received attention. Nevertheless, the facilitation of trade and investment among Northeast Asian countries still lacks institutional guarantee. Therefore, it is necessary for us to study the impact of establishing a China–Japan–ROK FTA and explore China's strategic countermeasures to promote trade and investment facilitation and regional cooperation in Northeast Asia.

5.1 Economic and Trade Cooperation in Northeast Asia Under the Conditions of Economic Globalization

Following the overall trend of world economic globalization and regional economic integration, Asia, as one of the three major economic regions in the world, is lagging in the process of regional economic cooperation compared with Europe and North America. Although Northeast Asia, as a subregion of the Asian economy, has achieved rapid economic development, the quantity and quality of its economic cooperation can hardly meet the needs of the development in this region. Especially in recent years, Northeast Asian countries have been witnessing rapid economic development, which in turn poses higher demand for regional economic cooperation. Hence, a new historical opportunity for regional cooperation in Northeast Asia has appeared.

5.1.1 Stable economic development in Northeast Asia

From the rise of Japan's economy to the rapid development of China after World War II, the speedy economic development of Asian countries, especially Northeast Asian countries, attracted worldwide attention.

5.1.1.1 *Economic growth*

Since the early 1990s, Northeast Asia has been playing an important role in the world economy. In terms of GDP, the proportion of total economic volume of Northeast Asia in the world declined due to the impact of the Asian financial crisis in 1997. However, from the end of the 20th century onward, the total economic volume of Northeast Asia began to show relatively stable growth and maintained a good momentum of growth and gradually got rid of the influence of the economic crisis. Despite the financial crisis in 2008, the GDP of Northeast Asia was relatively stable in terms of both its total amount and its global proportion and showed an upward trend in the last seven years (from 2007 to 2013). (see Table 5.1 and Figure 5.1 for details).[1] Although there is still a gap between the total economic capacity of Northeast Asia and that of the EU and NAFTA, the gap is narrowing year by year, with Northeast Asia's capacity reaching US$17.43 trillion in 2012, exceeding the EU's US$17.25 trillion and not far from the NAFTA's US$19.17 trillion.

China and Japan are the most important forces of economic growth in Northeast Asia. China's position has become increasingly prominent, gradually replacing Japan, which can be observed from the fluctuations in

---

[1] Since relevant data are not available, the data on the DPRK are not included in the data on Northeast Asia in this section.

Table 5.1. GDP comparison of Northeast Asia, the EU, and NAFTA (Unit: US$ trillion).

Year	Northeast Asia	EU	NAFTA	World
2004	7.95	13.69	14.06	43.42
2005	8.49	14.31	15.12	46.98
2006	9.07	15.27	16.13	50.89
2007	10.28	17.66	16.98	57.35
2008	12.04	19.01	17.36	62.88
2009	12.15	17.00	16.68	59.56
2010	14.05	16.93	17.63	65.24
2011	16.34	18.31	18.47	72.13
2012	17.43	17.25	19.17	73.52
2013	17.57	17.96	19.86	75.62

Source: World Bank, http://da//data.worldbank.org/indicator/NY.GDP.MKTP.CD, and the International Monetary Fund, http://www.imf.org/externaVpubs/ft/weo/2015/01/weodata/index.aspx.

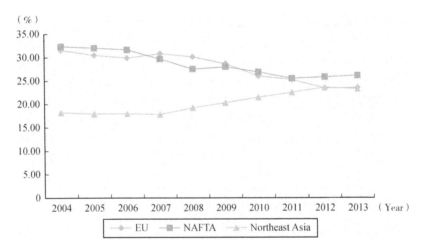

Figure 5.1. Comparison trend of global GDP shares of Northeast Asia, the EU, and the NAFTA from 2004 to 2013.

Source: The data in Table 5.1.

the overall GDP of Northeast Asia and that of China. As shown in Table 5.2 and Figure 5.2, the share of the total GDP of Northeast Asia followed the fluctuating trends of Japan before the end of the 20th century. Since the start of the 21st century, the total GDP of Northeast Asia fell

Table 5.2. Total GDP of Northeast Asian countries (Unit: US$100 million).

Year	China	Japan	The ROK	Russia	Mongolia	Countries in Northeast Asia	World
1994	5,592.24	48,503.48	4,587.04	3,950.87	9.26	62,642.89	276,386.74
1995	7,280.08	53,339.26	5,593.30	3,955.28	14.52	70,182.43	305,925.36
1996	8,560.85	47,061.87	6,034.13	3,917.21	13.46	65,587.52	312,474.00
1997	9,526.53	43,242.78	5,604.85	4,049.27	11.81	62,435.24	311,547.86
1998	10,194.62	39,145.75	3,764.82	2,709.53	11.24	55,825.96	310,296.19
1999	10,832.79	44,325.99	4,863.15	1,959.06	10.57	61,991.56	321,842.91
2000	11,984.75	47,311.99	5,616.33	2,597.08	11.37	67,521.52	332,273.28
2001	13,248.07	41,598.60	5,330.52	3,066.03	12.68	63,255.89	330,328.65
2002	14,538.28	39,808.20	6,090.20	3,451.10	13.97	63,901.74	343,174.23
2003	16,409.59	43,029.39	6,805.21	4,303.48	15.95	70,563.62	385,397.24
2004	19,316.44	46,558.03	7,648.81	5,910.17	19.92	79,453.37	434,213.66
2005	22,569.03	45,718.67	8,981.34	7,640.01	25.23	84,934.28	469,752.73
2006	27,129.51	43,567.50	10,117.98	9,899.31	34.14	90,748.43	508,906.20
2007	34,940.56	43563.47	11,226.76	12,997.05	42.35	102,770.19	573,457.98
2008	45,218.27	48,491.85	10,022.16	16,608.44	56.23	120,396.96	628,782.08
2009	49,902.34	50,351.42	9,019.35	12,226.44	45.84	121,545.38	595,606.37
2010	59,305.02	54,953.87	10,944.99	15,249.16	62.00	140,515.05	652,378.05
2011	73,218.92	59,056.31	12,024.64	19,047.93	87.61	163,435.41	721,286.10
2012	82,294.90	59,544.77	12,228.07	20,174.71	103.22	174,345.67	735,211.55
2013	92,402.70	49,195.63	13,045.54	20,967.77	115.16	175,726.81	756,218.58

Source: World Bank, http://data.worldbank.org/indicator/NY.GDP.MKTP.CD.

along with the fall of Japan's GDP, but with a gentler slope due to the increase in China's GDP. After 2007, the total GDP share of Northeast Asia began to show a significant upsurge with the rapid growth of China's GDP, diverging from Japan's decline.

The economic development in Northeast Asia is reflected not only in the steady increase in the total GDP but also in the relatively sustained and stable GDP growth rate. According to Table 5.3 and Figure 5.3, the GDP

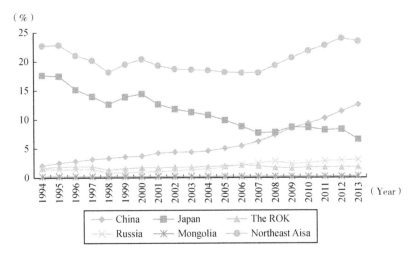

Figure 5.2. Comparison trend of the proportion of GDP of Northeast Asian countries 1994 to 2013.

Source: The data in Table 5.2.

growth rate of Northeast Asian countries is relatively stable, except that of Russia and Mongolia. Japan's GDP growth rate has been hovering around 1% because its economy has not walked out of the long time depression after its foam economy. The ROK on the whole has shown good growth of total GDP, except for a few years of drastic fluctuations. China's GDP growth has been the strongest, with the exception of 7.62% in 1999, which is lower than the ROK's 10.73%. China has taken the leading position in Northeast Asian countries. In 2009, the growth of most countries and economic groups was zero or even negative due to the economic crisis, but China's economic growth still reached 9.21%. Compared with the GDP growth of the world's major economies, such as the EU and NAFTA, the GDP growth of the major Northeast Asian countries has been better in most years.

Despite the high GDP growth, the GDP per capita of Northeast Asian countries is unsatisfactory. Even though the GDP per capita of Japan and the ROK has long been above the average worldwide GDP per capita, that of Russia, China, and Mongolia are lower than the global average. In 2013, the GDP per capita of China, Japan, the ROK, Mongolia, and

Table 5.3. GDP growth rates of Northeast Asian countries and major global economic groups (Unit: %).

Year	China	Japan	The ROK	Mongolia	Russia	NAFTA	EU	World
1994	13.08	0.87	8.77	2.13	−12.57	4.08	2.86	3.12
1995	10.92	1.94	8.93	6.38	−4.14	2.72	2.66	2.91
1996	10.01	2.61	7.19	2.24	−3.60	3.62	1.99	3.29
1997	9.30	1.60	5.77	3.90	1.40	4.46	2.68	3.70
1998	7.83	−2.00	−5.71	3.34	−5.30	4.43	3.03	2.55
1999	7.62	−0.20	10.73	3.07	6.40	4.80	3.00	3.38
2000	8.43	2.26	8.83	1.15	10.00	4.17	3.88	4.26
2001	8.30	0.36	4.53	2.95	5.09	1.04	2.19	1.81
2002	9.08	0.29	7.43	4.73	4.74	1.87	1.31	2.06
2003	10.03	1.69	2.93	7.00	7.30	2.74	1.48	2.79
2004	10.09	2.36	4.90	10.63	7.18	3.73	2.52	4.15
2005	11.31	1.30	3.92	7.25	6.38	3.33	2.06	3.57
2006	12.68	1.69	5.18	8.56	8.15	2.66	3.42	4.11
2007	14.16	2.19	5.46	10.25	8.54	1.79	3.07	3.93
2008	9.63	−1.04	2.83	8.90	5.25	−0.14	0.48	1.48
2009	9.21	−5.53	0.71	−1.27	−7.82	−2.80	−4.41	−2.08
2010	10.45	4.65	6.50	6.37	4.50	2.60	2.13	4.08
2011	9.30	−0.45	3.68	17.51	4.26	1.68	1.76	2.79
2012	7.65	1.75	2.29	12.40	3.44	2.26	−0.40	2.27
2013	7.67	1.61	2.97	11.74	1.32	2.20	0.06	2.29

Source: World Bank, http://data.worldbank.org/indicator/NY.GDP.MKTP.KD.ZG.

Russia were US$6,807.43, US$38,633.71, US$25,976.95, US$4,056.40, and US$14,611.70, respectively (see Table 5.4, Figures 5.4 and 5.5). However, judging from the long-term development trend, Russia has exceeded the global average since 2006, while China and Mongolia are moving closer to the global average, with the gap narrowing year by year.

As for national income (GNI), whether it is the growth of GNI, the increase of its share in the world, or the performance of GNI per capita, there is a trend similar to the relevant data of GDP. Thus, the relevant analysis is not repeated herein (see Table 5.5, Figures 5.6 and 5.7 for details).

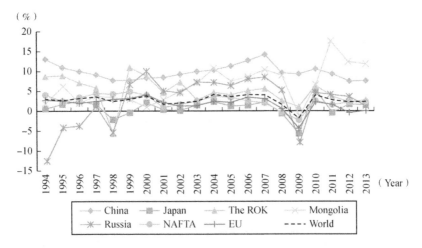

Figure 5.3. Comparison trend of GDP growth rates of Northeast Asian countries and major global economic groups.

Source: The data in Table 5.3.

Table 5.4. The GDP per capita of Northeast Asian countries and the world (Unit: US$).

Year	China	Japan	The ROK	Mongolia	Russia	World
2004	1,490.38	36,441.50	15,921.94	798.02	4,109.38	6,771.66
2005	1,731.13	35,781.17	18,657.46	998.76	5,338.41	7,238.23
2006	2,069.34	34,075.98	20,917.04	1,333.88	6,947.50	7,748.53
2007	2,651.26	34,033.69	23,101.44	1,631.90	9,145.45	8,629.03
2008	3,413.59	37,865.62	20,474.83	2,135.81	11,699.68	9,350.24
2009	3,748.50	39,322.61	18,338.71	1,715.36	8,615.67	8,753.71
2010	4,433.34	42,909.25	22,151.21	2,285.65	10,709.77	9,476.72
2011	5,447.31	46,203.70	24,155.83	3,181.10	13,324.29	10,356.43
2012	6,092.78	46,679.27	24,453.97	3,691.05	14,090.65	10,438.63
2013	6,807.43	38,633.71	25,976.95	4,056.40	14,611.70	10,613.45

Source: World Bank, http://data.worldbank.org/indicator/NY.GDP.PCAP.CD.

5.1.1.2 *Foreign exchange reserves*

Foreign exchange reserve is one of the important indicators of a country's economic strength, which has the function to maintain a country's international balance of payments, stabilize the exchange rate of its own

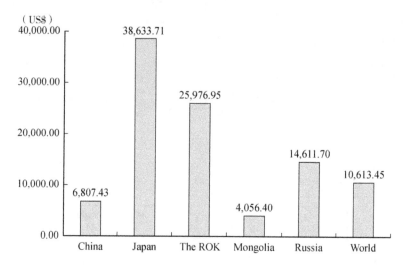

Figure 5.4. Comparison of GDP per capita of Northeast Asian countries and the world in 2013.

Source: The data in Table 5.4.

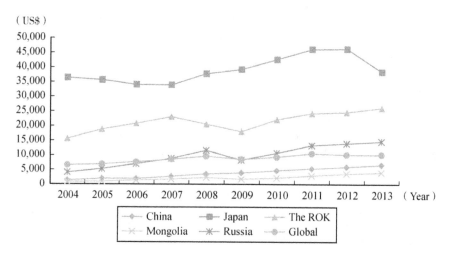

Figure 5.5. Comparison trend of GDP per capita of Northeast Asian countries and the world from 2004 to 2013.

Source: The data in Table 5.4.

Table 5.5. National Income in Northeast Asia and the world (Unit: US$100 million).

Year	China	Japan	The ROK	Mongolia	Russia	Northeast Asia	World
2004	19,361.98	47,463.37	7,516.33	18.94	4,905.82	79,266.44	422,787.11
2005	22,656.51	50,016.24	8,569.66	22.64	6,384.71	87,649.77	473,950.41
2006	26,698.73	49,314.12	9,665.85	28.62	8,301.40	94,008.71	510,489.77
2007	32,616.18	48,121.19	10,917.24	36.46	10,799.83	102,490.90	553,329.58
2008	40,407.56	48,355.53	11,186.45	47.35	13,685.94	113,682.82	600,971.18
2009	48,082.92	47,979.84	10,373.79	47.82	13,184.95	119,669.32	609,384.21
2010	56,694.46	53,766.02	10,533.01	51.55	14,251.23	135,296.26	644,598.57
2011	65,926.64	57,756.33	11,257.87	64.58	15,470.09	150,475.51	682,902.08
2012	77,457.29	61,015.79	12,321.64	86.18	18,240.88	169,121.79	728,558.63
2013	89,053.36	58,999.05	13,015.75	107.06	19,877.38	181,052.60	761,192.65

Source: World Bank, http://data.worldbank.org/indicator/NY.GNP.ATLS.CD.

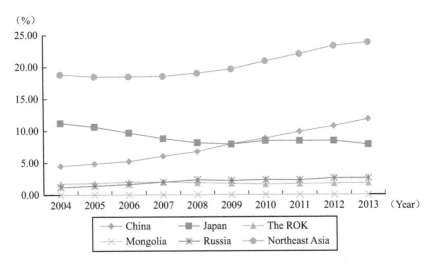

Figure 5.6. GNI proportions of Northeast Asian countries and Northeast Asia in the world.

Source: The data in Table 5.5.

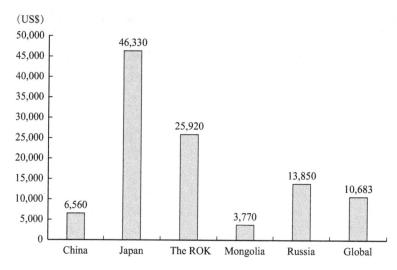

Figure 5.7. GNI per capita in Northeast Asia and the world in 2013.
Source: World Bank, http://data.worldbank.org/indicator/ny.gnp.pcap.cd.

currency, and pay the international debt. It is the most important component of a country's international liquidity. Due to historical reasons, the major countries in Northeast Asia have adopted distinct economic development models, such as the catch-up model, the government-led model, and the export-oriented model. Moreover, the painful lessons of the 1997 crisis forced the Northeast Asian countries to accrue relatively sufficient foreign exchange reserves in recent years. Especially in the 21st century, the total foreign exchange reserves of these countries have exceeded the sum of the EU and the NAFTA, reaching 45.05% of the world total in 2011. Among them, China contributed the most with its foreign exchange reserves reaching US$3.25 trillion in 2011, accounting for 27.37% of the world's total (see Table 5.6 and Figure 5.8). Sufficient foreign exchange reserves provide adequate safeguard for Northeast Asia against financial shocks.

Although the sufficient foreign exchange reserves of Northeast Asian countries provide protection for the region to cope with external financial shocks, a heavier reserve burden has been imposed on the countries in this region. Exchange rate changes in reserve currency issuing countries have a far-reaching impact on reserve currency holders, which brings about uncertainties to Northeast Asia's ability to cope with external financial

Table 5.6. Foreign exchange reserves of Northeast Asian countries and the world (including Gold) (Unit: US$100 million).

Year	China	Japan	The ROK	Mongolia	Russia	Northeast Asia	World
2000	1,717.63	3,616.39	962.51	2.02	276.56	6,575.12	22,314.71
2001	2,200.57	4,019.58	1,028.75	2.07	363.03	7,613.99	23,533.17
2002	2,977.39	4,696.18	1,214.98	2.67	483.26	9,374.48	27,857.54
2003	4,161.99	6,735.54	1,554.72	2.04	784.09	13,238.38	34,771.14
2004	6,229.49	8,446.67	1,991.95	2.08	1,262.58	17,932.77	42,003.16
2005	8,314.10	8,468.96	2,105.52	3.33	1,822.72	20,714.63	47,800.89
2006	10,807.56	8,953.21	2,391.48	7.20	3,037.73	25,197.18	57,938.61
2007	15,463.65	9,732.97	2,625.33	10.02	4,788.22	32,620.18	73,933.86
2008	19,660.37	10,307.63	2,015.45	6.57	4,262.79	36,252.81	80,719.95
2009	24,528.99	10,489.91	2,704.37	13.27	4,393.42	42,129.96	94,104.53
2010	29,137.12	10,960.69	2,921.43	22.88	4,792.22	47,834.34	107,908.88
2011	32,546.74	12,958.39	3,069.35	28.44	4,974.10	53,577.02	118,316.10

Source: International Monetary Fund, http://hvww.imf.org/external/pubs/ft/weo/2012/02/weodata/index.aspx.

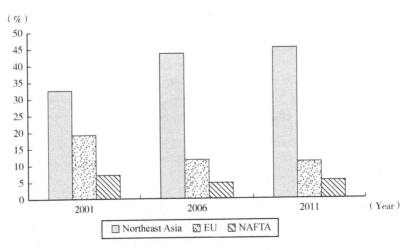

Figure 5.8. Comparison trend of foreign exchange reserves in Northeast Asia and major economies in the world.

Source: The data in Table 5.6.

Table 5.7. Inflation rates measured by GDP deflator in Northeast Asian countries and major global economies (Unit: %).

Year	China	Japan	The ROK	Mongolia	Russia	EU	NAFTA	World
2004	6.93	−1.35	2.98	16.69	20.28	2.95	3.28	5.46
2005	3.92	−1.25	1.03	20.10	19.31	2.56	3.22	5.49
2006	3.81	−1.12	−0.14	21.99	15.17	2.95	3.07	5.41
2007	7.64	−0.93	2.40	11.63	13.80	3.04	3.24	5.55
2008	7.76	−1.27	2.96	21.45	17.96	3.20	2.09	8.35
2009	−0.61	−0.50	3.54	1.83	1.99	1.83	0.33	2.39
2010	6.64	−2.16	3.16	20.03	14.19	1.04	1.23	4.60
2011	7.80	−1.85	1.58	12.13	15.91	1.73	2.06	5.66
2012	2.00	−0.93	1.04	12.44	7.48	1.61	1.80	3.48
2013	1.70	−0.55	0.70	12.08	5.90	1.39	1.40	2.34

Source: Bank for International Settlements, http://www.bis.org/statistics/index.htm; the IMF, http://www.imf.org/external/pubs/ft/weo/2012/02/weodata/index.aspx.

shocks. As a result, part of the momentum for economic development in Northeast Asia has been grabbed by external economic groups. Therefore, it shows that there is no mature international currency in Northeast Asia. Although the Japanese yen has become an international currency, its weight in the international monetary system is not consistent with Japan's economic power in the world, which means that the Japanese yen fails to play its due role in the global foreign exchange reserves. Moreover, though the renminbi internationalization strategy has been gradually promoted, it is far from being a truly internationalized currency. Yet the currencies of other countries in Northeast Asia are far from being internationalized.

5.1.1.3 *Inflation rate control*

According to the inflation rate of Northeast Asia and the major economies in the world by GDP deflator as indicated in Table 5.7 and Figure 5.9, the inflation rates of China, Japan, and the ROK, the major economies in Northeast Asia, are generally lower than the global average except those of Russia and Mongolia. Compared with the overall level of the NAFTA and the EU, the inflation rates of China and the ROK have been higher in

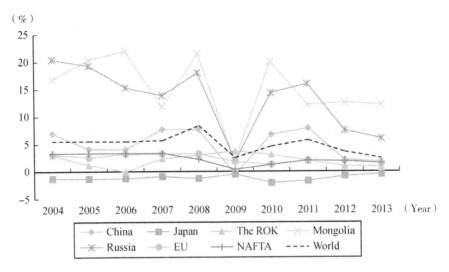

Figure 5.9. Comparison trend of inflation rates of Northeast Asian countries and major global economies measured by GDP deflator.

Source: The data in Table 5.7.

some years, while Japan's inflation rate has been negative for a long time due to its economic stagnation.

5.1.2 Growing trade and investment in Northeast Asia

5.1.2.1 *Foreign trade*

In the 21st century, the total import and export in Northeast Asia have been increasing. In the 10 years from 2005–2014, the total volume increased from US$3.78 trillion to US$8.92 trillion. At the same time, the proportion of Northeast Asia's foreign trade in the world also increased, from 14.90% in 2005 to 19.14% in 2011 (see Tables 5.8–5.9 and Figure 5.10 for details). China's total foreign trade topped the list in Northeast Asia in 2000 and has been steadily growing, reaching US$4.69 trillion in 2014, accounting for 10.06% of the world's total foreign trade and making the greatest contribution to the growth of foreign trade in Northeast Asia. The proportions of the ROK and Russia showed a relatively flat upward trend, rising from 2.56% and 1.71% in 2005 to 2.94% and 2.13% in 2014, respectively. Mongolia's total foreign trade has been less than 0.03% of the world's total

Table 5.8. Total foreign trade in Northeast Asia (Unit: US$1 trillion).

Year	China	Japan	The ROK	Mongolia	Russia	Northeast Asia	World
2005	1.4163	1.2776	0.6488	0.0031	0.4332	3.7789	25.3623
2006	1.7380	1.3943	0.7607	0.0039	0.5427	4.4395	29.0923
2007	2.2027	1.5187	0.8893	0.0050	0.6741	5.2897	33.8754
2008	2.6383	1.7655	1.0428	0.0068	0.8897	6.3431	39.0738
2009	2.3005	1.3147	0.8351	0.0049	0.5903	5.0456	31.1883
2010	3.0724	1.6585	1.0604	0.0073	0.7628	6.5614	37.1287
2011	3.7994	1.8995	1.3392	0.0130	0.9835	8.0346	44.0896
2012	4.1447	1.9252	1.3699	0.0133	1.0345	8.4876	44.6902
2013	4.4822	1.7856	1.3675	0.0126	1.0631	8.7110	45.8773
2014	4.6897	1.8539	1.3718	0.0129	0.9936	8.9220	46.6128

Source: UNCTAD database, http://unctadstal.unclad.org/ReportFolders/reportFolders.aspx.

Table 5.9. Proportion of total foreign trade of Northeast Asian countries (Unit: %).

Year	China	Japan	The ROK	Mongolia	Russia	Northeast Asia
2005	5.58	5.04	2.56	0.01	1.71	14.90
2006	5.97	4.79	2.61	0.01	1.87	15.26
2007	6.50	4.48	2.63	0.01	1.99	15.62
2008	6.75	4.52	2.67	0.02	2.28	16.23
2009	7.38	4.22	2.68	0.02	1.89	16.18
2010	8.28	4.47	2.86	0.02	2.05	17.67
2011	8.62	4.31	3.04	0.03	2.23	18.22
2012	9.27	4.31	3.07	0.03	2.31	18.99
2013	9.77	3.89	2.98	0.03	2.32	18.99
2014	10.06	3.98	2.94	0.03	2.13	19.14

Source: UNCTAD database, http://unctadstat.unctad.org/ReportFolders/reportFolders.asp.

due to the small scale of its economy. Although Japan's total foreign trade increased from US$1.28 trillion in 2005 to US$1.85 trillion in 2014, its share in global trade decreased from 5.04% in 2005 to 3.98% in 2014, showing an apparent dwindling influence.

Economic and Trade Relations in Northeast Asia 251

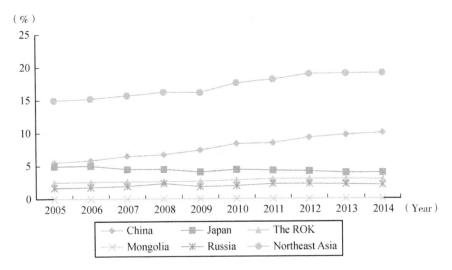

Figure 5.10. Comparison trend of total foreign trade of Northeast Asian countries.
Source: The data in Table 5.9.

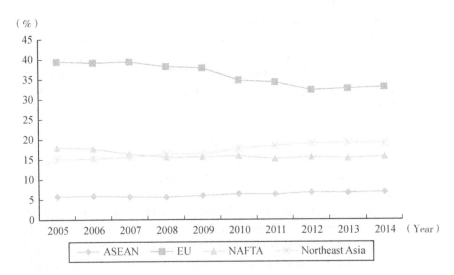

Figure 5.11. Comparison trend of total foreign trade proportion of major economic groups in the world.
Source: Based on the data from UNCTAD database, http://unctadstat.unctad.org/ReportFolders/reportFolders.aspx.

Table 5.10. Total foreign trade volumes of the major economic groups in the world (Unit: US$1 trillion).

Year	ASEAN	EU	NAFTA	Northeast Asia	World
2005	1.4532	9.9576	4.5775	3.7789	25.3623
2006	1.6794	11.3455	5.1180	4.4395	29.0923
2007	1.9161	13.3221	5.5813	5.2897	33.8754
2008	2.2562	14.9028	6.0784	6.3431	39.0738
2009	1.8583	11.7351	4.8585	5.0456	31.1883
2010	2.3763	12.9329	5.8127	6.5614	37.1287
2011	2.8298	15.0070	6.6650	8.0346	44.0896
2012	2.9785	14.3976	6.9011	8.4876	44.6902
2013	3.0262	14.9267	6.9909	8.7110	45.8773
2014	3.0570	15.3564	7.1941	8.9220	46.6128

Source: Based on the data from UNCTAD database, http://unctadstat.unctad.org/ReportFolders/reportFolders.aspx.

Compared with the foreign trade data of major economies in the world, it can be seen that the proportion of total foreign trade of the EU and the NAFTA in the world has been declining slowly, which is in sharp contrast to the stable growth in Northeast Asia (see Figure 5.11). Northeast Asia officially surpassed the NAFTA in 2008 with a total trade volume of US$6.34 trillion that year. Although there is still a big gap, with the stable performance of the EU accounting for about 40% of the global foreign trade, the gap between the two is narrowing year by year with a slow decline of the EU's share and a steady rise of the Northeast Asia's share worldwide. In 2014, Northeast Asia's total foreign trade volume was close to 2/3 of the EU's total, compared with less than half of the latter in 2005 (see Table 5.10).

While the total foreign trade in Northeast Asia has increased rapidly and its share in world import and export trade has also increased rapidly, the share of intra-regional trade in foreign trade has not increased. It shows a slight decline (see Table 5.11, Figures 5.12 and 5.13 for details) from 23.98% in 2004 to 21.06% in 2013, maintaining a low level of about 20% on the whole. Thus, it is clear that economic dependency among Northeast Asian countries remains low, dependence on intra-regional trade is relatively low, and the degree of intra-regional economic

Table 5.11. Comparison of intra-regional commodity trade proportion among Northeast Asia and other major economic groups.

Year	Commodity trade in Northeast Asia (US$100 million)	Total commodity trade of Northeast Asian countries (US$100 million)	Proportion of commodity trade in Northeast Asia (%)	Proportion of commodity trade in EU (%)	Proportion of commodity trade in NAFTA (%)
2004	7,038.08	29,347.34	23.98	68.57	55.88
2005	8,159.83	34,475.00	23.67	67.77	55.74
2006	9,367.75	40,898.82	22.90	68.08	53.85
2007	10,981.34	47,970.60	22.89	68.10	51.29
2008	12,703.80	57,056.74	22.27	67.19	49.47
2009	10,200.12	45,031.74	22.65	66.56	47.96
2010	13,714.25	59,613.42	23.01	64.89	48.69
2011	16,372.70	72,344.60	22.63	63.75	48.30
2012	16,275.77	74,709.04	21.79	61.96	48.55
2013	16,079.86	76,352.92	21.06	61.21	49.19

Source: Based on the data from UNCTAD database, http://unctadstat.unctad.org/ReportFolders/reportFolders.aspx.

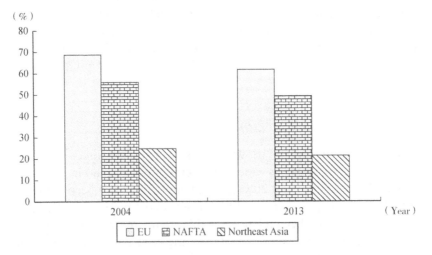

Figure 5.12. Comparison of commodity trade proportion among Northeast Asia and other major economic groups.

Source: The data in Table 5.11.

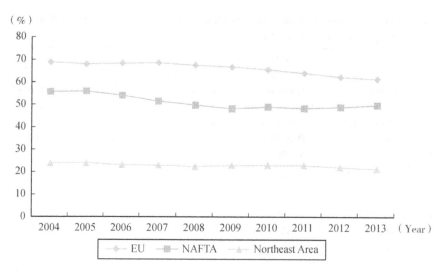

Figure 5.13. Trends of commodity trade proportion among Northeast Asia and other major economic groups.

Source: The data in Table 5.11.

cooperation is still at a relatively low level. Consequently, regional economic cooperation in Northeast Asia is not good.

The root cause of this phenomenon is that the foreign trade growth in Northeast Asia is not the result of the industrial division of labor but the result of production and consumption. It has closer relation with the external markets. In other words, economic cooperation in Northeast Asia lacks an internal dynamic mechanism, that is, a regional production and consumption network.

5.1.2.2 *International investment*

In terms of foreign capital inflow, the inflow of foreign direct investment (FDI) in Northeast Asia has shown an overall upward trend in fluctuation since the 1970s. In the past 20 years, although there have been noticeable fluctuations in the proportion of FDI inflows in the world, the FDI inflow in Northeast Asia has been relatively stable, compared with the drastic ups and downs in FDI inflows in the EU and the NAFTA. At the same time, the total inflow of FDI into Northeast Asia has been growing steadily and swiftly from US$160 million in 1970 to US$219.744 billion in 2013,

Table 5.12. FDI inflows of major economic groups in the world (Unit: US$100 million).

Year	Northeast Asia	ASEAN	EU	NAFTA	World
1973	−0.38	12.45	95.06	57.62	206.46
1978	1.77	13.79	133.07	102.24	343.58
1983	15.16	32.93	149.32	157.11	504.59
1988	40.03	70.66	581.37	675.76	1,646.45
1993	297.76	165.85	781.29	597.83	2,227.01
1998	574.25	209.26	2,854.63	2,099.94	7,071.57
2003	749.28	297.84	2,870.82	795.26	6,043.03
2008	2,195.52	503.00	5,514.13	3,962.31	18,188.34
2013	2,197.44	1,254.35	2,462.07	2,881.38	14,519.65

Source: Based on the data from the database of UNCTAD, http://unctadstat.unctad.org/ReportFolders/reportFolders.aspx.

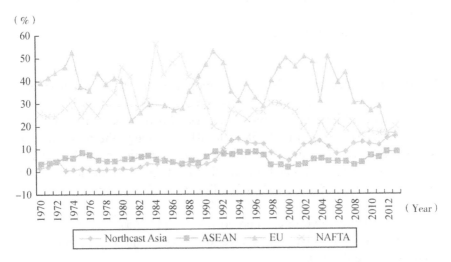

Figure 5.14. Comparison trend of FDI inflows of major economic groups in the world.
Source: The data in Table 5.12.

which is very close to US$288.138 billion for the NAFTA and US$246.207 billion for the EU with steadily narrowing gaps (See Table 5.12, Figures 5.14 and 5.15 for details).

With regard to attracting foreign investment, the amount of investment from Northeast Asia in foreign countries has also shown similar

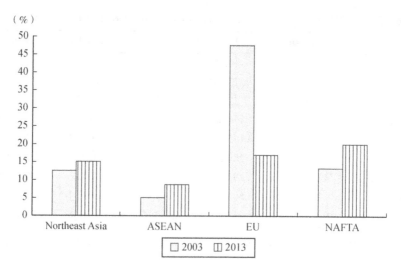

Figure 5.15. The Proportion of FDI inflows into the world's major economies in 2003 and 2013.

Source: Based on the data in Table 5.12.

fluctuations. Since the 1970s, as the amount of Northeast Asian investment in foreign countries has increased rapidly, its overall proportion in the world's total investment abroad has also shown an upward trend, rising from 2.51% in 1970 to 25.58% in 2013. Although the proportion of Northeast Asia's investment abroad has shown drastic ups and downs in the past 20 years, there has been an obvious trend of a quick rise since 2006, up from 7.36% in 2007 to 25.58% in 2013, while that of the EU dropped from 55.50% to 17.75% in the same period. Despite the fact that the NAFTA's investment abroad rose from 20.57% to 27.92%, its fluctuation is still relatively severe in a long run (see Table 5.13, Figures 5.16 and 5.17).

From the perspectives of foreign trade and international investment, Northeast Asia has shown a trend of rapid growth in total volume and a significant rise in global status. Compared with the EU, NAFTA, and other major economic groups, Northeast Asia has shown a significant increase in terms of total trade volume and has become increasingly prominent in global trade circulation, but its internal trade has not increased. There was an obvious upward trend in attracting foreign capital

Table 5.13. Investment abroad of major economic groups (Unit: US$100 million).

Year	Northeast Asia	ASEAN	EU	NAFTA	World
1973	19.06	0.26	110.60	125.19	259.35
1978	24.02	1.20	173.39	185.03	393.21
1983	38.74	3.04	180.82	121.20	377.00
1988	370.12	3.82	934.68	248.62	1,825.46
1993	207.78	43.07	938.43	828.39	2,427.73
1998	322.76	48.35	4,217.98	1,667.17	6,893.70
2003	464.01	56.18	2,946.06	1,535.30	5,806.95
2008	2,592.31	339.58	9,836.01	3,887.30	19,993.26
2013	3,608.78	563.61	2,504.60	3,938.76	14,108.10

Source: Based on the data of the World Trade Organization, http://stat.wto.org/GountryProfile/WSDBcountryPFExportZip.aspx?Language=E; and the United Nations Conference on Trade and Development, http://unctadstat.unctad.org/ReportFolders/reportFolders.Aspx.

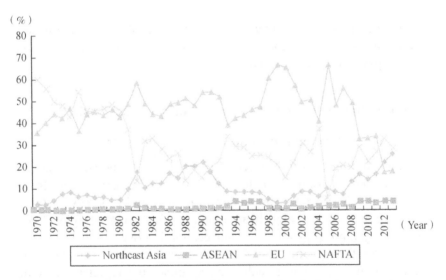

Figure 5.16. Trends of the proportion of investment abroad of major economic groups in the world.

Source: Based on the data in Table 5.13.

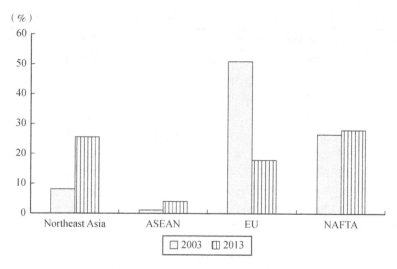

Figure 5.17. The proportion of FDI outflows from major economies in the world in 2003 and 2013.

Source: The data in Table 5.13.

and making investments abroad in Northeast Asia, showing that this area is accelerating its integration into the global production chain and gradually occupying a more important position in world production.

5.1.3 Further economic cooperation in Northeast Asia

5.1.3.1 *Regional economic and trade ties are improving*

Although Northeast Asia is currently the region with the largest population, area, and economic strength in the Asia-Pacific region, it is also an area with relatively loose cooperation in politics and economy. With the deepening of economic globalization and the furthering of regional economic integration, plus the incessant economic crises, Northeast Asian countries are facing common political and economic problems that need tackling promptly. Against such a background, the regional economic cooperation in Northeast Asia is moving toward institutional economic integration. China, Japan, the ROK, and other countries have merged into a process of regionalization.

While the economy of Northeast Asian countries is developing rapidly, various forms of economic cooperation in the region are also continuously developing and deepening. Economic cooperation is promoted via various bilateral and multilateral agreements. For example, China and the ROK signed the China–ROK Government Trade Agreement and China–ROK Investment Protection Agreement. The partnership between China and Russia was upgraded from a constructive partnership in 1994 to a comprehensive strategic cooperative partnership for a new era in 2019. On October 14, 2004, China and Russia jointly signed the China–Russia Joint Statement and Implementation Outline of the China–Russia Treaty of Good Neighborliness and Friendly Cooperation in Beijing. Of all the bilateral and multilateral trade and investment agreements that Northeast Asian countries have signed and are negotiating, the focal point is economic cooperation among China, Japan, and the ROK. In a summit attended by China, Japan, and the ROK in November 1999, the concept of Northeast Asian Economic Cooperation was put forward, which set off a discussion on institutional cooperation among the three countries. In 2002, the leaders of the three countries agreed to launch a study on the establishment of a free trade area among China, Japan, and the ROK. The three countries then conducted a 10-year study on this issue. On March 22, 2012, the negotiations on a China–Japan–ROK investment agreement were successfully concluded. On May 2, 2012, the Ministry of Commerce of China and the Ministry of Foreign Affairs and Trade of the ROK jointly issued a ministerial statement and officially announced that negotiations on a free trade agreement had commenced. On May 13, China, Japan, and the ROK formally signed an agreement among their governments on the Promotion, Facilitation, and Protection of Investment (hereinafter referred to as China, Japan, and the ROK Investment Agreement). It is the first legal document and institutional arrangement among the three countries to promote and protect investment and to provide an important foundation for the construction of China, Japan, and the ROK FTA. On November 20 of that year, the leaders of China, Japan, and the ROK agreed to launch trilateral FTA negotiations. If a free trade agreement can be reached, it would be the first important legal document in economic cooperation among China, Japan, and the ROK. The establishment of the FTA among China, Japan, and the ROK (also known as the CJKFTA) will push forward trilateral economic and trade cooperation and greatly promote economic cooperation in Northeast Asia. However, the Diaoyu Dao issue between China and Japan has cast a shadow over the prospect of the trilateral FTA. In this context, the governments of China and the ROK formally signed a Free Trade Agreement on June 1, 2015. This agreement covers the widest range of topics and involves the largest volume of trade between two countries among all the free trade agreements signed by China to date. It is a mutually beneficial agreement and achieves the goal of ensuring "generally balanced, comprehensive, and high-level interest." At the same time, the two parties promised to continue negotiations on trade by working out the negative list after the agreement was signed and put into force. They also agreed to conduct investment negotiations based on the pre-establishment national treatment and the negative list.[2] The signing of the China–ROK Free Trade Agreement will surely speed up the CJKFTA talks and negotiations, thus promoting economic cooperation in the entire Northeast Asian region.

5.1.3.2 Regional economic cooperation moves forward steadily

(1) Greater Tumen River Regional Cooperation
In December 1995, China, the DPRK, and Russia signed the Agreement on the Establishment of the Coordination Committee for Tumen River Area Development. China, Russia, the DPRK, the ROK, and Mongolia signed the Agreement on the Establishment of the Coordination Commission for the Development of the Tumen River Economic Development Zone and Northeast Asia and the Memorandum of Understanding on Environmental Criteria for the Tumen River Economic Development Zone and Northeast Asia. At the same time, the "Consultative Committee for Tumen River Area Development" and the "Coordination Committee for Tumen River Area Development" were established and became the main consultative bodies for cooperation and development in the Tumen River area.

In 2005, the member states agreed to extend the validity of the memorandum and upgrade the development to the Greater Tumen River area. After more than ten years, remarkable achievements have been made in the development of the Tumen River area in infrastructural construction, energy, communications, and transportation. The most important achievement is the formation of a cooperation mechanism at the local government level. The United Nations Development Programme thus set up a secretariat for the International Development Project for the Tumen River in Beijing. Moreover, a dialogue and meeting mechanism was established to

---

[2] The Free Trade Agreement Between the Government of the People's Republic of China and the Government of the Republic of Korea was officially signed on June 1, 2015, http://city.ce.cn/2015cspd/csl/jjdl/201506/02/120150602_2547438.shtml, Xinhua News Agency, June 2, 2015.

tackle problems in economic cooperation among the involved governments. On November 17, 2009, China officially approved Outlines for the Cooperative Development in the Tumen River Region: To Establish the Changchun-Jilin-Tumen Development and Opening-up Pilot Zone, thus enhancing all-round cooperation between China and Northeast Asian countries.

(2) Northeast Asia regional economic cooperation under the ASEAN Plus Three Framework
At the end of the 20th century, the Asian financial crisis hit East Asian economies hard. The crisis not only slowed down the rapid economic development in East Asia but also drove East Asian countries to explore economic cooperation. In this way, the economic cooperation in this region with function of crisis-management began to develop among East Asian countries. The cooperation is marked by the meeting of ASEAN, China, Japan, and the ROK (ASEAN plus Three Summit Meeting) in 1997. After that, a regular meeting mechanism of ASEAN plus Three leaders came into being. After more than ten years, the original informal ASEAN plus Three mechanism was institutionalized. The three countries of Northeast Asia set up meetings for promoting regional economic cooperation. Under the ASEAN plus Three framework, Northeast Asian countries strengthened their cooperation and development in the fields of trade, investment, monetary finance, food, energy, technology information, etc. For example, Northeast Asian countries signed a series of bilateral currency swap agreements under the Chiang Mai Initiative, which contributed to establishing a solid economic cooperation framework for the Northeast Asian region.

(3) Regional economic cooperation in Northeast Asia under the framework of Asia-Pacific Economic Cooperation (APEC)
APEC and Northeast Asia share the same characteristics of diversity, openness, and informality. Moreover, China, Japan, the ROK, and Russia are also APEC members. In the process of actively participating in the trade and investment liberalization propelled by APEC, regional economic cooperation in Northeast Asia has also deepened. For example, the Bogor Declaration, Manila Declaration, and other important documents signed by China, Japan, the ROK, and Russia under the APEC greatly reduced the overall tariff level and gradually phased out restrictions on capital flows in investment, thus effectively enhancing trade and investment liberalization in Northeast Asia. Although the United States, an

important member of APEC, does not belong to Northeast Asia, the economic development of Northeast Asian countries cannot be separated from the final product consumption market provided by the United States due to the close political, economic, and trade ties between the United States and major countries in Northeast Asia. It is through the APEC that the United States has played an indispensable role in further regional economic cooperation in Northeast Asia.

In Northeast Asia, regional economic cooperation is not mature and independent, but the cooperation framework of the APEC and ASEAN plus Three in East Asia is improving the situation. The economic cooperation in the Greater Tumen River region will be one of the important frameworks for regional economic cooperation in Northeast Asia.

5.1.3.3 *Local cooperation and coordination mechanisms emerge in Northeast Asia*

The reason why Northeast Asian countries are able to establish increasingly close economic and trade ties is not only due to the joint efforts made by international organizations and local governments but also due to the impetus from various regional forums and institutional mechanisms. These forums serve as venues for government officials, experts, scholars, and people from financial and business circles to convene. They hold consultations and dialogues on various issues in the process of economic cooperation through different types of gatherings, such as academic meetings, trainings, and discussions on certain economic cooperation projects. Thus, economic cooperation mechanisms are introduced and formulated in Northeast Asia by means of semi-official and non-governmental channels. Of the above-mentioned economic cooperation mechanisms, the important and influential ones are as follows[3]:

(1) Meetings of Heads of Local Governments for International Exchanges and Cooperation in the Region Around the Japan Sea
In 1994, local leaders of Jilin Province of China, Tottori Prefecture of Japan, Gangwon-do of the ROK, and Primorsky Krai of Russia convened in Gangwon-do and established the "Local Summit System around the

---

[3] Chen Zhiheng, Study on Regional Economic Integration in Northeast Asia-From the Perspective of Transaction Cost Theory, Changchun: Jilin People's Publishing House, 2006, pp. 91–92.

Japan Sea." In 2000, Tuv Province of Mongolia also became a full member. The summit meeting is held once a year and has aided all-round cooperation in numerous fields. For some projects, contracts have been signed and implemented. Economic cooperation around the Japan Sea has been promoted from particular functional areas to comprehensive regional economic cooperation.

(2) The Northeast Asia Economic Forum (NEAEF)
The Northeast Asia Economic Forum, established in 1990, is a regional cooperative organization. Its participants consist of the national governments, colleges and universities, research institutions, and business and enterprises of seven countries including the US. The United Nations Development Programme, the World Bank, and the Asian Development Bank have also participated in and observed this forum. The forum studies bilateral and multilateral economic cooperation in Northeast Asia through dialogue and consultation and has held regular Young Leaders Programs (YLPs) every year since 2006. The Northeast Asia Economic Forum has made substantial achievements in promoting economic cooperation in Northeast Asia. On October 28, 2008, the 17th annual meeting of the Northeast Asia Economic Forum held in Tianjin issued the Tianjin Binhai Declaration, reaching a consensus on the establishment of the Northeast Asia Cooperative Development Bank with participants from all countries.

(3) The Northeast Asia Economic Conference
Held by the Japan Sea Rim Economic Research Institute in Niigata Prefecture, Japan, the conference has taken place annually since 1990 with participants from China, Japan, the ROK, Russia, Mongolia, the United States, and other countries and regions. The conference provides a grand platform for inviting investment, conducting commodity trade, and holding seminars for transborder investment, trade, and research.

(4) The China, Japan, and the ROK Local Government Exchange Conference
In 1999, the Chinese People's Association for Friendship with Foreign Countries, the Chinese Association for International Friendship Cities, the Council of Local Authorities for International Relations (CLAIR) of Japan, and the International Consortium of the ROK's Local Self-Government Organizations held a China–Japan–ROK Local Government Exchange Conference. The conference was intended to discuss the role of

international exchanges between governments in revitalizing the local economy and promoting regional cooperation.

(5) The Mayor's Meeting of East Asian Cities (the Yellow Sea rim)
In November 1993, the first meeting of mayors of East Asian cities (around the Yellow Sea) was held in Kitakyushu, Japan. It was stipulated that an annual meeting and a biennial meeting of mayors be held, involving nine cities in China, Japan, and the ROK. Committees, bureaus, and other institutions were set up, showcasing regional economic cooperation around the Yellow Sea and the Bohai Sea.

(6) The Trilateral (China, Japan, and the ROK) Cooperation Secretariat
During the "10 + 3" leaders' meeting of ASEAN and China, Japan, and the ROK in 1999, economic cooperation among China, Japan, and the ROK was established. In order to boost cooperation among the three countries in a more efficient and systematic way, according to the Agreement on the Establishment of the Trilateral Cooperation Secretariat. Among the Governments of the People's Republic of China, Japan, and the Republic of Korea, a Trilateral Cooperation Secretariat was officially established in Seoul on August 1, 2011. The aim of it is to provide administrative and technical support for the operation of the consultation mechanism among the three countries and enhance the economic cooperation among the three countries. Within the framework of this cooperation mechanism, China, Japan, and the ROK established more than 50 intergovernmental consultation mechanisms, including 17 trilateral ministerial meetings. The Trilateral Cooperation Secretariat has become the most important international organization for subregional cooperation in Northeast Asia.

Although various cooperation and coordination mechanisms have been established in Northeast Asia, the overall level of cooperation is not high. The establishment of FTA cooperation mechanisms among China, Japan, and the ROK will be a qualitative improvement in the level of cooperation in the region.

5.1.3.4 *Major fields of Northeast Asia regional economic cooperation*

In addition to the above-mentioned trade and investment cooperation in Northeast Asia, countries in the region have also launched cooperation in other fields for specific economic cooperation projects, including financial cooperation, energy cooperation, and environmental cooperation.

(1) Financial Cooperation in Northeast Asia

Regional financial cooperation in Northeast Asia began in the 1990s. The outbreak of the Asian Financial Crisis facilitated economic cooperation among East Asian countries. Since East Asian economic cooperation is obviously set up to handle the crisis, the economic cooperation in East Asia and even in Northeast Asia aims first at finance. Northeast Asian countries have launched financial cooperation under the "10 + 3" framework, mainly in the form of a series of bilateral and multilateral mechanisms.

Bilateral financial cooperation in Northeast Asia is mainly among China, Japan, the ROK, and Russia.

China–Japan financial cooperation: The major channels of financial exchange between China and Japan are the China–Japan High-level Economic Dialogue Mechanism launched in April 2007 and the China–Japan Finance Ministers Dialogue Mechanism launched in March 2006, both of which provide platforms for meetings and consultations on the macroeconomic situation and policies, economic cooperation, international financial cooperation, etc., between the two countries. The major achievement of bilateral financial cooperation is the currency swap agreement signed in 2002 with a limit of US$3 billion between the renminbi and yen. In September 2007, the two countries renewed the swap agreement, deepening cooperation between the two central banks and the entire monetary and financial fields of the two countries.

China–ROK financial cooperation: One of the great achievements of China–ROK financial cooperation is the signing of bilateral currency swap agreements. On December 12, 2008, China and the ROK announced the signing of the RMB180 billion/KRW38 trillion bilateral currency swap agreement, providing short-term liquidity support to the financial systems of the two economies which had sound fundamentals and operations. On October 26, 2011, the two countries renewed the currency swap agreement and expanded it to RMB 360 billion/KRW64 trillion. China and the ROK agreed to explore the possibility of converting the swap currency into major reserve currencies. The renewal of the swap agreement helped China and the ROK strengthen bilateral financial cooperation, promote bilateral trade and investment, and safeguard regional financial stability.

China–Russia financial cooperation: China and Russia have been deepening exchanges and cooperation in the field of finance since the 1990s. Under the framework of summit meetings and regular meetings between the two countries, the bilateral financial cooperation mechanism includes the China–Russia Prime Ministers' Regular Meeting Committee (the Sub-Committee for Financial Cooperation), China–Russia Financial Ministers Dialogue Mechanism, China–Russia Financial Cooperation Forum, and China–Russia Economic and Business Summit Forum. Through these mechanisms, financial cooperation between China and Russia achieved remarkable results. Firstly, direct currency transactions between the two countries in the inter-bank foreign exchange market were realized, providing important support for currency internationalization on both sides. Secondly, the two countries increased the number of financial institutions mutually, that is to say, Beijing set up more financial institutions dealing with the ruble and Moscow did the same for renminbi transactions. Finally, the local currency settlement system and the related legal system of the two countries were promoted and improved.

Other bilateral financial cooperations: Firstly, a series of bilateral currency swap agreements were signed between Northeast Asian countries. On May 6, 2011, China and Mongolia signed a bilateral local currency swap agreement worth RMB5 billion to promote trade and provide short-term liquidity for financial systems. On March 20, 2012, the two countries expanded the swapping scale to RMB10 billion/MNT2 trillion. On October 19, 2011, the scale of the bilateral currency swap agreement between Japan and the ROK increased from US$13 billion to US$70 billion.

The multilateral financial cooperation mechanism in Northeast Asia mainly consists of the meeting of leaders of China, Japan, and the ROK that began in 1999, the meeting of finance ministers of China, Japan, and the ROK that began in 2009, and the meeting of central bank governors of China, Japan, and the ROK that started on December 10, 2008. Through these cooperation mechanisms, China, Japan, and the ROK have jointly worked out and agreed on important documents, such as the Joint Statement on the International Finance and Economy, the Action Plan for Promoting China, Japan, and the ROK Cooperation, and 2020 China–Japan–ROK Cooperation Outlook. They have reached an agreement on the distribution ratio of a regional foreign exchange reserve pool plan, regional financial integration, and the reform of the international financial system. They believe that close financial cooperation can promote the recovery and growth of the regional economy.

Apart from the cooperation framework of China, Japan, and the ROK, another important cooperation framework is the ASEAN Plus

Three (APT), i.e., the "10 + 3" mechanism. Since the first meeting in 1997, 13 meetings of finance ministers had been held by 2010 to strengthen cooperation on the establishment of a regional fund rescue mechanism, promote the development of regional bond markets, and ensure the surveillance of short-term capital flows. An important outcome of the "10 + 3" finance ministers' meeting was the Chiang Mai Initiative, reached in 2000, which established a bilateral currency swap mechanism and network in East Asia to help member countries with short-term foreign exchange liquidity or balance-of-payments difficulties during the financial crisis. On March 24, 2010, the Chiang Mai Initiative Multilateralization Agreement came into effect.[4]

In addition, Northeast Asian countries also hold talks and negotiations on issues such as international monetary and financial cooperation and the reform of the international financial system through various international and regional economic institutions. These international dialogue mechanisms include the APEC Finance Ministers' Meeting, International Monetary Fund, Regular Meeting for Central Bank Governors of the Bank for International Settlements, G20 Finance Ministers and Central Bank Governors Meeting, Executives Meeting of East Asia and Pacific Central Banks (EMEAP), East Asia Summit Financial Cooperation Mechanism, and Asia-Europe Finance Ministers Meeting Mechanism.

At present, China, Japan, and the ROK are the main participants in financial cooperation among Northeast Asian countries. Financial cooperation is carried out at bilateral and multilateral levels and has achieved positive results. This has created a favorable environment for economic recovery and development in Northeast Asia and has laid a solid foundation for economic cooperation in Northeast Asia.

(2) Regional Energy Cooperation in Northeast Asia
Energy, as the blood of the economy, is an indispensable and important area for economic cooperation and development in Northeast Asia. China, Japan, and the ROK are all highly dependent on energy imports. In order to obtain sufficient energy support for regional economic development, Northeast Asian countries need to deepen cooperation to avoid the impact of energy price fluctuations.

---

[4]Ren Weitong, Financial Cooperation in Northeast Asia, recorded in Wang Shengjin, *Northeast Asia Development Report* (2010), Changchun: Jilin University Press, 2011, p. 166.

The new energy strategy of Russia: In this field, as a major energy exporter, the energy strategy of Russia has a decisive influence on energy cooperation in Northeast Asia. The western European market has always been the focus of Russia's energy strategy, and Russia's oil and natural gas were exported to Europe as a priority. In recent years, Russia has gradually shifted its development strategy from Europe to Asia. It has begun to implement an eastward development strategy, building infrastructure and increasing energy exports to Asia. In December 2009, the Eastern Siberia Pacific Ocean oil pipeline (ESPO) officially transported oil to the Asia-Pacific region, effectively expanding Russia's energy market. In terms of natural gas, Russia is also stepping up its efforts to tap the Asian market. Gazprom will make two of its three major investments in the next few years in the Asia-Pacific market. The eastward move of Russia's energy strategy will greatly promote energy cooperation in Northeast Asia and in the whole region.

Energy cooperation among Northeast Asian countries: Energy cooperation in Northeast Asia is carried out with Russia as the center and Russia is the world's largest energy exporter. In terms of China–Russia energy cooperation, a crude oil pipeline (Skovorodino–Mohe–Daqing line) has been put into operation. The building of the second line of the China–Russia crude oil pipeline is being planned. When the second line is finished, the annual fuel flow of the China–Russia crude oil pipeline will reach 30 million tons.[5] The two countries have also made important progress in natural gas cooperation. In 2014, PetroChina and Gazprom signed a purchase and sale agreement for Russian Gas Supply via the Eastern Route and also signed the Western Route Gas Supply and Sales Framework Agreement. Russia will supply 38 billion cubic meters of natural gas per year and 30 billion cubic meters per year to China through the China–Russia Eastern Route and Western Route pipelines, respectively. In addition, Russia also exports other energy sources to China such as electrical energy and coal. As for Japan–Russia energy cooperation, oil and gas cooperation projects between the two countries mainly include the "Sakhalin-1" and "Sakhalin-2" projects, of which the "Sakhalin-1" project has a crude oil reserve of 9.626 million tons and a natural gas output of 8.22 billion cubic meters. The "Sakhalin-2" project has a crude oil

---

[5] *The Orderly Advance of the Second Line of China-Russia Crude Oil Pipeline* by PetroChina News Center. http://news.cnpc.com.cn/system/2016/05/12/001592052.shlml, May 12, 2016.

reserve of 140 million tons and a natural gas output of 684 billion cubic meters, which will constitute Japan's important imported energy reserve.

In short, energy cooperation in Northeast Asia has great potential. It not only provides energy security for the economic development of the countries in Northeast Asia but also provides a greater thrust to the deepening of economic cooperation in Northeast Asia.

(3) Regional Environmental Cooperation in Northeast Asia

As the global environmental pollution becomes more and more serious, and countries pay more attention to sustainable development, environmental cooperation has become a new way of economic cooperation among countries. Environmental cooperation in Northeast Asia began since the adoption of the Rio Declaration and Agenda 21 in 1992, focusing on the prevention and control of cross-border air pollution and marine pollution. After more than 20 years of efforts, environmental cooperation in Northeast Asia has led to bilateral collaborations, regional collaborations, and multilateral collaborations with international organizations.

Bilateral cooperation is the most common and fruitful form of environmental cooperation in Northeast Asia, leading to a number of agreements and projects. For example, China and Japan signed the Environmental Protection Cooperation Agreement in 1994 and the Joint Communique on Environmental Cooperation Facing the 21st Century in 1998. China and the ROK signed the Environmental Cooperation Agreement in 1993 and set up a joint committee in 1994. Japan and the ROK signed the Environmental Protection Cooperation Agreement in 1993 and formed a joint environmental cooperation committee. Northeast Asian countries have carried out international environmental projects through various bilateral agreements.

On the basis of bilateral cooperation, multilateral environmental cooperation at the regional level has also been established, such as the Northeast Asia Conference for Environmental Cooperation (NEAC) launched in 1992, the Northeast Asia Subregional Programme for Environmental Cooperation (NEASPEC) launched in 1993, and a mechanism for the meeting of environmental ministers of China, Japan, and the ROK started in 1999. Besides, in November 2002, the ASEAN–China–Japan–ROK (10 + 3) environment ministers' meeting kicked off, with sandstorm monitoring and early warning system implementation.

Northeast Asian countries have also fully participated in environmental cooperation with international organizations, such as the Northwest Pacific Action Plan (NOWPAP) in 1991, the East Asian Acid Deposition

Monitoring Network set up in 1993, and the United Nations Environment Programme's Asia-Pacific Subregional Environmental Policy Dialogue established in 2003.

At the 14th meeting of environment ministers of China, Japan, and the ROK held in 2012, representatives of environmental agencies from the three countries signed the following environmental cooperation and mutual recognition agreements: the Agreement on Common Certification Rules for All-in-One Environmental Labeling Machines among China, Japan, and the ROK, the Agreement on Mutual Recognition and Certification Procedures for Environmental Labels among China, Japan, and the ROK, and the Implementation Rules for Mutual Recognition among China, Japan, and the ROK. All the agreements broke through international trade barriers, expanded the market for environmental protection products in Northeast Asia, and promoted regional economic cooperation on the basis of strengthening environmental cooperation.

Environmental cooperation in Northeast Asia has grown over the past 20 years. It has promoted communication among Northeast Asian countries and strengthened the building of environmental capacity and consciousness. The countries have gained common benefits, especially through the introduction of a clean development mechanism (CDM) and effective market-oriented operation modes. However, environmental cooperation in Northeast Asia is still in the initial stages. Therefore, the degrees of cooperation and participation of the countries are uneven, with much scope for better organization.

In all, because there is no independent and mature economic cooperation framework in Northeast Asia, the strategic height is rather limited. The areas for economic cooperation are scattered and links among the countries are loose. Promoting trade and investment facilitation among Northeast Asian countries and FTA cooperation across the region is an important way to improve the quality and raise quantity of economic cooperation in Northeast Asia.

5.2 Investment Facilitation and FTA Cooperation of International Trade Centers in Northeast Asia

Countries in Northeast Asia are important trading partners and have established close economic and trade relations. Many measures have been taken to facilitate trade and investment facilitation and construct free trade areas. Under the framework of the APEC, ASEAN Plus Three, China, Japan, and the ROK have started trade and investment cooperation. The investment agreements reached by China, Japan, and the ROK have created a stable and transparent investment environment for mutual investment. The three countries are also pushing forward negotiations for free trade areas.

5.2.1 Development of trade and investment facilitation in Northeast Asia

5.2.1.1 *Trade and investment facilitation development from a global perspective*

International trade and international direct investment are important components of international economic relations. The facilitation and liberalization of trade and investment constitute an important driving force to promote global economic development. Although the definition of trade and investment facilitation is not as clear and uniform as liberalization (see Table 5.14),[6] practical activities have already started. International organizations such as the World Customs Organization, United Nations, WTO, and World Bank have formulated or are in the process of formulating binding conventions or agreements for their members to actively promote facilitation in the field of international trade and international direct investment. In the following, the APEC and WTO are taken as examples to analyze the development of global trade and investment facilitation.

---

[6] It is generally believed that trade facilitation refers to "simplifying and coordinating international trade procedures and accelerating the cross-border flow of factors." It is quoted from the research report of the Foreign Economic Research Department of the Development Research Center of the State Council of the People's Republic of China, written by Zhang Qi and Xu Hongqiang, *Trade Facilitation in Regional Trade Arrangements among China, Japan, and the ROK*. Regarding investment facilitation, APEC (2008) refers to a series of actions or practices taken by the government to attract foreign investment and maximize its management effectiveness and efficiency at all stages of the investment. It includes market approval, investment treatment, performance prohibition requirements, dispute resolution, and investment protection.

Table 5.14. Definitions of trade facilitation by major international (regional) economic organizations.

APEC (1999)	Through specific measures, coordinate and simplify trade-related procedures or barriers, reduce costs, and promote better circulation of goods or services, mainly involving four major areas, namely, customs procedures, harmonization of standards, mobility of business personnel, and e-commerce.
WTO (1998)	The systematization and coordination of international trade procedures, including the activities, practices, and procedures for collecting, providing, communicating, and processing data necessary for the flow of international trade in goods.
OECD (2001)	In international trade, the simplification and standardization of procedures and related information flow required for goods to flow from the seller to the buyer and to pay the other party.

Source: According to relevant documents.

(1) Trade and Investment Facilitation Process Promoted by the APEC

Trade and investment facilitation is one of the three pillars of the APEC.[7] Up to now, APEC's key areas to promote trade and investment facilitation have included tariff concessions, reduction of non-tariff measures, and opening up service and investment markets.[8] APEC's actions can be divided into the Individual Action Plan (IAP), the Collective Action Plan (CAP), the Pathfinders Approach,[9] and a mixture three approaches.[10] The main achievements are as follows:

---

[7]The other two are trade and investment liberalization and economic and technological cooperation.
[8]Gong Zhankui and Yu Xiaoyan, APEC trade and investment liberalization in 20 Years: Achievements and prospects. *Contemporary Asia Pacific*, 2009, 4.
[9]The Pathfinder Approach is a new initiative put forward in *Shanghai Consensus* in the 2001 APEC meeting. It aims to encourage some APEC members to take the lead in adopting actions or measures to promote trade and investment liberalization and facilitation, and gradually expand it to all APEC members after the experience is accumulated or conditions are ripe.
[10]Lyu Gang, Facilitation measures of China, Japan, and the ROK under APEC framework. *Development Research*, 2010, 3.

In terms of trade facilitation, the APEC established the Bogor Goals in 1994 and proposed that the developed members and developing members realize liberalization of trade and investment in 2010 and 2020, respectively. To implement the Bogor Goals, the APEC adopted the Osaka Action Agenda in 1995, which set out principles, mechanisms, and specific areas for trade and investment facilitation.[11] Then, relevant institutions were established one after another. In 1996, the Osaka Action Agenda was implemented by signing the Manila Action Plan. According to the Manila Action Plan, each member promised to gradually reduce the trade costs caused by differences in product standards and technical control and implement the trade facilitation goals of the APEC. The individual action plan of each member is very substantive. Subsequently, at the Montreal Meeting in 1997, APEC members further reached a consensus to simplify the customs procedures, coordinate customs valuation, and effectively implement the intellectual property agreement.

Since 1999, the APEC has further sought to promote the facilitation process by establishing faster customs clearance procedures, promoting transparency of customs system and application of e-commerce, simplifying business travel, and other measures. The most important results are the signing of two action plans, namely, the First Action Plan on Trade Facilitation (launched in 2003 and successfully completed in 2006) and the Second Action Plan on Trade Facilitation (2007–2010).

As for investment facilitation, the APEC formally launched the Investment Facilitation Action Plan (IFAP) in 2009.[12] This is the first large-scale action taken by the APEC in the field of investment facilitation, which aims to reduce investment barriers for international investors and encourage investment in the Asia-Pacific region. Shen, a researcher, says in his paper that "since then, investment facilitation activities within

---

[11] The main areas of APEC's trade and investment facilitation stipulated in the Osaka Action Agenda include tariffs, non-tariff measures, services, investment, standards and conformance, customs procedures intellectual property rights, competition policy, government procurement, deregulation/regulatory review, WTO obligations (including rules of origin), dispute mediation, mobility of business people, information gathering and analysis, transparency, and Regional Trade Agreements / Free Trade Agreements (RTAs/FTAs).
[12] IFAP is the first large-scale action taken by the APEC in the field of investment facilitation, aimed at reducing trade barriers for international investors and encouraging investment in the Asia-Pacific region.

the APEC have been gradually on the right track," and the progress has also been accelerating, "emphasizing supervision and evaluation mechanism, capacity building and cooperation."[13]

(2) Trade and Investment Facilitation Process Promoted by the WTO

The WTO does not have special trade facilitation agreements, and the relevant provisions are scattered across several agreements, such as the Agreement on Rules of Origin, the Customs Valuation Agreement, the Technical Barriers to Trade Agreement, and the Pre-shipment Inspection Agreement. There are obvious defects in the facilitation process within the WTO framework as it has only specified the principles, which are too abstract in the operation sense. Besides, as provisions are scattered in various agreements, it is difficult for countries to coordinate.

Although trade facilitation negotiations have made some progress (see Table 5.15), it is evident that there are still great differences in issues like whether to formulate the binding multilateral rules and whether the rules can be used in the dispute settlement mechanism. Moreover, due to the great differences in the economic development level among members, the difficulty in negotiations involves sensitive commodities, such as agricultural products, as well as the influence of factors such as the increasing political sensitivity of the negotiations and the different nature and scope of their respective commitments. There is less and less room for compromise among all parties, and collective negotiations on trade facilitation issues under the WTO framework will become more and more difficult.[14]

In December 2013, at the 9th WTO ministerial conference, the Doha round of negotiations was restarted and the Bali Package Agreement was reached. It was the first multilateral trade agreement since the WTO was established. It was the breakthrough of zero in 12 years. In December 2015, the 10th WTO ministerial conference made a breakthrough in agricultural negotiations. All members reached a consensus on agricultural export competition, which is of the greatest concern to developing members such as African countries. For the first time, all WTO members promised to eliminate agricultural export subsidies completely. Among them,

---

[13] Shen Minghui, APEC investment facilitation process-based on investment facilitation action plan. *International Economic Cooperation*, 2009, 4.

[14] Among them, the United States, Japan, the ROK, and other countries formed a group to advocate and promote the negotiation of trade facilitation rules (that is, the Colorado Group). However, when submitting the proposal, they did not effectively reduce the difficulty of the negotiation.

Table 5.15. Trade facilitation process under the WTO framework.

Year	Issue	Feature
1996	The first WTO ministerial meeting formally raised the issue of trade and investment facilitation, aimed at exploring ways to reduce cumbersome procedures and customs clearance costs.	Developed members advocate low-cost customs clearance for global trade and reduced obstacles to the cross-border flow of commodities. Developing members demand respect for the existing customs structure and functions, which may differ from developed members.
2001	Trade facilitation was included in the agenda of the 4th Doha Ministerial Conference. The conference considered it necessary to speed up the flow, delivery, and customs clearance of goods and to improve technical assistance and capacity-building in this field.	Developing members are not enthusiastic, and the expected progress has not been made in the field of trade facilitation.
2004	A framework agreement for the Doha round of trade negotiations was reached to simplify unnecessary trade procedures, publish trade system information in an open and transparent manner, reasonably levy fees, reduce trade costs, shorten customs clearance time for goods, and improve trade efficiency.	Developing members believe that the outcome of the negotiations is only instructive and cannot be applied to the dispute settlement mechanism, while developed members hold that the outcome of the negotiations should be a mandatory and binding rule, and the dispute settlement mechanism should be applied.

Source: Based on relevant documents.

developed members promised to immediately eliminate most of their agricultural export subsidies, while developing members were to follow suit in 2018.[15] At present, the main members of the WTO, including China, all hope to push forward the conclusion of relevant negotiations as soon as possible and strive to take forward trade facilitation.

---

[15] WTO Agricultural Negotiations Breakthrough, Prospects for Doha Round to be Observed, http://news,xinhuanetcom/world/2015-12/20/c_1117520089.htm, Xinhua News Agency, December 20, 2015.

5.2.1.2 Measures and progress of trade and investment facilitation in Northeast Asia

(1) Facilitation Measures between China and ASEAN, Japan and ASEAN and the ROK and ASEAN under the ASEAN plus Three Framework

The first is China's facilitation measures under the framework of the China–ASEAN Free Trade Area. The China–ASEAN FTA is the first free trade area for China and the first area that the ASEAN as a whole has negotiated with foreign countries. Since China and the ASEAN started negotiations on a free trade area in 2002, the two sides have signed three important documents, namely, the Agreement on Trade in Goods, the Agreement on Trade in Services, and the Agreement on Investment[16] in 2004, 2007, and 2009, respectively.

In October 2009, the two sides showed that they would jointly promote extensive development of trade facilitation at the China–ASEAN Customs and Business Cooperation Forum. Since January 1, 2010, the China–ASEAN Free Trade Area has been formally established. China and the six original ASEAN members (Singapore, Malaysia, Thailand, Indonesia, the Philippines, and Brunei) have implemented substantial tariff concessions.

The second point is Japan's facilitation measures under the framework of the Japan–ASEAN FTA. Japan and the ASEAN reached a free trade agreement in Manila in August 2007. After the agreement entered into force, Japan implemented measures to eliminate tariffs or make tariff concessions on goods imported from the ASEAN,[17] but rice, sugar, and some dairy products were regarded as "special commodities" and were not put on the list due to "political sensitivity."

---

[16] Agreement on Investment is committed to establishing a free, convenient, transparent, and fair investment system under the China–ASEAN Free Trade Area, which includes 27 clauses. The two sides promise to grant each other national treatment, most-favored-nation treatment, and fair and just treatment for investment, improve the transparency of investment-related laws and regulations, provide an institutional basis for creating more convenient investment conditions, and provide adequate legal protection for investors of both sides.

[17] 90% of the products will be subject to zero tariffs, and the tariffs for the other 3% will be phased out within ten years while the tariffs for the other 6% will be reduced.

The last point is the ROK's facilitation measures under the framework of the ROK–ASEAN Free Trade Area. In October 2003, at the ROK–ASEAN Leaders Summit, the ROK proposed the establishment of the ROK–ASEAN Free Trade Area, after which the two sides held multi-party talks. In July 2006, five countries, Brunei, Indonesia, Singapore, Malaysia, and the Philippines, together with ROK, implemented tax reduction measures. According to the goods trade agreement, general products from ROK and six ASEAN countries (Brunei, Indonesia, Singapore, Malaysia, Thailand, and the Philippines) would achieve zero tariffs by 2010. In November 2007, the two sides signed a service agreement and completed the free trade negotiation process in less than a year and a half.

For investment facilitation, a bilateral investment agreement between the ASEAN and the ROK has been formally signed. According to the provisions of the investment agreement, the ASEAN and the ROK both promise to open their investment areas and provide preferential treatment to each other's investments. The governments of ASEAN member countries and the ROK cannot take over the assets of enterprises without giving fair and adequate compensation. In terms of investment disputes, investors will be able to deal with these issues through domestic courts or international arbitration institutions.

(2) Progress in Trade Facilitation among China, Japan, and the ROK
China, Japan, and the ROK account for 74% of the population in East Asia and 22% in the world, 90% of the total economy in East Asia and 20% in the world, 70% of the total trade volume in East Asia and 20% in the world. Moreover, China, Japan, and the ROK are geographically close, and their economy and trade are closely interdependent. They play an important role in promoting trade and investment cooperation in East Asia. Due to the establishment of the China–ROK FTA and the onset of the CJKFTA negotiations, in-depth cooperation on trade facilitation among the three countries will be promoted.

Previously, trade facilitation among China, Japan, and the ROK was mainly promoted under the frameworks of the WTO, the APEC, and the APT (10 + 3), specifically including the construction of free trade areas and the signing of trade and investment agreements. For example, as APEC members, China, Japan, and the ROK actively participated in many important processes to promote trade and investment, such as the Action Plan on Trade Facilitation and the Action Plan on Investment Facilitation. However, there has been almost no collective action among China, Japan, and the ROK, which is one of the manifestations of the slow progress in economic integration in Northeast Asia.

As for the construction of free trade areas, on the initiative of China, the leaders of China, Japan, and the ROK agreed to carry out a feasibility study on the establishment of a free trade area among China, Japan, and the ROK at the end of 2002. After that, the research institutions of the three countries conducted comprehensive studies on the impact of the free trade area and worked out a common policy proposal. In May 2010, a governmental, industrial, and academic joint study on CJKFTA was officially launched, and formal negotiations on the free trade area were launched in November 2012.

In terms of customs cooperation, a mechanism of the trilateral customs leaders' meeting among China, Japan, and the ROK was formally established in 2007. There are four working groups under the mechanism: one working group on intellectual property rights (IPR) protection, one on customs enforcement and intelligence, one on authorized economic operator (AEO), and one on customs procedures. These mechanisms provide an essential platform for the three customs to strengthen coordination and cooperation.

In the area of intellectual property protection, the customs authorities of the three countries have adopted the IPR Action Plan, and have made progress in exchanging information, sharing legislation and law enforcement experience, raising public awareness, and enhancing cooperation with IPR holders.

For transportation and logistics construction, China, Japan, and the ROK have held three conferences of maritime transportation and logistics ministers. The first conference was held in Seoul, the ROK, in September 2006, in which the three countries decided to establish a mechanism for China–Japan–ROK a Ministerial Conference on Maritime Transport and Logistics, and hold the meetings in a rotating manner every two years. The Ministerial Conference also adopted 12 concrete action plans. The second conference held in Okayama, Japan, in May 2008 adopted an action plan for future work and identified three major goals for trilateral cooperation in transport and logistics: creating a seamless logistics system, developing environment-friendly logistics, and achieving a balance between logistics security and efficiency. The third conference was held in Chengdu, China, in May 2010 during which the initiative for building a Northeast Asia logistics information service network was put forward.

The Northeast Asia Logistics Information Service Network (NEAL-NET) was officially launched in December 2010.

(3) Progress in Investment Facilitation in China, Japan, and the ROK
Although bilateral investment agreements among China and Japan, China and the ROK, and Japan and the ROK have been signed in 1988, 1992, and 2002, respectively, a common investment agreement among the three countries was not formally signed until 2012. As for industries, although China, Japan, and the ROK already have a relatively mature production network and their foreign investment amounts are as high as US$67.6 billion, US$115.6 billion, and US$20.4 billion, respectively, in 2011, the mutual investment among the three countries only accounted for about 6% of the total investment.

In October 2003, the leaders of three countries agreed to conduct an informal joint study on the possible modes of trilateral investment arrangements. In order to carry out the joint study, a joint research group was formed in 2004 with participants coming from the government, the business community, and academic circles. Furthermore, in November of the same year, the leaders of the three countries reached a consensus to implement the recommendations of the research group so as to improve the business environment and strengthen mutual investment.

In May 2005, the three countries established a mechanism to improve the business environment. On the basis of this mechanism, the three countries signed the Action Plan for Improvement of Business Environment in December 2008. Each country promised to improve the business environment and promote investment. The areas covered in the Action Plan are as follows: transparency of laws and regulations; establishment of a public appraisal system and a response system on applications; intellectual property protection; dispute settlement mechanisms including at the local level; investment promotion and related services; and management consistency between central and local administrations.

On May 13, 2012, after 13 rounds of formal negotiations and several informal consultations within five years, a China–Japan–ROK Investment Agreement was finally signed in Beijing. The agreement was to provide a more stable and transparent investment environment for investors from the three countries. According to previous experience, trade agreements often precede investment agreements. That is to say, trade liberalization is generally realized first and then followed by the facilitation and liberalization of capital, technology, and human resources. Lan, a research, says in his article that "however, breaking the conventional rules, the investment agreement among the three countries has broken the conventional rules and is signed before the trade agreement."[18]

The agreement consists of 27 articles and an additional protocol, including all the essential contents normally contained in international investment agreements, such as investment definition, the scope of application, most-favored-nation treatment, national treatment, collection, transfer, subrogation, taxation, general exception, and dispute resolution.

The significance of the agreement is that it is the first legal document and institutional arrangement for China, Japan, and the ROK to promote and protect investment among the three countries through collective actions. In addition, although the China–Japan–ROK Investment Agreement is not equivalent to an investment agreement in the future free trade area negotiations, it is the basis for the future negotiations of the CJKFTA investment agreement. Li, a researcher, says in his essay that "it is an independent treaty to promote, facilitate and protect the investment of the three countries. Besides promoting international investment among the three countries, it also aims to further promote negotiations and consultations on the free trade area among the three countries, which is vital to China."[19]

5.2.1.3 Measurement of trade and investment facilitation in Northeast Asia

Since the definition of trade and investment facilitation is not uniform, it is extremely difficult to measure it quantitatively. Therefore, based on *The Global Enabling Trade Report 2012* by the World Economics Forum[20] and the *Doing Business 2012* report by the World Bank, we have made a general assessment of the facilitation levels of China, Japan, and the ROK.

---

[18] Lan Qingxin, China–Japan–ROK investment agreement has milestone significance. *International Business News*, May 16, 2012.
[19] Li Guoxue, Characteristics, problems, and implications of China–Japan–ROK investment agreements. China Market, 2012, 33.
[20] Robert Z. Lawrence, Margareta Dizeniek Hanouz, and Sean Doherty. The global enabling trade report 2012: Reducing supply chain barriers. *World Economic Forum*, 2012.

Table 5.16. The ETIs of China, Japan, and the ROK.

Item	China	Japan	The ROK
ETI	4.22	5.08	4.65
Global ranking	56	18	34

Source: Lawrence, R. Z., Hanouz, M. D., and Doherty, S. (2012). The global enabling trade report 2012: Reducing supply chain barriers. *World Economic Forum*, p. 32.

(1) The Establishment of Trade Facilitation Indicators and the Evaluation of China, Japan, and the ROK

According to *The Global Enabling Trade Report 2012*, the Enabling Trade Index (ETI),[21] which represents the overall level of trade facilitation, includes market access, customs administration, transport and communication infrastructure, and business environment. At the same time, each index mentioned contains nine sub-indicators to ensure the coverage of trade facilitation contents as much as possible, namely, domestic and external market entry, customs management efficiency, import and export procedure efficiency, administrative transparency, accessibility and quality of transportation infrastructure, accessibility and quality of transportation services, accessibility and application of information and communication technologies, regulatory environment, and safety. There are several indicators under each sub-indicator amounting to fifty.

The three most important countries in Northeast Asia, China, Japan, and the ROK, not only have frequent economic and trade exchanges but also initially formed a unified production network. The trade facilitation levels of these three countries directly determine the level and depth of economic and trade development in Northeast Asia. The ETIs of China, Japan, and the ROK are shown in Table 5.16.

It can be seen that in the ranking released by the World Economic Forum (WEF), the ETI of Japan is 5.08, higher than that of China and the ROK, and relatively high in the global ranking. The ETI of the ROK is 4.65, ranking 34th in the world, while the ETI of China is only 4.22, ranking 56th in the world.

We will further examine the performance of China, Japan, and the ROK in the sub-indicators (see Table 5.17).

---

[21] World Economic Forum (WEF), headquartered in Geneva, compiles ETI ranking reports every two years.

Table 5.17. Trade facilitation level of China, Japan, and the ROK in terms of nine sub-indicators.

Item	China (global ranking)	Japan (global ranking)	The ROK (global ranking)
Domestic and external market access	3.6(108)	3.8(98)	3.4(115)
Customs management efficiency	4.6(38)	5.7(13)	5.0(30)
Efficiency of import and export procedures	4.8(63)	5.8(16)	6.2(5)
Transparency of administrative management	3.6(61)	6.0(13)	4.4(40)
Availability and quality of transportation infrastructure	3.6(94)	5.6(18)	5.5(21)
Accessibility and quality of transportation services	3.8(64)	5.4(6)	5.0(14)
Accessibility and application of information and communication technology	4.1(58)	5.5(20)	6.2(5)
Regulatory environment	3.6(72)	4.8(23)	3.8(59)
Safety	5.3(44)	5.6(31)	5.1(53)

Source: Based on the data of the World Economic Forum world trade promotion report 2012, see Robert Z Lawrence, Margareta Dizeniek Hanouz, and Sean Doherty. The global enabling trade report 2012: Reducing supply chain barriers. *World Economic Forum*, 2012, p. 32.

According to the above-mentioned data, China, Japan, and the ROK did differ in several aspects as indicated. They ranked 108, 98, and 115, respectively, in the world in terms of domestic and external market access and belonged to the lower echelon. In terms of customs management efficiency, China, Japan, and the ROK are in the middle level in the world, ranking 38, 13, and 30, respectively. As for the efficiency of important import and export procedures, Japan and the ROK presented well, ranking 16 and 5, respectively, while China ranked 63. In terms of the regulatory environment, China and the ROK performed poorly, ranking outside 50, while Japan ranked 23.

Generally speaking, the trade facilitation of China, Japan, and the ROK is lagging behind and can hardly meet the needs of increased trade volume. Specifically, Japan has the highest level of trade facilitation, followed by the ROK, while China's level of trade facilitation is still far lower than that of the two countries.

(2) Setup of Investment Facilitation Indicators and Assessment of China, Japan, and the ROK

In *Doing Business 2012* report, the World Bank examined the business environment in various countries from 10 aspects, i.e., the establishment of enterprises (4 sub-indicators involved), construction permits (3 sub-indicators involved), access to electricity (3 sub-indicators involved), registered ownership (3 sub-indicators involved), credit certification (4 sub-indicators involved), protection of investors (4 sub-indicators involved), taxation (3 sub-indicators involved), cross-border trade (6 sub-indicators involved), execution of contracts (3 sub-indicators involved), and bankruptcy settlement (3 sub-indicators involved).

Table 5.18 presents the global ranking and specific values of China, Japan, and the ROK in terms of the business environment (the ranking is listed first, and then the specific values of sub-indexes are shown in brackets).

Based on the data analysis, it can be seen that the ROK has done the best among the three countries in investment facilitation and ranks first in the world. Japan ranks 20th, while China lags far behind Japan, the ROK, and many other countries in the world. For examples, in the process of setting up an enterprise, 14 procedures are needed in China, 8 in Japan, and 5 in the ROK. Besides, setting up an enterprise in China takes the longest time, 38 days. But it takes only seven days, the shortest time, in the ROK with 23 days in Japan. The situation remains the same with construction permits.

In general, the ROK has the highest level of investment facilitation among the three countries and ranks among the top 10 in the world. Then comes Japan, while China is far from Japan and the ROK with much room for improvement.

5.2.2 Trade and investment facilitation in Northeast Asia

5.2.2.1 *Problems in trade facilitation*

The WEF conducted a survey of import and export business people in countries around the world, by which several prominent factors hindering

Table 5.18. Comparison of business environment among China, Japan, and the ROK.

Item	China	Japan	The ROK
Global ranking	91	20	8
Establishing a business (procedures, time-cost, cost, minimum capital)	151 (14 items, 38 days, 3.5%, 100.4%)	107 (8 items, 23 days, 7.5%, no minimum capital limit)	24 (5 items, 7 days, 14.6%, no minimum capital limit)
Getting permits (procedures, time-consuming)	179 (33 items, 311 days)	63 (14 items, 193 days)	26 (12 items, 30 days)
Obtaining electricity (procedures, time-consuming, cost)	115 (5 items, 145 days, 640.9%)	26 (3 items, 117 days, 0.0%)	11 (4 items, 49 days, 38.6%)
Registering for ownership (procedure, time-consuming)	40 (4 items, 29 days)	58 (6 items, 14 days)	71 (7 items, 11 days)
Getting credit	67	24	8
Protecting investors	97	17	79
Paying	122	120	38
Doing cross-border trade (the number of import and export documents required)	60 (5 pieces, 8 pieces)	16 (5 pieces, 3 pieces)	4 (3 pieces, 3 pieces)
Implementing contracts	16	34	2
Solving bankruptcy	75	1	13

Notes: Cost refers to the percentage of the cost of setting up enterprise of the foreign investors in the per capita income of the country. The minimum capital is the percentage of the minimum capital of setting up enterprise of the foreign investors in the per capita income of the country.
Source: World Bank, IFC: *Doing Business 2012*.

foreign trade were summarized, and accordingly countries were ranked and factors listed. According to the survey, we can get the following results.

Firstly, as for China, in terms of exports, 13.3% of the total number of Chinese interviewees think that foreign technical requirements and standards have greatly affected China's exports, which is the most prominent problem. At the same time, it shows that non-tariff barriers have a strong blocking effect on China's goods export to the international market. 9.4% of the total number of interviewees regard that high costs and delays caused by poor international transportation hinder China's exports and 11.2% think an obstacle to China's exports is inappropriate product techniques and technologies. 8.6% of the total number of interviewees regard failure to meet the buyer's requirements for the quantity and quality of goods into consideration, 6.5% regard the complicated export procedures and foreign corruption, 4.8% regard the requirement for the source area from foreign countries, and 9.6% regard access to trade finance accounts as causes hindering China's exports. As far as imports are concerned, 22.2% of the total Chinese interviewees regard tariff and non-tariff barriers as the biggest obstacles, 14.2% regard domestic technologies and standards, and 13.1% and 13.7% regard high costs and delays caused by poor domestic and international transportation, respectively, as the obstacles to China's imports. As high as 19.9% of the interviewees choose complicated import procedures and only 2.6% regard inappropriate telecommunication infrastructure as a hindrance to China's imports. Though the last number is small, considering the rapid development of e-commerce, this factor will seriously affect China's foreign trade environment in the future.

Secondly, as for Japan, as far as exports are concerned, 10.9% of the total number of Japanese businessmen interviewed regard foreign technical requirements and standards have a greater impact on Japan's exports. Non-tariff barriers are also the first hindrance factor in Japan's exports of goods. 10.6% of the interviewees regard the failure to meet the buyer's requirements for the quantity and quality of goods, 10.2% regard the high costs and delays caused by poor international traffic, 8.6% regard the foreign requirements for origin, and 8.7% regard cumbersome export procedures and foreign corruption as obstacles to Japan's exports. For imports, 23.7% of the total number of interviewees regard tariff and non-tariff barriers, 22.9% regard the domestic technologies and standards, 13.8% and 16.8% regard the high costs and delays caused by poor domestic and international traffic, respectively, 20.4% regard the cumbersome import procedures, and 1.2% regard the inappropriate telecommunication infrastructure as the causes hindering Japan's imports.

Thirdly, as for the ROK, as far as exports are concerned, 13.8% of the total number of interviewees think that foreign technical requirements and standards have a greater impact. 14.9% of the interviewees regard the failure to meet the buyer's requirements for the quantity and quality of

Table 5.19. Trade efficiency of China, Japan, and the ROK.

Country	Import/export time (days)	Total number of import/export formalities (items)
China	24/21	6/7
Japan	11/10	11/10
The ROK	8/8	6/4

Source: Based on Shen Minghui's: *Measurement of Trade Facilitation Level in East Asian Countries and After-Thoughts*.

goods, 3.9% regard requirement for source area from foreign countries, and 7.7% regard the complicated export procedures and foreign corruption as the obstacles to the exports of the ROK. For imports, 24.6% of the total number of interviewees regard tariff and non-tariff barriers, 17.1% regard the domestic technologies and standards, 24.7% regard the complicated import procedures, 17.7% regard the high costs and delays caused by poor international traffic, and 2.7% regard the inappropriate telecommunication infrastructure as the obstacles to the imports of the ROK.

At present, there are still some problems to be solved in terms of trade efficiency, market approval, customs administration, and control measures in Northeast Asian countries. To better illustrate the import and export efficiency, Table 5.19 lists the trade efficiency data of China, Japan, and the ROK in terms of the import and export time consumption and the import and export procedures.

As shown in Table 5.19, import and export time consumption in China is 2 to 3 times greater than that in Japan and the ROK, which is not conducive to improving the efficiency of the foreign trade industry and calls for further improvement of customs management efficiency. Yet, Japan has far more import and export procedures than China and the ROK, which also needs improving.

What's more, according to Table 5.17, China, Japan, and the ROK are far from satisfactory in terms of several important indicators, some of which are far behind other countries in the world.

In the aspect of domestic and external market access, China scores only 3.6, ranking 108th in the world. Japan is higher than China and the ROK, but it scores only 3.8, ranking 98th in the world. The ROK scores 3.4, ranking 115th in the world. All these indicators show that China, Japan, and the ROK have still not done enough in terms of market access and there is much room for improvement.

For customs management efficiency, the three countries perform better than in market access, but the overall level is still not satisfactory, with China, Japan, and the ROK ranking 38th, 13th, and 30th, respectively, in the world. For the efficiency of import and export procedures, China falls behind with a score of 4.8 and a global ranking of 63rd. Japan and the ROK are better and among the world's top countries. This is an area in which China needs to exert great efforts in the future.

For the regulatory environment, China and the ROK scored lower than Japan, which is not satisfactory. This shows that the three countries have very tight control. It is worth noting that although Japan has a high score, it is not more open because there are many invisible controls, such as the insularity of social traditions and ethnic customs, which are difficult to reflect in quantitative indicators.

5.2.2.2 Focal issues in investment facilitation in China, Japan, and the ROK

The China–Japan–ROK Investment Agreement signed by China, Japan, and the ROK through trilateral joint actions is one of the most important investment facilitation measures in Northeast Asia. Its characteristic is that "it basically follows the 'high standard' of the bilateral investment agreement of American style, but it is more pragmatic and flexible in the cooperation of the three countries in the field of international investment in terms of investment promotion and relevant dispute settlement mechanisms."[22] The biggest shortcoming of the agreement is that the dispute on the "negative list" and the "pre-establishment national treatment" has not been resolved, and both will likely be mentioned again in the FTA negotiations.

The pre-establishment national treatment and the negative list are two interrelated issues and the focus of China, Japan, and the ROK investment agreement negotiations.[23] The so-called "pre-establishment national

---

[22] Li Guoxue, Characteristics, problems, and implications of China-Japan-ROK investment agreements. *China Market*, 2012, 3.

[23] According to Zhao Yumin, "Pre-establishment national treatment is the most important difference between the control mode adopted in the traditional investment agreement and the free mode in the open investment system. Giving pre-establishment national treatment to foreign investors means a further commitment to investment liberalization." Pre-establishment National Treatment in the International Investment System: Looking at the Development Trend of International Investment Rules from Japanese and the ROK's Investment National Treatment, *International Trade*, 2012, 3.

treatment" refers to the treatment given to foreign investors and investments before the investment is established, which should be no more or less than that given to domestic investors and investments under similar circumstances. The so-called "negative list" mean the list of areas which are not open up to foreign investment, the other areas are "allowed if not listed." China should list its current and future reservations, and those that are not listed must be opened up.

The core of the pre-establishment national treatment is to grant the right of admission to foreign capital, which means canceling the examination and approval that are part of the establishment and merger of foreign enterprises. It is in fundamental conflict with China's current foreign capital management system. Even if it does not mean giving up the power of examination and approval completely, it will greatly decentralize the government's power in terms of foreign investment.

The agreements signed by Japan, the ROK, and their FTA/EPA partners all contain the principle of the pre-establishment national treatment.[24] However, the opening up of their domestic fields for foreign investment is very limited, with heavy restrictions on foreign investment extremely strict supervision, especially due to the parochialism of national traditions and social atmosphere. Such invisible control severely restricts China's investment in Japan and the ROK and is not conducive to further development of investment facilitation in the three countries.

The China–Japan–ROK Investment Agreement (2012) has not settled disputes over the negative list and the pre-establishment national

---

[24] According to Zhao Yumin, "After Japan and the ROK signed a bilateral investment agreement in 2002 that included the pre-establishment national treatment of investment, most of their economic partnership agreements signed in recent years have adopted the pre-establishment national treatment. By February 2011, Japan had signed a total of 12 free trade economic partnership agreements, 10 of which contained investment rules, and all agreements containing investment rules promised to grant pre-establishment national treatment. By the end of 2010, the ROK had signed a total of 93 bilateral investment agreements, of which only the bilateral investment agreement signed with Japan in 2002 contained a clause on pre-establishment national treatment. At present, the ROK has signed free trade agreements with eight countries and regions. Except for the agreements with the EU that do not cover investment, the other seven agreements all contain investment chapters, and these investment chapters all include provisions on the pre-establishment national treatment." Pre-establishment National Treatment in the International Investment System: Looking at the Development Trend of International Investment Rules from Japanese and the ROK's Investment National Treatment, *International Trade*, 2012, 3.

treatment. China has not made any promise on these two items. From the legal perspective, the China-Japan-ROK Investment Agreement is not equal to the investment agreement in future FTA negotiations, but it is the basis for the future investment agreement. Therefore, China is still facing high pressure in the investment agreement negotiations.

In addition, the closeness and exclusiveness of the economic systems of Japan and the ROK have seriously impeded capital flows from other countries. The impediments are caused by the tangible measures of the governmental legal regulations and intangible factors from society. This makes it difficult for Chinese enterprises to adapt. The unique investment protectionism of Japan and the ROK will not help the implementation of the existing China–Japan–ROK Investment Agreement. Although in the past few years, Japan and the ROK have successively relaxed foreign investment and adopted some measures conducive to investment facilitation, they still utilize strict supervision in important economic sectors, even in the manufacturing industry, which occupies a dominant position in Japan and the ROK. Taking Japan as an example, although it has implemented capital liberalization, it mainly introduces indirect investment and strictly regulates direct investment that does not account for a large proportion to prevent economic control from falling into the hands of outsiders.

5.2.2.3 *The development potential of trade and investment facilitation among China, Japan, and the ROK*

Firstly, China, Japan, and the ROK have close economic ties, which is of great significance to all countries. They have been closely linked by a large-scale cross-border production network. However, the great potential of economic complementarity among the three countries is far from being realized under the current trade and investment conditions.

In 2011, the foreign trade volume of China, Japan, and the ROK accounted for about 1/5 of the total global trade volume. However, the current intra-regional trade volume among China, Japan, and the ROK is 20%, much lower than the 60% of the EU and the 40% of the NAFTA. China, Japan, and the ROK are struggling in economic scale and transnational investment. Still, mutual investment among the three countries accounts for only 6% of the total investment abroad of the three countries. If we can find areas of common interest to the three countries and come up with targeted and feasible improvement plans, we will greatly improve economic and trade cooperation in Northeast Asia.

Secondly, paradoxically, the relative shortage of collective action leaves much room for cooperation. From the substantive process of facilitation in the three countries, we can see that China, Japan, and the ROK have taken many individual substantive actions and measures to promote facilitation. However, there are few trilateral joint actions, leaving much room for further cooperation. In fact, this is also an obvious deficiency in the facilitation process under multilateral frameworks such as the WTO and APEC. In short, China, Japan, and the ROK will make faster and greater progress in the field of facilitation once joint actions can be taken. One field they can work on together is to establish a paperless trading environment.[25] In addition, actions can be taken to coordinate and simplify the customs procedures of the three countries, apply information technology, and improve the transparency of customs procedures. In this way, cooperation among the customs authorities of China, Japan, and the ROK will be secured.

Thirdly, the institutional construction among China, Japan, and the ROK is relatively poor with high tariff barriers and restricted investment and trade exchanges. So, the great potential for economic complementarity among the three countries is far from being realized. From this analysis, it can be seen that the non-tariff trade barriers and complicated import and export procedures have had the greatest impact on the international trade of the three countries. In the future trade facilitation and the construction of the free trade area, joint actions to remove non-tariff barriers and other barriers blocking goods, capital, and personnel, promote further facilitation of customs clearance, and reduce unnecessary approval procedures will definitely benefit all countries.

5.2.3 From facilitation to liberalization: FTA strategy of Northeast Asian countries

5.2.3.1 *The influence of facilitation on FTA construction*

FTA is becoming more and more complicated and comprehensive as it develops. Besides the traditional negotiations on trade agreements in

---

[25] Lu Gang, Facilitation measures of China, Japan, and the ROK under APEC framework. *Development Research*, 2010, 3.

goods, services, and investment, countries, especially developed economies, are currently devoting more and more attention to other aspects of free trade agreements, such as environmental protection, labor standards, intellectual property protection, and government procurement agreements. The Joint Study Report on the Feasibility of the China–Japan–ROK Free Trade Area (CJKFTA) points out that the future CJKFTA will cover not only areas such as trade in goods, services, and investment but also issues such as sanitary and phytosanitary measures, technical barriers to trade, IPRs, transparency, competition policy, dispute resolution, industrial cooperation, consumer safety, e-commerce, energy and mineral resources, fisheries, food, government procurement, and environmental protection.[26]

It can be seen that the trade investment facilitation is the foundation of the trade investment liberalization. The facilitation and liberalization have the same contents on many issues. The facilitation of trade in goods and services and of movement of persons, capital, and information is an important part of the FTAs/ETAs signed by China, Japan, and the ROK. Simplification and coordination of customs procedures and other facilitation measures will be another important part of future FTA negotiations.

5.2.3.2 *FTA strategy of China, Japan, and the ROK*

In August 2008, the Doha round of the WTO negotiations failed to make any progress, and many countries were very disappointed with this multilateral system and were more determined than ever to strengthen regional cooperation. A free trade area strategy is a national strategy for each member to meet its own actual needs and diversified intentions.

(1) FTA Strategy of China

Due to the rapid development of the domestic economy, China is in dire need of a stable raw material market and export market. Therefore, China signed an FTA agreement for favorable domestic economic development and the establishment of China's role in East Asian economic integration.

---

[26] Department of International Affairs. Ministry of Commerce of the people's Republic of China, Preparatory Meeting for Launching a Joint Study on a Possible FTA among China, Japan, and the ROK, website of the Ministry of Commerce of the People's Republic of China, http://image.Mofcom.gov.cn/gjs/accessory/201203/1333096957493.pdf, March 30, 2012.

China conducts early planning, participates in trade in goods and services step by step, and does not sign all the FTA agreements at one time. China regards regional economic cooperation and strengthening the construction of FTAs as new approaches to open up to the world.

Though "China has not yet established a set of national FTA strategies with clear themes, orderly arrangements and specific measures,"[27] this does not hinder the practice of China's regional economic cooperation. China has become an important force in the construction of the Asia-Pacific free trade area. At present, China has signed FTAs with New Zealand, the ASEAN, Chile, Singapore, Peru, Pakistan, Costa Rica, Australia, Switzerland, and Iceland. FTA negotiations between China and the Gulf Cooperation Council (GCC), the Southern African Customs Union (SACU), and Norway are in progress.[28]

From the actual process, China's FTA strategy has the following characteristics:

Firstly, priority is given to neighboring countries and regions, especially East Asia. At present, the guidelines for China's diplomatic relations are that "the major powers are the key, the periphery the primary, developing countries the foundation and multilateral diplomacy the important stage." China also puts forward the principles of "building friendship and partnership with neighboring countries" and "fostering an amicable, secure and prosperous neighborhood." Most of the economies with which China has reached an agreement are located in East Asia, such as the ten member countries of the ASEAN. This was done to meet China's needs for raw materials and external markets and to avoid trade friction.

A research group of the International Economic Research Institute from the University of International Business and Economics of China lists China's FTA partners in order according to their economic, political and diplomatic, geographical, and time standards as shown in Table 5.20.

---

[27] Zhang Fan, On the construction of China's FTA strategy. *China Opening Journal*, 2004, 5: 74–77.

[28] Department of International Affairs. Ministry of Commerce of the People's Republic of China, *Joint Feasibility Study Report on China-Japan-ROK Free Trade Area*, website of the Ministry of Commerce of the People's Republic of China, http://image.Mofcom.gov.cn/gjs/accessory/201203/1333096957493.pdf, March 30, 2012.

Table 5.20. Schedule of China's FTA partner selection.

Time	Target cooperation countries
Short term	Ten ASEAN member countries, Australia, six Gulf countries, Mexico, and five South African allies
Medium term	The ROK, India, and Russia
Long term	Japan, EU, and USA

Source: Research group of International Economic Research Institute with University of International Business and Economics, *China's Free Trade Area Strategy-Neighborhood First*, University of International Business and Economics Press, 2010, p. 197.

Secondly, progressive, pragmatic, and flexible ways are adopted. In FTA negotiations with partner countries, instead of accomplishing an action overnight, China chooses to reach a comprehensive agreement in a gradual way according to the national conditions and as acceptance to partner countries by reducing tariffs and diminishing non-tariff barriers. China starts with trade in goods and then expands to services and investment. For example, Early Harvest Plans are always firstly signed to reduce tariffs on some commodities, and then cooperation will be deepened to cover investment, services, and trade facilitation. This helps partner countries benefit from FTA construction as early as possible. It shows China's sincerity and helps build confidence in the bilateral cooperation.

(2) FTA Strategy of Japan

Entering the 21st century, Japan changed its past practice of excluding regional trade groups and has actively established and negotiated various bilateral free trade agreements. It has formulated a clear strategy for regional economic integration. By October 2013, Japan signed an Economic Partnership Agreement (EPA) with Singapore, Mexico, Malaysia, Chile, Thailand, Indonesia, Brunei, ASEAN, Philippines, Switzerland, Vietnam, India, and Peru. Japan is conducting EPA negotiations with ten economies including the ROK, the Gulf Cooperation Council (GCC), Canada, Mongolia, and Australia.

In 2002, Japan's Ministry of Foreign Affairs published Japan's FTA Strategy, which for the first time showed its basic principles and guidelines for the future construction of FTAs. "According to Japan's FTA Strategy and the Basic Principles for Promoting EPA in the Future, the main criteria for Japan to choose the negotiation partner are as follows. Firstly, the negotiation will ensure its own economic interests. Secondly, the negotiation will form a favorable political and diplomatic environment for Japan. Thirdly, there is the possibility of success."[29]

Japan's FTA strategy lays more emphasis on the construction of the EPA system.[30] Besides trade, it also pays much attention to investment. However, hindered by the excessively high protection from its farm product sector, Japan is very limited in choosing its partner countries. In practice, Japan's FTA strategy takes East Asia as the center and ASEAN as the foundation, with limited consideration to the ROK and major ASEAN members. It will not give much consideration to trans-regional regions and countries, such as Mexico, Chile, and Switzerland.

Japan's strategic objectives for establishing FTAs mainly lie in the following three aspects. For economic objectives, Japan can maintain a good external operating environment with FTAs, so as to enable Japanese foreign investment enterprises to obtain higher returns, reduce trade barriers, increase freedom to carry out business activities, improve foresight, and protect investor interests. For political objectives, domestic structural reform can be promoted through FTAs. Japan's domestic postal privatization reform, agricultural policy reform, administrative reform, and other structural reforms have encountered many obstacles due to the extensive interest groups involved. Therefore, Japan not only needs a good external economic environment to support its reform but also needs external stimulation. For security objectives, Japan regards FTAs as a complex entity of economy, diplomacy, and security. The reason for Japan's participation in FTAs is not only due to economic interests but also due to diplomatic, security, and political considerations. The history of Japan's post-war

---

[29] Xu Mei, Zhang Shuying, and Zhao Jianglin, *Study on the Establishment of Free Trade Area between China and Japan*, Beijing: Economic Press China, 2009, pp. 21–22.

[30] According to Japanese domestic parlance, regional economic cooperation includes free trade agreements and economic cooperation agreements. To avoid sensitive domestic sectors such as agriculture and highlight overseas investment, Japan prefers the Economic Partnership Agreement (EPA) with a wider extension in the FTA strategy it promotes. This is mainly because the degree of trade liberalization and openness of the EPA mode may be lower than the requirements of WTO rules in some fields. It helps Japan foster strengths and circumvent weaknesses, obtain maximum economic benefits at the lowest cost, and at the same time meet the needs for Japanese capital of partner countries, especially in East Asian countries and regions. Japan's overseas entities have huge investments.

investment abroad shows that Japan has always attached great importance to Southeast Asia. Southeast Asia is not only a resource supply area for minerals that Japan is in extreme lack of and the external market for Japan but is also important to ensure the safety of Japan's maritime transport routes. In the eyes of some Japanese politicians, Southeast Asian countries can be instigated to join its actions to contain China and curb China's expanding influence. This can be proved by Japan's attitude to participating in TPP negotiations.[31]

(3) FTA Strategy of the ROK

The Joint Study Report on the Feasibility of China–Japan–ROK Free Trade Area (CJKFTA) points out that there are three objectives for the ROK's active participation in the FTA. They are promotion of trade growth, economic efficiency, and welfare.[32]

The ROK's FTA strategy is very different from that of Japan. The fundamental reason is that the ROK has the least influence and is the weakest compared with China and Japan. So, the ROK has divided its FTA strategy into three steps. The first step is to sign an FTA agreement with the United States, which has been completed. The second step is to sign FTA agreements with the EU and ASEAN, which are currently underway. The third step is to negotiate on an FTA with China. The reason for placing the negotiation with China after the EU and the United States is that the ROK hopes to learn from the advanced trade system of the EU and the US, the two most developed economic bodies. It hopes to achieve an advanced trading system, increase domestic competition, promote economic growth, improve the production efficiency of the ROK's enterprises, and get rid of the heavy dependence on the China–Japan trade. It also hopes to enter the US market ahead of schedule, attract US investment, improve its domestic economic environment, and strive for a favorable position in the negotiation process with China and Japan.

---

[31] 《日本のFTA戦略》, http://www.mofa.go.jp/mofaj/gaiko/fta/policy.html, October 2002.

[32] Department of International Affairs, Ministry of Commerce of the People's Republic of China, Joint Feasibility Study Report on China-Japan-ROK Free Trade Area, website of the Ministry of Commerce of the People's Republic of China, http://image.Mofcom.gov.cn/gjs/accessory/201203/1333096957493.pdf, March 30, 2012.

5.3 China's Strategic Conception of Promoting Trade and Investment Facilitation and Regional Cooperation in Northeast Asia

Countries in Northeast Asia are important economic and trade partners and have set up close interdependent relationships. However, the level of trade and investment facilitation and liberalization in Northeast Asia is still not high. Therefore, it is important to adapt to the development trend of economic globalization and regional integration, strengthen the construction of trade and investment facilitation, and promote the construction of a free trade area in Northeast Asia. It will help deepen the economic cooperation in Northeast Asia and promote stable economic development.

5.3.1 China's policy to promote trade facilitation in Northeast Asia

Northeast Asia includes not only Japan and the ROK, two developed countries, but also emerging economies and developing countries such as China, Russia, Mongolia, and the DPRK. As these countries are at different stages of economic development, the level of development of trade facilitation varies from country to country. As the world's second-largest economy, compared with other countries in Northeast Asia, China is in a leading position in the development of trade facilitation and has always attached importance to international and regional cooperation in this regard, accumulating more experience. Therefore, China should play a more active role in promoting trade facilitation in Northeast Asia by strengthening collaboration with neighboring countries.

China has always advocated active participation in and promotion of East Asian regional economic cooperation on the basic principles of "consultation on an equal basis, mutual benefit and reciprocity, proceeding in an orderly way, openness and inclusiveness." Its theme coincides with the principles of voluntariness, consultation, flexibility, transparency, and openness advocated by the APEC. Because of the different advantages and disadvantages in specific areas of trade facilitation in Northeast Asian countries, we can learn from the APEC approach, especially the Path Finders' Approach. Besides, the realistic factors affecting trade facilitation cooperation in Northeast Asia mainly come from "hard constraints" represented by insufficient infrastructure and "soft barriers" posed by the lack of institutional construction. Compared with "hard constraints," "soft barriers" cover a wide range of aspects, such as technical regulations, trade procedures, domestic systems, and policies, which have a more significant impact on the interests of the countries. Therefore, China should put forward and realize short-term, medium-term, and long-term goals in stages according to the ease of implementation in the process of promoting regional trade facilitation.

In the short term, China proposes facilitation initiatives in specific and key areas to carry out more specific and targeted activities and help in developing countries in the region to implement needed measures.

For the medium term, China aims to cooperate with countries in the region, organize and coordinates trade facilitation cooperation, and solve problems in implementing trade facilitation measures.

For the long term, Northeast Asian countries will jointly build a more transparent, convenient, and efficient trade management system and gradually shift to institutional cooperation.

At present, compared with the complexity and difficulty of building a regional system, it is more practical and feasible to give priority to developing cooperation in key areas and establishing a trade facilitation coordination body. China should take the lead in these two areas.

5.3.1.1 *Giving priority to cooperation in key areas*

(1) Infrastructure Construction

One of the important conditions for trade facilitation is infrastructure construction. Without a certain amount of infrastructure investment, trade facilitation is not possible. Infrastructure construction in a country means not only the construction of new roads or railways but also the maintenance of ports, airports, and bridges, improvement of transportation capacity and facilities management systems with information technology, and continuous and consistent transportation policies.

For most developing countries, the cost of achieving these goals in a short period is too high, which often requires foreign capital or assistance. At present, Northeast Asia countries, especially less developed countries, are weak in the construction of roads, railways, and air transportation, and improvement is needed in transportation services, such as the transformation of the tools, tracking and tracing of cargo, postal services, and logistics. From another perspective, there is a huge demand for infrastructure financing in the region. To this end, China proposed the establishment of the Asian Infrastructure Investment Bank to provide financial support for infrastructure construction in developing countries in the region.[33] Chinese enterprises follow the national "going global" strategy and actively participate in infrastructure construction in Northeast Asia, especially projects related to trade facilitation, so as to create conditions for further development of trade among countries in the region. Moreover, China and other countries can gradually narrow the gap between Japan and the ROK, promote the free flow of goods and capital in the region, and reduce the difficulty of cooperation in the field of trade facilitation by improving the quality of ports, air transportation, and internet infrastructure.

(2) Customs Procedures
Customs is an important part of the chain of international trade. Increasing the speed of implementation of customs is the main problem that all countries, regional economic organizations, and the WTO face. With the development of economic globalization and economic integration, traditional non-tariff barriers have been further restricted, while complex customs procedures and regulations have been regarded as non-tariff measures by the global business community and relevant international organizations, and even assessed as the biggest obstacle to trade facilitation equivalent to tariffs.[34]

In promoting its own trade facilitation, China's customs should increase the efficiency of customs clearance at ports, hasten the construction of the electronic port system, promote the new supervision mode of "customs declaration in advance and release upon arrival," and make a transition to a new integrated management system at ports. First of all, China will continue to push forward the construction of large-scale customs clearance at ports, raise the level of supervision and service quality, simplify the examination and approval procedures, shorten the time for customs clearance, and reduce the trade costs of enterprises. Secondly, we will continue to deepen the construction of local electronic ports, expand the scope of internet applications, and strengthen information exchange and sharing among government departments. Thirdly, on the premise of ensuring effective supervision, we will actively adapt to the requirements

---

[33] Xi Jinping, Deepen Reform and Opening up and Work Together for a Better Asia Pacific: Address to the APEC CEO Summit (October 7, 2013), *People's Daily*, October 8, 2013.
[34] Fan Ying, East Asian Trade and Investment Facilitation Cooperation in the Post-Financial Crisis Era. *Journal of International Economic Cooperation*, 2011, 3.

of regional economic integration, widen the application scope of possession declaration and port check out, and facilitate inbound and outbound logistics. Finally, we will work toward closer cooperation with other relevant government departments like transportation, commerce, and finance, and strengthen communication with enterprises related to import and export, freight forwarders, customs declaration, and production to ensure the safety and convenience of the entire trade supply chain.

In promoting regional trade facilitation, China should strive to overcome various barriers in customs procedures, standardization, business flow, and regulatory environment, and expand the scope and depth of customs cooperation with other countries. Under the current economic situation, China's customs department takes trade development as the goal and enhances international customs cooperation through mutual recognition of supervision, mutual assistance in law enforcement, and exchange of information. In doing so, China's customs department makes efforts to standardize and manage the enterprises in their developing market and provide conveniences and services for them. China can run training programs for personnel in customs procedures and systems, such as training Mongolian customs officials in regulations, supervision, and risk management techniques. It is also possible to improve the level of customs information technology in recipient countries through the provision of customs information equipment and the construction of information networks, for example, the China–Mongolia cross-border project.[35]

In addition, China can exert its influence in regional customs cooperation and introduce its mature trade facilitation practice at an appropriate time. China's trade facilitation practice can gradually become the standard for the regional customs trade facilitation and establish it's leading position. Northeast Asian countries should also learn from the experience of international customs in promoting trade liberalization, improving regional customs cooperation by raising the level of bilateral exchanges, and finally deepening people's participation in multilateral cooperation affairs.[36]

---

[35] See Progress Report and Work Plan on Trade Facilitation Planning (2011–2012) of the 11th CAREC ministerial conference on central Asian regional economic cooperation.
[36] Zhou Yang, A Discussion on Improving the Customs Trade Facility System of China: A Perspective from the United States. *International Business Research*, 2010, 6.

(3) Standardization and Consistency

Among the current measures to promote international trade cooperation, adopting uniform international standards is the simplest, most feasible, and most effective way of eliminating technical barriers to trade. At the same time, standards and consistency are also important parts of trade facilitation. China, Japan, the ROK, and Russia all are members of the APEC. Standards and consistency are an important component of the APEC Trade Facilitation Action Plan II. Therefore, it is an inevitable requirement to construct and perfect a set of scientific and reasonable technical standard systems in line with international standards. The specific measures are as follows. Firstly, China and other countries should try their best to bring their domestic standards in line with international standards. Secondly, they should format a series of rules, regulations, and procedures that affect the mutual recognition of goods between countries. Thirdly, in the compulsory and voluntary fields, bilateral or multilateral agreements on conformity assessment should be reached. Fourthly, they should maintain consistency in trade agreements, domestic laws, and regulations concerning international standards. Fifthly, they should strengthen multilateral and bilateral cooperation and strive for regular exchanges between countries to ensure transparency in the standardization.

It should be noted that the standards for trade facilitation should not be set too high. Otherwise, developing countries will face great difficulties with insufficient funds, workforce, and technology. In addition, regarding the differences in customs environments and regulatory environments among Northeast Asian countries, we should give priority to mutual recognition of national standards instead of setting up a unified set of standards with undue haste.

(4) E-commerce

When the trade facilitation levels of various countries are compared, e-commerce is usually one of the indicators to measure whether a country has sufficient communication and information infrastructure and whether it can use the information to improve business efficiency and promote economic activities. Electronic commerce is an important means to simplify trade procedures and promote the development of international trade. Therefore, whether new information technologies can be adopted in a timely manner is also an aspect of trade facilitation.[37]

---

[37] Shen Minghui, Measurement and thinking of trade facilitation level in East Asian countries. *Journal of International Economic Cooperation*, 2009, 7.

In Northeast Asia, the gap between Japan and the ROK in e-commerce is not very large. Russia and other countries are still lagging behind in adopting new technologies to improve trade facilitation. China can propose that all countries work together to formulate an overall development plan for e-commerce in Northeast Asia, adopt a strategy of combining the guidance of supervision departments, form a leading group of experts and governmental officials on e-commerce policies, and establish corresponding e-commerce management agencies. For the construction of regional internet, countries can first complete their own network infrastructure and then strive to build an e-commerce cooperation framework in Northeast Asia by promoting intergovernmental dialogue and consultation. In addition to state investment, funding from local governments and private companies can also be encouraged for the construction of the basic network. Moreover, China and other countries should speed up the research and formulation of relevant laws and regulations in the region to promote the legal construction of e-commerce to the needs of rapid economic development in Northeast Asia.

(5) Business Personnel Flow

With the development of economic globalization and the increase of international trade activities, business activities among countries are increasing. The flow of business people with goods and capital affects all aspects of international trade and reflects the level of trade facilitation.

Northeast Asian countries can learn from trade facilitation talks of various regions and organizations, especially the APEC Trade Facilitation Action Plan. Northeast Asian countries can work out measures in terms of the business flow procedures and the use of information and communication technologies. For business flow procedures, measures should first be taken inside the companies to make the visa or review requirements simple and easy. Standardization can be carried out in the aspects of travel document inspection, professional services, security (and processing system), immigration regulations, and so on, which can shorten the processing time for business and work visas. Business travel cards, visa exemption arrangements, or multiple-entry visas for short-term business visitors can be implemented.[38] In the use of information and communication

---

[38] According to the APEC Business Travel Card Program, cardholders can enjoy various forms of short-term visa-free entry with a maximum duration of 60 days within the membership of the program without applying for visas or entry permits. Cardholders also enjoy the right to enter and leave the country quickly through special passages at APEC's major

technology, measures should be taken to ensure that all countries share the latest information on customs entry on the internet and business travel manuals. The advanced passenger information systems can be used in countries where economic and technological conditions permit and customs clearance upon arrival can be made quick and easy.

5.3.1.2 *Establishing a trade facilitation coordination agency*

In order to ensure the smooth progress of trade facilitation cooperation in Northeast Asia, China should propose and take active and effective measures to improve the organizational structure of trade facilitation inside China and in the region. First of all, trade facilitation committees should be gradually established in China and other countries to promote and improve the level of trade facilitation in each country. Secondly, coordination agencies among regional governments or trade facilitation coordination mechanisms at the national level should be set up to increase the impetus of trade facilitation and solve the problems existing in the implementation of trade facilitation agreements. Finally, a steering committee on trade facilitation cooperation in Northeast Asia with substantive functions should be set up in the region to be fully responsible for cooperation among members in the field of trade facilitation. The steering committee is not only responsible for transmitting and implementing the instructions of regional conferences but also undertakes information communication, resource sharing, progress monitoring, and other work among various countries and between the public and private sectors. At the same time, the committee should regularly report on the latest development of cooperation among countries in the field of trade facilitation and actively put forward policy suggestions for improvement.

Besides, developing countries in Northeast Asia have not yet been able to effectively participate in WTO negotiations and various forums sponsored by the United Nations and the World Customs Organization to formulate new standards for trade facilitation. In response to this situation, China can cooperate with Japan, the ROK, and other countries by holding regional seminars and adopting a series of measures to help these

---

airports. At present, China, Japan, the ROK, and Russia, have already taken part in the program.

countries, such as exchanging views on trade facilitation and solving practical problems.[39]

5.3.2 China's policy to promote investment facilitation in Northeast Asia

Under the background of a slowdown or even decline in global FDI growth, the FDI situation in Northeast Asia has managed to remain the same, with much room for investment facilitation. First of all, Northeast Asia is an important destination for global FDI. From 2008 to 2013, the flow of FDI in the world decreased by 20.17%, while the flow of FDI in Northeast Asia remained stable, accounting for 20.84% of the total flow of FDI in the world, up from 16.20%.[40] In 2013, China's FDI inflow reached US$123.911 billion, ranking second in the world after the United States. Russia ranked third with US$79.262 billion.[41] Secondly, the status of host countries of FDI in Northeast Asia has also been raised. In 2008–2013, FDI outflows from Northeast Asia showed a high growth momentum, with the proportion of FDI outflows in the world rising from 16.33% to 33.09%. In addition to Japan, the traditional major investment country, China, Russia, and the ROK have also gradually increased their foreign investment, ranking 3rd, 4th, and 12th, respectively, among the world's 20 largest investment economies in 2013.[3] However, the investment share of the countries outside Northeast Asia is higher than that of the countries in the region and because of this, the countries in Northeast Asia have less desire to enhance regional investment facilitation cooperation.

In view of this, China can still learn from the APEC, especially the APEC Investment Facilitation Action Plan. We can establish an investment area in Northeast Asia by signing a framework agreement on investment cooperation with Japan, the ROK, Russia, Mongolia, and the DPRK so as to reduce various restrictions on direct mutual investment and promote the level of investment facilitation in the region.

---

[39] The trade-related technical assistance work plan issued by the WTO in 2003 involves the substance of trade facilitation, which is helpful for members to understand the problem more accurately.

[40] UNCTAD. *World Investment Report, 2014*. United Nations Publication, 2014. Data on FDI in Northeast Asia include Japan, China, the DPRK, the ROK, Mongolia, and Russia.

[41] *Ibid*.

At the bilateral level, China has signed investment agreements with its neighboring countries.[42] The agreements are providing important policy guarantees for facilitating mutual investment between countries. However, these investment agreements play a very limited role in promoting direct mutual investment. In addition, the number of recently signed bilateral investment agreements in the world has continued to decline, and more and more countries and regions are formulating international investment rules through regional rather than bilateral means.[43]

At the multilateral level, the leaders of China, Japan, and the ROK signed an agreement for the Promotion, Facilitation, and Protection of Investment on May 13, 2012. The agreement consists of 27 articles and a protocol, which comprise all the important contents normally specified in international investment agreements, such as definitions, promotions and protection of investment, most-favored-nation treatment, national treatment, collection, transfer, subrogation, taxation, general exceptions, and dispute resolution. This is the first legal document and institutional arrangement for China, Japan, and the ROK to promote and protect investment among the three countries, providing an important foundation for the construction of a free trade area among the three countries. On May 17, 2014, the China–Japan–ROK Investment Agreement entered into force. The agreement will enhance government transparency, improve dispute resolution mechanisms, and strengthen intellectual property protection so as to provide a more stable and transparent investment environment for investors from the three countries.

At the regional level, China, Japan, the ROK, and Russia can strive to improve investment facilitation in their respective countries by reaching

---

[42] On August 27, 1988, China and Japan signed an agreement Concerning the Encouragement and Reciprocal Protection of Investment. On August 26, 1991, China and Mongolia signed an agreement Concerning the Encouragement and Reciprocal Protection of Investments. On September 30, 1992, China and the ROK signed a bilateral investment agreement and on September 7, 2007 signed an agreement on the Encouragement and Reciprocal Protection of Investments. On March 22, 2005, China and the DPRK signed an agreement on the Promotion and Protection of Investments. On November 9, 2006, China and Russia signed an agreement on the Promotion and Reciprocal Protection of Investments.

[43] UNCTAD. *World Investment Report, 2013*. United Nations Publication, 2013. In 2012, a total of 20 bilateral investment treaties were signed, the lowest number of treaties reached in 25 years. Eight of the 10 "other international investment agreements" reached are regional agreements.

the goals established by the APEC, thus accumulating experience for the future. However, there are great differences in the economic development levels and foreign policy priorities of Northeast Asian countries, making it difficult to reach an agreement in the short term.

Therefore, the Chinese government should start from the multilateral level in the short term, making full use of the positive role of the China–Japan–ROK Investment Agreement to attract Japanese and the ROK enterprises to invest in China, vigorously promote Chinese enterprises to invest in Japan and the ROK, and further promote investment facilitation among the three countries. In the medium and long terms, a series of actions and measures should be taken to reduce the economic and non-economic factors that restrict investment cooperation in Northeast Asia.

At present, the main factors restricting investment cooperation in Northeast Asia are in the following aspects. Firstly, as there are large gaps in the economic development levels of the countries in the region, leading to different investment opportunities and economic benefits. This leads to difficulty in coordination for the construction of the investment zone in terms of investment funds and preferential policies. Secondly, the lack of organizational structure and institutional guarantee in regional investment cooperation and the different complicated standards of the existing laws and policies directly affect the healthy and effective development of international direct investment. Thirdly, regional cooperation lacks an evaluation mechanism for investment facilitation. If investment facilitation is promoted in the absence of an evaluation mechanism, it will increase the uncertainty of some countries to strengthen cooperation in the investment field. Fourthly, regional territorial disputes, historical issues, differences in political systems, national interests, and other reasons lead to frequent political friction between countries, which will affect the process of investment cooperation in Northeast Asia.

To tackle these problems and challenges, China and the governments of Northeast Asian countries should further strengthen their political will and adopt feasible policies and measures to seek peace, maintain stability, and promote development for all. Specifically, by improving the investment environment in Northeast Asia, advocating capacity-building and cooperation, and improving the quantitative evaluation mechanism, the development gap between countries in the region will be gradually narrowed, regional investment cooperation will be enhanced, cooperation levels will be upgraded, and regional investment will be jointly promoted.

5.3.2.1 *Improving the institutional environment*

The ultimate goal of investment facilitation is to ensure the effective flow of investment and the efficient use of funds. In this process, the government can take a series of actions and measures to attract foreign investment and improve the efficiency of the entire investment cycle. Therefore, coordinating various investment policies and maintaining their consistency, simplifying investment approval procedures, and reducing investment risks have become the current top priority for investment facilitation cooperation in Northeast Asia.

Firstly, the openness and transparency of investment policymaking and management should be strengthened. The government should provide investors with all laws and information related to investment policies and inform them in advance of the investment policies being changed. When formulating rules and regulations related to investment, simple and understandable language should be used. Regarding the operation of the existing management system, the evaluation results should be published regularly in official publications or government websites. These policies and measures can improve the interest and confidence of enterprises that will make timely business decisions and set business expectations according to changes in investment policies.

Secondly, the stability of the investment environment and the safety of property should be improved. The government should provide a stable political and economic environment and establish a fair dispute resolution mechanism with laws and regulations to protect investors' property rights, reduce non-commercial risks related to investment, improve the financing capacity of small and medium-sized enterprises, and increase enterprises' confidence in the domestic legislative system.

Thirdly, the predictability and consistency of investment policies should be improved. The government should set up special agencies to formulate investment rules and regulations and clearly divide the functions of investment management agencies to maintain the consistency of domestic laws and regulations on investment and reduce discriminatory bureaucratic practices in the interpretation of investment-related policies. For enterprises, the predictability and consistency of investment policies can not only simplify business transactions and reduce business operating costs and corruption but also enhance business confidence and improve their competitiveness.

Fourthly, the efficiency and effectiveness of the investment process should be enhanced. The government should speed up the investment process by simplifying it, encouraging and promoting institutional cooperation and coordination, and establishing a competent one-stop responsible organ. Clear responsibilities at all levels of government are necessary to avoid repetitive management of the investment process. The principle of minimum investment for investors should be guaranteed to reduce the operating costs of enterprises and provide more opportunities for small and medium-sized enterprises.

In addition, governments should take policies to coordinate relations with enterprises and set up investment supervision and evaluation mechanisms to stimulate the enthusiasm and social responsibility of enterprises. Specifically, the government should encourage enterprises to invest in research and development or technological and procedural improvement activities, and use new technologies to improve the investment environment in the region.

5.3.2.2 *Advocating capacity-building and cooperation*

There are big gaps in investment facilitation among Northeast Asian countries, so China should actively advocate capacity-building and technical cooperation with other countries to help developing countries in the region. The specific measures are as follows:

Firstly, the Northeast Asian countries should hold seminars on best cases in and outside Northeast Asia and run training programs for administrative officials to help the developing countries in the region select and determine the most suitable facilitation measures based on their national conditions.

Secondly, the Northeast Asian countries should learn from and follow APEC's investment facilitation capacity-building projects and establish corresponding indicators such as "minimum capacity-building needs" to evaluate the progress in various countries. Countries in this region can also set up cooperation mechanisms to help the less developed countries reach their capacity-building targets. The help may come from a country, the cooperation activities in the region, or from international and regional institutions.

Thirdly, the Northeast Asian countries should strengthen the cooperation between the government and the private sector to ensure that the action measures for investment facilitation have a direct interest relationship with enterprises, and encourage enterprises to make their own voices heard in order to improve the investment environment in Northeast Asia and offer suggestions on promoting the development of investment facilitation.

Fourthly, the Northeastern Asian countries should actively participate in various activities of regional and international organizations such as the APEC, UNCTAD, OECD, and the World Bank, strengthen capacity-building cooperation with these organizations in the field of investment facilitation, accept assistance and learn from their successful experiences, and integrate the goal of capacity-building into concrete actions of investment facilitation in Northeast Asia.

5.3.2.3 *Improving the quantitative evaluation mechanism*

Cooperation in trade and investment facilitation is obvious to reduce the management cost for the government and the operating cost for enterprises and increase trade income. However, there are many obstacles to trade and investment facilitation. It is generally difficult to simply conduct a cost–benefit economic analysis. Compared with trade facilitation, the establishment of a quantitative evaluation framework for investment facilitation and the selection of evaluation indicators are even more difficult.

China, Japan, the ROK, and Russia, who are all members of the APEC, should strongly support and actively participate in the investment facilitation action plans, pay close attention to the evaluation framework and key performance indicators stipulated by the plans, and use them as an important institutional guarantee for substantial progress in investment facilitation.

Firstly, they should develop key performance indicators and use the World Bank's Doing Business database as specific quantitative criteria to measure the progress of investment facilitation.

Secondly, they should set up a regular reporting mechanism and an independent evaluation expert group, including government departments, officials, business representatives, and scholars, to regularly report on the progress made in investment facilitation in various countries and regions every year.

Thirdly, they should hire independent experts to evaluate the realization of the investment facilitation objectives in the region.

Fourthly, they should strengthen research on quantitative models, evaluation methods, and standards for investment facilitation to avoid technical factors affecting the accuracy of evaluation.

5.3.3 China's strategic conception of promoting regional economic cooperation in Northeast Asia

As one of the most dynamic and economically complementary regions in the world, Northeast Asia has been falling behind in regional cooperation for a long time without a formal economic cooperation mechanism. Apart from the unstable political situation and the large gap in economic development levels among countries in the region, the major influence of the United States and the lack of dominant position of the core countries in the region are also factors affecting the economic integration in the region.

As a major country in Northeast Asia, China's total economic volume surpassed that of Japan and ranked second in the world in 2010. Its economic growth shows the potential to change the international power pattern. China has always followed the policy of equality, consultation, peace, and communication in international relations and has no intention of becoming a hegemonic country in the region. China has actively promoted regional cooperation in Northeast Asia for strategic considerations. On the one hand, China has been building a harmonious society at home for economic and social development. At the same time, China has also been promoting bilateral and multilateral cooperation to enhance its international position in Northeast Asia. Based on these efforts, China is likely to become a global power while enhancing its economic strength. On the other hand, China's current capability to handle the international affairs determines its future international position. China must ensure that its international influence rises as it economy rises. So it is important for China to hold the discourse power. Promoting regional cooperation in Northeast Asia and participating in the formulation of regional cooperation rules will help China exert and enhance its influence in the region, and promote and expand its soft power on the basis of strength to shape its leading position in Northeast Asia. Therefore, China should make "common development, shared responsibility and active participation" part of its world outlook and actively participate in regional affairs with the goal of expanding and consolidating its national strategic interests and giving full play to the responsibility of being a major country in the region.

At present, the bilateral relations of other countries in Northeast Asia are generally good except for the normalization of relations between the DPRK and the ROK, as well as the DPRK and Japan. China has traditionally friendly relations with Russia, the DPRK, and Mongolia, and it is a very close neighboring country of Japan and the ROK. China, Japan, and the ROK have frequent exchanges and close cooperation. Russia has achieved relatively normal exchanges and cooperation with Japan and the ROK. Mongolia has established partnerships with China, Japan, the ROK, and Russia. Generally speaking, the normalization of the relations between Northeast Asian countries has laid a good foundation for regional economic cooperation.

FTAs are a good cooperation mechanism in Northeast Asia when the actual economic situation of the region is considered. Before the mid-1990s, Northeast Asian countries, especially China, Japan, and the ROK, did not pay due attention to FTAs. Japan has always regarded the promotion of the multilateral free trade system as the basis of its foreign trade policy and had not taken a positive attitude toward the issue of the bilateral and regional FTAs. The ROK as a latecomer industrialized country fully enjoyed the benefits of the multilateral free trade system, so it had no intention of getting involved in FTAs. China was initially too busy applying for WTO membership and naturally had no time to think about FTAs.[44] However, with the outbreak of the Asian financial crisis, difficult WTO multilateral trade negotiations, and the rapid rise and expansion of FTA cooperation in various regions of the world, Northeast Asian countries have realized the importance of strengthening regional cooperation, and China, Japan, and the ROK have accelerated the pace of establishing FTAs. By June 2015, China, Japan, and the ROK signed 40 FTA agreements. All three countries regard FTAs as an important way to expand international economic cooperation and promote the multilateral free trade system.[45] In addition to signing and negotiating FTA agreements with countries in Oceania, Europe, North America, and South America, China, Japan, and the ROK are actively cooperating with Asian countries. Comparatively, the construction of free trade areas among Northeast Asian countries is slow. It is undoubtedly a good way to promote bilateral cooperation in the Southeast Asian region through the bilateral cooperation outside the region. And it is also a good way to use the bilateral cooperation in the region to promote the multilateral cooperation within the region. Most of the bilateral FTAs that Northeast Asian countries signed have been

---

[44] Chen Jian'an, The feasibility and economic effect of China-ROK-Japan free trade area agreement. *World Economy Studies*, 2007, 1.

[45] See the websites of the Ministry of Commerce of China, Japan, and the ROK. The data are from June 2015. http://fta.mofcrnn.gov.cn, http://www.mofa.go.jp/policy/economy/fta, http://www.fla.go.kr/main/.

between developed countries with low tariff levels and developed and developing countries or regions with low tariff levels. The economic effect of establishing FTAs among these countries is not significant. On the contrary, if a free trade area is established among Northeast Asian countries, the tariff level of developing countries can be greatly reduced. In addition, the Northeast Asian countries have obvious political and security considerations in setting up free trade areas. The deep-level regional economic integration requires good political relations and common interests and these are what the Northeast Asian countries need.[46]

Judging from the current situation, China–ROK FTA covers the widest range of topics and involves the largest amount of the trade of a specific country.[47] According to the agreement, in terms of the level of openness, both sides have liberalized their trade in goods by more than 90% of tax items and 85% of trade volume, covering 17 areas such as trade in goods, trade in services, investment, and rules. The signing of the China–ROK FTA will not only provide a more favorable institutional environment for the economic and trade cooperation between the two countries but also play a role in promoting the ongoing negotiations in the China–Japan–ROK FTA and the integration of the entire Northeast Asian region. The strategic choice of China's FTA in Northeast Asia should firstly be to promote the establishment of China–Japan–ROK FTA as soon as possible based on the China–ROK FTA. At the same time, China should further carry out bilateral FTA negotiations with Japan and Russia as soon as possible. Then, China should integrate several bilateral agreements to promote multilateral arrangements, gradually adding Mongolia and the DPRK to the free trade area and forming multiple trilateral mechanisms, such as China–Japan–ROK, China–Russia–ROK, and China–DPRK–Russia, and even multilateral mechanisms like China–Japan–ROK–Russia. Finally, there will be a transition to a free trade area covering all the member countries in Northeast Asia. This strategy can effectively reduce the difficulty of multilateral FTA negotiations.[48]

---

[46] Wang Shengjin and Yu Xiao, The current situation and trend of the establishment of free trade area (FTA) in Northeast Asia. *Northeast Asia Forum*, 2007, 4.

[47] China–ROK Free Trade Agreement Signed, Website of the Ministry of Commerce of the People's Republic of China. http://fta.mofcom.gov.cn/article/chinakorea/kore-anews/201506/21837—1.html, June 1, 2015.

[48] Zhao Jinlong, China's FTA strategic choice in Northeast Asia: A comparative study based on CGE model. *Northeast Asia Forum*, 2008, 5.

However, China will face great resistance and difficulties in implementing this strategy. Firstly, China's FTA strategy will trigger competition and cooperation between Japan and the ROK. In order to compete with China for dominance in Northeast Asia and even East Asia, Japan and the ROK will accelerate FTAs with other countries. As each bilateral FTA has its own trade liberalization arrangement, these multiple complicated regulations will eventually lead to the Spaghetti Bowl Effect. The Spaghetti Bowl Phenomenon originated from Bhagwati's book *US Trade Policy: The Infatuation with FTAs* published in 1995. It means that different preferential treatments and various agreements are like spaghetti in a bowl — tangling in disorder. It actually refers to that when the preferential trade agreements, such as the bilateral free trade agreements (FTA) and regional trade agreements (RTA), emerge in large numbers and in disorder, the import and export enterprises and export commodity manufacturers feel at a loss to know what to do.[49] Secondly, there are some problems in China's FTA strategy. Compared with Japan and the ROK, China has neither a clear FTA strategy nor a special negotiation or in-depth research department on FTA. Faced with the competitive advantages of the manufacturing industries of Japan and the ROK, many industries in China are not well prepared. In addition, China's current average tariff rate is higher than that of the ROK and even higher than that of Japan. Once the China–Japan FTA or the China–Japan–ROK FTA is established, China's industry will endure a greater impact. Thirdly, China's FTA negotiations are not going smoothly. After eight years of careful preparation, successively conducting a folk feasibility study and a government-led joint study, it was not until May 2012 that the FTA negotiations between China and the ROK officially started and it took another two and a half years to complete. The decision of China, Japan, and the ROK to shelve territorial disputes and start negotiations on free trade agreements reflects their maturity in promoting political and economic separation and giving priority to solving practical problems. However, since the three countries have different considerations on this issue, it can be assumed that the negotiation will not be smooth. Russia has bypassed China and led its Eurasian integration alliance to sign an FTA with Vietnam. This also reflects the concerns of developing countries in the region about the impact of

---

[49] Lee, C.J., Jeong, H.G., Kim, H.S., *et al.*, From East Asian FTAs to an EAFTA: Typology of East Asian FTAs and implications for an EAFTA. Seoul: Institute for International Economic Policy, 2006.

Chinese manufacturing products such as automobiles, textiles, and household appliances on their domestic markets.

Therefore, China's FTA strategy in Northeast Asia must aim at steady profits and should not blindly rush forward. Under the trend of more and more FTA negotiations and more complicated negotiation contents, it is necessary for China to formulate specific FTA principles and policies and establish a special FTA negotiation department, adopting flexible and diverse ways to gradually establish an FTA cooperation network on the basis of scientific analysis. Of course, the change from the bilateral cooperation, trilateral cooperation, quadrilateral cooperation and multilateral cooperation to finally the establishment of FTA in Northeast Asia needs a long time of quantity change to final quality change. Northeast Asian countries should also aim to improve their own national conditions and work together to promote the construction of the Northeast Asian Free Trade Area.

5.4 The Construction of the China–Japan–ROK FTA and China's Strategic Countermeasures

At present, despite the close economic and trade relations among China, Japan, and the ROK, the development potential of the economic and trade relations has not been fully realized due to the relatively high trade barriers between them. The establishment of the CJKFTA means that all kinds of tariff and non-tariff barriers must be removed, and more convenient conditions must be created for the movement of people and capital. With the constant development of trade relations among the three countries, trade frictions and disputes may occur from time to time. Dealing with trade disputes quickly and reasonably has become an unavoidable and important issue in promoting the development of trilateral economic and trade relations. The establishment of the CJKFTA and a trade dispute coordination and settlement mechanism is of great significance for promoting the development of China–Japan–ROK economic and trade relations. The construction of the China–Japan–ROK FTA will also promote trade and investment facilitation and regional integration in the entire Northeast Asia region.

5.4.1 Favorable factors for FTA construction among China, Japan, and the ROK

The construction of the CJKFTA is conducive to promoting more liberalization and facilitation of trade as well as the stable and healthy development of trade relations among the three countries. There are both positive and negative factors in the construction of the CJKFTA. The basis for promoting the construction of the CJKFTA is to complement each other's advantages and avoid individual disadvantages.

5.4.1.1 *Economic and trade relations with good development trend*

(1) Economic and Trade Relations Between China and Japan

Since the normalization of diplomatic relations between China and Japan, bilateral trade has maintained a high-speed development trend (see Figures 5.18 and 5.19). According to China's customs statistics, the bilateral trade volume between China and Japan was US$25.36 billion in 1992 and US$312.25 billion in 2014, which increased 11.31 times with an average annual growth rate of 12.09%. With the development of China–Japan trade relations, the two countries have become each other's most

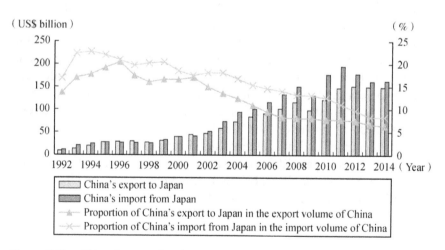

Figure 5.18. China–Japan trade volume and its proportion in China from 1992 to 2014.
Source: Calculated according to the yearbook data of *China Customs Statistics*.

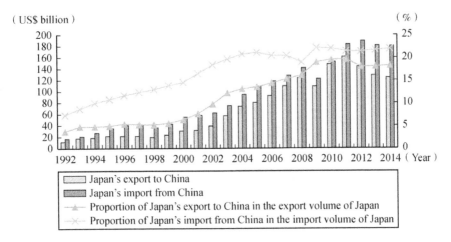

Figure 5.19. China–Japan trade volume and its proportion in Japan from 1992 to 2014.

Source: Calculated according to the *Trade Statistics* of Japan's Ministry of Finance for each year.

important trade partners. Although the proportion of China's exports to Japan and imports from Japan in China's trade volume shown a downward trend in recent years, and since 2004 Japan has fallen from China's largest trading partner to its third-largest trading partner, according to China's customs statistics, the bilateral trade volume between China and Japan is still on the rise. Among Japan's trading partners, China's status has been continuously elevated. According to the trade statistics of Japan's Ministry of Finance, China has become Japan's largest source of imports since 2002 and Japan's second-largest export market since 2001, with an increasing proportion of its trade volume both in Japan's exports to China and imports from China.

(2) Economic and trade relations between China and the ROK

Since China and the ROK established formal diplomatic relations in 1992, the two governments successively signed trade agreements and investment protection agreements. Cooperation at the government level is a powerful impetus to the development of substantive economic and trade relations. In particular, the China–ROK Free Trade Area negotiations were officially launched in May 2012, deepening the development of the strategic partnership between the two countries. Before 1992, the China–ROK trade was mainly conducted indirectly through third places. Since the establishment of formal diplomatic relations, China and the ROK

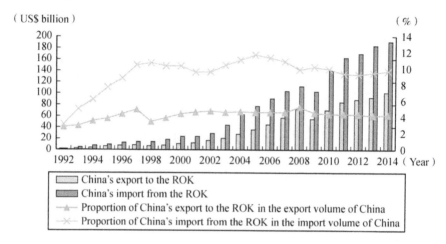

Figure 5.20. China–ROK trade volume and China's proportion from 1992 to 2014.
Source: Calculated according to the yearbook of *China Customs Statistics*.

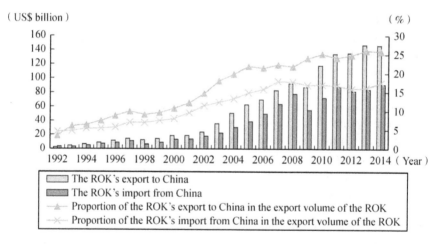

Figure 5.21. The ROK–China trade volume and ROK's proportion from 1992 to 2014.
Source: Calculated according to the *Trade Statistics* of the ROK's Trade Association each year.

entered the stage of direct trade and the trade relations between the two countries followed the track of rapid development (see Figures 5.20 and 5.21). According to Chinese customs statistics, the trade volume between China and the ROK in 1992 was US$5.03 billion, of which China's exports to the ROK amounted to US$2.41 billion, and imports from the

ROK amounted to US$2.62 billion. In 2014, the above-mentioned three numbers rose to US$290.44 billion, US$100.335 billion, and US$190.105 billion, respectively. From 1992 to 2014, the bilateral trade volume between China and the ROK increased 56.74 times; China's exports to the ROK increased 40.63 times and China's imports from the ROK increased 71.56 times. The average annual growth rate in the bilateral trade volume, China's exports to the ROK, and China's imports from the ROK were 20.25%, 18.47%, and 21.50%, respectively. During this period, China's total foreign trade grew 25.99 times, with an average annual growth rate of 15.95%. The ROK's total foreign trade increased 5.94 times, with an average annual growth rate of 9.20%. It can be seen that the speed of development of the bilateral trade between China and the ROK far exceeded the speed of the overall foreign trade development of China and the ROK. With the rapid development of the China–ROK trade, the two countries became each other's most important trade partners. At present, the ROK is China's third-largest trading partner, third-largest export market, the largest source of imports, and the fourth-largest source of foreign direct investment. China's position among the ROK's trading partners is rising and it has become the ROK's largest trading partner, largest export market, largest source of imports, and largest investment destination.

(3) Economic and trade relations between Japan and the ROK
Since the establishment of formal diplomatic relations between Japan and the ROK in 1965, the cooperation between Japan and the ROK in politics, economy, culture, and other aspects made great progress, especially the remarkable achievements in trade (see Figures 5.22 and 5.23). According to statistics from Japan's Ministry of Finance, the bilateral trade volume between Japan and the ROK was US$29.35 billion in 1992, of which Japan's exports to the ROK amounted to US$17.77 billion and imports from the ROK amounted to US$11.58 billion. In 2014, the total volume of trade, Japan's exports to the ROK, and Japan's imports from the ROK increased to US$85.064 billion, US$50.488 billion, and US$34.576 billion, respectively. From 1992 to 2014, the bilateral trade volume between Japan and the ROK increased by 1.90 times, with a 1.84 times increase in Japan's exports and a 1.99 times increase in Japan's imports. The average annual growth rate of the total volume of trade, Japan's exports, and Japan's imports was 4.96%, 4.86%, and 5.10%, respectively, during the 22 years. We can see that bilateral trade between Japan and the ROK was

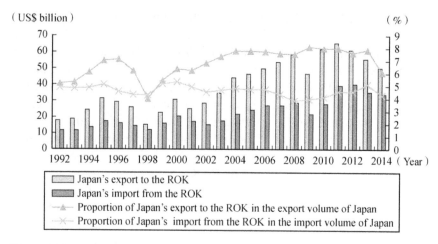

Figure 5.22. Japan–ROK trade volume and Japan's proportion from 1992 to 2014.

Source: Calculated according to the *Trade Statistics* of Japan's Ministry of Finance for each year.

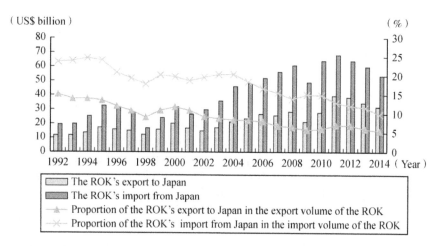

Figure 5.23. The ROK–Japan trade volume and the ROK's proportion from 1992 to 2014.

Source: Calculated according to the *Trade Statistics* of the ROK's Trade Association each year.

developing rapidly, and the scale of trade was constantly expanding. With continuous expansion of trade between Japan and the ROK, the two countries became each other's most important trading partners. Japan has always been a very important trading partner for the ROK. Although the

ROK's exports to Japan and imports from Japan as a proportion of the ROK's trade volume generally showed a downward trend, the total trade volume was fluctuating upward. In 2002, Japan was downgraded from the ROK's largest export market to the third largest, but in the same year, it rose from the ROK's second-largest import market to the largest import market. The ROK has been in a relatively important position among Japan's trading partners with top ranks in both export trade and import trade. The amount of Japan's imports from the ROK remains stable in the total amount of Japan's total imports.

5.4.1.2 *The active attitude of Japan and the ROK in participating in regional economic cooperation*

The establishment of a free trade area among China, Japan, and the requires close cooperation and coordination of three countries. The regional economic integration strategies and policies of the three countries directly affect the establishment of the FTA. On the whole, China has increasingly attached importance to the development of regional economic cooperation with its neighboring countries and has taken a positive attitude toward the establishment of a free trade area among China, Japan, and the ROK. In recent years, the ROK has also shown a positive attitude toward participating in regional economic cooperation in Northeast Asia, especially the establishment of a free trade area among China, Japan, and the ROK. Although the Japanese government has not made the establishment of a free trade area with China an important part of its foreign economic policy, it has transformed from a firm critic of the regional economic grouping policy to a prudent practitioner.

(1) Japan's Changing Attitude Toward Regional Economic Cooperation
For quite a long time after the end of the World War II, Japan always adhered to a regional cooperation policy characterized by refusing to join in any international group. Japan had not participated in any closed reciprocal trade agreements, instead it often criticized economic groupings for being against the multilateral reciprocal trade principles established by the GATT. It was not until the 1980s that Japan began to pay real attention to regional cooperation with relevant countries and regions in East Asia.

In 1999, a white paper *on Trade* published by Japan's Ministry of Communications and Industry pointed out that Japan needs to take more flexible and constructive measures in signing free trade agreements. In October 2002, Japan's Ministry of Foreign Affairs issued a report entitled Japan's FTA Strategy, which is Japan's first government document on regional integration strategy. The report briefly summarizes the Japan's understanding of the nature of FTA/EPA and its relations with WTO's multilateral trading system, expounds the political and economic significance of Japan's promotion of regional integration and matters needing attention, indicates the contents and characteristics that Japan should include in the regional integration agreements signed with relevant countries, and explains the selection criteria of the target countries for regional integration cooperation. It also puts forward the basic direction of promoting regional cooperation with the ROK, ASEAN, China, Australia, Mexico, and other countries as well as the possibility of signing FTAs/EPAs.

In December 2004, the Japanese government convened a cabinet meeting on promoting economic cooperation, which approved the basic guidelines for promoting economic partnership agreements in the future. The basic guideline clearly put forward Japan's strategic focus of regional integration and economic partnership with East Asia and specifically expounded the selection criteria of negotiation objects from three aspects, namely, creating a favorable international environment for Japan, protecting Japan's overall economic interests, and analyzing the specific conditions of relevant countries and regions and the possibility of concluding EPAs/FTAs with Japan. The guidelines mainly contained the following three aspects. Firstly, Japan's regional integration strategy was officially defined as the EPA strategy, which defined the main areas of Japan's promotion of regional economic integration with relevant countries. Secondly, it formally put forward the strategy of the regional integration with East Asia as the center and changed the old policy of giving priority to promoting economic integration with East Asian countries in order to reduce the trade barriers in East Asia. Thirdly, it further clarified and enriched the selection criteria for the targets of regional integration and clearly reflected the comprehensive characteristics of Japan's regional integration strategy, that is, to realize various economic, diplomatic, and political purposes through the establishment of economic partnerships. Since then, the Japanese government and relevant departments have gradually specified the timetables for the implementation of the regional integration strategy in accordance with the guidelines.

In May 2006, the Japanese government issued a report entitled Globalization Strategy submitted by the economic and financial advisory meeting. In May 2007, the Progress Plan for EPA Negotiations released by Japan's Economic and Financial Advisory Conference reaffirmed the relevant objectives of the Strategic Outline for Economic Growth and also proposed corresponding progress plans for different countries and regions that were the targets of the negotiations. For the first time, it was proposed that Japan sign EPA agreements with more than 12 countries within two years after January 2007. Since then, Japan formed a systematic regional integration strategy, including basic guidelines for promoting regional integration, the main areas of economic cooperation, the selection criteria of targets, and the promotion path and timetable.[50]

(2) The More Positive Attitude of the ROK toward Regional Economic Cooperation

Before the Asian financial crisis in 1997, the ROK government's FTA strategy emphasized the principle of multilateralism. It is only after the financial crisis hit that the ROK government began to pay more attention to bilateral free trade agreements and showed an increasingly positive attitude toward regional economic cooperation. Chile became the first target country of the ROK for negotiations to implement an FTA strategy in November 1998 and the first partner country to formally sign a free trade agreement in February 2003, which entered into force in April 2004. After the ROK–Chile FTA as implemented, the rapid development of trade relations between the two countries further strengthened the determination of the ROK government to support and participate in regional economic cooperation. Although the deadlock in the ROK–Japan FTA negotiations from December 2003 to December 2004 led to a decline in the ROK's enthusiasm for signing FTAs, negotiations resumed since 2005. Special agencies such as the FTA Non-governmental Promotion Committee and the Free Trade Agreement Bureau (FTA Bureau) were set up promote FTA institutionalization. At present, the ROK has signed FTAs or is negotiating FTAs with many countries and organizations in the world such as ASEAN, Singapore, India, China, the GCC, the EU, the

---

[50]Lian Xiaomei, Geopolitical Motives and Countermeasures of Japan's Regional Integration Strategy Excluding China, *Northeast Asia Forum*, 2006(6).

European Free Trade Association (EFTA), the United States, Canada, Chile, Peru, Colombia, Mexico, New Zealand, and Australia.

At the same time, the FTA negotiations among China, Japan, and the ROK have been progressing gradually. In addition, the ROK is considering and hopes to start FTA negotiations with Russia, Türkiye, Mercosur (the Southern Common Market), Israel, the Southern African Customs Union (SACU), and other countries. We can see that the ROK has become one of the most active countries in the world in signing bilateral free trade agreements with other countries. Although negotiations between the ROK and Japan are still on hold, the China–ROK FTA negotiations have been concluded and a formal agreement has been signed on June 1, 2015. The ROK's policy adjustment and positive attitude toward signing bilateral free trade agreements are of great significance and provide a favorable environment for an FTA among China, Japan, and the ROK.

5.4.2 Negative factors in FTA construction among China, Japan, and the ROK

5.4.2.1 *No effective mechanism of political mutual trust in the region*

Northeast Asia is one of the regions with the most complicated international relations in the world today. There are not only many unresolved territorial disputes but also big differences in understanding historical issues among major countries in the region. Besides, Northeast Asia is also one of the regions influenced to the largest extent by the remnants of the Cold War mentality. In particular, disputes over the territorial sovereignty among China, Japan, and the ROK have seriously damaged the political mutual trust among the three countries and will be a big obstacle to their cooperation. Territorial disputes are bound to cause unpredictable variables to a large extent whether or not the FTA negotiations among the countries can achieve the expected results.

5.4.2.2 *Obvious geopolitical tendency in Japan's regional economic cooperation strategy*

The development of regional economic cooperation cannot be separated from the mutual coordination and active promotion of major regional countries. There are some examples. France and Germany played key roles in promoting the establishment and development of the EU (the original European Community, EC). The NAFTA was established with the active promotion of the United States. As an important economic power in Northeast Asia, the influence of Japan on regional economic cooperation in Northeast Asia cannot be ignored. In recent years, Japan has changed from a critic of economic regionalism to a prudent practitioner, but such a change is limited. In fact, Japan's negative attitude toward regional economic cooperation, especially in Northeast Asia, has become one of the important obstacles to the breakthrough of regional economic cooperation. There is still an obvious tendency by Japan to exclude China in regional economic cooperation. Firstly, Japan's policy orientation to protect its vulnerable agriculture has not been fundamentally adjusted, so it will not give up its traditional policy of protecting the interests of backward agricultural farmers in the short term. Therefore, it is difficult to establish economic groups such as free trade zones with large and powerful agricultural countries unless the countries concerned do not require Japan to open up the agricultural product market substantially in the process. Secondly, Japan's main foreign policy axis of maintaining a coordinated political and economic relationship with the United States has not changed. US–Japan relations are the main axis of Japan's foreign political and economic relations. Therefore, Japan has been depending on the United States in dealing with Northeast Asian countries, and its tendency to follow the US foreign policy has not changed. In that sense, the attitude and policies of the United States are still the key factors influencing Japan's policies in Northeast Asia and East Asia. Thirdly, there is an obvious tendency to oppose and exclude China in the process of Japan's participation in regional economic cooperation. So far, Japan has not actually identified China as the object of negotiation, and the Japanese government plans to hold negotiations with China after reaching economic partnership agreements with other East Asian countries. For example, with regard to China's proposal to establish the CJKFTA, although the three governments of China, Japan, and the ROK have signed the investment agreement, the Japanese government has not shown a substantial sense of cooperation, and it is still difficult to judge whether the China–Japan–ROK FTA negotiations can make real progress.[51]

---

[51] Lian Xiaomei, Geopolitical motives and countermeasures of Japan's regional integration strategy excluding China. *Northeast Asia Forum*, 2008, 6.

5.4.2.3 Difficulties faced by weak industries in dealing with regional trade liberalization in the three countries

There are obvious differences in the economic development levels and economic structures in the three major economies, i.e., China, Japan, and the ROK. In terms of total economic output (PPP), according to statistics of the International Monetary Fund (IMF), China's total economic output is US$17.632014 trillion, ranked the second globally, and its GDP per capita is US$12,893.43, ranked 80th globally in 2014. Japan's total economic output with US$4.788.033 trillion ranked third in the world and its GDP per capita is US$37,683.05, ranked the 27th. The ROK's total economic output, with US$17.89758 trillion, ranked 14th in the world and its GDP per capita is US$35,485.07, ranked 31st worldwide. From the perspective of economic structure, Japan has the highest level of industrialization with competitive, capital-intensive and technology-intensive industries. However, it lacks natural resources and has high labor and land costs. The ROK has high-level capital and technology-intensive industries and certain financial strength, but its natural resources are relatively poor. And with the rising wage costs and land costs, the development of labor-intensive industries in the ROK is increasingly slow. Although the level of industrialization is the lowest and funds are low in China, it enjoys abundant labor resources and rapidly developing labor-intensive industries. Due to the great differences in the development stages, levels, and resource endowments, the difficulties of the vulnerable industries in the region in coping with the liberalization of the regional trade are extremely prominent. Firstly, Japan's fragile agricultural sector is its biggest obstacle to market opening. Japan is a country with a large population but limited land and low agricultural productivity. Its agricultural sector mainly relies on various government subsidies and various tariff and non-tariff barriers to protect and maintain production. Without tariff and non-tariff barriers, Japan's agriculture will suffer an unbearable blow. Within Japan's current electoral system, a small number of farmers have large political influence. Opposed by parliamentarians from agriculture and forestry sectors, the Japanese government can hardly make any substantial concession in opening up the agricultural product market. Secondly, the ROK's agricultural sector is also one of the obstacles to market opening. Although agricultural development in the ROK is a little better than that of Japan, it is also a highly sensitive sector. Japan is an important agricultural export market for the ROK. Over the years, the ROK has been running a huge trade deficit with Japan, but there is a large surplus in agricultural trade. However, compared with China's agricultural products, the ROK obviously lacks advantages in the price of the agricultural products. In recent years, China's export of agricultural products to the ROK has grown rapidly, which has also led to trade frictions between China and the ROK. Thirdly, the difficulties of the capital- and technology-intensive industries of China are obstacles to market opening. The industrial field is an especially sensitive sector in China, particularly the capital-intensive and technology-intensive industries. Compared with Japan and the ROK, there are obvious disadvantages in the automobile manufacturing industry, steel industry, petrochemical industry, and high-tech industry in China. A full market opening in these fields in a short period of time will have a very severe impact on the markets of these industries. It can be concluded that the differences in the vulnerable and sensitive industries of countries in Northeast Asia make it extremely difficult to reach a common agreement on market opening in this region.[52]

5.4.2.4 *The negative impact of the US' return to the Asia-Pacific*

The "pivot to Asia" policy implemented by the Obama administration refers to East Asia rather than the whole of Asia. The so-called "pivot" does not mean returning after withdrawal because the United States never withdrew its military deployment from East Asia and never stopped its participation and intervention in East Asian affairs. The fact is that the influence of the United States in East Asia has obviously declined for various reasons. Therefore, this "pivot" is actually the United States' desire to enhance its influence in the East Asia region in an all-round way by further consolidating and expanding its alliance in the region, participating in East Asia regional cooperation, and seeking to establish its own regional cooperation organization — the Trans-Pacific Partnership Agreement (TPP) — which it hopes will play a leading role. The policy has had a profound impact not only on the security pattern and regional situation in East Asia but also on regional economic cooperation in many aspects. The establishment of the TPP is one of the important measures taken by the United States to "pivot to Asia" and

---

[52] Lian Xiaomei, On the restrictive factors in the establishment of China–Japan–ROK free trade area. *Contemporary Economy of Japan*, 2004, 4.

encourage economic cooperation in the Asia-Pacific region. On February 4, 2016, 12 countries — the United States, Japan, Australia, Brunei, Canada, Chile, Malaysia, Mexico, New Zealand, Peru, Singapore, and Vietnam — formally signed the TPP Agreement. The impact of the signing of the TPP Agreement on regional economic cooperation in Northeast Asia, especially the China–Japan–ROK FTA, cannot be ignored. Firstly, it affects the enhancement of regional cohesion and the formation of regional consensus. As mentioned earlier, the conflicts among China, Japan, and the ROK are numerous and complicated, leading to low regional cohesion, which directly restricts the development of deep-rooted regional cooperation among the three countries. The 12 countries that signed the TPP agreement are all APEC members, eight participate in the East Asia Summit, and 1 is a Northeast Asian country. The ROK is currently pushing forward the second round of TPP preparatory negotiations. The promotion of TPP by the United States will definitely split the existing cooperation mechanisms among the APEC, East Asia, and Northeast Asia and restrict the formation of regional consensus. Secondly, the efforts of China, Japan, and the ROK for economic cooperation in the region have been reduced to a certain extent. In recent years, Japan and the ROK have begun to shift the focus of their regional cooperation strategy to assess the impact of the TPP and analyze how to deal with it. Under such circumstances, the promotion of the China–Japan–ROK FTA will inevitably be ignored to a certain extent. Thirdly, the Spaghetti Bowl Phenomenon will be intensified in East Asian regional economic cooperation. At present, there are already too many bilateral and multilateral regional trade agreements and cooperation mechanisms in East Asia. The promotion of the TPP by the United States will further aggravate the Spaghetti Bowl Phenomenon in East Asia regional cooperation, thus affecting the establishment and development of the CJKFTA.

5.4.3 China's strategic countermeasures for promoting FTA negotiations among China, Japan, and the ROK

5.4.3.1 *Countermeasures for contents in the China–Japan–the ROK FTA*

Taking into account the great differences in economic development levels among China, Japan, and the ROK, China should insist that the regional economic integration agreement of the three countries include the promotion of trade and investment liberalization and economic and technical cooperation; that is to say, the three countries should sign a comprehensive economic cooperation agreement with trade liberalization as the core. Economic and technical cooperation is also commonly called development cooperation, which is an indispensable and important aspect of many bilateral or multilateral regional economic cooperation agreements. For example, under the framework of the APEC, economic and technological cooperation is regarded as one of the two wheels that promote APEC's continuous development, as important as trade and investment liberalization and facilitation. In recent years, the vast majority of bilateral regional cooperation agreements signed by countries in East Asia have also included economic and technical cooperation. In the framework of the China–ASEAN Free Trade Area agreement, it is clearly stipulated that China and ASEAN countries will strengthen cooperation in the fields of agriculture, information and communication technology, human resources development, and Greater Mekong River Basin development. The economic cooperation agreements signed by Japan with Singapore, Malaysia, and the Philippines also contain similar clauses. Considering the economic development levels of China, Japan, and the ROK and the common interests of the three countries, China should actively promote that the three countries carry out economic and technological cooperation in finance, investment protection, intellectual property protection, international labor service, scientific and technological development, tourism, and environmental protection.

5.4.3.2 *Countermeasures for the range of the trade liberalization*

According to the bilateral free trade agreements that Japan signed with other countries or regional organizations, the scope of trade liberalization will become a difficult issue for the three countries to negotiate. Several bilateral free trade agreements currently signed by Japan basically exclude agricultural products, aquatic products, and some sensitive industrial products from the scope of trade liberalization. As it is also a country with relatively backward agriculture, the ROK is likely to follow Japan and reserve the vast majority of agricultural products as an exception to trade liberalization. If China agrees with Japan and the ROK's request, it means that the establishment of an FTA among China, Japan, and the ROK is simply a unilateral trade privilege given by China to Japan and the ROK. Therefore, China must insist on the elimination of tariffs and other commercial regulations on the vast majority of trade, earnestly promote free trade among China, Japan, and the ROK, and narrow the scope of commodities as exceptions to free trade as much as possible. To be specific, China's proposal to expand the scope of trade liberalization as much as possible can be realized in the following ways. Firstly, China should set a basic quantitative standard for the scope of trade liberalization. Before negotiations, China should carefully calculate the proportion of sensitive industries that Japan and the ROK may list in their trade with China. Then, according to the proportions, China should speculate on the quantitative indicators of the trade liberalization scope that Japan and the ROK can accept to the greatest extent and put forward its negotiation indicators accordingly. Secondly, China should try to reduce the types of commodities that are exceptions to trade liberalization by agreeing to extend the transition time of trade liberalization as a countermeasure. There should be few exceptions, limited to a few key vulnerable industries as far as possible. The problem of the remaining vulnerable industries should be mainly solved by extending the market transition period and protecting the adjustment time.

5.4.3.3 *Countermeasures for rules of origin of products*

As different countries participate in the international division of labor in different ways, their attitudes to maneuvering the application of the principle of origin are different. In regard to the complete acquisition or production of goods, the differences among the three parties are not much. The most complicated issue is the decision of the origin of products assembled and processed with raw materials or parts outside the region. Generally speaking, most of Japan's industrial exports are processed products and raw materials from outside the region are used. The domestic added value of the relevant products will be far higher than the raw materials or the cost of them. In addition, for processing and assembling products, although Japan imports more and more parts and accessories, it has a dominant position in the production of technology-intensive high-value-added parts. This makes the added value of Japan's own production of such products higher than that of imported products. Therefore, Japan generally advocates stricter rules of origin to protect its own market. From the analysis of several free trade agreements that the ROK has already signed, the ROK's requirements on rules of origin for products are not strict, because the imported raw materials and spare parts contained in the ROK's export products are also of high value, and extremely strict rules of origin are not conducive to its expansion of exports. China is the world's most important processing and assembling base. Most of its exported products contain imported parts and even key parts. The imported raw materials, parts, and accessories account for a very high proportion of commodity prices. Among the industrial products exported by China, more than 50% belong to the products produced by enterprises that have transnational investors. If extremely strict rules of origin of products are set up, it will definitely affect the preferential treatment of free trade enjoyed by China and hinder direct foreign investment in China. Therefore, China should appropriately lower the standard of the rules of origin to promote a reasonable division of labor among enterprises in East Asia, especially among China, Japan, and the ROK. Therefore, China should strengthen coordination and communication with the ROK and try to control the rules of origin to an appropriate level. In addition, the rules of origin in the China–Japan–ROK free trade agreement should be as simple and clear as possible to improve administrative efficiency and reduce commercial costs.

5.4.3.4 *Countermeasures for liberalization of service trade*

Since trade liberalization in regional free trade is no longer limited to the trade in goods, it has become one of the core contents of many regional free trade agreements to actively promote the mutual opening of service markets and liberalization of service trade. China's measure for this issue is to make reasonable arrangements and set a reasonable timetable for opening up the service industry market. In view of the development of China's service industry, the Chinese government may adopt the following measures in the negotiation. The first measure is to separate the liberalization of trade in goods from the liberalization of the service industry in negotiation. China might settle the relevant contents of the liberalization of trade in goods and implement them, and then restart the negotiation on the opening up of the service trade market. This is the best result one can hope for. The second measure is that China and its FTA partners might link the liberalization of the service industry with the liberalization of trade in agricultural products in negotiations. In the establishment of the CJKFTA, Japan and the ROK face the greatest challenges in the liberalization of agricultural trade, while China does not want the service trade market to be fully opened up in a short period. Therefore, China can combine the two. If Japan and the ROK promise to liberalize the agricultural market, China can accelerate the liberalization of trade in the service industry. The third measure is that China will strive for a longer transition period for market opening in the service trade field as far as possible. All parties can gradually open up the service trade field within 10–15 years, thus creating convenient conditions for their own industrial adjustment and enterprise reorganization.

5.4.3.5 *Countermeasures for trade protection*

Since China, Japan, and the ROK each have some weak industries, the three countries should hold discussions and reach an agreement on the conditions, procedures, and specific types of trade safeguard measures that can be adopted. At the same time, the agreements reached by the three countries should prevent any of them from abusing trade safeguard measures and hindering normal free trade in the region in an attempt to avoid excessive and intense industrial impact in a short period. Regarding trade safeguard measures, China's countermeasures may mainly include the following three aspects. Firstly, China should require that the China–Japan–ROK free trade agreement specify clearly what can be regarded as a major industrial impact from a qualitative perspective and what specific criteria can be regarded as a major industrial impact from a quantitative perspective. Secondly, China should clearly put forward in the relevant negotiations which procedures should be followed in adopting trade safeguard measures and what kind of explanatory responsibilities the governments of the countries concerned have toward other members of regional trade agreements. Thirdly, China should advocate for the setting of a reasonable timetable for the implementation of trade safeguard measures. If there are new impacts after the expiration and cancellation of safeguard measures, the countries concerned can start a new round of trade safeguard measures.

5.4.3.6 *Countermeasures for a trade dispute settlement mechanism*

Trade dispute settlement mechanisms are important parts of most regional free trade agreements. The reason why regional free trade agreements should make clear provisions on this is to improve the efficiency of settling trade disputes, resolve trade disputes in a timely manner, and ensure healthy development of trade relations among the countries concerned. In the negotiation process of establishing a free trade area among China, Japan, and the ROK, China should insist on making clear provisions on the trade dispute settlement mechanism. The ideal plan is to set up a trade dispute coordination body composed of trade experts from the three countries, which will be responsible for coordinating and arbitrating trade disputes. If the agency is unable to resolve trade disputes effectively, the parties concerned can directly conduct intergovernmental consultations. If intergovernmental consultations still fail to resolve the problems, negotiations and arbitration can be conducted through the WTO dispute settlement mechanism. In this way, a multi-level and efficient trade dispute settlement channel and mechanism should be established, which will be conducive to the settlement of trade disputes among the three countries.

Bibliography

Alan S. Blinder, Andrew W. Lo, and Robert M. Solow, *Rethinking the Financial Crisis*, Russell Sage Foundation, 2013.
Alastair Iain Johnston, What (If Anything) Does East Asia Tell Us About International Relations Theory?, *Annual Review of Political Science*, 2012, 15.
Alessio Patalano and James Manicom, Rising Tides: Seapower and Regional Security in Northeast Asia, *Journal of Strategic Studies*, 2014, 37.
Alexander E., Farrell, Hisham Zerriffi, and Hadi Dowlatabadi, Energy Infrastructure and Security, *Annual Review of Environment and Resources*, 2004, 29.
Alexander Wendt, *Social Theory of International Politics*, New York: Cambridge University Press, 1999.
Allen S. Whiting, Chinese Nationalism and Foreign Policy after Deng, *The China Quarterly*, 1995, 142.
Andrew Mark and John Ravenhil (eds.), *Pacific Cooperation: Building Economic and Security in the Asia-Pacific Region*, Boulder: Westview Press, 1995.
Andrew O'Neil, *Nuclear Proliferation in Northeast Asia: The Quest for Security*, Palgrave Macmillan, 2007.
Andrew Phillips, *War, Religion and Empire: The Transformation of International Orders*, New York: Columbia University Press, 2011.
Anthony D. Smith, *Nations and Nationalism in a Global Era*, Trans. Gong Weibin, Liang Jingyu, Beijing: Central Compilation & Translation Press, 2002.
Arase David, Non-Traditional Security in China-ASEAN Cooperation: The Institutionalization of Regional Security Cooperation and the Evolution of East Asian Regionalism, *Asian Survey*, 2010, 50(4).

Artyom Lukin, Russia and the Balance of Power in Northeast Asia, *Pacific Focus*, 2012, 27(2).

Atsuko Ichijo, Book Review: Political Theory: Nation-States and Nationalisms, *Political Studies Review*, 2015, 13(3).

Ba Dian-jun and Shen He, Transition of International System and Geopolitical Dilemma of East Asia, *Jilin University Journal Social Sciences Edition*, 2014, 3.

Ba Dianjun, Analyzing Japan's Strategic Choice of Foreign Policy from a Cultural Perspective, *Japanese Studies*, 2010, 4.

Bader, Jeffrey A, *Obama and China's Rise: An Insider's Account of America's Asia Strategy*, Brookings Institution Press, 2012.

Barry Buzan, Ole Waever, *Regions and Powers: The Structure of International Security*, Trans. Pan Zhongqi *et al*., Shanghai: Shanghai People's Publishing House, 2010.

Benedict Anderson, *Imagined Communities: Reflections on the Origin and Spread of Nationalism*, Trans. Wu Ruiren, Shanghai: Shanghai People's Publishing House, 2005.

Boris G. Saneev, Energy Cooperation Between Russia and Northeast Asian Countries: Prerequisites, Directions and Problems, *Global Economic Review*, 2003, 32.

Bruce Gilley, *Middle Power and the Rise of China*, Georgetown University Press, 2014.

Byong-kuen Jhee, Public Support for Regional Integration in Northeast Asia: An Empirical Test of Affective and Utilitarian Models, *International Political Science Review*, 2009, 30(1).

C. Riznin (С. Жизнин), Wen Gang. Russia's Foreign Energy Cooperation in Northeast Asia, *Russian Studies*, 2010, 3.

Cai Jian, DPRK's Nuclear Crisis Rising Again, How China Should Deal with It, *World Affairs*, 2009, 9.

Carlton J.H. Hayes, *The Historical Evolution of Modern Nationalism*, Trans. Pamir, Shanghai: East China Normal University Press, 2005.

Charles L. Pritchard, John H. Tilelli Jr., Scott A. Snyder, U.S. *Policy Toward the Korean Peninsula: Independent Task Force Report*, Council on Foreign Relations, 2010.

Chen Dingding, Domestic Politics, National Identity, and International Conflict: The Case of the Koguryo Controversy, *Journal of Contemporary China*, 2012, 21(74).

Chen Fengjun, Wang Chuanjian, *Major Powers in Asia-Pacific and Korean Peninsula*, Beijing: Peking University Press, 2002.

Chen Hanxi, Sun Xuefeng. Debates on the Future of East Asian Security Cooperation, *World Economics and Politics*, 2008, 3.

Chen Jian'an, The Feasibility and Economic Effect of China-ROK-Japan Free Trade Area Agreement, *World Economy Studies*, 2007, 1.

Chen Yue, China's Current Diplomatic Environment and Its Correspondence, *Contemporary International Relations*, 2010, 11.

Chen Yue, The Reform and Trend of the Current International System, *Foreign Affairs Review*, 2015, 6.

Chen Zhiheng. *Study on Regional Economic Integration in Northeast Asia: From the Perspective of Transaction Cost Theory*, Changchun: Jilin People's Press, 2006.

Chi Lo, *China After the Subprime Crisis: Opportunities in the New Economic Landscape*, Palgrave Macmillan, 2010.

Chih-Yu Shih, Breeding a Reluctant Dragon: Can China Rise into Partnership and Away from Antagonism? *Review of International Studies*, 2005, 31(4).

China Institute of Contemporary International Relations, *Global Strategic Structure: China's International Environment in the New Century*, Beijing: Current Affair Press, 2000.

China Institute of International Studies, *International Situation and China's Foreign Affairs (2012)*, Beijing: World Affairs Press, 2012.

China Institute of Contemporary International Relations, *Security Cooperation Mechanism in Northeast Asia*, Beijing: Current Affair Press, 2006.

Choon-ho Park, *East Asia and the Law of the Sea*, Seoul: Seoul National University Press, 1983.

Christopher P. Twomey and M. Taylor Fravel, Projecting Strategy: The Myth of Chinese Counter-intervention, *The Washington Quarterly*, 2015, 37(4).

Cui Shunji, Beyond History: Non-traditional Security Cooperation and the Construction of Northeast Asian International Society, *Journal of Contemporary China*, 2013, 22(83).

Cui Wanglai, Xi Jinping's Ideology on Oceans, *Journal of Zhejiang Ocean University (Humanities Sciences)*, 2015, 2.

Danish Institute for International Studies, North Korea's Security Policy: Implications for Regional Security and International Export Control Regimes, *DIIS Report*, 2008, 31.

David C. Kang, *China Rising: Peace, Power, and Order in East Asia*, New York: Columbia University Press, 2007.

David Shambaugh, China Engages Asia: Reshaping the Regional Order, *International Security*, 2005, 29.

Department of Policy Planning, Ministry of Foreign Affairs of the People's Republic of China, *China's Foreign Affairs (2014)*, Beijing: World Affairs Press, 2014.

Diao Xiuhua, *Progress of Economic Cooperation between Russia and Northeast Asia: from the Perspective of Energy Cooperation and China-Russia Regional Cooperation*, Dalian: Dongbei University of Finance & Economic Press, 2011.

Diao Xiuhua, Research on Energy Security in the Process of Revitalizing and Developing Northeast China: Also on Energy Cooperation between Northeast China and Russia, *Siberian Studies*, 2009, 1.

Diao Xiuhua, Zhou Yiying, Energy cooperation between Russia and Northeast Asia, *Northeast Asia Forum*, 2006, 6.

Edward N. Luttwak, *The Rise of China vs. the Logic of Strategy*, The Belknap Press of Harvard University Press, 2012.

Elie Kedourie, *Nationalism*, Trans. Zhang Mingming, Beijing: Central Compilation & Translation Press, 2002.

Elizabeth Wishnick, Energy in Northeast Asia: Resources for Conflict or Cooperation? An Introduction, *East Asia*, 2008, 25.

Ely Ratner, Rebalancing to Asia with an Insecure China, *Washington Quarterly*, 2013, 36(2).

Ernest Gellner, *A Typology of Nationalism*, Trans. Han Hong, Beijing: Central Compilation & Translation Press, 2002.

Ernst B. Haas, International Integration: The European and the Universal Process, *International Organization*, 1961, 15(3).

Ernst B. Haas, What is Nationalism and Why Should We Study it?, *International Organization*, 1986, 40(3).

Eugenio Andrea Bruno, *Global Financial Crisis: Navigating and Under-standing the Legal and Regulatory Aspects, Globe Law and Business*, 2009.

Evelyn Goh, *The Struggle for Order: Hegemony, Hierarchy and Transition in Post-Cold War East Asia*, New York: Oxford University Press, 2013.

Evelynl Goh, The United States in Asia: Reflections on Deterrence, Alliances, and the "Balance" of Power, *International Relations of the Asia Pacific*, 2012, 12(3).

Fan Ying, East Asian Trade and Investment Facilitation Cooperation in the Post-Financial Crisis Era, *Journal of International Economic Cooperation*, 2011, 3.

Fang Changping, *The Theory and Practice of International Conflict: Contemporary World and China's International Strategy*, Beijing: Social Sciences Academic Press (China), 2015.

Fang Guangshun and Wu Yaowei, New Development and Strategic Choice of Energy Security Situation in Northeast Asia, *Crossroads: Southeast Asian Studies*, 2008, 7.

Fang Ning, Wang Bingquan, *On Nationalist Thoughts*, Beijing: Higher Education Press, 2004.

Fang Tingting, Energy Cooperation between Russia and the Asia-Pacific Region and China's Response, *Forum of World Economics & Politics*, 2010, 4.

Fumio Ota, Red Star over the Pacific: China's Rise and the Challenge to U.S. Maritime Strategy, *The China Journal*, 2011, 66.

Gaye Christoffersen, Russia's breakthrough into the Asia-Pacific: China's Role, *International Relations of the Asia Pacific*, 2010, 10(1).
Gerald P. Dwyer and Paula Tkac, The Financial Crisis of 2008 in Fixed-In-come Markets, *Journal of International Money and Finance*, 2009, 28(8).
Gil Delannoi, *Sociologie De La Nation*, Trans. Zheng Wenbin, Hong Hui, Beijing: SDX Joint Publishing Company, 2005.
Glenn H. Snyder, *Alliance Politics*, Ithaca: Cornell University Press, 1987.
Glenn Kessler, North Korea Tests U.S Policy of Strategic Patience, *The Washington Post*, 2010.
Gong Li and Wang Hong (eds.), *China's Diplomatic Strategy in the New Era*, Beijing: The Central Party School Press, 2014.
Gong Zhankui and Yu Xiaoyan, 20 Years of Trade and Investment Liberalization in APEC: Progresses and Prospects, *Journal of Contemporary Asia-Pacific Studies*, 2009, 4.
Goo Cheon-seo, *Northeast Asia Community Dream*, Beijing: Peking University Press, 2014.
Gui Yongtao, Rise of Nationalism in East Asia and the Changing Relations between China and Its Neighbors, *Journal of International Security Studies*, 2013, 2.
Guo Ming, Charm of Mongolia's Mineral Resources, *China Land and Resources News*, July 27, 2004.
Guo Rui, The Transformation of International System and the Project of Multilateral Institution Arrangement in Northeast Asia, *Journal of Tongji University (Social Science Section)*, 2008, 6.
Gwyn Prints (ed.), *Threats Without Enemies*, London: Earthscan, 1993.
Hal S. Scott, *The Global Financial Crisis*, Foundation Press, 2009.
Han Aiyong, Coordination between Great Powers in Northeast Asia and the Establishment of a Complex Security Cooperation Framework, *Journal of Contem-porary Asia-Pacific Studies*, 2013, 6.
Han Lihua, Multilateral Cooperation Must Be Taken to Ensure Energy Security in Northeast Asia, *Journal of Eurasian Economy*, 2005, 6.
Han Lihua, Northeast Energy: From Competition to Cooperation, *International Petroleum Economics*, 2005, 1.
Han Lihua, Research on the Problem of Energy Security and Cooperation in Northeast Asian, *International Business*, 2006, 1.
Hans Morgenthau, *Politics Among Nations: The Struggle for Power and Peace (Seventh Edition)*, Trans. Xu Xin, Hao Wang, Li Baoping, Beijing: Peking University Press, 2006.
Hans Morgenthau, The National Interest of the United States, *American Political Science Review*, 1952, 46(4).
Hazel Smith, International Politics and Security in Korea, *Pacific Affairs*, 2009, 82(1).

He Huigang, Comparative Analysis of Euro Model and Dollarization Model and Its Implications for Monetary Cooperation in East Asia, *Industrial Economic Review*, 2005, 11.

He Zhigong, An Xiaoping, *Regional Cooperation in Northeast Asia: The Road toward an East Asian Community*, Current Affairs Press, 2008.

Henry Kissinger, *Diplomacy*, Trans. Gu Shuxin, Lin Tiangui, Haikou: Hainan Publishing House, 1998.

Henry Kissinger, *Does American Need a Foreign Policy? Toward a New Diplomacy for the 21st Century*, Trans. Hu Liping, Ling Jianping et al., Haikou: Hainan Publishing House, 2009.

Henry Kissinger, *On China*, Trans. Hu Liping, Lin Hua, Yang Yunqin, Zhu Jingwen, Beijing: China CITIC Press, 2012.

Henry Kissinger, *World Order*, Trans. Hu Liping, Lin Hua, Cao Aiju, Beijing: China CITIC Press, 2015.

Howard Davies, *The Financial Crisis: Who's to Blame?* Polity Press, 2010.

Hsieh, Alice Langley, *Communist China's Strategy in the Nuclear Era*, Kessinger Publishing, 2011.

Huang Fengzhi (ed.), *Annual Report on Politics and Security in Northeast Asia (2012)*, Beijing: Social Sciences Academic Press (China), 2012.

Huang Fengzhi and Jin Xin, A Multidimensional Survey of China's Security Interest in Northeast Asia, *Northeast Asia Forum*, 2011, 2.

Huang Fengzhi and Jin Xin, Review of the Six-Party Talks on the DPRK's Nuclear Issue, *Contemporary International Relations*, 2012, 12.

Huang Fengzhi, Gao Ke, and Xiao Xi. *Study on Security Strategy in Northeast Asia*, Changchun: Jilin People's Press, 2006.

Huang He, Wu Xue, Adjustment of China's Foreign Policy towards the DPRK under New Situation, *Northeast Asia Forum*, 2011, 5.

Huang Ping and Ni Feng (eds.), *Annual Report on American Studies (2013): Build-ing up a New Type of China-U.S. Big Power Relations*, Beijing: Social Sciences Academic Press (China), 2013.

Huang Ping and Zheng Bingwen (eds.), *Annual Report on Research of U.S.A. (2014): The Third-Party Issues in China-U.S. Relationship*, Beijing: Social Sciences Academic Press (China), 2014.

Huang Xiaoyong, Su Shuhui, and Xing Guangcheng (eds.), *Annual Development Report on World Energy (2014)*, Beijing: Social Sciences Academic Press (China), 2014.

Hyon Joo Yoo, The China factor in the US-South Korea Alliance: The Perceived Usefulness of China in the Korean Peninsula, *Australian Journal of International Affairs*, 2014, 68(1).

Hyun Jinv Choi, Fueling Crisis or Cooperation? The Geopolitics of Energy Security in Northeast Asia, *Asian Affairs An American Review*, 2009, 36(1).

Igor Ivanov, *Russia's New Diplomacy: A Decade of Foreign Policy*, Trans. Chen Fengxiang *et al.*, Beijing: Contemporary World Press, 2002.

Ikuo Kabashima, *The Track of Japanese Politics after World War II: Formation and Changes of Liberal Democratic Party System*, Trans. Guo Dingping, Tian Xuemei, Zhao Ridi, Shanghai: Shanghai People's Publishing House, 2014.

Isak Svensson, East Asian Peacemaking: Exploring the Patterns of Conflict, *Asian Perspective*, 2011, 35(2).

Isak Svensson, Management and Conflict Settlement in East Asia, *Asian Perspective*, 2011, 35.

J. Miles, Chinese Nationalism, US Policy and Asian Security, *Survival*, 2000, 42(4).

J. R. V. Prescott, Maritime Jurisdiction in East Asian Seas, Occasional Papers of the East-West Environment and Policy Institute, East-West Center, No. 4, 1987.

Jae-Seung Lee, Towards Green Energy Cooperation in Northeast Asia: Implications from European Experiences, *Asia Europe Journal*, 2013, 11.

Jaewoo Choo, Energy Cooperation Problems in Northeast Asia: Unfolding the Reality, *East Asia*, 2006, 23(3).

James Doherty, Robert Pfaltzgraff Jr., *Contending Theories of International Relations: A Comprehensive Survey*, Trans. Yan Xuetong, Chen Hanxi *et al.*, Beijing: World Knowledge Press, 2003.

Jane Perlez, China Bluntly Tells North Korea to Enter Nuclear Talks, *The New York Times*, 2013.

Jeanne L. Wilsona, Soft Power: A Comparison of Discourse and Practice in Russia and China, *Europe-Asia Studies*, 2015, 67(8).

Jennifer Lind, Democratization and Stability in East Asia, *International Studies Quarterly*, 2011, 55(2).

Ji Zhiye, Russia's Northeast Asian Policy, *Northeast Asia Forum*, 2013, 1.

Ji Zhiye, The Evolution and Trend of Russian Policy towards Korean Peninsula, *Contemporary International Relations*, 2003, 2.

Jim Garamone, Gates: North Korea Becoming Direct Threat to U.S., *American Forces Press Service*, 2011.

Jin Canrong, The New Situation of China's Diplomacy in 2010, *Contemporary International Relations*, 2010, 11.

Jin Dukkyu: Nationalism in South Korea, Seoul: Contemporary Thoughts Press, 1976.

Jin Jingyi and Jin Qiangyi, Transition of Northeast Asian International Order and the Role Orientation of Great Powers, *Northeast Asia Forum*, 2013, 1.

Jin Xiangbo, Analysis of Energy Cooperation in Northeast Asia and China's Energy Countermeasures, *Changbai Journal*, 2008, 3.

Jin Xide, Connotation and Trend of Japan's Political Power Strategy, *Contemporary World*, 2007, 7.

Joerg Friedrichs, East Asian Regional Security, *Asian Survey*, 2012, 52(4).

John Bolton, How to Answer the North Korean Threat, *The Wall Street Journal*, 2013.

John E. Endicott and Alan G. Gorowitz, Track-II Cooperative Regional Security Efforts: Lessons from the Limited Nuclear-Weapons-Free Zone for Northeast Asia, *Pacific Review Peace Security & Global Change*, 1999, 11.

John Ikenberry and Chung-in Moon, *The United States and Northeast Asia: Debates, Issues and New Order*, Rowman & Littlefield, 2008.

John King Fairbank, *The Chinese World Order: Traditional China's Foreign Relations*, Trans. Du Jidong, Beijing: China Social Sciences Press, 2010.

Joseph Y.S. Cheng, China's Regional Strategy and Challenges in East Asia, *China Perspectives*, 2013, 2013(2).

Junji Banno, *Envisioning Modern Japan*, Trans. Cui Shiguang, Wang Junying, Beijing: Social Sciences Academic Press (China), 2014.

Karla S. Fallon, Promoting an Energy Partnership in Northeast Asia, *Pacific Focus*, 2006, 21(1).

Kathleen Collins, The Limits of Cooperation: Central Asia, Afghanistan, and the New Silk Road, *Asia Policy*, No. 17, 2014.

Kei Koga, The US and East Asian Regional Security Architecture: Building a Regional Security Nexus on Hub-and-Spoke, *Asian Perspective*, 2011, 35(1).

Kim Jang-soo *et al.*, National Identification, Regional Identification and Foreign Cognition of Northeast Asia, *Contemporary Republic of Korea*, 2010, 4.

Kim Wootae, Research on Nationalism in South Korea, Busan: Pusan National University Press.

Kiyofumi Nakauchi, The Delimitation of the East China Sea and the Sea of Japan, Trans. Shao Jin, *Peking University Law Journal*, 1980, 4.

Kyu-sung Yi, Th*e Korean Financial Crisis of 1997: Onset, Turnaround and Thereafter*, World Bank, 2011.

L. Nichols, Expansion and Contraction in developed Northeast Asian Nations, *Hydrocarbon Processing*, 2015, 94(10).

Lee Youngho: Values of South Koreans, Iljisa, 1979.

Li Baoguo and Lin Bohai, A Study on the Contemporary China Nationalism with the Marxism Perspective, *Forward Position*, 2012, 5.

Li Guoxue, Characteristics, Problems and Implications of China-Japan-ROK Investment Agreements, *China Market*, 2012, 33.

Li Hanmei, *A Study of the Forms of Japanese Nationalism*, Beijing: The Commercial Press, 2012.

Li Jianming, Discussion about the ROK's Nationalism and China-ROK Relationship under its Affection, *Theory Research*, 2008, 18.
Li Junjiang and Fan Shuo, Status and Outlook of China-DPRK Trade and Economic Relation, *Northeast Asia Forum*, 2012, 2.
Li Kaisheng and Li Xiaofang, Trend of the DPRK's Nuclear Issue From the Perspective of Security Structure, *Pacific Journal*, 2011, 4.
Li Shenming and Zhang Yuyan (eds.), *Annual Report on International Politics and Security (2015)*, Beijing: Social Sciences Academic Press (China), 2015.
Li Wen, *The Cultural Causes of East Asian Cooperation*, Beijing: World Affairs Press, 2005.
Li Xiangyang (ed.), *Annual Report on Development in Asia-Pacific: Belt and Road Initiative (2015)*, Beijing: Social Sciences Academic Press (China), 2015.
Li Xiangyang (ed.), *Annual Report on Development in Asia-Pacific: The Surroundings around China (2014)*, Beijing: Social Sciences Academic Press (China), 2014.
Li Xianzhong, *Study on Russian Nationalism*, Beijing: Social Sciences Academic Press (China), 2015.
Li Yongquan (ed.), *Annual Report on Development of Russia (2013)*, Beijing: Social Sciences Academic Press (China), 2013.
Li Yutan, Chen Zhiheng, and Yin Lichun, *A Study of Regional Economic Development and Cooperation Mechanism Innovation in Northeast Asia*, Changchun: Jilin People's Press, 2006.
Li Zhonghai, Analysis on Ruble Internationalization Strategy and on China-Russia Trade in Domestic Currency Settlement, *Russian Studies*, 2011, 4.
Li Zhonghui, An Analysis of the Binary Structure of Contemporary the ROK's Nationalism, *People's Tribune*, 2011, 26.
Lian Xiaomei, Motivation and Countermeasures of Japanese Regional Integration Strategy Exclude Chinese Geopolitics, *Northeast Asia Forum*, 2006, 6.
Lian Xiaomei, On the Restrictive Factors in the Establishment of China-Japan-ROK Free Trade Zone, *Contemporary Economy of Japan*, 2004, 4.
Liang Yunxiang, A Comparative Study of Nationalism between China and Japan, *The Journal of International Studies*, 2009, 1.
Lin Jun, *A History of Russian Diplomacy*, Beijing: World Affairs Press, 2002.
Lin Yueqin and Zhou Wen, *Annual Report on Social Development of BRICS Countries (2011)*, Beijing: Social Sciences Academic Press (China), 2011.
Liu Boran and Huang Fengzhi, The Adjustment and Impact of Diplomatic Strategy toward Northeast Asia of the Park Geun-hye Government, *International Forum*, 2014, 3.
Liu Ge, Energy Security Situation in Northeast Asia and South Korea's Strategic Choice, *Contemporary Republic of Korea*, 2009, 2.

Liu Ge, The ROK's Energy Security: Vulnerabilities and Strategy Options, *Northeast Asia Forum*, 2009, 5.

Liu Guobin, Strategic Study of Constructing Northeast Asian Bridgehead Group based on the "Belt and Road" Plan, *Northeast Asia Forum*, 2015, 2.

Liu Hong, Development and Tendency of Japanese Nationalism, *People's Tribune*, 2012, 31.

Liu Hui and zhao Xiaochun, *Annual Report on China's National Security Studies (2014)*, Beijing: Social Sciences Academic Press (China), 2014.

Liu Jiangyong, *Twenty Lectures on China-Japanese Relations*, Beijing: China Renmin University Press, 2007.

Liu Qingcai (ed.), Study on *Russia Northeast Asia Policy: Geopolitics and State Relations*, Changchun: Jilin People's Press, 2006.

Liu Qingcai and Dai Hui, Transcend the Cold War Ideology and Construct the New Harmonious Order of Northeast Asian Region, *Northeast Asia Forum*, 2008, 1.

Liu Qingcai and Liu Tao, The Development Strategy of Russian Far East Region and China-Russia Regional Cooperation under the Background of Western Sanction, *Northeast Asia Forum*, 2015, 3.

Liu Qingcai and Liu Wenbo, Transformation of Northeast Asian International System and Opportunities and Challenges Facing China, *Jilin University Journal Social Sciences Edition*, 2011, 3.

Liu Qingcai and Zhao Xuan, Strategic thought about China-Russia promotion of the establishment of Asia-Pacific regional security and cooperation architecture, *Northeast Asia Forum*, 2014, 3.

Liu Qingcai et al., *Russia's Asia-Pacific Policy in the Early 21st Century*, Beijing: Social Sciences Academic Press (China), 2013.

Liu Qingcai, Cheng Fang, Pushing Forward the Establishment of the Asia-Pacific Regional Security Cooperation Framework: Strategic Planning and Approach, *Jilin University Journal Social Sciences Edition*, 2015, 5.

Liu Qingcai, Gao Ke et al., *Geopolitics in Northeast Asia and China's Geostrategy*, Tianjin: Tianjin People's Publishing House, 2007.

Liu Shuchun et al., *Contemporary Russian Political Parties*, Beijing: Central Compilation & Translation Press, 2006.

Liu Sisi, Belt and Road: New Paths in Research on Theories of Cross Border Sub-Regional Cooperation, *South Asian Studies*, 2014, 2.

Liu Xuelian and Li Xiaoxia, China's major country diplomacy with Chinese characteristics and its developing features in East Asia, *Northeast Asia Forum*, 2015, 6.

Liu Xuelian and Wang Yong, Main Factors Affecting the Transformation of East Asian International System and China's Strategic Choices, *Jilin University Journal Social Sciences Edition*, 2011, 3.

Liu Zhongmin, Zuo Caijin, and Luo Suqing, *Nationalism and Contemporary International Politics*, World Affairs Press, 2006.
Lu Yaodong, The Nationalistic Characteristics of Japanese Political Right-deviation, *Japanese Studies*, 2014, 3.
Luo Peng, Bai Fuchen, and Zhang Li, The Forecast of Marine Economy Prospects in China, *Fisheries Economy Research*, 2009, 2.
Lyu Gang, Facilitation Measures of China, Japan and ROK under APEC Framework, *Development Research*, 2010, 3.
M. Titarenko, Zhu Xianping, and Zhang Xinyu, Security and Stability of Asia-Pacific Region and the Interests of Russia and China, *Northeast Asia Forum*, 2012, 6.
Ma Lian, Thinking of China's Grand Strategy: Chinese Perspectives, *International Relations of the Asia Pacific*, 2013, 13(1).
Makot Iokibe, *Japanese Diplomatic History after World War II (1945–2010)*, Trans. Wu Wanhong, Beijing: World Affairs Press, 2013.
Makoto Iokibe, *History of Japan-US Relations*, Trans. Zhou Yongsheng et al., Beijing: World Affairs Press, 2012.
Maria Elena Romero-Ortiz, Asia Pacific Regionalism: The Strategies of Japan and China in the Region, *Latin American Journal of International Affairs*, 2010, 2(3).
Mario Giovanoli and Diego Devos, *International Monetary and Financial Law: The Global Crisis*, Oxford University Press, 2010.
Masahiro Kawai, East Asian Economic Regionalism: Progress and Challenges, *Journal of Asian Economics*, 2005, 16(1).
Mei Xinyu, Inspiration from DPRKa's Energy Problem, *China SOE*, 2014, 11.
Men Honghua and Shin Jung-seung, *Cooperation in North East Asia and China-South Korea Relationship*, Beijing: China Economic Publishing House, 2014.
Men Honghua, *China's Strategy in the Next Decade*, Beijing: China Economic Publishing House, 2015.
Men Honghua, On *The East Asian Order: Regional Change, Power Game and China's Strategy*, Shanghai: Shanghai People's Publishing House, 2015.
Miao Jiafu, *Globalization and Ethnic Cultural Diversity*, Beijing: People's Publishing House, 2005.
Michael Alan Brittingham, The "Role" of Nationalism in Chinese Foreign Policy: A Reactive Model of Nationalism & Conflict, *Journal of Chinese Political Science*, 2007, 12(2).
Michael Lumbers, Whither the Pivot? Alternative U.S. Strategies for Responding to China's Rise, *Comparative Strategy*, 2015, 34(4).
Michael Yahuda, Chinese Dilemmas in Thinking about Regional Security Architecture, *The Pacific Review*, 2003, 16(2).

Mikyoung Kim and Barry Schwartz, *Northeast Asia's Difficult Past: Essays in Collective Memory*, Palgrave Macmillan, 2010.
Natasha Kuhrt, The Russian Far East in Russia's Asia Policy: Dual Integration or Double Periphery? *Europe-Asia Studies*, 2012, 64(3).
Ni Jianmin, *National Energy Security Report*, Beijing: People's Publishing House, 2005.
Ni Jianping, Russian Energy Strategy and Energy Security Cooperation in Northeast Asia: A Perspective of Regional Public Goods, *Social Sciences in Heilongjiang*, 2011, 1.
Ni Shixiong et al., *Contemporary Western Theory of International Relations*, Shanghai: Fudan University Press, 2009.
Nick Bisley, Securing the "Anchor of Regional Stability"?: The Transformation of the US-Japan Alliance and East Asian Security, *Contemporary Southeast Asia*, 2008, 30(1).
Niklas Swanstrom, *Regional Cooperation and Conflict Management: Lessons from the Pacific Rim*, Department of Peace and Conflict Research, Uppsala: Institutionen for freds-och konfliktforskning, 2002.
Nikolai Berdyaev, *Russian Thought: Main Issues of Russian Thought from the 19th Century to the Beginning of the 20th Century (Second Edition)*, Trans. Lei Yongsheng, Qiu Shoujuan, Beijing: SDX Joint Publishing Company, 2004.
Ou Minggang, Ten Years after the Financial Crisis: A New Starting Point for East Asian Financial Cooperation, *World Economics and Politics*, 2007, 11.
Pan Weijuan, *Compilation of Important World Security Documents in 2013*, Beijing: Current Affairs Press, 2014.
Pan Zhongqi, *From Following the Shi to Shaping the Shi: China's International Orientation and Strategic*, Shanghai: Fudan University Press, 2012.
Pang Zhongying, China's Role in the Transformation of the Asian Regional Order, *Foreign Affairs Review*, 2005, 4.
Park Jianyi, *China's Periphery Security Environment and the Korean Peninsula Issue*, Beijing: China Minzu University Press, 2013.
Peter Hays Gries, China New Nationalism: Pride, Politics, and Diplomacy, *The China Journal*, No. 53, 2005.
Peter J. Katzenstein, Takashi Shiraishi, *Beyond Japan: The Dynamics of East Asian Regionalism*, Trans. Wang Xingyu, Beijing: China Renmin University Press, 2015.
A. Pettigrew, H. Thomas, and R. Whittington, *Handbook of Strategy and Manage-ment*, Sage Publications, 2006.
Philip Gannon, Obama and China's Rise: An Insider's Account of America's Asia Strategy, *Political Studies Review*, 2013, 11(3).

Pritchard Charles L., Snyder Scott A., and Tilelli John H., U.S. *Policy Toward the Korean Peninsula: Independent Task Force Report*, Council on Foreign Relations, 2010.

Putin's Collected Works (2002–2008), Beijing: China Social Sciences Press (China), 2008.

Putin's Collected Works (2008–2014), Beijing: World Affairs Press, 2014.

Putin's Collected Works, Beijing: China Social Sciences Press (China), 2002.

Qi Huaigao, *Building East Asia's Future: China-US Institutional Balancing and Transformation of East Asian System*, Beijing: China Social Sciences Press, 2011.

Qi Wenhai, On the Construction of Northeast Asia Energy Cooperation Community, *Journal of Eurasian Economy*, 2004, 4.

Qiu Shengyan and Gu Lina, Discrimination of the Concepts of Dodson Doctrine, Regionalism and Bilateral Doctrine, *Economic Review Journal*, 2007, 10.

Qu Wei, Liu Shuang, and Da Zhigang, *China-Northeast Asia Yearbook*, Harbin: Heilongjiang People's Publishing House, 2012.

Ramon Pacheco Pardo, China and Northeast Asia's Regional Security Architecture: The Six-Party Talks as a Case of Chinese Regime-Building, *East Asia*, 2012, 29(4).

Ren Dongbo, Nationalism and Regionalism, *Northeast Asia Forum*, 2005, 5.

Richard A. Posner, *A Failure of Capitalism: The Crisis of '08 and the Descent into Depression*, Harvard University Press, 2009.

Richard J. Samuels, *Securing Japan-Tokyo's Grand Strategy and the Future if East Asia*, Cornell University Press, 2008.

Robert A. Scalapino, *The United States and Asia: Lectures at Peking University*, Trans. Hao Ping et al., Beijing: Peking University Press, 2002.

Robert E. Kelly, The "Pivot" and Its Problems: American Foreign Policy in Northeast Asia, *The Pacific Review*, 2014, 27(3).

Robert Gilpin, *War and Change in World Politics*, Trans. Wu Jun et al., Beijing: China Renmin University Press, 1994.

Robert J. Shiller, *The Subprime Solution: How Today's Global Financial Crisis Happened, and What to Do about It*, Princeton University Press, 2012.

Robert Jervis, Dilemmas About Security Dilemmas, *Security Studies*, 2011, 20(3).

Robert W. Kolb, *Lessons from the Financial Crisis: Causes, Consequences, and Our Economic Future*, Wiley, 2010.

Roselyn Hsueh, *China's Regulatory State: A New Strategy for Globalization*, Cornell University Press, 2011.

Ross A. Hammond, Robert Axelrod, The Evolution of Ethnocentrism, *The Journal of Conflict Resolution*, 2006, 50(6).

Samuel P. Huntington, *The Clash of Civilizations and the Remaking of World Order*, Trans. Zhou Qi *et al.*, Beijing: Xinhua Publishing House, 1999.
Sergey Sevastyanov, The More Assertive and Pragmatic New Energy Policy in Putin's Russia: Security Implications for Northeast Asia, *East Asia*, 2008, 25.
Shao Yiping, *Korean Peninsula: Challenges of Geo-Environment*, Shanghai: Shanghai Classics Publishing House, 2005.
Shen Dingchang, *Restructuring of International Relations in Asia*, Beijing: Social Sciences Academic Press (China), 2008.
Shen Dingchang, *The ROK's Diplomacy and the United States*, Beijing: Social Sciences Academic Press (China), 2008.
Shen Minghui, APEC Investment Facilitation Process-Based on Investment Facilitation Action Plan, *Journal of International Economic Cooperation*, 2009, 4.
Shen Minghui, Measurement and Thinking of Trade Facilitation Level in East Asian Countries, *Journal of International Economic Cooperation*, 2009, 7.
Shi Yuan-hua and Wen Enxi, On Factors of the United States in China-ROK Strategic Cooperative Partnership, *Northeast Asia Forum*, 2012, 5.
Shunji Cui, Problems of Nationalism and Historical Memory in China's Relations with Japan, *Journal of Historical Sociology*, 2012, 25(2).
Simg-han Kim, Environment-Security Nexus in Northeast Asia, *Global Economic Review*, 2001, 30.
Simon S. C. Tay, *Asia Alone: The Dangerous Post-Crisis Divide from America*, Wiley, 2010.
Soichi Itoh, TPP Changes Energy Pattern in Northeast Asia, *China Entrepreneur*, 2013, 8: 40–41.
Steen Thomsen, Caspar Rose and Ole Risager, *Understanding the Financial Crisis: Investment, Risk and Governance*, Sim Corp Strategy Lab, 2009.
Stephen G. Nelson, Peter J. Katzenstein, Uncertainty, Risk, and the Financial Crisis of 2008, *International Organization*, 2014, 68(2).
Stephen Krasner (ed.), *International regime*, Cornell University Press, 1983.
Su Changhe, Periphery System and Peripherism: China's Approach to Regional Governance in East Asia, *World Economics and Politics*, 2006, 1.
Su Qin and Xiao Jing, Comparison of Banking Reform Performance and Experience Reference between China and Russia, *Inquiry into Economic Issues*, 2013, 12.
Sun Chunri, The ROK's Expectation for the Security Mechanism in Northeast Asia in the Next 15 Years from "The ROK's National Strategy 2020", *Journal of Contemporary Asia-Pacific Studies*, 2006, 11.
Sun Xia, Northeast Asia Regional Security Complex: Dynamics and Challenges. *International Forum*, 2006, 3.
Sun Xuefeng and Huang Yuxing, China's Rise and the Evolution of the East Asia Regional Order, *Journal of Contemporary Asia-Pacific Studies*, 2011, 1.

Tang Xiaohong, *World Important Security Documents Compilation 2010*, Beijing: Current Affairs Press, 2011.

Tang Yanlin, Building a Multilateral Energy Cooperation Mechanism in Northeast Asia in the Context of International Politics. *Siberian Studies*, 2006, 4.

Tang Yongsheng and Xu Qiyu, *To Obtain the Balance in the Complexity*, Beijing: World Affairs Press, 2004.

Tsuneo Akaha, International Cooperation in Establishing a Regional Order in Northeast Asia, *Global Economic Review*, 1998, 27.

Tsutomu Toichi, Energy Security in Asia and Japanese Policy, *Asia-Pacific Review*, 2003, 10(1).

Ukeru Magosaki, *The Truth of Japan-US Alliance*, Trans. Guo Yina, Beijing: Xinhua Publishing House, 2014.

Victoria Ivashina and David Scharfstein, Bank Lending during the Financial Crisis of 2008, *Journal of Financial Economics*, 2010, 97(3).

Vladimir I. Ivanov, Prospects for Russia's Energy Diplomacy in Northeast Asia, *Global Economic Review*, 1999, 28(1).

W. T. Tow and B. Taylor. What is Asian Security Architecture, *Review of International Studies*, 2010, 36(1).

Wang Chuanjian, The Korean Peninsula Issue and China-US Relations, *The Journal of International Studies*, 2005, 3.

Wang Fan, *New Development: Complex Systems Thinking and China's Diplomatic Strategic Planning*, Beijing: World Affairs Press, 2014.

Wang Jun, *Nationalism and International Relations*, Hangzhou: Zhejiang People's Publishing House, 2009.

Wang Junsheng, Multilateral Security Mechanisms in Northeast Asia: Progress and Solutions, *World Economics and Politics*, 2012, 12.

Wang Lian, *On Nationalism*, Beijing: Peking University Press, 2002.

Wang Luolin, Zhang Yuyan and Sun Jie, *World Economy Analysis and Forecast (2015)*, Beijing: Social Sciences Academic Press(China), 2015.

Wang Sheng, An Analysis of the ROK's Nationalism, *Contemporary International Relations*, 2010, 2.

Wang Sheng, Analysis on the Situation of the ROK Estranged the U.S.A and Close to China, *Northeast Asian Forum*, 2006, 2.

Wang Sheng, *The Study on Contemporary Nationalism in Republic of Korea*, Beijing: Social Sciences Academic Press (China), 2015.

Wang Shengjin and Yu Xiao, The Situation and Prospect of FTA in Northeast Asian, *Northeast Asia Forum*, 2007, 4.

Wang Shengjin, *Report on Northeast Asia Development*, Changchun: Jilin University Press, 2013.

Wang Shengjin, The Development Trend and Path Choice of Northeast Asian Regional Economic Cooperation, *Jilin University Journal Social Sciences Edition*, 2007, 7.

Wang Shuang, The Influence of Japan's Investment Trend on China, *Dongyue Tribune*, 2011, 2.

Wang Wenqi, Nationalism and Regional Order in Northeast Asia in the Post-Cold War Era, *Northeaster Asian Forum*, 2012, 4.

Wang Xiangsui, Currency-Politics: The Changes and Future of the World Situations, *World Economics and Politics*, 2011, 4.

Wang Yizhou, *Global Politics and China's Foreign Policy*, Beijing: World Affairs Press, 2003.

Wang Zhili, Deeply Thoughts of Contemporary China's Nationalism, *Journal of Jiangsu Normal University (Philosophy and Social Sciences Edition)*, 2012, 4.

Wei Liang and Faizullah Khilji, *China and East Asians Post-Crisis Community: A Region in Flux*, Lexington Books, 2012.

Wei Min, *The Interaction Between Nationalism and Regionalism: A New Prospective on Asia*, Beijing: Peking University Press, 2005.

Wen-lung Laurence Lin, The U.S. Maritime Strategy in the Asia-Pacific in Response to the Rise of a Seafaring China, *Issues & Studies*, 2012, 48(4).

William T. Tow, Brendan Taylor. What is Asian Security Architecture?, *Review of International Studies*, 2010, 36(1).

William T. Tow, The United States and Asia in 2013: From Primacy to Marginalization, *Asian Survey*, 2014, 54(1).

Woo-sang Kim, Rising China, Pivotal Middle Power South Korea and Alliance Transition Theory, *International Area Studies Review*, 2015, 18(3).

Wu Xiaoling, East Asian Financial Cooperation: Causes, Progress and Development Direction. *Studies of International Finance*, 2007, 8.

Wu Xinbo, *Asia-Pacific Regional Order in Transformation*, Beijing: Current Affairs Press, 2013.

Xi Jinping, *The Governance of China*, Beijing: Foreign Languages Press, 2014.

Xia Yishan, *China's Perspective on International Energy Development Strategy*, Beijing: World Affairs Press, 2009.

Xiang Qing, *Nationalism of Japan in Modern Time*, Beijing: Social Sciences Academic Press (China), 2007.

Xiao Xi, *Non-traditional Security in Northeast Asia: An Issue-area Analysis*, Beijing: China Economic Publishing House, 2015.

Xiao Xi, Non-traditional Security of Northeast Asia: Its Problem Domain and Cooperation Model, *Northeast Asia Forum*, 2010, 2.

Xiao Xi, The Transformation of the East Asian Order after the Cold War and the East Asian Strategy of China and the United States, *Jilin University Journal Social Sciences Edition*, 2010, 1.

Xu Jin, A Multilateral Security Cooperation Framework for Northeast Asia: Problems and Considerations, *Journal of Contemporary Asia-Pacific Studies*, 2011, 4.

Xu Mei, Zhang Shuying, and Zhao Jianglin, *Study on the Establishment of Free Trade Area between China and Japan*, Beijing: China Economic Publishing House, 2009.

Xu Ning and Huang Fengzhi, Objective Quantification of Moisture Transport that Influences Summer Rainfall in the Middle and Lower Reaches of the Yangtze River. *Northeast Asian Forum*, 2014, 3.

Xu Wansheng, *Japanese Politics and Foreign Relations*, Beijing: People's Publishing House, 2006.

Xu Xiangmei, Energy Security and Multilateral Energy C Cooperation in Northeast Asia, *International Petroleum Economics*, 2004, 10.

Yan Xuetong, *Shift of Power in the World: Political Leadership and Strategic Competition*, Beijing: Peking University Press, 2015.

Yan Xuetong, The Instability of China-US Relations, *World Economics and Politics*, 2010, 12.

Yang Bojiang, An Analysis on the Foreign Strategic Direction of the Democratic Party of Japan, *Contemporary International Relations*, 2012, 2.

Yang Jiemian, *The Construction and Innovation of China's Diplomatic Theory and Strategy*, Shanghai: Shanghai People's Publishing House, 2015.

Yang Jun, *The Formation and Evolution of Koguryo Nation and State*, Beijing: China Social Sciences Press (China), 2006.

Yang Li, Russia and Northeast Asia, *International Studies*, 2005, 1.

Yang Ningyi, Nationalism in the View of World History, *History Teaching*, 2005, 10.

Yang Zewei, China's Energy Security: Challenges and Responses, *World Economics and Politics*, 2008, 8.

Yange Geng, On Multilateral Perspective Analysis of Checks and Balances of Power Structures and Interests of the International Political System in Northeast Asia, *Journal of Inner Mongolia University for Nationalities (Social Sciences)*, 2010, 1.

Yasu Seishu, *Japan's Drifting Politics*, Trans. Gao Ke, Beijing: Social Sciences Academic Press (China), 2011.

Yu Changshen, Track-Two Diplomacy and Security Cooperation in the Asia-Pacific Region, *Southeast Asian Studies*, 2003, 5: 44.

Yu Jianhua, ROK's Energy Security Strategy of and Its Energy Cooperation with China, *International Relations Studies*, 2014, 2.

Yu Xintian, China and Northeast Asian regional Security Cooperation, *Asia-Pacific Review*, 2005, 12(2).

Yuan Gujie, *The Theory and Practice of the International Maritime Delimitation*, Beijing: Law Press China, 2001.

Zbigniew Brzezinski, *The Grand Chessboard: American Primacy and Its Geostrategic Imperatives*, Trans. China Institute of International Studies, Shanghai: Shanghai People's Publishing House, 2007.

Zhang Dongning, Nationalism and Security Framework in Northeast Asia, *Journal of International Security Studies*, 2014, 2.

Zhang Haibin, Review and Prospect of Environmental Cooperation in Northeast Asia, *The Journal of International Studies*, 2000, 2.

Zhang Huizhi, Strategic Adjustment on the Korean Peninsula and Interaction between Northeast Asian Powers, *Social Science Front*, 2012, 4.

Zhang Jian, On the "Trustpolitik" by the Park Geun-hye Administration, *Contemporary Republic of Korea*, 2013, 4.

Zhang Jingquan, The International System and Japan's Alliance with the Outside World, *Japanese Studies*, 2005, 3.

Zhang Lihua, *Chinese Culture and Diplomacy*, Beijing: Intellectual Property Publishing House, 2013.

Zhang Xuegang, China's Border Sea Situation and Policy Choice, *Contemporary International Relations*, 2012, 8.

Zhang Yuguo, American-Japanese Relations in New Era: Retrospect and Prospect, *Journal of Foreign Studies*, 2004, 3.

Zhang Yuguo, Improvement of the Japan-US Alliance by Noda Regime, *Journal of Foreign Studies*, 2011, 4.

Zhang Yunling, *China and Its Neighbors: Making New Partnership*, Beijing: Social Sciences Academic Press (China), 2008.

Zhang Yunling, East Asia and Community Building: Ways and Means, *Crossroads: Southeast Asian Studies*, 2008, 11.

Zhang Yunling, Northeast Asian Regional Cooperation and the Construction of a New Order, *Social Science Front*, 2015, 3.

Zhao Chuanjun, *Research on Three Major Relations of Northeast Asia: Economy and Trade, Politic, Security*. Beijing: Social Sciences Academic Press (China), 2006.

Zhao Huasheng, China-Russia Treaty of Good-Neighborliness, Friendship and Cooperation and China-Russia Relations, *Russian Studies*, 2001, 3.

Zhao Jinlong, The Direction of China's FTA Strategy in Northeast Asia: A Comparative Research of CGE Model, *Northeast Asia Forum*, 2008, 5.

Zhao Lixin, *Contemporary Nationalism in East Asia and Inter-State Relations: Conflict and Integration of Nationalism in China*, Beijing: Social Sciences Academic Press (China), 2012.

Zhao Lixin, The Potential Obstacle in East Asia Regional Cooperation: Demands of China-Korea-Japan Nationalism and Its Impact, *Northeast Asian Forum*, 2011, 3.

Zhao Mingwen, China-Russia Relationship: In the Face of Challenges and Opportunities, *Peace and Development*, 2012, 3.

Zhao Suisheng, China's Global Search for Energy Security: Cooperation and Competition in Asia-Pacific, *Journal of Contemporary China*, 2008, 17.

Zhao Yumin, Pre-establishment National Treatment in the International Investment System-Looking at the Development Trend of International Investment Rules from Japanese and the ROK's Investment National Treatment, *Intertrade*, 2012, 3.

Zheng Xianwu, Constructing a Concert of Powers in East Asia: Normative, Realistic Foundation and Path Selection, *World Economics and Politics*, 2013, 5.

Zheng Yongnian, *The Big Picture: China's Rise Should Surpass Emotion and Ideology*, Beijing: The Oriental Press, 2014.

Zhou Fangyin, China's Rise, the Transformation of East Asian Structure and Directions for the Development of the East Asian Order, *Journal of Contemporary Asia-Pacific Studies*, 2012, 5.

Zhou Fangyin, China's Understanding of World Order and International Responsibility, *International Economic Review*, 2011, 3.

Zhou Yang, A Discussion on Improving the Customs Trade Facility System of China: A Perspective from the United States, *International Business Research*, 2010, 6.

Zhu Feng and Robert Rose, *China's Rise: From the Perspective of Theory and Policy*, Shanghai: Shanghai People's Publishing House, 2008.

Zhu Feng, China-U.S. Strategic Competition and the Future of East Asian Security, *World Economics and Politics*, 2013, 3.

Zhu Feng, DPRK's Nuclear Crisis after the Second Nuclear Test: Six-Party Talks and Compulsory Diplomacy, *Contemporary International Relations*, 2009, 7.

Zhu Feng, System Construction of Six-Party Talks and Multilateral Security Mechanism in Northeast Asia, *Contemporary International Relations*, 2007, 3.

Zhu Feng, The Security Situation in East Asia: New Situation, New Characteristics and New Trends, *Contemporary International Relations*, 2010, 12.

Zhu Xianping and Li Tianzi, Energy Cooperation in Northeast Asian: Its Status Quo and Prospects, *Jilin University Journal Social Sciences Edition*, 2006, 2.

Zhu Xianping and Li Tianzi, Ensure Our Country's Energy Safety Through the Cooperation of Energy in Northeast Asian Counties, *Northeast Asian Forum*, 2004, 6.

Zhu Xianping, The Cooperation of Energy between China and Russia and the Effect to Regional Economy of Northeast Asia, *Northeast Asian Forum*, 2004, 2.

Zong Liang et al., *Global Financial Reform After the Era of Crisis*, Beijing: China Financial Publishing House, 2010.

Zuo Fengrong, *Revitalizing Russia: Putin's Foreign Strategy and Policy*, Beijing: The Commercial Press, 2008.

Ивашенцов Глеб Александрович, Соаммит АТЭС-2012: Тихокеанские горизонты России. «Международная жизнь», №2-2012.

Ивашенцов Глеб Александрович, России нужна развернутая энергет ическая стратегия в АТР. «Международная жизнь», №3-2013.

Долгов Борис, Россия и Китай: стратегическое партнерство. «Между народная жизнь», №7-2014.

Петровский Владимир, Россия, Китай и новая архитектура междунаро дной безопастности в АТР. «Международная жизнь», №1-2013.

Бородавкин Алексей Николаевич, Восточное направление российской веншней политики-итоги и перспективы. «Международная жизнь», №1-2011.

Давыденко Андрей Иванович, Россия укрепляет связи с партнерами в Азии. «Международная жизнь», №3-2013.

Бруденц Карен, Россия и Азия. «Международная жизнь», №3-2011.

Николаев Михаил Ефимович, АТР и национальная безопастность России. «Международная жизнь», №4-2010.

Стратегия национальной безопастности Российской Федерации до 2020 года. 13 мая 2009 года, http://news.kremlin.ru/ref_notes/424.

В. Путин, Выступление на саммите Совещания по взаимодействию и мерами доверия в Азии 21 мая 2014 года, http://kremlin.ru/news/21058.

Концепция внешней политики Российской Федерации, 12 февраля 2013 г. http://www.mid.ru/bdomp/ns-osndoc.nsf/e2f289bea62097f9c352787a 0034c255/c32577ca0017434944257b160051bf7f! OpenDocument.

Петровский Владимир, Эхо Второй мировой в Восточной Азии: «ловушки» холодной войны и уроки коллективного действия. «Международная жизнь», №8-2014.

Стратегиия национальной безопастности Российской Федерации до 2020 года, http://archive.mid.ru/bdomp/ns-osndoc.nsf/e2f289bea62097f9c352787 a0034c255/8abb3c17eb3d2626c32575b500320ac4! OpenDocument.

Александр Лукин, Поворот России к Азии: миф или реальность? 4 номера 2016 года, http://interaffairs.ru/jauthor/material/1468.

Дмирий Лабин, В поисках стратегии успехов Северо-Восточной Азии, 31 октябр. 2012 года, http://www.ru.journal-neo.com/node/119518.

16. Людмила Захарова, Экономические отношения России и КНДР: курс на прорыв, 04. 06. 2014, http://ru.journal-neo.org/2014/06/04/e-konomi-cheskie-otnosheniya-rossii-i-kndr-kurs-na-prory-v/.

Послание Президента Федеральному Собранию, 3 декабря 2015 года, http://kremlin.ru/events/president/transcripts/messages/50864.

В. Путин, Стенографический отчёт о заседании сессии в рамках Делового саммиа форума «Азиатско-тихоокеанское экономическое сотрудничество» 10 ноября 2014 года, http://www.kremlin.ru/news/46988.

е министров иностранных дел стран-участниц Совещания по взаимодей ствию и мерам доверия в Азии, 28 апреля 2016 года, http://www.mid.ru/press_service/minister_speeches/-/asset_publisher/7OvQR5KJWVmR/content/id/2256996.

Юрий Райков, Восточная Азия и новый мировой порядок, 12 номера 2015 года, http://interaffairs.ru//jauthor/material/1419.
半田滋,「集団自衛権のトリックと安倍改憲」, 高文研, 2013年。
渡辺利夫,「日本の東アジア戦略：共同体への期待と不安」, 東洋経済新報社, 2005年。
渡辺昭夫,「アジア太平洋協力構想」, NTT出版社2005年版。
長島昭久, 「日米同盟の新しい設計図：変貌するアジアの米軍を見据えて」, 日本評論社, 2002年.
防衛省編,「防衛白書平成24年版」, 佐伯印刷, 2012年。
防衛省編,「防衛白書平成25年版」, 日経印刷, 2013年。
防衛省防衛研究所, 「東アジア戦略概観2013」, (有) 成隆出版, 2013年。
防衛省防衛研究所, 「東アジア戦略概観2014」, (株)時評社, 2014年。
防衛日報社編, 「自衛隊年鑑2013J, 防衛日報社, 2013年。
防衛年鑑刊行会編, 「防衛年鑑2013, 防衛メディプセンターJ, 2013年。
谷内正大郎編, 「日本の安全保障と防衛政策」, ウェッシ, 2013年。
河野収,「日本地政学：環大平洋地域の生きる道」, 原書房, 1983年。
江沢譲爾,「地政学研究」, 日本評論社, 1942年。
入江昭,「歴史家が見る現代世界」, 講談社, 2014年。
森本敏,「安全保障論：21世紀世界の危機管理」, PHP研究所, 2000年。
石破茂,「日本人のための「集団的自衛権」入門」, 新潮社, 2014年。
五百旗頭真, 「秩序変革期の日本の選択：「米・欧・日」三極システムのすすめ」, PHP研究所, 1991年。
外務省編, 「外交青書2013J, 日経印刷, 2013年。
小牧實繁, 「大東亞地政学新論」, 星野書店, 1943年。
小島朋之, 竹田いさみ,「東アジアの安全保障」, 南窓社, 2002年。
小原雅博, 「国益と外交」, 日本経済新聞出版社2007年版。
小沢一郎, 「日本改造計画」, 講談社1993年版。
信夫清大郎, 「日本外交史」, 商務印書館1992年版。
永野信利, 「日本外交全貌」, 耕文社1986年版。
永野信利,「天皇と鄧小平の握手」, 行政問題研究所1983年版。
猪口孝,「日本:経済大国の政治運営」, 東京大学出版会, 1993年。
猪口孝,「現代国際関係と日本」, 築書斎1991年版。
荒井利明, 「東アジアの日・米・中：平和と繁栄をどう確保するか」, 日中出版, 2007年。
ピルエモット着, 伏見威蕃訳, 「アジア三国志：中国・インド・日本の大戦略」, 日本経済新聞出版社, 2008年。
アーロン・フリードバーグ著, 住橋亮監修, 「支配への競争：米中対立の構図とアジアの将来」, 日本評論社, 2013年。
ニコラス・スパイクマン著, 奥山真司訳, 「平和の地政学：アメリカの大戦略の原点」, 芙蓉書房出版, 2008年。

ドミニク・モイシ著, 櫻井佑子訳, 「「感情」の地歌学: 恐怖・屈辱・希望はいかにして世界を創り変えるか」, 早川書房, 2010年.
コリングレイ, シェフリースローン著, 奥山真司訳, 「進化する地政学: 陸、海、空そして宇宙へ」, 五月書房, 2009年.
ケント・E. カルダー著, 杉田弘教誤, 「新大陸主義: 21世紀のエネルギーパワーゲーム」, 潮出版社, 2013年.
イアン・ブレマー, ジョセフ・ナイ, ハピエル・ソラナ, クリストファー・ヒル著, 「新アジア地政学」, 土曜社, 2013年.
노태구: ≪민족주의와 국제정치≫, 서울: 범학사, 2001.
김혜승: ≪한국민족주의: 발생양식과 전개과정≫, 서울: 比峰出版社, 2003.
정용녠, 승병철: ≪21세기는 중국의 시대인가: 민족주의, 정체성 그리고 국제관계≫, 과천: 문화발전소, 2005.
차기벽: ≪한국 민족주의의 이념과 실태≫, 파주: 한길사, 2005.
박찬승: ≪민족주의의 시대: 일제하의 한국 민족주의≫, 서울: 景人文化社, 2007.
곽진오: ≪세계화와 동아시아민족주의≫, 서울: 책사랑, 2010.
노태구: ≪한국민족주의와 국제주의≫, 서울: 경기대학교 민족문 제연구소, 1996.
유광진: ≪중국의 민족주의와 동양성≫, 수원: 경기대학교 민족문 제연구소, 1997.
王生: ≪동북아평화와 중한합작: 북한 핵 문제 해결을 위한 과정 중 중국과 한국의 역할을 중심으로 연구함≫, ≪韩国文化技术≫, 第八集, 韩国檀国大学文化技术研究所2009年12月出版.
최연식: ≪탈냉전기 중국의 민족주의와 동북아질시≫, 2004, 14(1).
남정휴: ≪중국 근대국가 형성과정을 통해서 본 중국의 민족주 의≫, 한국동북아논총, 2005, 37.
천성림: ≪20세기 중국 민족주의의 형성과 전개≫, 동양정치사상사, 2005, 5(1).
곽진오: ≪글로벌화와 일본민족주의≫, 일본학보, 2006, 67.
김경국, 외: ≪"大中华"论与当地중국민족주의 분석≫, 중국학논총, 2006, 21(1).
박의경: ≪동복아 협력의 모색과 21세기 한국 민족주의를 위한 제언≫, 한국동북아논총, 2006, 40.
노태구: ≪동북아시대와 한국민족주의≫, 한국의 청소년문화, 2006, 7.
이희옥: ≪중국민족주의의 발전의 이데올로기적 함의≫, 중국학 논총, 2009, 47.
장규식: ≪20세기 전반 한국 사상계의 궤적과 민족주의 담론≫, 한 국사 연구, 2010, 150.
한석희: ≪21세기 중국 민족주의의 딜레마≫, 신아세아, 2010, 17(1).

석한섭: ≪중국 대외정책형성에 미친 민족주의의 영향에 관한 연구≫, 조선대학교, 1993.
김월회: ≪20세기초 중국의 문화민족주의 연구≫, 서울대학교, 2001.
이빈: ≪중국 근대 민족주의 사상에 관한 연구≫, 원광대학교, 2007.
한주희: ≪중국의 부흥과 대외정책의 변화: 중국 민족주의와의 상관성을 중심으로≫, 부산대학교, 2010.

Index

A
Abe administration, 7, 10, 41, 61
Abe, Shinzo, 156
air movement, 106, 108
Alternative Energy Law, 197
Anti-Japanese War, 41
Anti-Monopoly Law, 221
APEC Trade Facilitation Action Plan, 301
ASEAN Plus Three (APT), 63, 266–267
ASEAN Regional Forum (ARF), 130
Asian Cooperation Dialogue (ACD), 130
Asian Infrastructure Investment Bank (AIIB), 12, 77
Asian premium, 215
Asia-Pacific Economic Cooperation (APEC), 63, 233, 261–262, 272–275
Asia-Pacific rebalancing strategy, 6–7, 22, 51, 56, 87, 92, 100, 111, 125
Asia-Pacific region, 11, 22, 189
Association of Southeast Asian Nations (ASEAN), 47

B
Beijing Six-Party Talks, 57, 66, 68, 124
Belt and Road Initiative, 184–185, 228
bilateral cooperation, 269
bilateral financial cooperation, 265
bipolar pattern, 36
Blue-Water Navy stage, 155
Bogor Declaration, 261
Bogor Goals, 273
British thermal unit (BTU), 213
Buddhism, 13
Burgess, Ronald, 102
business personnel flow, 301–302

C
capacity-building, 307–308
carbon emission reduction, 230
Catholicism, 13
Chiang Mai Initiative, 267
China–ASEAN Free Trade Area, 276
China Huaneng Group, 211

China–Japan disputes, 177–185
China–Japan financial cooperation, 265
China–Japan maritime cooperation, 183
China–Japan–ROK cooperation mechanism, 48–49, 59, 70, 89
China–Japan–ROK Free Trade Area (CJKFTA), 11, 80, 291, 295, 259, 313–331
China–Japan–ROK investment agreement, 48, 70, 259, 280, 288–289, 304
China–Japan–ROK Trilateral Cooperation Secretariat, 70
China–Kazakhstan oil pipeline, 229
China–Mongolia cooperation, 26, 95
China–Mongolia-Russia economic cooperation, 63
China–ROK Cooperation, 43
China–ROK financial cooperation, 265
China–ROK FTA, 19, 48–49, 311
China–ROK Joint Statement, 44
China–Russia cooperation, 26, 47, 211
China–Russia crude oil pipeline, 212
China–Russia energy cooperation, 217
China–Russia financial cooperation, 265–266
China–Russian border, 96
China–Russia oil pipeline project, 192
China–Russia strategic cooperative partnership, 113
China–Soviet relations, 154
China threat theory, 27, 37, 81, 83, 104, 136
China–US relationship, 93, 146
Chinese culture, 30
Christianity, 13
Cisco, 110

clean development mechanism (CDM), 270
Cold War, 1, 3, 8, 10, 15, 22, 36, 42, 44, 56, 85–87, 118, 121, 143, 155, 219, 322
Collective Action Plan (CAP), 272
collective security, 127–128
comfort women, 10
commodity trade proportion, 253–254
Communist Party of China (CPC), 14–15
complementarity, 232
comprehensive management, 121
Confidence Building Measures in Asia (CICA), 71
conflict management, 125
consensus, 121–122
continental shelf, 178–180
cooperation, 53–54, 74, 117, 307–308
cooperative security, 46, 66, 72, 112, 129
Council for Security Cooperation in the Asia Pacific (CSCAP), 131
Council of Local Authorities for International Relations (CLAIR), 263
cross-border pollution, 90, 106
cultural interests, 29–33
cultural soft power, 32–33
customs procedures, 298–299

D

Dai Bingguo, 97
Deep-Blue Navy stage, 155
Democratic People's Republic of Korea (DPRK), 3, 9, 39, 57, 88, 214, 309
development, 53–54
development cooperation, 327
dialogue, 74, 117

Diaoyu Dao issue, 9, 20, 28, 41, 96, 98–100, 111, 139, 141, 148, 154, 157, 159, 173–177
diplomatic strategy, 103
diversification strategy, 196
Dokdo, 9
DPRK-US bilateral dialogue, 134
Dvorkovich, Arkady, 234

E
East Asian Acid Deposition Monitoring Network, 269–270
East Asia Summit (EAS), 130
East China Sea, 9, 145, 148, 177–184
East China Sea Air Defense Identification Zone, 150–153
Eastern Orthodox, 13
Eastern Siberia Pacific Ocean oil pipeline (ESPO), 268
ecological security, 106
e-commerce, 300–301
economic and trade relations, 237–331
economic cooperation, 10–12, 19, 75–81, 162, 258–260
economic crisis, 189
economic globalization, 237–270
economic growth, 60, 238–243
economic integration, 19
economic interests, 16–21
Economic Partnership Agreement (EPA), 293
economic threat, 37
electronic commerce, 300–301
Enabling Trade Index (ETI), 281
energy, 233, 267
Energy Charter, 231
energy competition, 214–218
energy conservation policy, 196
Energy Consumption Promotion Committee, 204
energy cooperation, 209–221

Energy Cooperation Policy, 187–236
Energy Coordination Group (ECG), 196, 198
energy-saving technologies, 204
energy security, 187–236
energy strategy, 189–193, 200–205
environmental protection, 230
Environmental Protection Cooperation Agreement, 269
equality, 120
Europe, 189
European Union (EU), 58
external environment, 165
extremism, 46, 67, 69, 75, 85, 133

F
Far East, 234–235
fertilizer production, 208
financial cooperation, 265–267
financial crisis, 21
Five Principles of Peaceful Coexistence, 43, 64, 113
foreign direct investment (FDI), 254, 303
foreign exchange reserves, 243–248
Foreign Investment and Foreign Trade Agency (FIFTA), 206
Foreign Investment Law, 220
foreign trade, 249–254
Free Trade Agreement (FTA), 80, 211, 260, 270–295, 310, 312
Free Trade Agreement Bureau (FTA Bureau), 321

G
G20, 233
General Administration of Customs of the People's Republic of China (GACC), 157
General Security of Military Information Agreement (GSOMIA), 146

globalization, 15, 19
Greater Tumen Initiative (GTI), 48
Greater Tumen River regional cooperation, 260–261
gross domestic product (GDP), 17, 241, 243

H
Hong Kong SAR, 175–176
hydropower strategy, 209

I
inclusiveness, 120
Individual Action Plan (IAP), 272
inflation rate control, 248–249
informatization, 15
infrastructure construction, 297–298
institutional environment, 306–307
institutionalization, 133–135
internal affairs, 64
International Court of Justice, 170
international direct investment, 271–274
International Energy Agency (IEA), 196
International Energy Forum (IEF), 233
International Energy Plan (IEP), 198
International Energy Program Agreement, 196
international investment, 254–258
International Monetary Fund (IMF), 190, 324
international security mechanisms, 127
international system, 2–12
international trade, 271–274
intra-regional commodity, 253
investment facilitation, 270–295
Investment Facilitation Action Plan (IFAP), 273
investment facilitation process, 272–275
Island, 29

J
Japan, 7–8, 11, 193–199, 279–290, 309, 314–319, 327–328
Japan-US-Australia-India value alliance, 104
Jilin Province, 78
Joint Oil Data Initiative (JODI), 233

K
Kan, Naoto, 198
key spillover program, 167
Koguryo Kingdom, 31
Korea Electric Power Corporation, 211
Korean National Oil Corporation, 204
Korean Peninsula, 8–9, 27, 39–40, 45, 71, 88, 94, 96, 103, 211, 214
Korean War, 55
Kyoto Protocol, 230

L
Law of the Sea, 171
Law on International Peace and Cooperation, 156
Law on Surrounding Events, 156
Law on the Exclusive Economic Zone, 172
Liberal Democratic Party, 99
liberalization, 290–295, 329–330
liquefied natural gas (LNG), 188

M
Macao SAR, 175–176
Manila Declaration, 261
marine economy, 159–161
maritime delimitation, 174

maritime rights, 137–185
maritime security, 22–25
Maritime Silk Road, 79
Middle East, 224
military alliance mechanism, 128
Military-First Politics, 39
military security, 104–105
military threat, 37
Mining Law, 199
Ministry of Commerce, Industry, and Energy (MOCIE), 202
Mitrany, David, 132
Mongolia, 17, 205–209
Mongolia Plateau, 109
Moo-hyun, Rohm, 203
multilateral cooperation mechanism, 129
multilateral financial cooperation mechanism, 266
multilateral security cooperation, 130–131
multilateralism, 321
multi-polarization, 2–5, 35, 43, 113
mutual benefit, 53–54, 231–232

N
national defense forces, 172–173
national defense security, 22–25
National Development and Reform Commission, 78
National Energy Commission, 201
National Energy Conservation Promotion Committee, 204
national energy security, 187
national grand strategy, 181–182
national income, 245
national interests, 12–33
nationalization, 99, 143
national reunification, 16, 98
National Security Council, 23
National Security Law, 97, 111
National Security Strategy, 102

national unity, 16, 98–101
Natural Gas Development Plan, 191
natural gas energy, 198
Navigation Plan, 22
negative list, 288
neighborhood diplomacy, 50–52
New Energy and Industrial Technology Development Organization (NEDO), 197
non-tariff barriers, 285
non-traditional security interests, 105–110
non-traditional security threats, 89–92
North American Free Trade Area (NAFTA), 218, 323
Northeast Asia, 1–33, 137–185, 187–236
Northeast Asia Cooperation Dialogue (NEACD), 131
Northeast Asia Economic Conference, 263
Northeast Asia Economic Forum (NEAEF), 263
Northeast Asian Economic Cooperation, 259
Northeast Asian Energy Community, 232
Northeast Asian Energy Cooperation Forum, 232
Northeast Asian Regional Energy Cooperation Organization, 231
Northeast Asia Regional Economic Cooperation, 261
Northeast Asia Subregional Programme for Environmental Cooperation (NEASPEC), 269
Northern Territories, 86
North Pyongan Province, 207
North–South tension, 8
Northwest Pacific Action Plan (NOWPAP), 269

nuclear energy, 198
nuclear non-proliferation mechanism, 123
Nuclear Regulatory Commission, 198
Nye, Joseph, 167

O
Obama, Barack, 22, 69, 73, 91
open regionalism, 232
Organization for Economic Cooperation and Development (OECD), 198
Organization of the Petroleum Exporting Countries (OPEC), 233
Osaka Action Agenda, 273

P
Pacific Ocean, 69, 153
Pathfinders Approach, 272
Pax Americana, 5
peace, 52–53, 55–58, 135
People's Republic of China (PRC), 72
pivot to Asia policy, 22, 125, 325–326
political dilemma, 140–144
political interests, 13–16
population threat, 37
Potsdam Proclamation, 41
Power of Siberia pipeline, 212
pre-establishment national treatment, 287–288
Prism, 109–110

Q
quantitative evaluation mechanism, 308
quasi-domestic energy, 195

R
Rason Free Economic Zone, 211
Regional Comprehensive Economic Partnership (RCEP), 80

regional economic cooperation, 18, 258–262, 267–270, 309–313, 319–322
regional power dynamics, 5
regional sharing mechanism, 234
Regional Trade Agreements, 273
regional trade liberalization, 324–325
renewable energy, 197
Republic of Korea (ROK), 3, 18, 200–205, 214, 279–290, 314–319, 327–328
right-leaning policy, 216
ROK–Chile FTA, 321
Russia, 69, 189–193
Russia–DPRK Energy Bridge Project, 211
Russia–DPRK–ROK Economic Cooperation, 63
Russian Federation, 191

S
safeguarding national territorial sovereignty, 163–169
safeguarding peace, 27–29, 118
Sakhalin project, 217, 268
Sakhalin-2 project, 212, 268
security, 135
security dilemmas, 88–89
security interests, 21–29
security issues, 8–10
security mechanism, 117–136
security strategy, 85–136
Self-Defense Forces Law, 24, 156, 216
separatism, 46, 69, 75, 85, 133
Shanghai Cooperation Organization (SCO), 45, 69, 127, 133
Shanghai International Energy Exchange, 226
Silk Road Economic Belt, 76, 184, 226
Six-Party Talks, 28, 40, 45, 133–135

socialism, 15
soft barriers, 296–297
soft power, 3, 14, 29, 32, 35, 81, 174
solar cells, 197
Southern African Customs Union (SACU), 322
Southern Kurils, 86
South Hamgyong Province, 209
South Pyongan Province, 207
sovereign security, 97–98
Soviet Union, 3, 36, 39, 90, 145, 208
stable economic development, 238–243
State Council Information Office (SCIO), 164
State-owned Assets Supervision and Administration Commission of the State Council (SASAC), 235
strategic countermeasures, 313–331
Strategic Investment Law, 221

T

Tailored Access Operations (TAO), 110
Taiwan region, 175–176
Taiwan Strait, 58
territorial integrity, 16, 98–101
territorial sovereignty, 9, 137–185
terrorism, 46, 67, 69, 75, 85, 121
Thucydides' trap, 6–7, 68, 115
Tickell, Crispin, 91
track-II mechanisms, 124
trade cooperation, 47
trade dispute settlement mechanisms, 330–331
trade facilitation, 277–291, 296–303
trade protection, 330
trade relations, 314–319
transformation of international system, 2–12

Trans-Pacific Partnership Agreement (TPP), 12, 325
Trilateral Cooperation Secretariat, 264
trust-building, function of, 126
Tumen River Area Development Program (TRADP), 48, 77
Tumen River region, 77

U

UN Charter, 64–65, 73
UNCLOS, 171, 177–180
United Nations, 34, 271, 302
United Nations Convention on the Law, 171
United Nations Educational, Scientific and Cultural Organization (UNESCO), 31
United Nations Statistics Department (UNSD), 233
United States, 3, 5, 8, 15, 36, 56, 68, 86, 94–95, 100, 102, 141
US hegemony policy, 92–96
US-Japan bilateral alliances, 4, 24, 92, 100
US-Japan Defense Cooperation, 93
US-Japan relations, 323
US-Japan-ROK alliance, 104
US military alliance, 27
US military strategy, 7
US-ROK bilateral alliances, 4, 147
US Taiwan policy, 93
US-Vietnam cooperative relationship, 101

W

war of aggression, 31
White, R. E., 165
winner-takes-all principle, 43, 54, 65
win-win cooperation, 30, 43, 67, 120
World Bank, 271, 283, 308

World Customs Organization, 271, 302
World Economic Forum (WEF), 281
world economy, 58
world powers, 34
World Trade Organization (WTO), 20, 26, 271
World War II, 6, 23, 37, 40–41, 145, 176, 183, 196, 224

Y

Yalta Agreement, 41
Yellow-Water Navy stage, 155
Young Leaders Programs (YLPs), 263

Z

Zarubino Port, 79
zero-sum game, 5, 54, 65, 81, 95, 119–121, 139, 141, 178
Zhang Zhijun, 143